Resisting the Third Reich

Resisting the
Third Reich

The Catholic Clergy in Hitler's Berlin

Kevin P. Spicer

NORTHERN

ILLINOIS

UNIVERSITY

PRESS

DeKalb

The picture of Josef Roth greeting Hitler was provided by the Federal Archives, Koblenz, Germany. All other figures are courtesy of the Diocesan Archive Berlin.

Library of Congress Cataloging-in-Publication Data

Spicer, Kevin P., 1965–

Resisting the Third Reich : the Catholic clergy in Hitler's Berlin / Kevin P. Spicer.

  p.   cm.

Includes bibliographical references (p.   ) and index.

ISBN 0-87580-330-X (hardcover : alk. paper)

1. Catholic Church. Diocese of Berlin (Germany)—History—20th century. 2. Catholic Church—Germany—Berlin Region—Clergy—History—20th century. 3. Berlin Region (Germany)—Church history—20th century. 4. Church and state—Germany—History—1933–1945. 5. National socialism and religion. I. Title.

BX1538.B4S65 2004

282′.43155′09043—dc22

2004001437

For my parents, John and Gloria Spicer, whose love and

encouragement over the years have helped me to persevere.

When I was a young child, my father, as a teacher and counselor,

inspired me with his dedication and commitment to education.

His love of history made this field come alive.

This work is dedicated to them.

Contents

Acknowledgments

A historian's task is often a solitary one. It requires dedication and concentration as he or she spends long hours sifting through primary source material in the covert recesses of an archive. It is, however, one in which I happily engage myself, reading through file after file, in anticipation of some new insight a document might reveal. Since 1996, I have been engaged in the historian's craft of researching and writing this work. I conducted the majority of my research in 1996–1997 in Germany, though subsequently I have made numerous trips back to Germany to continue my investigation of the Catholic clergy's activities under National Socialism. During these visits, I received assistance from many individuals to whom I wish to offer a sincere word of gratitude: first and foremost, I would like to thank Dr. Gotthard Klein, the archivist of the Berlin Archdiocese and his incredibly efficient staff, especially Rosemarie Rietz, Cristine Grünig, and Roswitha Reiser, who provided me with unending assistance in using their collection. Throughout the research and writing of this work, Dr. Klein, with his extensive knowledge and expertise, readily and continuously answered my innumerable questions by phone call and fax. I also would like to thank the staff of the Bundesarchiv Berlin-Lichterfelde, especially Maike Macrten, Jana Blumberg, and Heinz Fehlauer, for their help during my research there. In addition, I would like to thank Dr. Susanne Wittern, Brandenburgisches Landeshauptarchiv; Gisela Klauß, Geheimes Staatsarchiv Preussischer Kulturbesitz; and the personnel of the Bundesarchiv, Koblenz and Dahlwitz-Hoppegarten, and the Staatsbibliothek, Berlin-Mitte.

In addition to these institutions and individuals, I would like also to offer my gratitude to the following individuals associated with specific research institutions: Dr. John L. Heineman, Dr. Donald J. Dietrich, and Dr. Francis J. Murphy, Boston College; Brun Appel, emeritus archivist, Dr. Bruno Lengenfelder, archivist, and Dr. Franz Heiler, Diocese of Eichstätt Archive; Dr. Heinz Hürten, University of Eichstätt; Dr. Karl-Joseph Hummel, director, and Dr. Hans Günter Hockerts, Kommission für Zeitgeschichte, Bonn; Prälat Sigmund Benker, Emeritus Director, and Dr. Peter Pfister, director, Lic. theol. Susanne Kornacker, Archdiocese of Munich and Freising Archive; Gerhard Sander, archivist, Archdiocese of Paderborn Archive; Dr. Joachim Lauchs, Bavarian Hauptstaatsarchiv; Dr. Reinhard Weber, Staatsarchiv Munich; Dr. Roland Müller, Stadtarchiv Stuttgart; Dr. Stephen Janker, director, Diocese of Rottenburg-Stuttgart Archive; Dr. Martin Persch, director, Diocese of Trier Archive; Dr. Július Baláž, Vojensky Historical Archive, Prague; Reinhold Lenski, Stadt Böbingen Archive; Dr. Annmarie Fenzl, Archdiocese of Vienna Archive; Dr. Norbert Müller, Diocese of Graz-Seckau Archive; Marguerite McDonough, Boston College; and Regina Egan, Stonehill College.

It would have been impossible for me to conduct my research without the financial assistance of several groups. First and foremost, I would like to thank my religious community, the Congregation of Holy Cross Eastern Province, that primarily supported my initial year of research in Germany. I would also like to thank Theodore Z. Weiss and the Holocaust Educational Foundation for a fellowship that helped to support additional research overseas. In addition, I would like to thank Stonehill College, especially Mark Cregan, C.S.C., J.D., president; Dr. Katie Conboy, vice-president for academic affairs; Dr. Karen Talentino, dean of faculty; Bonnie Troupe, director of academic development; Elaine Melisi, assistant to the vice-president for academic affairs; my faculty colleagues for their continued support; and Stonehill's general administration, for providing me with faculty summer grants that have enabled me to continue my research and writing.

When I arrived in Germany, the Archdiocese of Berlin was the first diocese to welcome me and provide me housing. For the kindness I received there, I would especially like to thank Cardinal Georg Sterzinsky; Generalvikar Peter Wehr; Pfarrer Bernhard Motter; and Pfarrer Dr. Michael Höhle. I would also like to thank the following people and institutions both in Germany and in the United States: Peter Wagner, S.A.C.; emeritus Abt Dr. Odilo Lechner, O.S.B., Valentin Ziegler, O.S.B., and the Benedictine community of St. Bonifaz, Munich; Dr. John Pawlikowski, O.S.M.; Msgr. Peter Conley; Dr. Ludwig Brandl; Professor Ulrich Wagener; Dr. Virginia Reinburg; Elias Füllenbach, O.P.; Thomas Klosterkamp, O.M.I.; the late Robert A. Graham, S.J.; the late Roman Bleistein, S.J.; Fr. Walter Cuenin and the staff and parishioners of Our Lady's Church in Newton, Massachusetts; Dr. Peter Hayes; Dr. Jacques Kornberg; Dr. Lucia Scherzberg; Domkapitular Wolfgang Knauft; Dr. Raymond C. Sun; Eduard and Waltraud Burchat; Dr. James Kenneally; James Fenstermaker, C.S.C.; Dr. Thomas Gariepy, C.S.C.; Dr. Thomas Campbell, C.S.C.; Walter Jenkins, C.S.C.; and Bradley Beaupre, C.S.C.

In a special way, I would like to thank my editors, James William Chichetto, C.S.C., and Ilse Andrews, whose dedication to and support of my work have been invaluable. Both challenged me to make this a better book in every way possible. In particular, Jim has been the truest of friends and never lost faith in my work or abilities. Finally, I would also like to thank my editors at Northern Illinois University Press, Melody Herr and Martin Johnson, who along with the anonymous readers provided insightful comments that greatly assisted me when I was revising this work for publication.

Resisting the Third Reich

Introduction

On October 23, 1941, when Konrad von Preysing, bishop of Berlin, received word that the Gestapo (*Geheim Staatspolizei,* Secret State Police) had arrested one of his most outspoken priests, Monsignor Bernhard Lichtenberg, one can only wonder what went on in the good bishop's mind.[1] The Gestapo had arrested Lichtenberg for "hostile activity against the state." According to the National Socialist state, Lichtenberg had not legally followed everything that was expected of him as a citizen. That is, at a prayer service, he had prayed for Jews and for those imprisoned in concentration camps. Upset by what they had heard at the service, two students shared their experience with a friend, who later denounced Lichtenberg to her father—a member of the SS (*Schutzstaffel,* the elite corps of the Nazi Party). In no time, the Gestapo moved in, hoping that by arresting him it would deprive Lichtenberg of any "allegedly" moral and patriotic stance he had aspired to have as pastor of St. Hedwig's Cathedral, the main church of the Berlin diocese.

According to Nazi officials, there was nothing wrong with silencing an outspoken critic of the state, whether priest, layman, or laywoman. From their perspective, any word or action against the state was illegal. The arrest made Preysing particularly vulnerable. He was Lichtenberg's bishop. Because Germany had signed a concordat with the Vatican in 1933 promising recognition and protection of the Roman Catholic Church and its interests in Germany, Preysing and his fellow bishops had over the years tried to work out a pastoral policy for Catholics that would both preserve the Church's mission to save souls and maintain state law. Of course, such a policy was not foolproof. Preysing and his fellow bishops, for example, knew that there would be many gray areas within daily parish life where both priests and laity alike would have to make wrenching moral decisions that the concordat had never spelled out or considered. As it turned out, such decisions often departed from the daily adjustments that priests had to make in parish life. In Bernhard Lichtenberg's case, he had merely asked his parishioners to pray on a daily basis for Jews and for all those whom the laws of the state affected. Such an action, however, directly defied German laws against Jews. According to Nazi officials, Lichtenberg was more than just a loose cannon; he was also a traitor who had to be arrested because of his "defamations." He had elusively challenged the anti-Semitic policy of the Nazi state and had caused "unrest" among the German population. He had gone directly against the demands of the minister of propaganda, Joseph Goebbels, who challenged all German citizens to dedicate themselves totally to the Nazi state and ideology.[2] Now the state would have to act against Lichtenberg and anyone else who dared to speak out against Nazi policies.

In hindsight, Lichtenberg's arrest only now serves to illuminate the difficulties that committed clergy and citizens of all faiths had to face during this period. Certainly, this particular "disorder," which pitted Lichtenberg against the state, must have also inadvertently pitted Bishop Preysing against it as well. What actions could Preysing take in behalf of Lichtenberg? What actions did he take? Such questions—and so many more—only serve to highlight the subtle duel that existed between the German Catholic Church and Nazi state. Was the Church prepared for such a struggle or confrontation? Was the resistance of the Berlin German clergy to Nazi ideology the direct consequence of their theological education? To what extent did Lichtenberg's diocese resist or endorse the existing social and ethnic distinctions intrinsic to Nazism? How did diocesan priests engage in debate with the Nazis? How did priests resist the assault of Nazi ideology in their parishes, among their parishioners? How did Catholic teaching frustrate the efforts of some priests who were sympathetic to Nazism? Was there fractionalization among the priests? Among the bishops? These are some of the questions I hope to answer in this book.

When studying the history of the Catholic Church during the Third Reich, one must conclude that Church leaders, in their official capacity, never sought to overthrow the Nazi regime. Because their institution had not been forced underground, Church leaders instead undertook provisionally to adapt to the new regime.[3] In this process of adaptation, the bishops only sought to challenge the state in those areas where German officials or policy had taken exception to official Church teaching and had encroached upon the bishops' freedom to exercise their ministry. In their vigilance and negotiations, the bishops continually reverted to the stipulations of the 1933 Reich-Vatican concordat as their legitimate means of protest. The state, however, did not view these protests and complaints (i.e., pastoral letters, sermons, letters of petition used to protest or lodge a complaint) as valid. Rather, Berlin viewed them as a threat to the implementation of Nazi policy. From the perspective of the German state, there was only one weltanschauung in Nazi Germany. As Donald Dietrich has noted, what many modern-day historians have perceived "as capitulation or, at the very least, lack of resistance, was viewed by Nazi leaders as posing a very serious threat."[4]

Nevertheless, the question remains: did the Catholic Church and its leaders resist, check, or impede the ideology of National Socialism and the Nazi state? Ultimately, the answer to this question depends largely upon how one defines *resistance*. There is active resistance and passive resistance, an unambiguous stand and an oblique one, a vigorous opposition and a stoic one—each reflecting the knotty spirit of the resister. In his attempt to sketch the position of the Church in the Nazi state, Martin Broszat introduced a medical term, *Resistenz* (denoting immunity), both to broaden our almost homogeneous understanding of resistance and to mark out the action of those citizens who offered an "effective defense and demarcation" or restraint to "National Socialist control or its claims of control." He then contrasted *Resistenz* with *Widerstand*, the action of those who consciously opposed the Nazi regime on political grounds. Broszat's differentiation between these two forms of counteraction corresponds to the distinction I make between those clerics who indirectly checked the ubiquity of National Socialist control over Germany and those few clerics who directly challenged the regime for its racist policies against Jews and its anti-Church ideology.

Broszat located *Resistenz* in preexisting independent institutions, such as the churches, which continued to infuse potent religious values into a society dominated by National Socialist ideology. In addition, he considered a person's refusal to give the Hitler salute, a citizen's social contact with Jews, and membership in Church associations or youth groups (apart from state-coordinated groups) to be acts of civil disobedience and, consequently, occasions of *Resistenz*, the results of which inoculated an individual with an alternate set of moral prerogatives. This concept of *Resistenz* helped explain the behavior of many individuals and groups who expressed a partial affirmation of the regime, but who also opposed the regime on particular issues. Often, especially for Catholics, this opposition was directly tied to the defense of their ecclesiastical institution, structures, and biblical ideology.[5] In this respect, Broszat's concept has enabled me to categorize those individuals whose deeds did not fall directly into a more black-and-white category of resistance but whose actions nevertheless represented some mode of restraint or disobedience, thus falling somewhere between accommodation/adaptation and outright resistance.

In overseeing its daily rituals and educating the faithful according to the Roman Catholic faith, the Catholic Church in Germany provided a weltanschauung that stood in stark contrast to National Socialism. Recently, Vesna

Drapac highlighted this significant point in her work on the French Catholic Church under German occupation. According to Drapac, Catholic teaching often went beyond mere regional parochialism to include a more universal proclamation of the gospel and a clear-cut declaration of moral values that ran counter to National Socialism. She also argued that French Catholics' faith often translated their beliefs into action.[6] Although Drapac was dealing with a Church and a people under occupation, with more reasons and motivation for resistance, her argument, which has also been proposed by German scholars, is equally valid for German Catholics. Scholars such as Heinz Hürten and Ulrich von Hehl and individuals such as Walter Dirks, who lived during the Nazi regime, have suggested that through its teaching and parochial associations the Church enabled German Catholics to maintain a critical distance from the weltanschauung of National Socialism.[7] Hehl identified this distance as a "place of ideological immunization."[8] Even critics such as Richard Löwenthal and Karl-Egon Lönne, who are more exacting and critical about the lack of active resistance by Church leaders, have conceded that through its teaching and preaching the Church provided for its believing members an estranged oasis and ideological distancing that screened them from the worst seductions of the National Socialist weltanschauung.[9]

The duty of all Catholics to proclaim the Christian Gospel, which often reclaimed for them an "ideological immunization" from the National Socialist worldview, forced many Catholics in leadership positions to make daring statements and become more involved in activities that state officials deemed acts of political resistance. The majority of these committed Catholics, however, rejected any label associated with resistance. Rather, they argued that their actions were made solely to protect the interests of their Church and to secure pastoral freedom to care for their parishioners. Despite persecution, many of these individuals also pledged their allegiance to the German state and continued to hope and strive for good relations with state officials. Thus, the average German priest was not prepared to break entirely with the state and work for its demise. Instead, the majority of the parish priests limited their criticisms to situations that either directly affected their sacramental ministry or threatened the promulgation of Church doctrine and teaching.

In their public preaching (often in allegories) and in their local rebuttals with Nazi officials, most of whom were often suspicious of a cleric's attempt to energize religious education or reorganize disbanded associations, Catholic priests were, from their sacramental perspective, primarily fulfilling a pastoral mandate instituted by Christ. This mandate included proclaiming the gospel, administering the sacraments, ministering to the sick and dying, and ensuring that a new generation be instructed in the truths of the Catholic faith. Any limitation placed on the exercise of these ministries was seen as hostile, anti-Catholic, and a direct threat to the mission of the Church and its continuity in Germany. For these reasons,

Church leaders normally did not perceive the pastoral role of the Catholic Church as political. Indeed, seldom did they take it upon themselves in their official capacity as ministers of the Church to speak directly about political issues that did not expressly concern the welfare of their Church. According to this worldview, Catholics took care of Catholics, Protestants took care of Protestants, and Jews took care of Jews. Their worlds rarely met, except when similar issues or events overlapped and affected more than one religious community.

Monika Hellwig and Beate Ruhm von Oppen have recently encouraged historians to examine more carefully the priest's ministerial role and his self-understanding of pastoral ministry in relation to the Church's response to the Nazi state. Ruhm von Oppen has stressed that during the Nazi period many Catholics, including bishops, clearly recalled how officials of the Bismarck Kulturkampf had deprived Catholics of their clergy and how these policies affected whole regions. According to Ruhm von Oppen, many Catholics did not wish to repeat this period of deprivation, which forcefully separated Catholics from their means of salvation—sacramental grace.[10] Reflecting on her own experience as a youth in Berlin and later in the district of Limburg in the Netherlands, Hellwig reinforced Ruhm von Oppen's observations by stating that the majority of Catholics' concerns and hopes were related "exclusively to a goal after death." They strengthened these hopes through "exercises of piety and the observance of the commandments" in their daily lives.[11]

Thomas Breuer was one of the first scholars to recognize the facets of this cultural-theological worldview, linking period history to theological insularity. In particular, Breuer has explored how German bishops and priests in Nazi Germany viewed the continuity and preservation of the Church's ecclesiological mission to the world as their primary task.[12] According to Breuer, this particular self-understanding, which maintained a "pronounced primacy of ideology before ministry," guided the response of the Church's ministers to the state.[13] Any attack or encroachment upon this ecclesial ideology, he concluded, from whatever source—be it from Communism, Socialism, Liberalism, or National Socialism—was viewed as an assault on the Church itself and, consequently, subject to a vigorous counterattack in the form of a barrage of pulpit denunciations, pastoral letters, and invectives in the religious classroom. Naturally, Breuer was not the first person to emphasize that institutional continuity and self-preservation motivated Catholic resistance. Georg Denzler, Guenter Lewy, John S. Conway, and Klaus Scholder have also argued that Catholic resistance was a form of "institutional protectionism."[14] In their view, anything could be and was done, including signing a concordat with the Nazi state, to protect the institution of the Church. Unlike Breuer, however, these authors have carelessly neglected to highlight the importance of theology as a motivational and formative factor in the pastoral life of Catholic priests.

In assessing the importance of the sacraments and the role of doctrine in Church life, Breuer has made a significant contribution. His recognition of the importance of Catholic continuity, its uninterrupted record of Catholic witness in the sacramental and ritual life of the German Catholic Church, is essential to an understanding of the mindset of a parish priest in Germany of the 1930s and 1940s. Of course, any Catholic priest, by virtue of his ordination promises, is bound to celebrate the customs and rites of his tradition, despite the personal cost. In spite of his important insight, Breuer overlooks the deeply internalized effect and profound psychological impact the Catholic Church—as an ecclesiastic body—had on its members, especially the clergy. The Church made God sacramentally present, elucidated the faith of believers, and was the extension of the heavenly Christ himself. It also held the repositories of eternal life. Only by being grafted into this Church would people be saved. As a result, preservation of this institution demanded, especially from among the clergy, an uncommonly loyal following—indeed, adherents with an almost instinctive assurance and forthright boldness. Instead of causing the Church to succumb to Nazism, the spiritual practices and programs of the Church, on the contrary, provoked Catholic priests to confront the state directly. Often, the primary motivation for the actions of the priests was the exercise of pastoral freedom, but more often than not, these confrontations with the German state led members of the clergy to see the inherent and broader dangers of Nazi ideology and the fatal implications of its politics for the faithful.

Through his ministry, and especially by conferring the sacraments, the Catholic priest, as a representative of Christ in the world and leader in the Church, controlled the essential means of salvation for the Catholic faithful. Any individual or group who attacked or threatened the continuation of this mission exercised by the priest—dispensing the sacraments, affirming Catholic associations, preaching, and cultivating religious education that supported and educated the faithful in the sacraments—had, in the view of Church leaders, to be forcefully challenged. In his study of religious institutions, Gary Lease has pointed out that any deviation from the "norms and expectations" of a particular institution is not only a "failure to conform but also a dangerous threat to the continued existence of the system and its community."[15] Although Lease focused his concerns primarily on conformity from within a particular institution, his comments help explain the Catholic Church's response to Nazi encroachment in ecclesiastical areas. In the view of its leaders, the Catholic Church alone held the absolute truth that Christ had bequeathed to it. It alone had the right to safeguard its scripture, doctrine, and teachings on morality. To ensure the continuation of this faith in its unadulterated form and to protect it from any further pollution, the German Catholic hierarchy, along with the lower clergy, felt compelled to challenge and reject any person or worldview that countered it. In Nazi Germany, the bishops and priests, therefore, believed it was their duty to challenge the National Socialist weltanschauung and the Nazi state whenever its ideology and committed officials threatened any aspect of the sacramental or ministerial life of the Church.

It is important to remember here, however, as Detlef Schmiechen-Ackermann has pointed out, that there was not a consistent, overall resistance within the German Catholic milieu. Instead, there were "significant forms of refusal and political opposition" at various points and successive gradations throughout the Third Reich.[16] The hierarchy encouraged these forms of opposition through their statements and pastoral letters, which parish priests read and interpreted individually. Although the content of these statements was never meant to encourage the overthrow of the Nazi regime, it was definitely meant to halt the encroachment of Nazi ideology upon the Church's infrastructure and prevent dilution of the Church's sacramental life. In this regard, Church officials primarily reacted only to state measures that affected only the institution and life of the Church. Only through gradual reflection, however, did the German bishops, as Church leaders attempting to guard the moral fiber of German society, speak out on the importance of general human rights. Their statements, however, never clearly addressed the persecution and murder of European Jews or the multiple injustices committed against other minority groups outside of the Catholic Church. Despite these limitations, individual priests did find the moral resources from within their faith tradition to address issues of injustice.

This book examines the lives and choices of individual parish priests, specifically in the diocese of Berlin during the Third Reich. A case study of the Catholic Church in Berlin is an excellent entry to understanding the difficulties that Catholics, especially Catholic priests, had to face in a diaspora diocese where Protestants outnumbered Catholics almost ten to one.[17] Similarly, this work reveals that, even though Catholics held a minority status in Berlin, their clergy participated in similar forms of *Resistenz* alongside the clergy of other dioceses where the Catholic population was the majority.[18] Finally, it is important to see that even at the epicenter of German state government, in the Reich *Hauptstadt* (capital) with the headquarters of the SS and the Gestapo at hand, Berlin Catholic clergy were still willing to engage in acts of *Resistenz* to protect their local Catholic milieu and prized ministerial freedom. The majority of these priests viewed their ministry, and more specifically the sacramental life of the faithful, as their most important task.[19] They perceived themselves as the ordained representatives of Christ on earth whom the Church had charged with Christ's mission.

For most priests, the concerns of the state encroached upon their lives only when political affairs pertained directly to the rights of the Church and their freedom to minister to the faithful. This was not a selfish or narrow viewpoint. Rather, it was regarded as the accepted method of ministry for German Catholic priests; however, other factors such as their provincial background, theological education, family situation, nationalism, and prejudices likewise influenced the way these priests responded to the state. The variety of their responses attests to their individuality and reveals how difficult it is today to espouse one conclusive thesis that would unravel the complex actions and external circumstances of hundreds or even thousands of priests situated in the Nazi state. All we know is that there was an array of complex responses to the state in parish life. Whereas some priests resisted, others acquiesced, protesting only when state measures affected their own parishes. Still others apparently never challenged the state, because the extant records reveal nothing about their activity during the Third Reich. Finally, there were a few priests who embraced National Socialism and joined its ranks.

In the pages that follow, I explore the context and milieu of German Roman Catholicism, first examining the relationship of the Church, specifically in the diocese of Berlin, with the National Socialist Party from 1930 to 1934. I argue that the bishops initially adopted a conditional ban that differed from diocese to diocese in regard to Catholic membership in the Hitler movement. Once Hitler came to power and offered assurances to the Church, especially through signing the concordat with the Holy See, however, the bishops willingly rescinded their prohibition and attempted to work provisionally with the state. What were the results? I examine that outcome as well as the kind of instructions the Church hierarchy provided for its priests in their interaction with the state, the consequences of which prove compelling and achieve historical significance to this day.

I next focus on the relationship between the Church and state from 1934 through 1945. I approach this connection by showing how the consequences of the Röhm Purge of June 30, 1934, enabled not only the Church hierarchy but many Germans as well to view the realities of National Socialism differently. Did this event cause the bishops to turn dramatically against the state or make them take a more subtle approach? I will examine this in light of the rights guaranteed to the Church by the concordat of 1933. For example, did the reaction of the bishops greatly concern state officials such as Joseph Goebbels? To what degree did they fear public unrest and increased resistance against state measures? I will cover these questions. I will also show that the disagreements among the German bishops prevented them as a united body from issuing any joint statements that called upon Catholics to resist the state openly.

To explain this relationship between the Church and state, I use specific examples, such as how priests had to negotiate daily with state authorities—namely, officials of the Gestapo—to protect the rights of the Church and minister to its parishioners. I argue that these priests did not view themselves as resistors, but as pastoral operants who simply endeavored each day to maintain their pastoral ministry to their membership. In carrying out their normal pastoral activities, these priests often directly contradicted state ordinances or challenged Nazi ideology. Doing so, in turn, brought them into unwelcome conflict with the Gestapo. In this regard, I will also show that enforcement of state laws varied regionally, depending upon the whims of local officials. In addition, I will show that what was tolerated in 1935 was labeled treasonous by 1943, especially as the course of the war turned against Germany.

By way of background, I critically examine Catholic perceptions of Jews, specifically in the diocese of Berlin. Through an analysis of instructional guidebooks, catechisms, and sermons I will show that, though Catholics included Jews as their neighbors and generally tolerated "religious, observant Jews," they vehemently rejected "secular Jews," whom they linked with liberalism and blamed for the moral decline of German society. Alongside this perception, I will explore the degree to which anti-Semitism, inherently present within the Church itself, did not encourage Catholics to treat Jews as neighbors. Was this civic posture the norm? Though there were a few heroic individuals who risked their lives for their Jewish neighbors, why did the majority of clergy ignore the plight of Jews in Nazi Germany? Why were some more inclined to assist Catholics of Jewish descent? Why would a priest rarely extend himself for a Jew who did not profess Catholicism? Why did the majority of priests consider such an action beyond their pastoral concerns? In contrast to the many priests who simply refused to comment publicly on the situation of the Jews, a small group of priests openly embraced Nazism's anti-Semitic ideology. I examine the lives of these particular "brown" priests (referring to the color favored by the Nazis) in the diocese of Berlin. These clerics were either outright members of the Nazi Party or such overt supporters of the movement that their political efforts were noted either by their parishioners or by the Nazi state itself. Although they were not significant in number, to what degree did brown priests cause their bishops great consternation? To what extent did their presence reveal that clergy members were not immune to the allure of extreme nationalism and virulent anti-Semitism? These questions imply final options that put priests in an adversarial position within their dioceses.

Finally, I focus on the life and choices of one unique individual, Monsignor Bernhard Lichtenberg, whom the Catholic Church has recently distinguished as "blessed." In his ministry, Lichtenberg recognized the deeper reality and broader implication of the gospel message, which impelled him to speak in behalf of all those whom the Nazis oppressed, including the Jews. Unfortunately, in Germany, he was an isolated prophet, a lonely voice, for few priests had the courage to risk their lives in this heroic manner.

I hope that, through an examination of the lives and choices of individual clerics, this book will provoke new reflections on the varied postures priests assumed and on the provisional adjustments they made to sustain their ministry during the Third Reich. In accomplishing their

Church-appointed tasks, some priests compromised their principles, whereas others remained unaffected. Some were heroic, and others were criminal. All, however, had to put to use a common set of Catholic defenses and operative values in order to survive Nazism. Whether they did so at the expense of their faith (and souls) or because of it is left to the Almighty to decide. This study, however, should put at risk any belief that all German priests acquiesced to (or resisted) the Third Reich in the same manner. The broad categories into which these priests fell, standing with and against each other, form a comprehensive picture of a Church engaged in the lethal world of Nazism in an effort to survive and carry out its sacramental mission.

one

Initial Encounters

On June 21, 1931, at three in the afternoon, thousands of German Catholics from the diocese of Berlin gathered at the Festival Convention Hall in Stettin to hear Dr. Josef Schnippenkötter, a leading Catholic educator from Essen, speak. The *Märkische Katholikentag*, the weekend event to which he was invited, was an all-important one, dedicated that year to the promotion of the Catholic faith. Schnippenkötter's topic was relevant: "*Katholikentag* in a Time of Distress." Earlier that spring, organizers of the event had asked Schnippenkötter, known for his honesty and bluntness, to address the current crisis of Catholicism in Germany. True to form, as if he knew the issues the Church had to sort out with itself, Schnippenkötter spoke of the "terrible national distress" facing Germany. He also spoke of the lost world war that Germany had endured, the confusion and disorder that followed in its wake, and the current escalating tension fostered by the different competing religious, philosophical, and ideological groups within Germany. For him, however, a far more insidious threat than a lost war, social tension, and even economic depression lay at the root of Germany's troubles: the absence of God. According to Schnippenkötter, God had become "negated" in the current world. In God's place, he argued, stood a new "godless heathenism" snaring the attention of all: Russian Bolshevism and its conniving twin, German National Socialism. Both these ideologies, he stated, introduced new, enchanting weltanschauungen that threatened Catholic life. He especially feared the influence of National Socialism, which he believed presented itself as a "religion or even more, a substitute religion." Nevertheless, Schnippenkötter conceded that "within the ranks of National Socialists" there existed "a vastly more noble longing for more ideal conditions" that would benefit all of Germany. These yearnings also seemed to fit the body and soul of any political party open to promoting the best interests of the fatherland. Still, he argued, the way to reach these goals was not through belligerence, pitting one group of citizens against another, or through the adoption of a "radical race theory" like the one already at work in National Socialism. Instead, he contended, German Catholics needed to foster balance and see the future in terms of its own religious traditions. Indeed, he argued, Catholics were not in a "position to cross out the Old Testament" simply because Jews had "played a major role within it."[1]

Immediately following Schnippenkötter's speech, Christian Schreiber, bishop of Berlin, took the podium and addressed the same topic, "The Catholic Church and the Distress of our Age." Echoing Schnippenkötter's concerns, Bishop Schreiber also spoke of political and social distress that tore the country apart as politicians placed their political and private interests "above the interest of the *Volk*" (people, encompassing racial, ethnic, and national unity). Similarly, Schreiber observed that individuals often ignored the fact that politics were "subject to God's moral law," and, therefore, "lies and slander, injustice and one-sided representation of interests, hate and force" were as unlawful "for the politician as for every other person." And although religion did "not interfere in single political questions," it still had the obligation to remind individuals that even politicians were subject "to the Ten Commandments of God." Schreiber stopped at this point, however, and did not explore the implications of his comments. Nor did he, like Schnippenkötter, directly address the dangers of National Socialism. Even though a perfect opportunity had existed to address the inconsistencies of National Socialism with Catholic teaching, Schreiber condemned only "liberalism, Marxism and Bolshevism," especially in their attack on the "rights of the parents and the Church with reference to the education of children."[2]

The two different approaches of Schnippenkötter and Schreiber indicate the diversity of responses in the German Catholic Church to National Socialism. Very few Catholics fully recognized the inherent evil of National Socialism and the devastation it would bring to Germany and the world. Some, like Schnippenkötter, who from the start realized that there were inherent contradictions between National Socialism and the teachings of Catholicism, did address them and made an effort to challenge these incongruities publicly. Nevertheless, even a Catholic such as Schnippenkötter was not prepared to condemn National Socialism entirely. Like some Catholics at the time, he always left room for the Church to accept its promises for a revitalized Germany. Unfortunately, however, most people were all too willing to ignore or minimize the tenets of National Socialism that went directly against their own beliefs. Instead, they preferred to embrace its glorification of German nationalism and its promises of economic and social rebirth for the German fatherland. As a result, the majority of these individuals appropriated Bishop Schreiber's posture toward Nazism—a wait-and-see attitude offered the Hitler movement the benefit of the doubt.

This predicament exposed both the balance and disproportion of the relationship between German Catholicism and National Socialism, especially in the Berlin diocese prior to Hitler's appointment as chancellor. During this time—January 30, 1934, through the summer of 1934—the National Socialist leaders and the Catholic hierarchy were attempting to reach a modus vivendi in order to coexist peacefully in Germany. The desire to create legal agreements with secular states to ensure the free exercise of the Church in a particular country obsessed Catholic Church leaders, especially Eugenio Pacelli, the Vatican secretary of state. On June 29, 1933, this trial period yielded a concordat between the Vatican and Germany. Throughout the roundabout process, mistrust and hope-filled expectation would exist simultaneously on both sides. Although the Church hierarchy had clear reservations with regard to the Hitler movement, they never put forth any uniform response to condemn it. Instead, the Church hierarchy chose to oppose only those aspects of National Socialism that directly challenged the authority or freedom of the Catholic Church to exercise its pastoral mission among its members. As a result, the hierarchy sent mixed messages to its priests and laity in regard to its acceptance or rejection of National Socialism. This lack of clarity in dealing with political issues was also implicitly evident in the Church's many-sided instructions to its clergy. Members of the clergy often found themselves uninformed in regard to forging a unified political stance.

Prior to the early 1930s, the National Socialist Party had not garnered enough support to worry the Church. In the 1930 Reichstag election, however, the Party took 18.3 percent of the vote, which gave the Nazis 107 seats. In the 1932 election, the Nazi showing improved—they drew 37.3 percent of the vote and earned 230 seats—and the electorate brought the Hitler movement to the forefront of German political, cultural, and religious life.[3] Despite these electoral successes, the Nazi Party's vicious attacks on the Catholic-sponsored Center Party, its drive to hinder legislation backed by Center Party coalitions, and the Church's criticism of the Party's weltanschauung (especially criticism of its racial teaching), led some members of the Catholic hierarchy to reject Nazism and prohibit Catholics from joining its ranks.[4]

The Church's rejection of National Socialism was a gradual one. It began publicly in the fall of 1930, when the pastor of the parish in Kirchhausen bei Heppenheim (in the diocese of Mainz) declared in a sermon that no Roman Catholic could be a member of the Nazi Party. The pastor also stated that National Socialists could no longer, in a corporate way, take part in Church gatherings and that any active member of the Nazi Party could be refused the sacraments. Upon inquiry into these statements, the chancery of Mainz sided with the pastor against the Nazi Party.[5] This public declaration of the diocese of Mainz against Nazism heightened the tension between the Catholic Church and Hitler's party.

The point of dispute centered primarily on the failure of Nazi leaders to clarify their ambivalent stance toward the Church. Sporadically throughout Germany, regional Nazi Party leaders, without documented direction from Hitler or headquarters in Munich, aimed critical comments in their speeches at the Catholic Church. In addition, Hitler had failed to explain the meaning of the twenty-fourth point of the National Socialist Party platform. According to the platform text, Nazism professed an undefined "positive Christianity" and promised "freedom for all religious denominations in the state," on condition that "they do not threaten the state's existence nor offend the moral feelings of the German race."[6] The bishops feared such a statement might eventually mean state control of the Church. This was something that they refused to accept.

Although the diocese of Mainz decided to act against members of the National Socialist Party, not every diocese was ready to undertake such measures. The diocese of Berlin was no exception in this regard. In addition, a papal decree had only recently created the Berlin diocese, on August 31, 1930.[7] Previously, it was part of the Breslau archdiocese. Berlin's first bishop, Christian Schreiber, was also still in the process of establishing himself in the diocese: many difficult and time-consuming internal pastoral matters were deflecting him from national concerns. Nevertheless, Schreiber did take the time to comment on National Socialism publicly. Following the outcome of the September 1930 Reichstag election, Schreiber agreed to an interview with a correspondent of the *8 Uhr Abendblatt* evening newspaper. In the interview, Schreiber directly attributed the outcome of the election to unrest in the youth brought on by the "current distress and deplorable state of affairs" in the economy. He believed it was "in no way the work of a destructive weltanschauung," such as National Socialism.[8] Here Schreiber appeared unwilling to challenge the Nazi weltanschauung. Later, an October 13 article in the Berlin *Montag-Morgen* newspaper only confirmed this reluctance and noted that the Berlin chancery had stated earlier that the diocese of Mainz had no authority to determine policy or make recommendations for Catholics in other dioceses.[9] Several French newspapers, including *Le Temps,* reported this discrepancy and portrayed Schreiber in direct conflict with Ludwig Maria Hugo, bishop of Mainz. Schreiber, who was in Rome at the time, immediately attempted to straighten out this confusion and spoke with a correspondent of the Catholic Parisian newspaper *La Croix*. In the October 21, 1930, edition of the paper, Schreiber denied "formally and absolutely" any contradiction between his stance and that of the bishop of Mainz, insisting that he had only made one statement in regard to Germany in the *8 Uhr Abendblatt*. In *La Croix,* he reiterated the "pressing duty to maintain external peace, and a need to establish total internal agreement, without the anti-Christian exclusion of Semitic elements" that was "advocated by the Hitler people." Schreiber also added that he saw these reports as an "abominable maneuver to raise opposition between Catholic bishops who are supremely of one mind."[10] According to newspaper reports, however, some time in October, Schreiber's own chancery, in reply to an inquiry made by a committed National Socialist, publicly stated that one could be a member of the Nazi Party as long as the Party did not force the individual to stray from Catholic teaching and practice. In addition, the chancery also gave "convinced" National Socialists permission to receive the sacraments as long as they did not personally support the "anti-Catholic and unchristian ideas" regularly printed in Nazi-sponsored publications.[11]

On March 17, 1931, in reaction to diocesan statements critical of the National Socialist weltanschauung and prohibiting membership of Catholics in the Party, the Nazi-sponsored *Westdeutscher Beobachter*—to the dismay of the Berlin chancery—printed the October reply of the Berlin chancery under the bold headline "Bishop of Berlin Confirms Catholics May Be Members of the NSDAP [National Socialist German Workers' Party]."[12] The Berlin chancery quickly responded in a public letter on March 20, 1931, by stating that Schreiber stood with the bishops of Breslau, Cologne, Paderborn, and Bavaria, who had criticized National Socialism for its ideological errors. The chancery then acknowledged that five months earlier it had replied to an individual National Socialist and stated that membership in the Nazi Party was contingent on specified "fundamental conditions," such as the rejection of anti-Catholic ideas and respect for Church teaching and practice. Following this period of "observation and examination," however, the Berlin chancery eventually determined that the Nazi Party had not met these conditions; nor had Hitler offered any clear pronouncement on the Party's relationship with the Catholic Church. Therefore, the Berlin diocese felt compelled to agree with the German dioceses of Breslau, Cologne, Paderborn, and Bavaria. The article, however, did not clearly condemn National Socialism or specifically prohibit Berlin parishioners from joining the Nazi Party.[13]

Although Schreiber's chancery issued the statement of clarification on the position of the diocese in relation to National Socialism, the *Westdeutscher Beobachter*'s headlines were not completely inaccurate. At the beginning of 1931, in a lesser public light, Schreiber had encouraged the Cartel Federation of German Catholic Student Associations, which had made Schreiber an honorary member in three local branches, to rescind their prohibition against membership in the NSDAP. Schreiber believed that a "well-informed" Catholic might be able to work within the Nazi Party to counteract any views that were critical of the Catholic Church. In addition, Schreiber had a past history of involvement in political matters. For example, in his 1924 Lenten pastoral letter, he spoke out "against the occupying forces in the Rhineland, against the 'war guilt lie' of the Versailles Treaty, against rebellious workers, and against the unjust wage policy of employers."[14] Because Schreiber concerned himself with such issues in his pastoral letters and believed the effects of the depression were devastating for his people, he saw something promising in National Socialism.[15] Nevertheless, the refusal of National Socialism to define its relationship with and future plans for Christianity signaled to Schreiber that he had to alter his stance. More important, the unwanted press surrounding his previous comments on National Socialism made Schreiber appear in conflict with his fellow bishops. Schreiber did not wish to perpetuate this image of himself, especially since it was at variance with the National Socialist movement and its goals. Therefore, it was not difficult for him to reverse any previous position he had held in favor of Hitler's party. By early 1932, he also advised the members of the cartel to do likewise and ban membership in the Nazi Party. Schreiber now argued that an individual could only work from outside the party to influence any change.[16]

Ultimately, Schreiber fell in line with his fellow German bishops who earlier had published statements critical of Hitler's party.[17] On March 21, 1931, he presented the priests of his diocese with his own version of "Pastoral Directives Concerning National Socialism," which he based on guidelines that other German dioceses had issued earlier. Schreiber's guidelines primarily challenged National Socialist ideology, but only when it rejected the "essential teachings of Catholic belief" or projected false interpretations of them. He feared, he stated, that the National Socialists wanted "to establish a new weltanschauung in the place of Christian faith," because they placed "race higher than religion" and rejected "the revelation of the Old Testament." Here Schreiber was clearly not exalting the Hebrew Scriptures or defending Judaism or even Jews. Rather, he was defending the Christian reliance on the Old Testament for its interpretation of God's revelation in the New Testament and the role of Christianity as the basis for the German state. Moreover, Schreiber assailed those National Socialists who wished to create what he called "a dogmatically empty German National Church." For him, such misinterpreted and misguided "positive Christianity," which was represented in the Nazi Party platform, no longer represented "the Christendom of Christ." Instead, the Christianity that the party advocated called for the "rejection of every concordat, the demand for nondenominational school, the radicalization of national thought and the resistance against the protection of unborn life." He instructed his priests to explain simply and clearly to their parishioners that National Socialism had "increasingly veered toward the cultural arena" and had taken a "Kulturkampf position against the Church and its bishops." In turn, he "strongly prohibited" Catholic priests from working with the Nazi Party in any fashion. He stated that the Church, through its actions, had in no way "come to terms with National Socialism."[18]

Even though Schreiber used very strong language to criticize aspects of National Socialism that directly contradicted Church teachings, he refused to prohibit Catholics from partial participation in the movement and from voting for the Nazi Party. Instead, he instructed the clergy to permit an individual who wore an insignia of the Nazi Party to attend Mass so long as his or her presence was in no way seen "as a demonstration and in no manner" interrupted the service. He also granted priests leeway to determine whether they could administer the sacraments to known National Socialists. He did, however, prohibit the participation of National Socialists "in events of worship in closed columns with uniforms and flags."[19]

The guidelines with which Schreiber and his fellow bishops provided the priests of Germany highlight the difficulties Church leaders had when dealing with the political posture of National Socialism. For years, members of the Catholic clergy had involved themselves in politics through membership in the Center Party. For some priests, this even led to their holding elected offices, both regionally and nationally. Thus, in no way can anyone argue that the Church and its clergy did not have a political orientation.[20] With this point in mind, however, one also must understand why the clergy involved themselves in politics in the first place. This legacy of political involvement can be traced back to the period of persecution against the Church and its clergy under the legislation of the Bismarckian Kulturkampf. Neither the Church hierarchy nor the laity wished to repeat this time of repression and dishonor. Therefore, Catholic bishops encouraged their clergy and laity to involve themselves in the political process and in the foundation of the Center Party. Catholics, in general, wished to ensure that the Church would always have a venue to protect its freedom and to serve its members. Clerical involvement in the Center Party was primarily focused on civic concerns, such as education or the legislation of public morality, both of which directly affected the pastoral mission or teaching of the Church. At times, the sermon during Sunday Mass became the rallying point for Catholics to press for certain issues that the Church hierarchy wanted the laity to support or reject. Despite this clear tie with politics, there was still a hesitancy among Church leaders to involve themselves directly in political issues that appeared entirely separate from the Church's primary concern bearing upon salvation.

In Berlin, one may trace this hesitancy back to the theological education that the majority of Berlin priests received at the University of Breslau. Although the theology professors taught the seminarians that the priesthood was "an institution created and established by Jesus Christ" and "nothing less than a living continuation and operation of Christ's high priesthood," and that it, along with the Church, was necessary to continue the "mediation of grace and salvation" begun by Christ, they also instructed them that there were practical limits to the power and influence of their priesthood in secular society.[21] In essence, the Breslau professors, such as

Father Franz Schubert, a professor of pastoral theology (1920–1937), taught seminarians that as priests they had to learn to establish a relationship of "peace, mutual respect, and mutual appreciation" with the secular authority. According to him, they must always honor the "authorized decrees of the authority" and "refrain from disrespectful censure and offensive criticism." In turn, he instructed them to encourage "responsible obedience toward authority" among their parishioners. Schubert pointed out, however, that, as a priest, each had to "be careful that the authorities" respected his "status and his responsibilities as leader of the parish" and, therefore, "should and must reject harmful abrupt treatment" by them. Furthermore, Schubert stated that each future priest always had to exercise his ministry not out of personal consideration for himself, but from the viewpoint of the Church and his sacramental position as a priest. This included notifying supervisors whenever low-level bureaucrats acted in a way that spread "indifference, disbelief, seduction, and hostility toward the Church and its servants." In no case, he stressed, should one of them dishonor his office "through his conduct" toward civil authorities. Also, in the case of a serious dispute between Church and state, a priest should engage the state in discussion only after consulting with chancery officials. For Schubert, the latter was especially true in areas of "nationally mixed population," such as those in the eastern portion of the Berlin diocese, where he recommended a priest "should not drag national affairs" into his preaching and ministry; nor should he ever "provoke denominational quarreling without need."[22] Ultimately, Schubert taught seminarians to avoid conflicts with state officials and to challenge them only as a last resort, and only if a state official had directly impeded the freedom of a priest to carry out his pastoral duties. Such education, however, did not teach priests to question authority figures or resist state policy. Instead, it encouraged them to concern themselves solely with Church-related issues and to avoid politics if at all possible.

In his speeches and sermons, Bishop Schreiber offered his priests counsel that mirrored Schubert's advice. Schreiber wanted to ensure that the German government viewed both the priests of his diocese and the Catholics they served as good patriotic citizens of the state. For example, in a November 1930 address, Schreiber reminded not only priests but Catholics in general that the Church always recognized any legal form of government, whether it was "monarchical or republican, aristocratic or democratic." This included the current democratically elected government of the Weimar Republic, even though Schreiber on occasion regretted the "liberal character" of the Weimar constitution, which both "carried out the separation between Church and state" and failed fully to enact legislation to protect the denominational school and religious instruction in schools. Despite these reservations, Schreiber acknowledged that the Church must also accept the legally appointed or elected leaders of a state.

In the eyes of the Church, Schreiber argued, God granted and "vested in the legal bearer of state authority" the power to rule. Therefore, Schreiber instructed Catholics "to submit to state authority." Although Schreiber exhorted Catholics to recognize and obey the state, he also emphasized that the Church and state were "independent in their area of power." To this end, he wanted to ensure that the Church, without any interference by the state, maintained its freedom to serve its members, especially in regard to the sacraments and education. For this reason, he argued that the independence between the two was only "encroached upon if the Church illegally" interfered in "purely civic matters or the State in purely Church matters." Moreover, the Church had "no right in any way to interfere in the purely political affairs of the state," because the state was "independent in purely civic things." Still, Schreiber did not divorce the Church entirely from the political arena and, in his broad analysis, left an opening for the Church to criticize politics, especially in the area of ethics, because "all bearers of human nature" were subject to God's moral law.[23]

The Church's teaching on Church-state relations left the average parish priest in a dilemma. At first reading, a priest might conclude that he should stay out of politics altogether and avoid any situation that would bring himself in direct conflict with state authorities. He could conclude that any difficult situation with the state should be left for the bishop and chancery officials to deal with. By reflecting on the teaching as a whole and deciphering it to serve the laity who were also citizens of the State, however, a priest might also decide that he had to involve himself in political issues that in some way affected the freedom of the Church. Though he might chose the latter option, a priest still had to determine which issues were within the sphere of the Church and which were within province of the state. Naturally, he could call on diocesan chancery officials to offer him guidance, but ultimately the individual clergyman had to assess his pastoral situation and decide on his own what series of risks he needed to undertake to engage the combatants of the state successfully.

Before Hitler came to power, priests took fewer risks when they involved themselves in political issues and challenged supporters of National Socialism. For example, the bishops' pastoral guidelines for ministry to National Socialists, which were individually prepared, urged their priests to put pressure on parishioners not to join or support the Nazi Party. This, of course, would be one of the last times that priests received such a clear directive on how specifically to deal with National Socialists. Interestingly, this instruction galvanized many priests to refuse the sacraments to many well-known Catholic National Socialists. Although such an action today does not seem radical enough, remember, in the minds of believing Catholics then, such an action would have jeopardized their eternal salvation. Such a predicament happened in 1931 in Holzheim, when a pastor refused to offer a funeral mass for Peter Gemeinder, the regional NSDAP

Gauleiter (administrator). This action deeply troubled many Roman Catholics, including those who were supporters of the NSDAP, especially because they knew Gemeinder to be "a strongly believing Catholic." In lieu of a Catholic Mass and burial, his National Socialists comrades buried Gemeinder. Helen Radtke, a Catholic NSDAP supporter who had attended the burial, later stood at the grave and recalled: "We Catholics were under tremendous pressure from the Church. As I stood there, I thought that if the clergy did not stop acting in such an uncanonical spirit, I would have to leave the Church. It was a great spiritual struggle for me, but I did not lose my faith, even though the eternal forms of our Church were taken away from me. This sacrifice, too, had to be made."[24]

Even though Bishop Schreiber left some leeway for his priests to administer the sacraments to National Socialist Catholics, many priests chose to interpret the guidelines strictly and consequently withheld the sacraments from NSDAP members. The most prominent case involved Monsignor Bernhard Lichtenberg, provost of St. Hedwig's, the Catholic cathedral in Berlin, who publicly refused to admit known National Socialists to the sacraments. Lichtenberg's stance so outraged Dr. Bräutigam, a Catholic and member of the Nazi Party, that the doctor withdrew himself and his wife from the Church. Before he left, however, Bräutigam made sure that the press became aware of his displeasure over the situation.[25] In a separate case, Father Georg Gretz, associate pastor in Bernau, refused to bury an SA (*Sturmabteilung*, Storm Troopers) man unless his "brown shirt" was removed. After the event had been reported in the Nazi press, the diocesan newspaper published its own account of the event. Gretz explained that he had only followed the directives of Bishop Schreiber and, therefore, had refused burial because the man's SA comrades insisted upon wearing their uniforms, carrying flags, and processing in formation—all prohibited by the directives.[26]

In addition to National Socialism, the German Catholic bishops and leading members of the laity believed that there were other forces that threatened the existence and mission of the Catholic Church in Germany. In the early 1930s, German Catholics viewed Communism as the most terrifying of these forces.[27] Regularly, Bishop Schreiber bemoaned the godlessness that followed in the wake of a Communist upheaval. For example, in an April 1930 address, Schreiber even encouraged Protestants, Catholics, and Jews to create a "great united front of belief against disbelief" against the godlessness of Bolshevism.[28] Again on Christmas Day 1932, Schreiber, lamenting the secularism of the holiday and the failure of people to be in touch with the birth of Christ, reminded the members of his diocese that the Communists in the Soviet Union had even eradicated the secular celebration of Christmas.[29]

Bishop Schreiber also feared the rise of "cultural Bolshevism"—the removal of God and Christianity from everyday life—in German society. In a January 1930 address, he acknowledged that this move toward secularism was not always accomplished under the banner of Communism or liberalism but instead came from a variety of directions, including from Catholics themselves. He exhorted Catholics to stand true to their faith and avoid the challenges and temptations of society. Schreiber also encouraged Catholics to work diligently to uphold the natural law and to be faithful to their marriage vows while at the same time he condemned everyone who worked to make divorce easier or sought to legalize abortion and homosexuality.[30]

During this period, what Schreiber and his fellow bishops really feared was the pluralism of the democratically based Weimar Germany, even though its new constitution specifically protected freedom of religious expression.[31] Naturally, the activities of the Catholic Center Party in imperial Germany alerted the bishops to the larger possibilities of a parliamentary government. Nevertheless, in imperial Germany a power-wielding kaiser and his chancellor still dominated a government controlled by the traditional elites of German society. The establishment of the Weimar Republic and a new constitution, however, abruptly broke with the past tradition of monarchical government. For this reason, the German bishops simply had no experience negotiating with a democratically elected administration. As Stewart Stehlin concludes, the Weimar Republic was led by "an administration not based on tradition but a government which could be altered according to the wishes of the people and whose leaders were many times influenced by beliefs such as Liberalism or Socialism, whose philosophical foundations were often inimical to or which at least differed [from] those of the Church."[32] This uncertainty fostered the mistrust of the bishops toward the new government, which they feared at any moment could be swayed by the voters to limit the rights of the Church.

Even more detrimental to the relations between Church leaders and the Weimar government was the German hierarchy's perception of a new hedonism that they believed was widespread within Weimar culture and society. For German bishops, this hedonism not only posed a threat to Catholic morality but was also an assault on German sensibilities. Nowhere was this offensive voluptuousness more apparent than in Germany's capital city of Berlin.[33] After article 118 of the Weimar Constitution prohibited government censorship with the exception of obscenity, pornographers used this newfound freedom to test the limits of the new society and sell their wares freely.[34] The insouciant climate of the 1920s, coupled with economic instability, also increased the presence of prostitution and illegal drug sales in the city. Similarly, greater toleration of alternate lifestyles gave rise to nightclubs and bars dedicated to serving homosexuals and transvestites. These various factors combined led many bishops to conclude that Weimar culture was deleterious to the Catholic faithful.

In Berlin, this tension between Catholic morality and hedonistic culture placed an added burden on believing Catholics who were already attempting to cope with the tenuous position in which they lived. As early as 1918, Father Carl Sonnenschein, the "apostle to the city of Berlin" and advocate for the poor, declared that, although Berlin was "indeed a metropolis," the Catholicism there had "a damn small-town mentality."[35] As Sonnenschein and many of his contemporaries noted, Catholicism in Germany seemed more at home in the countryside than in the city.[36] Sonnenschein found a tension between a provincial church mentality, with its regional customs and traditions brought by immigrants to the city of Berlin, and the actual social and moral challenges that a large city placed upon Berlin Catholics.[37] He believed Catholics too often allowed themselves to accept the role of a hesitant minority in a city whose atmosphere lacked any sense of religiosity. For Sonnenschein, Berlin was a "dark city" into whose darkness he disappeared. It "invited no one. Observed by no one . . . The lonely die alone. . . . The city places thousands of temptations on thousands of street corners. . . . Against the spirit of what is Christian, what is civil, what is responsible living. Wrapping all life in anonymity . . . Christianity is not the atmosphere!" Most clearly, Sonnenschein saw this secularism particularly prevalent in the location of the churches. Instead of occupying the central squares of the city or other notable locations, Sonnenschein noted that churches were "rarely in open spaces," but instead were "wedged into street fronts. More frequently built in backyards. Behind houses."[38] These bleak observations offered Sonnenschein and others like him the challenge to steer Berlin Catholicism from its "ghetto" mentality toward an active semblance of unified parity, comparable to contemporary Protestantism. Through both the spoken and written word, Sonnenschein implored Berlin Catholics not only to live the gospel message of Christ but also to be proud of their confession of faith and to stand up for their rights afforded to them by God. He believed that the time of political discrimination and defensiveness had come to an end and, therefore, that Catholics should allow their isolation to be laid to rest.[39]

By 1931, Berlin Catholics had made some progress in their attempts to address Sonnenschein's concerns. Nevertheless, individuals such as Father Franz Rauterkus, S.J., still found sufficient minority feelings among Berlin Catholics to warrant addressing the issue in his writings; however, all his words were not negative. Rather, he viewed the hodgepodge of faith expression that resulted from a largely immigrant Church and the late foundation of the diocese as a rich blessing for Catholics. He argued that one did not hear the annoying clutter because it has "always been so." Consequently, people were more open to "a certain broad-mindedness, even a certain self-assurance."[40] Similarly, Dr. Erich Klausener, a Prussian government official and director of Berlin's Catholic Action, optimistically stressed the positive situation of Berlin Catholics. "Catholicism," according to Klausener, was "a religion of triumphant optimism that comes from its dogmatic basis. The Church founded by God will not be overcome. . . . It has survived all threats." For Klausener, the Catholic Church in Berlin was not solely an external institution made up of buildings and led by a distant hierarchy, but a "community" of "action." To Klausener "the strength of a community is based upon the strength of the individual personalities who work and live in it. The Church is not regarded as something different, distant; rather, we are the Church."[41]

This idea of community was not something new. For Berlin Catholics, it was instinctual. Since the founding of the Berlin diocese, Catholics had had to work together to have their voices heard in a very Protestant, but even more secular, culture. As Rauterkus stated, "The Berlin Catholic is Catholic in opposition. The Protestant and faithless environment makes unity urgent, forming a certain esprit de corps, an apostolic way of thinking, an incomparably greater interest in Church questions than ever before in the homeland." Rauterkus concluded that many lukewarm Catholics had "rediscovered their faith and their religious zeal" in this environment, even though Berlin air was "not favorable to Catholicism and not at all to religiosity."[42] Father Heinrich Lampe of St. Matthias stressed this point even more when he wrote, "Whoever comes to Berlin for the first time and sees the over-filled churches on a Sunday, suspects that for these people their belief and their confession have a vitality of the deepest meaning, since here in Berlin faith is still too often a real courageous confession."[43]

Because of the minority status of Catholics in the Berlin diocese, Catholic parishes often became the center of both spiritual and social life for practicing German Catholics. In 1933, there were only 538,096 Catholics in the diocese of Berlin among 6,963,709 non-Catholics. The diocese had seventy-eight parishes and eighty-nine additional chapels and communities of worship served by 358 diocesan and religious priests from eighteen religious communities to meet the spiritual needs of these Catholics.[44] An additional twenty-three communities of religious women also served in various ministries throughout the diocese. The parish communities ranged in size from the smaller parishes of the dispersed Catholic population of Brandenburg and Pomerania, such as the tiny St. James in Grimmen, Pomerania, with only 100 parishioners and one priest, to the huge city parishes of Berlin, such as St. Paul in the Moabit-Tiergarten district, with its 20,000 parishioners and four Dominican priests.[45]

Despite the commitment of a nucleus of Berlin Catholics who regularly practiced their faith and played an active role in the life of their parish and diocese, there were still many who rarely darkened a church door and some who could not even recall the name of their parish. This was the reality of Catholic life in a metropolis with a significant transient population. The size of the parishes did not ease the situation. Often, because of the huge number of parishioners, it was simply impossible for the pastor or his associates to visit all the newcomers personally and encourage them to become active members. The statistics compiled by Father Maximilian Kaller while he was pastor of St. Michael's parish in Berlin-Mitte (1917–

1926)—the largest parish at that time in Berlin, with 17,000 Catholics among 150,000 non-Catholics—revealed that few registered Catholics in the parish actually participated in a parish association. Kaller pointed out that, although the parish had 4,359 men, only 250 belonged to the Catholic Men's Association. The Women's and Mothers' Association fared a little better, with 1,130 members from among the 4,098 female parish-ioners. Of course, Kaller was disappointed by this number, stating that "all women and mothers should belong to it, especially the younger women." The Young Men's Association and Young Women's Association had even less participation in them than did the associations for older generations. Of the 2,849 young men, for example, only 100 belonged to the Young Men's Association, and of the 3,771 young women in the parish, only 615 were members of their respective organization.[46]

Mass attendance followed a similar pattern throughout the Berlin diocese. Kaller pointed out that during his tenure as pastor only two-thirds of the registered parishioners actually attended mass.[47] These data troubled him and other pastors throughout their ministry. For example, Father Wilhelm Frank offered an even more despairing statement concerning mass attendance at his parish: "I am convinced that not one third of the Catholics obligated to do so regularly attend Mass here on Sunday and holy days. I am convinced that at least half of all those obligated do not attend holy Easter communion. I have more than once given the opinion that half of all our new communicants even in the year following their first holy communion no longer receive their Easter communion."[48]

The statistics reported in the annual *Church Handbook for Catholic Germany* during the early years of the Third Reich support Frank's and Kaller's observations. In Berlin in 1933, out of a total Catholic population of 538,096, only 189,442 people (slightly more than 35 percent) received Easter communion—a fundamental obligation for Roman Catholics, even for those who attend church only once a year. This trend did not vary greatly from year to year and was far below that of the Reich national average of 61.84 percent. Regular weekly church attendance in Berlin was also the second lowest in Germany.[49] In 1933, for example, only 160,159, or 29.76 percent, of Berlin Catholics regularly attended mass. By contrast, in many German dioceses approximately 50 to 60 percent of the Catholic population attended weekly Eucharist. These figures remained relatively constant throughout the 1930s.[50]

These statistics alarmed the priests of the diocese, who, in turn, voiced their own concern to their congregations and to the diocese at large. In the extant writings of priests who served in parishes in Berlin during the 1920s and 1930s, there is an expressed fear of losing Catholic souls to other Christian denominations or to religious indifference (i.e., a total lack of participation in any faith). Commenting on this pastoral situation, Father Georg Puchowski, secretary general of Catholic Action Berlin, attributed this "increasing loss of faith" to the growth of materialism, immorality, and the general hatred "reflected in the hatred of classes and of parties, even in the hatred of individuals against one another." Puchowski also noted, "Despite all technical achievements one can hardly speak of advancement, but instead, it is clear that we find ourselves situated on descending paths with the future lying more ominous than rosy before us."[51] Activist priest Carl Sonnenschein not only shared Puchowski's concerns but also stressed far greater dangers: marriage outside the faith and the high rate of divorce. Sonnenschein stated that 69 percent of Catholic men who chose to marry wed non-Catholic women. The statistics for Catholic women were on par with Catholic men. Sonnenschein lamented that Catholics were only "ten per cent of the population! . . . [H]ow enormously have the emphasis and the safeguarding of our religious identity fallen!" The figures for divorce also disturbed him. He lamented the fact that the divorce rate for marriage between Catholics had quadrupled to 24.9 percent, "despite the Church's insistence on the indissolubility of marriage!" According to Sonnenschein, this high level of marital discord was the result of the greatest danger of his time, the political situation. As he put it, "Politics . . . disguises and distorts the spiritual reality."[52]

Monsignor Kaller offered similar observations about the pastoral problems at hand. Although he clearly stated that any "existing mixed marriages should in no way be belittled," he stated that mixed marriage "created misfortune" for the couple. He based this "on irrefutable facts." Kaller further argued that mixed marriages were "a great detriment to the Church life of the community" since most did not join congregations and associations, and either had no children or did not raise their children as Catholics. He concluded, "Mixed marriages infinitely harm the growth of the Catholic Church."[53] In addition to mixed marriages, Kaller was greatly concerned about the large number of single adults in his Berlin parish. Not only were these individuals difficult to reach because of their often transient lifestyles, but they, in turn, did not fall into the ideal model of Catholic life: marriage, the production of offspring, and the raising of a family according to the teachings of the Catholic Church.[54]

The German Catholic hierarchy was not alone in its negative evaluation of Weimar society and "cultural Bolshevism," especially as the latter attempted to whistle in the ears of German citizens. Ironically, many National Socialists also lamented society's perceived attack on marriage, reproduction, and family life. For example, in early January 1933, the *Tägliche Rundschau* newspaper reported that a recent production at the *Deutsche Theater Berlin* of "God, King and Farmer" had enraged "National Socialists who took offense" at the play's "degradation of imperial and princely dignity." Similarly, the diocese's weekly newspaper reported that "Catholics took offense" at the way the play debased "the pope's dignity."[55]

This was not the first time that Catholics and Nazis shared similar concerns over public morals and proper etiquette. Indeed, both groups fought regularly against many aspects of society that they perceived to be corrupt and the consequence of liberalism, especially in relation to the decline in marriages and births and the widespread diluting of morality. Despite these similar concerns in pre-Nazi Germany, there was also within the Catholic Church enough internal disagreement with the ideology of National Socialism to prevent the bishops from making a public overture to the Nazis. This became evident during a January 1931 Catholic youth rally in Berlin when featured speaker, Dr. Grundei, derided the anti-Christian attitude of both National Socialism and Communism. He believed that the issues facing the Catholic Church in the 1930s could eventually lead to a struggle that would make "the Kulturkampf of the 1880s" seem like "child's play."[56] For older Catholics, especially for those living in Prussia, the hate-provoking term *Kulturkampf* brought back bleak memories of repression and parishes without priests. In Berlin, it had even onerous meaning among Catholics because it reminded them anew of their minority status in the Reich capital and the surrounding areas. For younger German Catholics, evoking the term elicited memories of a kind of religious apartheid in which their grandparents were the victims. In the politically charged climate of the waning Weimar Republic, when political parties were literally fighting in the streets for power and constituents, it was an ominous rallying cry for any Catholic to hear. The radical outreach of the Nazis and Communists for the youth of Germany only compounded the growing panic provoked by such a dark memory.

Despite Hitler's appointment in late January as chancellor of Germany, the German bishops did not rescind their prohibitions against the Nazi Party. Nor, however, did the Prussian German Catholic bishops suggest that members of their dioceses could not vote for a specific party during the elections immediately before and after Hitler's ascendancy.[57] Rather, their statements, such as the pronouncement issued by the bishops of Prussia on July 12, 1932, just prior to the Reichstag election, stressed that they "did not want to carry the political party struggle into the sanctity of the Church." As a result, the bishops chose only to issue a word of warning, which requested the Catholic faithful to "choose representatives whose character and tried attitude" gave "witness to their support for peace and for the social welfare of the *Volk,* for the protection of the denominational schools, the Christian religion, and the Catholic Church." The bishops, however, did advise their followers to guard against agitators and parties that were "not worthy of the trust of the Catholic *Volk.*" In addition, they added that Catholics should draw their "advice from proven Catholic newspapers."[58] Because the majority of Catholic-sponsored newspapers, such as the Berlin-based *Germania,* supported the Center Party, a statement in that vein indirectly promoted Center Party candidates.[59]

For the Reichstag election on March 5, 1933, the Prussian Catholic bishops reissued their word of warning used during the July 1932 election. In his own diocese, Schreiber chose to have the Prussian bishops' statement not only published in the Berlin Catholic newspaper but also read aloud from the pulpits of all the churches in his diocese.[60] In their decision not to denounce the National Socialist Party directly, the bishops used caution and discretion to avoid antagonizing the party of the German chancellor. The outcome of the election gave the NSDAP 43.9 percent of the nationwide vote compared to the Center Party's 14.1 percent. It also placed more pressure on the bishops to alter their stance toward the Hitler party. Shortly after the election, Hitler, himself a Catholic, if only nominally, upset the German Catholic bishops even more when he refused to take part in the Catholic mass that marked the opening of the Reichstag. Earlier, a government official had publicly stated that Hitler would not take part in the mass because the Catholic bishops had described "the Führer and members of the National Socialist German Workers' Party as disloyal to the Church" and consequently would not be allowed "to receive the benefit of the sacraments."[61] Instead, Hitler, along with Joseph Goebbels, his minister of propaganda, visited the Luisenstadt Cemetery in Berlin and laid a wreath at the graves of their murdered SA comrades. This was an extremely awkward moment for German Catholics and especially for the entire German Catholic episcopacy. Hitler's clever move gave the impression to German Catholics that they could once again be excluded from civic activities, only this time from the National Socialist–led revitalization of Germany itself. Yet again, such actions awakened Kulturkampf feelings of inferiority and religious apartheid among Berlin Catholics.[62]

The events surrounding the opening of the Reichstag, including both Protestant and Catholic services in their respective houses of worship as well as a solemn state ceremony in the Garrison Church, offered the new Nazi-led government the perfect opportunity to show a face of civility and allegiance to tradition. The infamous picture that became a popular postcard depicting new Reich Chancellor Hitler bowing in respect to Reich President Hindenburg, as the latter shook his hand, only further reinforced this notion of trust. Then, on March 23, 1933, in a speech to the *Reichstag* deputies, Hitler finally made overtures to both Catholics and Protestants. The German bishops had been waiting for a clarification of the Party's stance toward Roman Catholicism, and now Hitler offered one. According to Hitler, the National Socialist government saw "in both Christian denominations the most important factors for the preservation of our *Volkstum* [ethnicity]." Therefore, the government would respect "the treaties concluded between them and the states." Their rights would not be infringed upon. Hitler also added, with specific emphasis for the sake of Catholics, "Likewise, the Reich government, which sees Christianity as the unshakable foundation of the moral and ethical life of the *Volk*, attaches the utmost importance to friendly relations with the Holy See and seeks to develop this relationship."[63] In this, he could not have been more solicitous to the German Catholic hierarchy. Now many Christians who were open to National Socialism more confidently believed that there was no need for hesitancy among them to join the NSDAP. Ironically, on the same day that Hitler promised cooperation with the churches, the Nazi-dominated German Reichstag, with the assistance of Center Party representatives, passed the Enabling Act, which transferred legislative power to Hitler's cabinet. In essence, Hitler now had dictatorial power to pass legislation without the consent of an elected body. Soon Germany would be a one-party state with political parties such as the Center disbanding after reviewing the futility of the situation.

A great deal of maneuvering took place before Hitler made his March 23 speech. Prior to this date, both party and government representatives went to great lengths to find out if the German bishops would change their position toward the National Socialist Party.[64] The Berlin chancery and Bishop Schreiber served as intermediaries for some of these overtures. Schreiber informed the government representative that the German episcopacy needed an official declaration that promised respect for the teaching and freedom of the Church and also recognized the role of the Catholic Church in the nation.[65] Shortly after Hitler's speech, the German episcopacy, in a March 28 declaration from their Fulda bishops' conference, which encompassed all the German bishops, announced the rescission of their ban against National Socialism, citing the "public and solemn declarations" that Hitler had given and that affirmed "the inviolability of the Catholic teaching on faith and the unchanging tasks and rights of the Church." The bishops, however, chose not to lift their "condemnation of definite religious-moral errors" in the ideology of National Socialism. In addition, they requested that no "political or party-associated demonstrations" occur in "houses of worship and during church functions."[66] Even with these cautions in place, the bishops chose to overlook much of the raw substance of Nazism, especially its blatant anti-Semitism and public violence that had been unleashed on a number of its political opponents.

On April 2, Bishop Schreiber publicly explained why the German bishops had changed their stance toward National Socialism. According to him, the bishops previously believed that the program of the National Socialists had exceeded "its political jurisdiction" and had made "claims to want to decide which teaching and institutions of the Church would be approved in the National Socialist State and which would not be approved according to the standpoint of a vague ethical and moral feeling of the German race." He also feared that the "National Socialists would infringe upon the inviolable rights of the Catholic Church," especially by rescinding treaties previously made by the Vatican with individual German states. Similarly, he worried about the effect of making "the ethical and moral feeling of the Germanic race the ultimate standard."[67] Now, however, Schreiber argued that Hitler's remarks of March 23 made it possible for the episcopacy to alter its stance toward National Socialism.[68] The bishops accepted Hitler's promises to respect the Church's autonomy and freedom and to work with the Holy See.

Along with his fellow bishops, Schreiber issued directives to his priests concerning National Socialism. He instructed his priests to offer the sacraments to members of the National Socialist Party. He also gave permission for party members to attend mass in party uniforms—even in large groups—but cautioned that by no means were masses or other liturgical celebrations to be used to promote political causes. Similarly, Schreiber prohibited priests from allowing anyone to carry flags of political organizations into a church and prohibited priests from holding special masses or prayer services for political parties. Furthermore, he asked his priests to ensure that political demonstrations following a funeral mass not obscure prayers during the final committal.[69]

The Church immediately experienced the effect of this modus vivendi with the National Socialist state. In July 1933, for example, the Ministry of Interior ordered that all civil servants, including the clergy, must offer the Hitler greeting, "Heil Hitler!"[70] The diocese complied with the order and published it (and similar laws) without any commentary in the *Amtsblatt,* a chancery publication used to inform priests of diocesan events and policies. By publishing the laws in this manner, the diocesan officials allowed the individual priests freedom to make their own decision concerning which directives to follow. On certain special occasions, however, chancery officials would publish in the *Amtsblatt* certain instructions to the clergy to assist them in planning events for the day. For example, on May 1, 1933, the Day of National Labor, the Berlin chancery ordered every diocesan parish to celebrate a Solemn High Mass, Benediction, and to ring the church bells at 9:00 a.m. for fifteen minutes. The chancery also requested that priests deliver a sermon stressing the "value and blessing of Christian work."[71]

Despite the attempt to work with the new state, the Berlin Church and its priests kept running into problems with state officials. Much of this may be attributed to the chaotic nature of National Socialist rule in Germany.[72] For example, it was common to find in some cities and towns state leaders who were open to the Church and who did not interfere in the activities of the Church's ministers. In other places, however, overzealous officials, wishing to impress their superiors and seek advancement, often strictly interpreted the laws of the state and encroached on Church freedoms. Enforcement of state law varied, even between the different districts of a city like Berlin. Upon viewing the gradual but continually heightened restrictions placed upon the Church's ministers and associations, the bishops realized that they needed some concrete means to hold Hitler to his promises of March 23.

Unfortunately, in Berlin, Bishop Schreiber was in no condition to face the situation fully. For some time, Schreiber had been suffering from a serious heart condition, and by the spring of 1933 his condition had deteriorated.[73] Nevertheless, the situation of the Church in Germany troubled him so much that, although weakened by his condition, he forced himself at the end of May to attend the annual bishops' conference at Fulda. There, Schreiber promoted his ideas for the protection of Catholic schools, youth groups, associations, and press and Catholic Action. He stressed the importance of natural and God-given rights and the respect necessary for these freedoms to flourish. He also declared that the state should work to promote justice and end all terror tactics, including the threat of concentration camps. Despite these demands, Schreiber still exhibited a willingness to work with the National Socialists and consequently became one of the bishops who agreed to the creation of a central office for the *Gleichschaltung* (coordination process in which organizations were brought in line with National Socialist principles) of Catholic associations. He believed this endeavor would promote a unified national process rather than individualistic regional ones.[74] Though the bishops rejected the coordination of Catholic associations according to state practice, they did agree to compose a letter detailing their grievances with the state. Cautious in tone, the German hierarchy pointed out that its "demands" were not in any way a "hidden reservation in opposition to the new state." In fact, the bishops avoided identifying National Socialism by name throughout the letter. Instead, they used such terms as "our age," the "new state," and "state authority" to identify National Socialist state under Hitler. First, the bishops praised the new state's desire to have Christianity serve as the basis of the nation and offered thanks to the state that Bolshevism would no longer be able to show its murderous face and "threaten and devastate the soul of the German *Volk* with its fanatical hatred of God." Quickly, however, by warning Catholics to reject extreme nationalism, the bishops expressed their concerns with the ideological tendencies of the NSDAP. That is, they exhorted Catholics to recognize their "natural and Christian tie with other peoples and families of peoples," who encompassed the "worldwide kingdom of God on earth." The bishops also questioned the new state's overemphasis of "organic integration" that often restricted "human freedom." Such policies, they argued, would ultimately lead to a "weakening and disintegration" of state authority.[75]

Today, after examining the pastoral letters written during the Third Reich, one might conclude that the bishops were not forthright in their condemnation of National Socialism. Examining the letters anew within the context of their times, however, shows that the bishops actually voiced more protests against the infringements of the state on institutional freedom than any other group. Nevertheless, the bishops concerned themselves only with those infringements and freedoms that directly related to the Church's sacramental mission and to the piety of its laity. What the bishops had done through their pastoral letters, however, was to identify those areas of state encroachment that were of concern to Catholics. In turn, those letters, as if slipped under closed doors, offered parish priests guidelines for their own ministry and for managing their own relations with the state.

In an effort to avoid further confrontations between the Catholic Church and the state and to ensure the pastoral interests of the Church, the German government and the Vatican agreed to sign a concordat. Signed on July 20, 1933, it was the culmination of efforts begun by Eugenio Pacelli, Vatican nuncio to the German Republic 1920–1929 and Vatican cardinal secretary of state from 1930 to 1939. Pacelli would later, in 1939, become Pius XII. During the Weimar Republic, only three individual states had concluded concordats: Bavaria (1924), Prussia (1929), and Baden (1932).[76] In their desire to protect the Catholic Church's freedom, influence, ministries, and work, the bishops were willing to overlook the difficulties in current church-state relations in order to conclude the concordat. The bishops hoped that this agreement would offer the Catholic Church in Germany a legal basis for protest against state infringements on its freedoms, especially in relation to lay associations, youth ministry, and the Catholic press.[77]

Hitler especially desired this concordat because it contained a clause that specifically prohibited Catholic clergy from participating in politics. Despite working out all the implications of the concordat, Hitler and other senior Nazi officials recognized that police could use such a stipulation to quell resistance among the clergy, especially their opposition to state measures. After the July signing, chancery officials instructed their priests to stay out of politics. In some dioceses, such as Würzburg and Eichstätt, chancery officials even sent out letters informing priests to avoid any conflict with the state whatsoever.[78] The Church had finally achieved its sought-after concordat and did not want to do anything to jeopardize its existence. On the part of the Church, there was a profound belief and hope that the state would honor the articles of the treaty. The words spoken on March 23 by Hitler were still fresh in the minds of Church leaders. Also, many still believed that their faith would be able to form the basis of morality and order in the new state.

Monsignor Paul Steinmann, vicar general for the Berlin diocese and soon to become administrator for the Berlin diocese after Bishop Schreiber's sudden death, was one of those churchmen who trusted in the promises that Hitler had made to the Catholic Church. Influenced by his two brothers, Monsignor Johannes Steinmann and Father Alphons

Steinmann, he exhibited an exceptional openness to National Socialism, especially after 1933. Monsignor Johannes Steinmann, a Church consultant (1921–1940) to the German embassy at the Vatican, had endeavored to promote friendly relations between the Vatican and Germany.[79] Alphons, a professor of New Testament exegesis at the State Academy in Braunsberg, had earlier joined the ranks of those theology professors at his university who openly supported National Socialism.[80] It is no wonder that Paul Steinmann, mirroring his brothers' zeal for Nazism at the time, fostered these same sympathies openly.

On August 20, 1933, following the signing of the concordat, Steinmann publicly revealed his support for the new Nazi state at a gathering of Catholic youth in Neukölln Stadium, Berlin. He made this revelation in the presence of more than 27,000 people, including 10,000 young people. Bishop Schreiber, who was severely ill, was not in attendance. In his remarks, Steinmann was particularly strong in his exhortation that Catholics not be left behind as the new Hitler state "awakened" the German nation. In no way did Steinmann want to reflect a lack of public enthusiasm for Hitler and the new government. Nor did he want Catholics absent from the Nazi polity. Therefore, in his rhetoric, he underscored Catholic willingness to work for the goals of the new state, all the while echoing words such as "manliness" and "sacrifice," which the Nazis continually used. Steinmann called on Catholics to be loyal not only to the Church but also to Germany. Catholics, he acknowledged, knew what their faith demanded of them, specifically, to "love your neighbor as you love yourself." Indeed, he continued, Catholics were to follow this commandment because as fellow citizens they were "children of this country, children of the German fatherland." Then he reminded his listeners that the German culture was "our culture" to which they were tied, the "history of the country is our history, for we were born out of it." To share this love of fatherland fully, Steinmann urged Catholics to develop the enduring characteristics by which "the German *Volk*" were so often "described by other peoples." Namely, "manliness, strength of will, and strength of character" to which was bound a "genuine spirit of sacrifice." If one did not maintain this character, Steinmann believed, "one could not fulfill one's duty to the fatherland." Then, as if parenthetically or as an afterthought, the vicar general alluded to the belief that Catholics also received their strength and courage "from prayer and from the Holy Sacraments."

Steinmann also urged Catholics not only to love their country and fellow Germans but to love especially the German state and its "Führer." He stated that it did not matter who the individual was behind the title. Rather, "we know that whoever stands at the helm was placed there as our Führer by God. And for God's sake we follow him loyally and conscientiously." For this reason, Steinmann declared, the Catholic Church did "not separate Church and state, Christ and citizens." Instead, Steinmann argued, the state and Church belonged together because "the Reich of Christ" comprised "both realms." Steinmann saw this unity between church and state best expressed in the Reich-Vatican concordat, given as a "gift to German Catholics by the Holy Father in Rome."[81]

Soon after he made this speech and after the death of Christian Schreiber on September 1, the Vatican called upon Steinmann to oversee the diocese until a new bishop was appointed. Immediately, Steinmann found himself embroiled in controversy and forced to defend his name from accusations made abroad. In October 1933, the *Kreuz Zeitung* printed a letter from Steinmann to the *Aurora und Christliche Woche,* a German-language newspaper published in Buffalo, New York. In his letter, Steinmann rebutted the newspaper's recent accusations that he offered an "undignified support for the Reich government of Adolf Hitler." Steinmann stated that he felt obligated to defend both the Church and his fatherland against those who had fully misjudged the "position of the Catholic Church in the new Germany and spread misunderstanding and disdain for Germany abroad." Steinmann believed that those abroad just did not understand the significance of the Reich-Vatican concordat, which guaranteed "the freedom of denomination and of public observance of the Catholic religion in the new Germany." Furthermore, he stated that, "if any friction between Catholic organizations and state authorities" existed, it was because "the German people" were in the "transitional stage" of a difficult process that would eventually enable them to adapt to "totally new forms." Indeed, there would be tensions in this process, but it had nothing to do with the desire of the state "to suppress the Catholic religion." In essence, Steinmann believed that any difficulties between church and state resulted from a "process in the national revolution" whose "magnitude had never before been known in modern history."

Steinmann also used the opportunity to defend Adolf Hitler, arguing that there could "be no doubt in any Catholic's mind that the Reich government of Adolf Hitler" was the "God-given authority for Germany" because Hindenburg had legally appointed Hitler as Reich chancellor. He stated that German Catholics had the obligation to "uphold loyalty and obedience toward the Reich government of Adolf Hitler." In addition, they had to support the government because it had recognized Christianity as the "unshakable foundation of our *Volk*'s ethical and moral life." These, however, were not the only reasons Steinmann supported Hitler and the new government. Hitler's new government had also "defeated Bolshevism, destroyed the Marxist movement of atheism, and liberated the German *Volk* from the pestilence of trash and smut in literature"—the same "evils" the Church hierarchy had fought against during the Weimar Republic. He concluded: "Some day, the future will recognize in gratitude that Germany, as a central country in Europe, erected a bulwark against Bolshevism and thus rescued the Occident from the red flood."[82]

The Vatican, of course, did not let Steinmann oversee the diocese for long. Early in 1934, it appointed Nicolaus Bares, former bishop of Hildesheim, the new leader of the Berlin diocese. Like his predecessor, Bares would suffer from serious health problems and serve only an abbreviated term. At the beginning of his term, however, his health did not hide his hesitancy to work with the Hitler state, though at first Bares attempted to show a positive attitude toward the new regime. For example, on January 31, 1934, during his oath of loyalty to the Reich government, which the concordat required of all diocesan bishops, Bares made known his ardent desire for a "peaceful and trusting cooperation between church and state with the lofty objective of involving the powerful fundamental forces of positive Christianity in the organic growth of the nation's life in the Third Reich—for the well-being of the people." Similar to his predecessor, Bares stated that he trusted in the promises of Hitler who had "repeatedly and publicly announced" his support for the Church "through the conclusion of the concordat with the Holy See."[83] Two weeks later, however, during a celebration at the Berlin Sport Palace in honor of Pius XI, Bishop Bares expressed more nuanced support of the new German state. Support, he said, did not hinge on the ideology of the National Socialist state, but rather on Christianity. Thus, if the German *Volk* were founded on Christ, "who through his appearance in the world not only offered the promise of eternal happiness, but also established the laws of human order in family, *Volk* and nations, in economics and society," it would be successful. Bares also said that he was Catholics' spiritual leader and exhorted them to "be loyal to the bishop. He is your guide and teacher—he is the watchman; if you follow him, you will not stray and you will remain united with Christ and the Church; for where the bishop is, there is the Church."[84]

Repeatedly, in his sermons as well as in his speeches, Bares was not afraid to challenge Nazi rhetoric in an effort to Christianize it. For example, during a 1934 youth rally, Bares proclaimed to the young people present, "My Catholic youth, Christ still stands before you today as your Lord and master, Christ is your true Führer." The bishop repeated this phrase two more times in his address that day.[85] In light of the tremendous pressure that the Nazi state had placed upon churches to incorporate their youth into Nazi youth programs, any efforts to redirect the focus of young people away from Nazi ideology was significant. Bares also centered his attention on adult Catholics, whom he addressed in a similar fashion in his first Lenten pastoral letter. In this letter, Bares called on Berlin Catholics to "stand firm in faith" by gathering closely around their "God-given pastors and teachers, the bishop and the priests, in confessing and living the faith." His words revealed the anxiety that many German Catholics had already felt toward the Nazi state. Now Bares used words such as "heroism" and "martyrdom" to describe the life of a believer in his diocese.[86] Gradually, it was becoming clearer to Bares and other members of the

German Catholic hierarchy that many state officials were not going to uphold the promises that Hitler had made to the Church in his speeches and through the concordat. In fact, the tensions between the Church and state over issues such as Catholic lay associations and youth programs were increasing at such a fast rate that some Catholic bishops began to express doubts as to whether the Vatican should ratify the final text of the concordat.[87]

Bares, however, was not prepared to turn Catholics against the Nazi state. For him, tensions with the state still revolved around a premature Nazi understanding of the Church's freedom to carry out its mission among Catholics. The bishop simply wanted the state to quit interfering with the activities of the Church, especially those involving young adults and the youth of the parishes. To help sustain their allegiance to the Church, Bares encouraged Catholics to receive Holy Communion, which he believed would strengthen them to keep and foster their "Christian faith, Christian courage, and Christian love."[88]

By the summer of 1934, National Socialism had made its full impact felt in almost every sphere of German society. Few realms continued to function apart from the influence of National Socialist ideology. The Catholic Church, however, was one of the few exceptions to this phenomenon. Because of its traditional institutional structure and its internal secretive manner of operation, it had successfully avoided the *Gleichschaltung* process that the National Socialists favored. The bishops also were not opposed to the pro-German nationalistic rhetoric that National Socialism cultivated and often incorporated it in their speeches and sermons. Nevertheless, the constant encroachment of the state on the freedoms that the Church enjoyed earlier, during the Weimar Republic, eventually alerted the bishops to the potential state hegemony that existed to stifle the Church and its mission to German Catholics. Still, most members of the German hierarchy were not yet ready to blame Hitler himself for the transgressions against the Church. Instead, they preferred to become his vigilant minions. The dire events of June 30, 1934, however, suddenly caused the bishops to change their minds.

two

Guiding the Flock

On the evening of June 30, 1934, Reinhard Heydrich, then the head of the SD (*Sicherheitsdienst*, Security Service), called an SS officer and a plain-clothes Gestapo agent into his office on the Prinz Albrechtstrasse and gave them orders to murder Erich Klausener. Hermann Göring, minister-president of Prussia and member of Hitler's cabinet, had singled out Klausener earlier for execution because during the Weimar Republic Klausener had made public statements against the National Socialist Party. Klausener was a director in the ministry for transportation and also the Berlin director of Catholic Action, an organization that promoted the active involvement of Catholic laity in the mission of the Church, and Göring's concern about Klausener seemed unfounded. At a recent large gathering of Catholics in Berlin's Hoppegarten Stadium, Klausener had publicly professed his willingness to work "for *Volk* and fatherland."

Despite Klausener's apparent loyalty, the two dealers of death immediately made their way with others to the transportation ministry building. They walked up a flight of stairs to Klausener's office and, after an abrupt encounter with his assistant, Herr Grunder, stormed into the director's office. Startling Klausener, they barked their demands to see his personal papers. Upon establishing his identity, the SS man accused Klausener of conspiring with SA leader Ernst Röhm to overthrow the government and ordered him to come with them to Gestapo headquarters. Realizing the hopelessness of his situation, Klausener complied and turned his back and began to pack his briefcase. Before he could turn around again, the SS officer took a pistol he had concealed in his coat and shot Klausener in the back of the head. The director's lifeless body fell to the floor. Hearing the commotion and gunshot, Grunder ran toward Klausener's office only to meet face to face with the SS officer, who immediately ordered him to go below and tell the other SS officers to come upstairs. Before venturing upstairs, they called Heydrich to report the deed. Pleased to hear the news, but fearful of reprisals because of Klausener's position in the Catholic community, Heydrich ordered his men to rearrange the death scene to make it appear to be a suicide. In its official findings, the state reported that Klausener, upon being accused of conspiracy, took his own life. To destroy any evidence to the contrary, Heydrich ordered Klausener's body to be cremated before anyone could investigate the cause of death.[1]

Klausener was not the only person murdered that evening. Members of the SS also murdered nearly two hundred others, including Röhm. The SS carried out these acts with the approval of Hitler, Göring, and Heinrich Himmler, *Reichsführer*-SS and deputy Gestapo chief in Prussia, all of whom wanted to consolidate power within both the government and the National Socialist Party and ultimately put an end to any remaining dissent against the regime.[2]

Klausener's death caught the Catholic bishops of Germany off guard. It also exposed to them the more ambiguous side of the concordat, the de facto side that necessitated the adoption of a more makeshift or provisional approach toward National Socialism. Consequently, after the summer of 1934, the bishops decided to focus on self-preservation. To accomplish this end, they would tolerate the Nazis to protect the freedoms the Church enjoyed in its ministry to Catholics. In their effort to preserve these freedoms, the bishops also had to tolerate the defects of self-preservation. That is, they had to turn a blind eye to any injustices and human rights violations that did not affect the Catholic Church directly. Theologically, of course, they could justify this posture on the basis of their belief that the Catholic Church had a relational integrity or completeness within itself, that because of the Church's divine origins, it was a perfect society whose primary duty was to save souls. Therefore, rather than view the Church as lagging behind National Socialism or at a standstill with the state, they preferred to view the state as wayward, evil, and in need of Christian reform. Thus, the bishops would continue to negotiate with the state in an effort to preserve the Church and its divine mission while at the same time hoping and praying that the state would eventually catch up with the Church (i.e., recognize the divine nature of the Catholic Church, which held the repositories of eternal life) and outgrow its evil aberrations. On the basis of this theology, the choices the German bishops made and the pastoral tactics they chose became significant, especially for parish priests who relied on the bishops for guidance in their negotiations with the state. The dynamics of the Church's deportment with the state and how this conduct played out with the clergy in the parishes formed much larger concerns for the Church.

More than any previous event, the murder of Klausener and others on June 30 revealed to the Church hierarchy that, although individuals might embrace German nationalism, the Nazi state expected much more radical loyalty from its citizens. It expected undivided loyalty to all its programs. In no way would the new regime tolerate public dissent. Previously, many bishops saw state restrictions on civic freedoms as a necessity to combat the Communist threat. Similarly, they had blamed local state authorities and individual regional Nazi Party members for intruding on Church affairs, but never had they blamed Hitler and high-ranking Nazi officials. Now, however, with the death of Klausener and others, it became very difficult for the bishops to remove the responsibility of the murders from Hitler himself, especially after his cabinet passed a law on July 3 legalizing all the murders that took place on June 30, 1934, "as measures of self-defense of the state."[3] As a result, the bishops became much more circumspect in their judgment of the state and the Nazi Party. The homicides revealed the harsh realities of the new regime. The deaths also struck a chord of fear in the bishops, who now realized that the regime would do whatever was necessary to maintain power. Klausener's death showed Catholic leaders firsthand that Nazi officials would not hesitate to take a life to retain their grip on power. Nevertheless, as a group, the bishops were unprepared and unwilling to challenge Hitler directly. In spite of everything, many of them placed considerable trust in the German chancellor and held out some hope in his promises. In their minds, Hitler was the person responsible for ending the menace of Communism in Germany. As a group, they also were just not convinced that he was behind the murders of June 30. There simply were too many differences among the German bishops to question Hitler, and besides, it was not their divine role. Nevertheless, Bishop Nicolaus Bares, whom the murder of Klausener directly affected, began to doubt Hitler's truthfulness.

Indeed, Bares refused to accept any part of the government's claim that Klausener had committed suicide. Not surprisingly, he immediately celebrated a memorial mass for Klausener in the house chapel of the Cathedral Chapter's residence.[4] Four days later, Bares attended a mass for the deceased held in the cemetery chapel of Klausener's home parish, St. Matthias. Afterward, the Bishop accompanied the family, the entire Cathedral Chapter, and Klausener's pastor, Father Albert Coppenrath, to the parish cemetery to bury Klausener's ashes. At the time, canon law prohibited ecclesiastical burials or memorial masses for Catholics who had committed suicide. Pastorally, however, many priests would argue that a person who had committed suicide suffered from some type of mental illness; therefore, they could make the pastoral decision to bypass this penalty. In the highly publicized case of Klausener, the Nazis claimed that he had intentionally taken his own life. Therefore, Bares's decision to grant Klausener both a memorial mass and a Christian burial signified that he had not accepted the claims of the state in regard to the cause of Klausener's death.[5]

On July 12, 1934, further infuriated by the Nazi charge of treason against Klausener, Bares addressed a letter directly to Hitler in which he stated that Klausener "was capable of neither suicide nor treason or even an illegitimate action against the present state."[6] Three days later, Bares made his belief public when he addressed the death of Klausener in the July 15 edition of the Berlin Catholic newspaper. In his printed statement, Bares attested to Klausener's loyalty to both his Church and his country by describing him as a "faithful Catholic and true German." Bares also exalted Klausener's character to dispel the charge of treason and claim of suicide, recalling "his love for church and fatherland," "his firm principles," and "his iron will," which always enabled him to stand firm in times of difficulties. Then Bares boldly stated that Klausener would receive salvation because "a beam of eternal light" shone on the urn containing the deceased's ashes. According to Bares, Klausener had embraced the cross of Christ and was a martyr for the faith.[7]

The Klausener murder caused great unrest among Catholics throughout the Reich, especially in the diocese of Berlin. Indeed, government claims that Klausener was a traitor who had committed suicide puzzled and dismayed the majority of Berlin Catholics. The government's story simply did not correspond with Klausener's personality or his recent public promises to work for *Volk* and fatherland. Nor could Catholics grasp that a practicing Catholic of Klausener's stature would choose to commit suicide rather than be arrested and tried in court. According to the reports of the Berlin SD, Klausener's death, following the Röhm Purge, became the central focus of discussion among clergy and laity. A July 1934 report, for example, noted that many newsstands that sold Catholic publications, such as the one in the vestibule of St. Hedwig, offered postcards with the imprint of Klausener, Bishop Bares, and other Catholic clergy offering the Hitler salute during the 1934 Katholikentag in the Hoppegarten. The SD feared that such actions would beget rumors that, in turn, would "endanger public law and order."[8]

Klausener's death greatly altered the climate of trust between church and state. Many Catholics agreed with Bishop Bares and concluded that Klausener had died a martyr's death. In particular, the feisty Father Coppenrath would not allow the government to dismiss the murder so easily and for years worked to construct a memorial for Klausener in his parish's cemetery. Despite this strong support for Klausener and the Church's refusal to accept the government's official line surrounding his death, Bishop Bares did not publicly condemn the events of June 30. Nor did any of his colleagues in the Fulda bishops' conference speak out strongly against the murders. Of course, Bares at least took the risk of protesting

Klausener's murder. While taking such a risk, however, Bares was concerned only with a murder that specifically involved someone who was active in the Church. Therefore, it may be argued that even in this instance Bares did not cross the concordat's narrow line to involve himself in state politics.

Even though the death of Klausener took a great deal of his time and energy, the tensions between the Church and the state forced Bares to address several other pressing concerns. In 1934, the most urgent concern of Bares and his fellow bishops was for the future of German Catholic youth. Although the government did not make membership in the Hitler Youth compulsory for all German youth until March 25, 1939, local and Nazi Party officials placed tremendous pressure on parents to allow their children to join the organization.[9] This activity alarmed the German bishops because the Hitler Youth leaders did everything possible to remove any outside influence from a young Catholic's life except all-encompassing National Socialism. For example, Hitler Youth leaders regularly scheduled meetings and rallies for Sunday mornings to compel children to pass up mass and other parish activities. Earlier, the Nazi state had suppressed the formal network of Catholic youth organizations. As a result, Church leaders feared that through such actions the Church and organized religion would lose all influence in the lives of young Germans, which, in turn, would have a negative effect on the number of practicing Catholics in Germany.

The Hitler Youth, however, was not the only means that the Nazi government used to spread its weltanschauung to German youth. In 1934, the Prussian Ministry of Culture established a program under the designation *Landjahr* (rural year), which the Reich Ministry of Education eventually took over. Under the *Landjahr* program, upon completion of their eighth year of education, boys and girls (especially those in the lower economic brackets) in certain school districts spent at least one year in the East Prussian countryside to learn the "joys" of agriculture and farming. In 1934, the Hitler Youth also established a similar program called *Landdienst* (rural service), which brought together splinter groups of the *Artamanen,* a former right-wing youth movement founded during the Weimar Republic. The *Landdienst* also took children from the city and brought them to live and work in the countryside. Hitler Youth leaders and former members of the *Artamanen,* many of whom were also members of the SA, ran the local groups associated with this program.[10] A third program, the *Reichsarbeitsdienst* (Reich Labor Service), which grew out of several volunteer labor services founded in the late Weimar Republic, also flourished. In March 1933, Hitler appointed Konstantin Hierl leader of this program, which now required all young men to do six months of manual labor or agricultural work and to live in camps administrated by Labor Service personnel. In 1936, the *Reichsarbeitdienst* also began to accept young women on a voluntary basis, until 1939, when the state made the half year of service mandatory.[11]

In all three of the programs, Nazi Youth leaders exposed the youth to the Nazi weltanschauung and, in later years, drilled them in paramilitary exercises. The German bishops, including Bares, were not against the idea of a program that offered youth a different living environment. They were, however, adamantly opposed to a program that brought Catholic youth from a Catholic environment to areas that were largely Protestant or far from a Catholic Church. In addition, the bishops resented the fact that, at times, local Gestapo officials or camp directors arbitrarily prohibited mass in the confines of the camps. In an October 23, 1934, address, Bishop Bares complained that the *Reichsarbeitsdienst* officials had located many of their camps far from a Catholic church. Bares believed it an impossible task to ask the few available local priests to travel a great distance to build makeshift altars for masses. According to Bares, it was "financially impossible" for his diaspora diocese to underwrite these costs. For Bares, the *Landjahr* program created even larger concerns because it often required the children to live in nondenominationally sponsored homes where "many dangers" existed. The location of these homes in areas that were largely Protestant, Bares explained, made it impossible to find Catholics to staff the programs. Even worse, Bares lamented, was the extreme distance—"up to sixty kilometers"—to the nearest Catholic church. Despite the appointment by Cardinal Adolf Bertram, the archbishop of Breslau and head of the Fulda bishops' conference, of four priests to offer pastoral care for these youths, Bares believed the number of priests was "still not enough" to meet the demand.[12]

Despite the fear of having a generation of mature Catholic youth who lacked proper instruction in their faith, the German bishops maintained a very nationalistic stance on issues involving foreign policy. In January 1935, for example, an opportunity arose for the bishops to express this nationalism by encouraging the inhabitants of the Saarland, which the Treaty of Versailles had separated from Germany, to join the Third Reich.[13] Along with the majority of the German population, the bishops viewed this question as a matter of national honor—not tied specifically to the Nazi government or Party but rather initiated to provide an occasion to nullify one of the despised terms imposed by the victors of the First World War. The overwhelming Catholic population of the Saar also offered the German bishops the opportunity to increase the number of Catholics in Germany. Although there was no lack of agreement within the German episcopacy as to how to formulate a joint declaration supporting the referendum, various Church provinces throughout Germany issued separate directives, very similar in nature. On December 31, 1934, Bares joined Cardinal Bertram and the other bishops of the Breslau Church Province, which included the Berlin diocese, to sign a declaration that encouraged Catholic support for the reunification of the Saar with Germany. The bishops argued that the conquering countries had "forcibly" separated the

Saar from the "German Reich through the coerced peace of the Versailles Treaty." According to the bishops, "No German can indifferently face this momentous decision for the future of our fatherland that will take place in the Saar in a few days. As German Catholics we are obliged to work for the greatness, welfare and peace of our fatherland." On the day of the referendum, the German bishops asked Catholics during the Sunday mass to pray the Lord's Prayer and the Hail Mary three times each "for a beneficial outcome of the Saar referendum for our German *Volk*."[14]

The people of the Saar voted overwhelmingly—90.76 percent in favor—to rejoin Germany. Throughout the campaign for reunification, Bishop Bares had allowed his name to be used in support of this national cause, which increased the land mass of the German Reich. He joined millions of other Germans who wished to see the Versailles Treaty eradicated. His gestures were not meant to be a stamp of approval of the Nazi regime as much as an effort to reach out to the German nation and people. Yet, by supporting this referendum, Bares assisted the Nazi government in the first of a series of land conquests that would eventually lead to the Second World War. It is doubtful, however, that in 1935 Bishop Bares had the foresight to anticipate where this step would lead. In either case, Bares's support for this national cause also gave permission for the clergy of his diocese to offer the same. By taking such a stance, Bares and his fellow bishops in the Breslau province made it possible for a Catholic priest or laymen to support a goal of the Hitler government.

On March 1, 1935, the Berlin diocese suffered a second major setback in leadership when, after a series of illnesses he had had since 1934, Bishop Bares died of a stomach infection.[15] The vacancy in the bishop's seat left Monsignor Paul Steinmann once again in charge of the diocese. At this point, the sixty-three-year-old Steinmann had his own health problems, which regularly caused him to delegate his duties to other chancery officials.[16] During this interim, Steinmann issued no pronouncements concerning the nature of the state as he had done earlier. Possibly he realized that the climate within Germany had changed. Restrictions placed upon the Church's ministry, especially in regard to youth, made it difficult even for Steinmann to support the intentions of the state expressly. Therefore, he limited himself primarily to issues of a pastoral nature.

Recognizing the urgency of the situation for new leadership in the Berlin diocese, the Vatican acted swiftly to replace Bares. In April 1935, Rome provided the Cathedral Chapter with three names from which to elect the new bishop. On April 28, the chapter elected Konrad von Preysing—a lawyer, Bavarian nobleman, and former bishop of Eichstätt (1932–1935)—to be the new bishop of Berlin. Preysing proved to be a wise choice to assume the bishop's office because very early on he had recognized the incompatibility between National Socialism and Catholicism. On May 31, 1933, for example, Preysing had warned the members of the

Fulda bishops' conference not to adopt language such as "new order" or "new state" in reference to the government. According to Preysing, any acceptance of the Nazi weltanschauung, which he believed was inconsistent with the Catholic faith and moral life, would only assist Nazi leaders to identify their party with the state.[17] Again in July 1933, Preysing voiced his objections, this time in a letter directed to Vatican Cardinal Secretary of State Pacelli, concerning the negotiations over the Reich-Vatican concordat. Preysing argued that article 32 of the concordat, which prohibited the involvement of clergy in politics, would enable the state to label as politically motivated the actions of any priest who challenged the weltanschauung of the state. Preysing stressed this could lead to arrests and convictions of priests who, with no political aspirations whatsoever, only wished to defend their faith.[18]

Interestingly enough, Preysing had been the favored episcopal candidate of Cardinal Pacelli, even though many churchmen in Berlin desired Clemens von Galen, the bishop of Münster, who had previously served at St. Matthias (1906–1929) in Berlin-Schöneberg.[19] Catholic National Socialists, including the outspoken Hermann von Detten, an NSDAP bureaucrat who dealt with church-related issues, had also suggested their own candidates for the Berlin Bishopric, including Franz Hartz, prelate of the Free Prelature Schneidemühl; Wilhelm Berning, bishop of Osnabrück; and Hellmuth Martin Brinckmann, pastor of Bonn-Kessenich's St. Nikolaus Church in the Archdiocese of Cologne.[20] Detten even wrote to both Hans Lammers, chief of the Reich chancellery, and Walther Funk, minister of economics, denouncing Preysing's candidacy.[21] On June 4, 1935, however, before either Lammers or Funk had the opportunity to act on Detten's expressed concerns, Bernhard Rust, Prussian and Reich minister for science, education, and culture, on behalf of Prussian Minister-President Göring, stated that, if a waiver could be obtained to exempt Preysing from the stipulations of article 14 of the concordat, there would be no "political objections" to Preysing's appointment. (A section in article 14 made it mandatory for all bishops to have studied at a university in Germany for at least three years before being appointed, and Preysing had completed his theology at the University of Innsbruck, in Austria.) Despite some further hesitation concerning the waiver, especially on the part of Johannes Schlüter, a counselor in the Prussian ministry for science, education, and culture, Preysing received the government's stamp of approval.[22]

The internal conflicts among state officials for control over the churches brought to light Preysing's name for the position. Despite the state's confirmation, a more significant problem lay in the fact that Preysing was not enthusiastic about this nomination and desired to remain in his beloved Eichstätt. Preysing traced his family's origins to an old, noble Bavarian family and did not wish to leave his home state, where Catholicism was part of the culture and daily rituals of life.[23] In early June 1935, he expressed this concern to Cardinal Pacelli, for whom he had worked as personal secretary when Pacelli was the Vatican nuncio in Munich (1917–1920).[24] Pacelli refused to heed Preysing's request and instead encouraged him to accept the appointment.[25] Despite current historians' denigration of Pacelli's choices during the Third Reich,[26] it is possible that the future pope urged Preysing's candidacy on the Berlin Cathedral Chapter because he realized that Preysing, as Catholic bishop of the Reich capital, a key episcopal position, had the strength to challenge the state. Preysing finally acquiesced, and on July 5, 1935, Pope Pius XI confirmed the appointment. Despite his compliance in taking the position, Preysing confided to Father Walter Adolph, a chancery official, that "you must at least once come to my homeland Eichstätt and get to know my previous diocese in order to understand how unfortunate I first felt here. The Berliners in this gigantic city cannot understand me if they do not know my homeland."[27]

By the time Preysing arrived in Berlin, in August 1935, to assume his new duties, church-state relations in Germany had grown increasingly strained. Tensions derived mainly from the state's infringements on the concordat and the clergy's bold attempt throughout Germany to challenge these encroachments. In mid-July, the Vatican entered this arena of church-state hostility when *L'Osservatore Romano*, a semiofficial Vatican newspaper, printed an article concerning the German government's violations of the Reich-Vatican concordat. *L'Osservatore* claimed that the Nazi government was excessively tolerant of certain elements in National Socialism, such as the writings of Nazi Party ideologist Alfred Rosenberg, which propagated anti-Semitism, neopaganism, and anti-Catholicism. The article especially took issue with the recent statements of Reich Minister of the Interior Wilhelm Frick, who accused Catholics of sabotaging German laws by their refusal to support the sterilization law, which legalized compulsory sterilization of anyone who suffered a serious congenital illness.[28] In particular, the article questioned Frick's accusation that Catholic organizations in Germany had created "denominational discord among the people." Furthermore, it challenged Frick's outspoken desire to remove religious influence in German society so, for example, "neither a Catholic nor a Protestant daily press, but one solely German," would exist. *L'Osservatore* also criticized the state's attempts to limit the activity of Catholic priests and religious to a role that only allowed them to proclaim and teach the doctrines and moral teachings of the Catholic faith. In each of these cases, the article pointed out that the state had violated the tenets of the concordat.[29] On Saturday, July 20, 1935, the chancery had the article published in the diocesan *Amtsblatt* and ordered it to be read aloud the following day during all masses throughout the diocese.[30]

During this same period, government officials were still attempting to determine how to handle the question of the churches. Until July 1935, around the time of Hans Kerrl's appointment to the newly created Ministry of Church Affairs, there was no one central government ministry that could deal specifically with church-related issues. Even after his official appointment, Kerrl never gained total control over church-state relations. Instead, both the Ministry of the Interior and the Ministry of Science, Education, and Public Instruction competitively bickered over matters relating to the churches. Further complicating this already complex and difficult arrangement were individuals, such as Rosenberg and Baldur von Schirach (leader of the Hitler Youth), who frequently made pronouncements that directly criticized the churches. In addition, the various police organs in the Nazi state did not have clear directives on how to handle clergy who publicly dissented from the regime. A May 27, 1935, letter from the Berlin headquarters of the Prussian Gestapo to its local bureaus noted this confusion in its clumsy attempt to bring some order to matters relating to clergy arrests. The letter, issued in reference to a previous decree by Frick regarding churches, specifically ordered the Gestapo to arrest clergy, Protestant or Catholic, but only after gaining the approval of a representative of the chief and inspector of the Prussian Gestapo. The order, of course, did allow for the immediate arrest of any clergy member who directly and immediately endangered public peace and order.[31]

Bothered by tensions between church and state, Prussian Minister-President Göring released a decree on July 16 to government officials, including the police president of Berlin, that addressed this difficult situation with the Catholic Church. Göring stated that the government would no longer tolerate any political dissent from within the Catholic Church. He specifically objected to the clergy's adaptation of National Socialist terms for the promotion of Church interests and organizations (i.e., H.J., the initials of the *Hitlerjugend* [Hitler Youth] for the youth group *Herz-Jesu Jugend* [Youth of the Sacred Heart]; and B.D.M., the abbreviation for the National Socialist *Bund Deutscher Mädel* [League of German Girls], for the Catholic girls' *Bund der Marienmädchen* [League of Marian Girls]). He also spoke against substituting "Jesus Christ" for "Hitler" when people offered one another the German greeting "Heil Hitler." Göring lamented, "It has gone so far that faithful Catholics leave mass with the impression that the Catholic Church" rejected all possible "manifestations of the National Socialist state because political questions and daily events are alluded to in polemical ways in the sermons." To counter the Church's actions, he reminded government officials and the Berlin police of their obligation to enforce the law because the bishops had taken an oath to uphold the state and had to be held accountable when they failed to fulfill this obligation. In that vein, he instructed them to use the legal system to employ "the full severity of existing punishment" to combat these infringements on the state's sovereignty. Furthermore, Göring argued that Catholic clergy who continued to "attack the Führer and his National Socialist State must be divested of their corrupting influence over the *Volksgemeinschaft* [ethnic community] by all necessary means." For him, this included ejecting priests from the classrooms and replacing them with teachers devoted to National Socialism, the prohibition of religious youth groups, and the outlawing of religious youth group uniforms. In all of these measures, however, Göring warned state officials and police to limit their reprisals. The government and party, he stressed, did not wish to enter into purely religious matters. He strongly emphasized that he neither wanted a renewed Kulturkampf nor wished to create new martyrs for the Church.[32]

Göring did not keep these new measures secret: he issued a version of the decree to the German press. This version stressed his singular desire to combat political opposition only. In no way, the report noted, did the state wish to create a new Kulturkampf with the Catholic Church. The press's version also left out the specific measures that the state and courts would have to take against politically hostile clergy.[33] Through the publication of an edited version of the measures, and without causing unrest among the churchgoers of Germany, Göring wanted to send a clear message: stop setting up roadblocks to state ordinances.

The Ministry of Justice took Göring's decree very seriously. On July 20, 1935, the ministry issued a letter to the chief public prosecutors in Germany, encouraging them to adhere strictly to Göring's decree. In particular, the justice ministry encouraged them to use the December 20, 1934, law against any treacherous attack on the state and party, and the February 28, 1933, decree of the Reich president for protection of the *Volk* and state, and to uphold similar laws that charged anyone who engaged in "political Catholicism" or perpetrated acts against the state.[34] On July 28, the provincial governor for Brandenburg also issued to local government and police officials his own interpretation of Göring's decree, acknowledging that the Catholic population was much smaller than the Protestant one and that efforts would have to be made to ensure that the clergy's political "agitation hostile to the state" taking place in the city of Berlin and "conducted under religious guise" did not spread to the countryside of Brandenburg. For that reason, the provincial governor ordered the Hitler Youth and all organizations of the party to work together closely to combat this political church activity. He also ordered officials associated with the legal system to enforce the law to its full extent against anyone who acted against the government. Finally, he commanded the police to observe the preaching and religious lectures of clergy, to review the content of Catholic newspapers, and to report immediately any infractions of the laws of the state.[35]

L'Osservatore Romano became aware of this publicly released version of Göring's memorandum and on August 4, 1935, printed a follow-up article concerning "the religious situation in Germany." On August 14, 1935, the Berlin diocese's *Amtsblatt*, in turn, published in its entirety *L'Osservatore's* second article concerning the concordat to alert Berlin priests of Rome's concern. This time, however, chancery officials did not order the article to be read in the churches of the diocese. That would have been too political a move. Nevertheless, the content of the article was important enough because it dealt specifically with the Church's involvement in political issues. For its part, *L'Osservatore* dismissed the label "political Catholicism" and stated that those churchmen who publicly expressed their concerns were doing so only as faithful Catholics attempting to abide by the provisions of the concordat. For that reason, their actions should not be seen as political or antipatriotic. The Church simply did "not delve in party politics." It did, however, emphasize that, if the politics expressed by the government affected the Church in a negative way, the Church had "the absolute right to defend itself." Indeed, stated the article, by its divine mission the Church had the right to concern itself with issues in the social sphere, especially with questions of morality. Therefore, the state could not limit the "jurisdiction of the Church to the realm of personal conscience and relegate it exclusively to the practice of mass." If the state continued in this direction, the article continued, it would be choosing to reject the Church's "apostolate" where it was needed the most.[36]

At the same time, it ought to be noted, the chaotic nature of the National Socialist administration prevented the Gestapo and local police from immediately implementing Göring's measures. For example, on September 19, 1935, the Ministry of Justice ordered the Ministry of Church Affairs to halt any legal proceedings against clergy until a uniform plan of action and punishment could be instituted. The justice ministry also requested that any proceedings against a German bishop be immediately discontinued in order to avoid public scandal. Instead, dialogue would be used to settle any future conflict between a German Catholic bishop and the German state.[37] In addition, during that same month, Minister of Church Affairs Kerrl, deciding to flex his own muscle, released an "urgent letter" to state and police officials throughout the Reich, requesting that they get his ministry's approval first before taking any further action against the Church or its personnel.[38] It was not until March 1936, however, that Kerrl provided comprehensive procedural guidelines for all matters related to church affairs.[39]

Even before the various agencies began issuing decrees for the handling of church-state relations, the Gestapo began to interpret any clergyman's action that questioned or challenged a law or principle of the state or party as an act of political resistance. This led to the increased arrest of clergy, primarily for their criticism of the state in their sermons and pastoral work. At the same time church-state relations were worsening, the Catholic bishops issued their annual Fulda joint pastoral letter, in which they reminded their clergy to limit their rebuttals to blatant anti-Church attacks on Catholic "dogmatic and moral teaching" and "to avoid all political confrontations and allusions from the pulpit, in the school, and in private discourse." In addition, they said, if a priest found it necessary "for local reasons to refute a false teaching or a lie against the faith and the Church," the clergyman had the obligation to "fight against the false teaching and the lie, but never against the mistaken and lying person."

Behind such statements, the bishops wanted to make it clear to their priests that they would stand alongside them in the face of an attack by elements who assailed the Catholic faith. Persecutions "against the priests are persecutions against the bishops," they stated. To withstand this onslaught, the bishops at the same time encouraged their priests to participate in "daily prayer, in daily mortification, and especially in the holy sacrifice on the altar." These actions, the bishops believed, enabled the priests "to be not only steadfast and loyal, but also to suffer joyfully and gladly for Christ, and, with Christ." Although the bishops provided room for priests to question the state's actions, their statements placed greater emphasis on restraint and patience than on action and involvement in regard to their counteractivity against the state.

Despite their awareness that certain Nazis, such as Göring and Rosenberg, worked against the mission and teaching of the Catholic Church, the bishops refused to separate themselves formally from the state or to denounce its actions directly. In one way, the Fulda letter revealed the bishops' bewilderment at the continued hostile actions of state officials against the Catholic Church in face of the hierarchy's effort to support the state. As an example of their goodwill toward the state, the bishops offered the weekly Sunday intercession for the fatherland and its leaders "that they might see the law in the light of God and enforce it through the authority of God." The joint episcopacy also assured their clergy that no stone would be left unturned in their efforts "to balance or certainly to lessen the existing unfortunate differences between church and state."[40] At this juncture, members of the German hierarchy seemed unable to distance themselves fully from the enterprise of the state, even though they realized that state officials were sometimes unrestrained in their criticism of the Church. After all, state officials wished to impose a single criterion of loyalty upon all institutions, including the Church. This desired state injunction put into question, among other things, the Church's right to follow the aims of its own pastoral mission. Thus, on the one hand, the bishops had to take a sharp stand against the government's actions and its religious intolerance, while, on the other hand, they continued to negotiate with it as problems arose. By taking his delicate path of tolerating the Nazis in order to protect the Church's freedoms, the bishops, however confusing or confounding it was for them, always risked alienating German Catholics who had already staked their political and economic well-being to the state. The bishops' own inherent nationalism and hesitancy to question governmental authority also tempered their decision to avoid any direct clash with the state. Thus, negotiation and the adoption of a provisional approach remained the norm.

In 1936, on the occasion of the reoccupation of the Rhineland and the subsequent March 28, 1936, plebiscite confirming the necessity of this aggressive action and prior to the August 1936 Olympics, the government issued two decrees in an effort to ease church-state tensions: on April 9, 1936, the government prohibited actions against members of the clergy (such as the curtailing of their right to speak in public and reside in a particular location), and on April 23, 1936, it enacted an amnesty law pardoning clergy who had been convicted of slander against the government or state leaders. Despite this overture, church-state relations did not ease.[41] In fact, the Berlin chancery had to offer further directives to their clergy concerning their interaction with the state. For example, an article issued by the Berlin chancery in the May 12 *Amtsblatt* ordered the Berlin clergy to avoid any disputes before a secular court. This article stated that, if a priest felt compelled to levy a charge or complaint against another person, he had to inform the chancery of the case and await approval for the action. The chancery also requested that priests inform the bishop of any action brought against them by another person. In either situation, the chancery asked that any disputes involving priests should, if possible, be settled in a Church court to avoid public scandal.[42]

Joseph Goebbels, Hitler's minister of propaganda, decided that the best way to attack the Church and break the "political" activity of its members was to create scandals involving members of the clergy. In the summer of 1935, the first opportunity presented itself when the state judiciary system, upon initiating legal action against diocesan clergy and religious communities, accused the latter of breaking the currency laws that governed foreign exchange. This was not hard to do. Many of the religious communities, for example, had their headquarters outside of Germany and regularly sent funds to other countries. Unfortunately, the technical nature of the laws governing currency made it quite easy for an individual who had little legal or commercial training to break the law.[43]

While the currency trials were underway, a runaway youth, apprehended by the German police in a burglary investigation, made accusations of sexual assault against a religious brother of the St. Francis Waldbreitbach religious community. This accusation led to further investigation of the religious brothers, who served at the Waldbreitbach Institution for Boys in Ebernach, near Cochem, in the Rhineland.[44] The police also discovered other incidents of sexual misconduct with students and began a massive arrest of members of this religious community. This, in turn, led to accusations and arrests of other brothers and even extended to suspected priests throughout Germany. Goebbels and the Nazi press exploited the sensationalistic nature of these accusations and subsequent trials. On May 26, 1936, the trials against the Waldbreitbach brothers and other male religious began in Koblenz and ended conveniently on July 17—just prior to the Berlin Olympics—with convictions against fifty-four Waldbreitbach brothers.[45] Following the Olympics, the courts initiated only one trial against a Waldbreitbach brother, after which tension seemed to ease.[46] From April to July 1937, however, when church-state relations broke down again, the government resumed the trials.[47]

Because there was some truth to the charges, especially against members of the Waldbreitbach community, the German bishops did not denounce the legal proceedings. They did, however, challenge, both individually and jointly, the biased use of propaganda by the press to attack all German religious and clergy. On June 14, 1936, Bishop Preysing critically assessed the situation in Waldbreitbach and had his comments read aloud on Sunday, June 21, during all masses. Preysing acknowledged the tragedy of the events, but also invited the members of his diocese to "practice mild caution in making severe judgments, in angry criticism, and not to raise carelessly an excessive, unfair or terrible attack on the Church and religious, on the priesthood and the sacrament of penance."[48]

On October 2, 1936, the bishops' conference at Fulda issued a similar statement concerning the legal proceedings against the Brothers of Waldbreitbach. In their statement, the bishops collectively condemned the actions of the accused "no less severely than the secular courts," but they made clear that the members of the Waldbreitbach community were lay brothers, not priests, and, therefore, Church members needed "decidedly and sharply" to reject all "slander and insults of the priesthood in connection with the trial in Koblenz." After making this clarification, the bishops turned to nationalistic sentiments, entreating Catholics to recall the faithful service that both the brothers of Waldbreitbach and the priests of Germany had given to the German people during World War I. The bishops noted that many priests had won medals of honor that marked them "as morally pure, brave men, loyal to their obligation to the Fatherland." In a similar vein, they attempted to portray the propaganda against the Church, stemming from the morality trials, as detrimental to the nation. According to the bishops, a nihilistic lack of faith resembling the destructive work of Bolshevism supported these attacks. Indeed, the bishops emphasized that anyone who either "intentionally or unintentionally" fought against the faith and the Church became a "collaborator of Bolshevism." By contrast, the bishops stated, the German Catholic Church stood in support of the Führer in his campaign against Bolshevism and his "endeavor for the preservation of peace and work for the rebuilding of our fatherland."[49] In this last statement, in which the bishops highlighted their own nationalism and placed themselves clearly on the side of Hitler, the German bishops perilously tried to adopt Nazi propaganda to their own advantage. Thus, their statements not only manipulated Nazi rhetoric to their assumed advantage and appealed to the state to desist from attacking the Church but also laid the groundwork for episcopal support of Hitler's nationalistic policies. No doubt the bishops' intent was to counteract recent claims by the Nazi press and officials that "the Catholic Church, the pope, the bishops and the priests" had "entered into relations with Bolshevism and Communism," but in doing so they unintentionally created a Catholic template for Nazi expansion.[50]

One cannot underestimate the Catholic Church's complex vision of world Communism during the 1930s as an almost apocalyptical evil. Catholic bishops saw Communism behind the pillaging of churches in Spain, Mexico, and the U.S.S.R. Its systematic hatred of the Catholic Church and all things religious put the bishops (in their minds) on the front lines of a cosmic Manichean conflict. For these reasons, the German bishops vehemently rejected the Nazi charge that they supported Communism. To a degree, they went out on a limb to make this point. They also rejected any attempt to portray themselves or their church as unpatriotic or working against the general well-being of Germany, especially a Germany free of Communists. If anything, the bishops believed there lay deeper social dependencies—however temporary—between Catholics and Nazis because of their mutual loathing of Communism. Indeed, Nazism's intense hatred of Communism was one of the central reasons why many Church leaders were provisionally willing to continue a dialog with the state, despite its continual encroachments on the Church. Therefore, in the fall of 1936, the Church took great offense when the state-sponsored German Newspaper Bureau widely disseminated an article accusing Catholic leaders of making "secret deals" with Communists and for failing to enter into the struggle against Bolshevism, especially in Spain. The article portrayed the German bishops as denominationally self-centered and obsessed with internal questions, such as the future of Catholic schools.[51] In October 1936, Bishop Preysing issued a rebuttal read in all the Sunday masses of his dioceses to reaffirm the Church's "most aggressive struggle against the mortal enemy of all religion—Communist Bolshevism."[52] In December 1936, the Fulda bishops' conference further defended the Church's stance by issuing a pastoral letter that condemned Bolshevism. The entire tone of the letter was defensive, not only against Bolshevism, but also against the charges orchestrated by the Nazi press. Bolshevism, they stressed, was a "Satanic power" that had to be combated with the weapons of faith. At the same time, however, the bishops promised to work with the state to eliminate Communism, for the good of the fatherland.[53]

Even though the German bishops did not want the state to portray the Church as separating itself from the goals of the state, they could not ignore continued encroachments by the state and the National Socialist Party against the Church's organizations and clergy. Therefore, on August

18, 1936, the Fulda conference wrote to Pope Pius XI to asked for an encyclical that would address the tense situation of the Catholic Church in
Germany.[54] The 1935 articles in the Vatican's *L'Osservatore Romano* had already revealed that Vatican officials were monitoring the situation of the
Church in Nazi Germany. In addition, since September 1933, the Vatican
had dealt with the Church question in Germany by sending "thirty-four
notes to the Berlin government, five *promemoriae*, three *aide-mémoires*, six
letters containing proposals and outlines for discussion and six other letters,
in all covering some three-hundred and sixty pages."[55] The lack of response
to these inquiries and complaints and the intense, manipulative propaganda that accompanied the currency and morality trials, coupled with the
plea by the German bishops, evidently convinced Vatican leaders that an
official Church document had to be issued against these injustices toward
the Catholic Church in Germany. Therefore, in late December 1936, Cardinal Pacelli, in behalf of Pope Pius XI, wrote to Cardinal Bertram, requesting
that he, Michael Cardinal Faulhaber of Munich and Freising, Karl Joseph
Cardinal Schulte of Cologne, and Bishops Galen and Preysing travel to
Rome to meet with the pope concerning the situation in Germany.[56]

During their meetings at the Vatican, the delegation of bishops spoke
against the Vatican's suggestion of ending the concordat. The concordat,
the bishops reasoned, at least afforded them a legitimate though provisional approach toward Nazism. Instead, they pleaded for an encyclical
from the pope. On January 21, Cardinal Faulhaber presented Cardinal Secretary of State Pacelli a draft in longhand for an encyclical.[57] Over the
course of the next month, Pacelli developed this text into a version acceptable to the Vatican. On March 14, 1937, Bishop Preysing received the
final version from Cesare Orsenigo, the Vatican nuncio to Germany, and
immediately sent his trusted friend Father Walter Adolph on a mission to
persuade Cardinal Bertram to order a universal reading of the papal encyclical on Palm Sunday in all the Catholic churches of the Reich. Hoping
to avoid conflicts during Holy Week, Bertram at first rejected this option
on pastoral grounds. Adolph, however, persisted in his plea, emphasizing
the possibility of Gestapo interference if he delayed the reading or permitted the reading to be made at different times in each diocese. Nuncio Orsenigo also visited Bertram to encourage the cardinal to approve a universal
reading on Palm Sunday. The nuncio stressed that the more they delayed
the reading the greater the possibility that the foreign press would obtain
and publish the contents of the encyclical or at least report about it,
which would then raise the suspicion of the Gestapo and cause greater risk
for the Church in Germany. Finally, Bertram relented and agreed to
Preysing's suggestions.[58]

In the diocese of Berlin, diocesan officials opted to have the Salvatorian
provincialate print the encyclical instead of the *Germania* press, in an effort
to avoid detection by the Gestapo. They also used a stencil process to hide

the site of the work. These factors were of particular importance because, prior to the public reading, the Gestapo had searched the *Germania* press for signs of the encyclical. They had apparently received some information from the foreign office, although the encyclical, when read, caught most of the Gestapo by surprise.[59] In the early morning of Palm Sunday, March 21, 1937, the day of the public reading, SD chief Reinhard Heydrich radioed his police to be on guard against the reading of the encyclical and to arrest anyone who was spreading copies of it. He also instructed the police to allow the printing of the encyclical in the diocesan *Amtsblatt* and then, without Church intervention, to confiscate the edition before its distribution.[60]

Immediately prior to the reading, Preysing sent the encyclical throughout his diocese via a courier service.[61] Upon receiving their copy, many pastors stored the papal encyclical in the Church tabernacle to prevent discovery and confiscation.[62] Along with each copy, Preysing enclosed a letter in which he instructed his priests to read the encyclical on Palm Sunday during all the masses in each parish. The encyclical was of such importance that he suggested that, in certain cases, the Passion be left out and the blessing of the palms put in its place. Preysing also recommended that they only read the introduction of the encyclical and the sections directed to the youth and the laity, and, if a pastor chose to condense the encyclical, Preysing ordered him to have a special afternoon service that included the reading of the more complex dogmatic sections.[63]

The encyclical, like the death of Klausener, took most people by surprise. One foreign observer stated that it "struck like a bomb."[64] The Nazi government viewed it as a direct assault on the state. On March 23, 1937, Reich Minister of Church Affairs Kerrl expressed this view in a letter to the German bishops, calling it "a serious breach of the provisions established in the Reich concordat." Furthermore, he stated that the encyclical "contained serious attacks against the welfare and interest of the German state" and sought "to undermine the authority of the German Reich government and to harm the welfare of the German state internationally."[65]

Though the encyclical was written by Faulhaber and Pacelli, Pope Pius XI's name appeared as the author, and it was addressed to the "archbishops and bishops of Germany and other Ordinaries in peace and communion with the Apostolic See."[66] Throughout the document, the pope limited his criticisms and concerns to areas that dealt specifically with state infringements on the concordat. He highlighted the German bishops' "own patriotic love" of their country to ensure that the comments would not be taken as political criticisms of the state. The pope also noted however, that, despite their love for country, the German bishops, in view of their responsibility to their office and the Church, had to share "reports of things hard and unpleasant." Then, using the words of the concordat, the pope noted how that contract had been agreed upon to uphold the German "people in a time of test and tribulation," but also "to secure for Germany the freedom of the Church's beneficent mission and the salvation of the souls in its care, as well as by the sincere wish to render the German people a service essential for their peaceful development and prosperity." In the eyes of the Church leaders, the Catholic Church, through its divine doctrine and moral teaching, in contrast to the imperfect Nazi state, offered Germany *the only* means for a peaceful and successful existence. The pope found that individuals, described as *enemies* of Holy Scripture, created "distrust, unrest, hatred, defamation" and expressed either an "overt or veiled" determined hostility against "Christ and His Church." These individuals, the pope stated, were responsible for the persecution of the Church.

Following these introductory remarks, the pope then spelled out in ten sections the specific infringements of the Nazi state against the guarantees contained in the concordat. A general theme running through these sections was encouragement. He wanted to fortify Christians to stand firm in their faith. To facilitate this, the pope condemned everything that challenged or directly attacked any practice or manifestation of the Catholic faith. He cited aggressive paganism, the drive for a national church, and state encouragement of individuals to resign from the Church. He encouraged young people especially to remain loyal in their profession of faith and exhorted the state not to misinterpret their loyalty to this faith as actions contrary to state goals. The pope pointed out that, even if the state deemed it necessary to organize a national youth organization (i.e., Hitler Youth), Catholics "must see that it is purged of anything anti-Christian." Furthermore, he demanded that the state allow young people the right to fulfill their Sunday obligation freely.

The pope also questioned the activities and weltanschauung of the state. He argued that whoever exalted "race, or the people, or the State, or a particular form of State, or the depositories of power, or any other fundamental value of the human community" divinized them and raised them "to an idolatrous level" and, therefore, distorted "an order of the world planned by God." Similarly, the pope told the state that it could not replace the moral law of God with the subjective opinion of a human being. To further emphasize this point, the pope stated that "no coercive power of the State, no purely human ideal, however noble and lofty it be, will ever be able to make shift of the supreme and decisive impulses generated by faith in God and Christ."

The pope accentuated the importance of the "sacred books of the Old Testament." The pope stated they were "exclusively the word of God" and constituted "a substantial part of his revelation." In the same paragraph, he also added that the Old Testament recorded "the story of the chosen people, bearers of the Revelation and the Promise, repeatedly straying from God and turning to the world. Eyes not blinded by prejudice or passion will see in this prevarication, as reported by the biblical history, the luminous splendor of the divine light revealing the saving plan which finally triumphs over every fault and sin." Those who reject this truth, the pope stated, "blaspheme the name of God." The pope, of course, did not speak in behalf of the Jewish people; nor did he condemn the legislation that the Nazis had passed against them in Germany. Instead, he spoke mainly against defaming the Old Testament, which Catholics viewed as a source of divine revelation and a precursor to the coming of Christ. This approach became more evident further along in the text when the pope stated, "The peak of the revelation as reached in the Gospel of Christ is final and permanent. It knows no retouches by human hand; it admits no substitutes or arbitrary alternatives such as certain leaders pretend to draw from the so-called myth of race and blood." In a protective gesture, the pope was alluding to and reviewing Rosenberg's philosophy of race and blood, which challenged Catholic teaching. Then, further along in the text, the pope was even more direct in challenging Rosenberg: "The Church founded by the Redeemer is one, the same for all races and all nations." All Christians, he stated, whether gentile or baptized persons of Jewish descent, were in solidarity with each other and with Christ. This was a distinction that the Nazis rejected. The pope did not, however, directly address the persecution of German Jews. Instead, he limited his comments to specific concerns pertaining to the articles of the concordat that affected the Church directly.

In the final two sections of the document, the pope addressed priests, religious, and laity. He praised the clergy and religious for their "guidance under duress" and encouraged them to continue "to serve truth and refute error in any of its forms." Failure to refute errors, the pope stated, was not only an act of "betrayal of God and vocation, but an offence against the real welfare of your people and country." Again in this statement, the pope insisted that the Church held the truth and served as the ultimate source for the positive welfare of any people or nation. Finally, he lauded those religious and members of the clergy who suffered persecution or were "imprisoned in jail and concentration camps." The pope also praised the efforts of the Catholic laity to uphold their faith in a time of stress and suffering. He exhorted parents to support Catholic education and their free right to choose this kind of upbringing for their children.

In his concluding section, the pope stated that he had "no greater desire than to see in Germany the restoration of a true peace between Church and state." He acknowledged, however, that if this did not come about, the Church of God would "defend its rights and its freedom in the name of the Almighty." The specific use of the term "true peace" is significant for any analysis. For the pope and the German bishops, a true peace between the Church and the state meant not only a cessation of all restrictions against and harassment of Catholic institutions and organizations, but also a suspension of neopaganism and the weltanschauung of National Socialism as propagated by Rosenberg, which was infiltrating

Catholic institutions. This propaganda included the Nazi teaching on race and how it affected Catholics of Jewish descent. Ultimately, because these racist doctrines were essential and unalterable features of the Nazi state and weltanschauung, the encyclical could rightly be seen by the state as the Church's declaration of war on Nazism to defend its rights and freedom against those individuals and organizations that threatened it.

Following the public reading of *Mit brennender Sorge* ("With Burning Concern"), the Nazi government resumed its morality trials with a vengeance.[67] The state levied accusations and charges against Catholic priests throughout Germany. Arrests of clergy on a variety of charges also increased. All of this took place in the marketplace, as it were, despite church affairs minister Kerrl's June 1937 plea to Goebbels to limit combat against the Church to the arena of the press. In attempting to halt the activities of the Church with regard to unresolved concordat problems, Kerrl argued that written warnings issued to the bishops brought no results. Furthermore, he clearly did not want to create further unrest among the Catholic population or in the foreign press and, therefore, spoke strongly against criminal proceedings against Church officials. For Kerrl, these actions were "still not possible" and were "unsuitable" on both ecclesiastical and political grounds.[68]

In July 1937, Bishop Preysing, realizing the difficult time his fellow Catholics and priests were having, issued a letter encouraging them once again to stand firm in their faith. According to Preysing, Christians in National Socialist Germany were in the midst of a struggle "between faith and infidelity, between Christianity and anti-Christianity." Therefore, it was his "holy duty" to tell them what was "valid today" and what was not valid. He reminded Berlin Catholics of the current devious methods that Nazis used to encourage them to stray from their Catholic faith and likened them to the persecution under Julian the Apostate, who, though he did not shed Christian blood, knew from his own Christian roots how deviously to undermine the faith. Christians, Preysing declared, were "pushed as it were into a ghetto, excluded from public life, and denied admission to higher education."

In his comments, Preysing showed how clearly he understood the intentions of the Nazi state, which were to usurp the authority of God and replace it with the singular authority of the state. He carefully stressed that his words did "not concern a question of state power" or "denominational peace." Rather, he questioned whether an earthly power was justified in claiming that its authority stood "above the authority of God whose commandments and laws" were "valid regardless of time and place, of land and race." This also caused him to reflect on whether an individual held "personal rights that no community and no state" was "allowed to take from him without causing injury to the will of God and endangering the welfare of individuals" and whether a person was free and should be allowed to be free. Also, he considered whether the "freedom of decision of conscience of the person" could be limited or even prohibited by the state. When the state or anyone acted in this manner, Preysing noted, they committed an "error in principle" by either deifying matter or declaring "the individual or the nation or blood and race . . . as the final aim and the final goal," which, in turn, placed a "false God in the place of the one, the only, the Trinity."[69]

In this and other documents, Preysing publicly made known that he recognized the seduction of Nazism and what the Nazi government was in the process of doing to religion: pushing it into the background and, he stated, not only "washing religion from politics" but, worse, turning "politics into a new religion—a replacement for religion." By restricting the activities of the Church, especially its organizations, the state was paralyzing "important measures of pastoral care" for German Catholics. According to Preysing, even "attendance at Sunday Mass, that for many used to have the character of a normal activity without spiritual involvement" was becoming more and more "a profession of the sacrifice of Christ, of salvation through the Cross." Therefore, Preysing encouraged the members of his diocese through vigilance, prayer, and sacrifice to remain loyal to their faith.[70]

While keeping both the Berlin Catholic clergy and laity informed of the difficult situation between the Church and state through pastoral letters, Preysing also endeavored to keep his clergy privately informed through memoranda delivered by couriers. For example, in February 1939, Preysing wrote a response to an anti-Catholic political tract called *The Huge Lie of Political Catholicism*, by Dieter Schwarz, and sent it to each member of the Berlin clergy.[71] In his lengthy response, Preysing refuted the charges made against the Catholic Church in the SS-sponsored booklet. He specifically dismissed the state's continued use of the label "political Catholicism" in reference to any activity of the Church that, in the state's view, contradicted the aims of the Nazi Party. Preysing argued that, "through the slogan 'political Catholicism,' the opponents of the Church believe they have established the legitimation for their struggle against the Catholic Church."[72] Prior to the mailing to the Berlin clergy, Preysing also sent copies of his response to his fellow German bishops and to representatives of the Reich government. On January 26, 1939, Kerrl replied to Preysing, accusing the Catholic Church of overstepping its religious bounds and regularly delving in the political arena.[73] At the same time, Kerrl also took the liberty of informing the German foreign office of Schwarz's pamphlet and of encouraging its bureaucracy to use the work for propaganda against the Catholic Church in foreign countries.[74]

Through his pastoral letters and memoranda, Preysing also revealed his willingness to voice his dissatisfaction publicly when it pertained to the way the Nazi regime treated the Catholic Church in violation of articles of the concordat. Preysing, however, did not limit his concerns to those issues that affected only the Catholic Church. He also spoke considerably about personal freedom versus state authority and control. He wanted the bishops to take a more forthright position against the actions of the state with regard to the Church and personal freedom. Preysing's adversarial stance, however, did not gain much support from most of his fellow bishops, especially from Cardinal Bertram.

On the occasion of the annexation of Austria by the German Reich, Preysing publicly stated his desire that the Catholic Church should take a stronger stance against the state. This was not the first time that Preysing had pushed for such a request. Previously, in October 1937, the West German Bishops' Conference rejected Preysing's appeal to alter the nature of the bishops' response to the state in the face of continued persecution. Up to this point, Cardinal Bertram's "Policy of Suggestion" *(Eingabenpolitik)*, which placed a great deal of trust in the state's willingness to abide by the Reich-Vatican concordat and which utilized assertive letters to high-ranking Nazi officials as a means of addressing wrongs committed by the state against the Church, had prevailed. Despite Preysing's request for a more adversarial line, Cologne's Cardinal Schulte, who supported Bertram's policy, refused to back Preysing's proposal. Bertram feared Preysing's reproachful action would lead to greater or total repression of the Church's pastoral care and its primary mission to administer the sacraments to German Catholics.[75]

This, however, did not deter Preysing. On March 31, 1938, the bishop, unlike many other bishops, informed his Berlin clergy that he had not ordered or permitted the diocesan newspaper to carry any special supplements concerning the annexation and that state authorities had ordered the publishing directors of *Germania* to issue the supplement.[76] Furthermore, Preysing demanded that no part of the supplement be read from the pulpit.[77] This action went directly against the spirit of the day, especially among Roman Catholics, who overwhelmingly rejoiced at the fact that the largely Catholic country of Austria had joined the German Reich—a desire many Catholics had shared since Bismarck unified Germany in 1871.

In April 1939, on the occasion of Hitler's fiftieth birthday, Preysing once again went against popular opinion and ordered his diocesan *Amtsblatt* not to carry any special mention of this celebration. He did not have to prevent publication of the event in the diocese's newspaper, however, because in September 1938 the Gestapo had already forced its editors to cease publication after a series of conflicts over the content of the newspaper that involved Goebbels's propaganda ministry and the Berlin Gestapo.[78] Later, the only mention of Hitler's birthday appeared in the calendar section of the *St. Peter's Calendar for the Diocese of Berlin,* alongside the births and deaths of other German leaders throughout history. The notice read simply "20 Thursday 1889 Birthday Adolf Hitler."[79] This lack of formal acknowledgment of Hitler's birthday was especially controversial because most extant diocesan newspapers and *Amtsblätter* contained articles dedicated to him. Some dioceses even requested that these articles of praise and well wishes be read during the Sunday Eucharist.[80]

In September 1939, Preysing took a similar stance in regard to the outbreak of war with Poland. Instead of praising the war or touting nationalism as some of his fellow bishops did, Preysing had his vicar general, Maximilian Prange, issue pastoral instructions to the Berlin clergy encouraging their parishioners, especially the soldiers, to receive the sacraments of penance and the Eucharist.[81] Prange did not encourage any extra prayers for victory in battle either; rather he requested that pastors continue the practice of reciting three Lord's Prayers and three Hail Marys to entreat "God's protection for *Volk* and fatherland." He also gave pastors permission to hold prayer services, at their discretion, for similar intentions in the churches.[82]

By the spring and summer of 1940, Preysing's relations with the state and his fellow bishops reached a breaking point. In April, as if there were not enough problems in church-state relations, Cardinal Bertram, on behalf of the Fulda bishops' conference, sent Hitler a birthday greeting that was more than flattering.[83] Bertram's move, especially his decision to write the letter in the name of all the Fulda bishops, infuriated Preysing. In fact, Preysing became so outraged that he debated whether to resign his office or leave the Fulda conference altogether. Indeed, Preysing's response to the letter enabled the members of the bishops' conference to see clearly two opposing camps emerging from within their ranks: those bishops who wished for a modus vivendi with the Nazi state and those who saw no sustainable need to work with it.[84]

Although not aware of the complexities of the internal debate of the German hierarchy over their relationship with the state, German government officials feared that the bishops might seek to replace the aging and complacent Bertram with a more outspoken candidate. Goebbels specifically revealed his apprehensions that Preysing might be the bishops' new leader when he wrote in his diary, "[T]he radical course of Bertram would be replaced by an even more radical course of Preysing. We have then definitely to wait and see what will happen in the near future." Nevertheless, Goebbels still felt that the state had the upper hand, especially if the bishops appeared to work against it in a time of war. He comforted himself by noting that "the more the Catholic Church and the clergy expose themselves, the better it is for us."[85]

The parish clergy, however, were, for the most part, not privy to the tensions that existed between Preysing and Bertram and the ensuing difficulties that these men created in the bishops' conference at Fulda. What the parish clergy were aware of, though, was the increasingly draconian nature of the state in restraining anyone it viewed as an enemy. To make matters worse, the war created a situation in which the state could eradicate any dissent against its policies, including any dissent from among the clergy. In 1941, the number of arrests and punishments inflicted on members of the Catholic clergy increased, equaling the number in 1937, the year of *Mit brennender Sorge*.[86] State officials encouraged this harassment and prosecution. In February 1940, Kerrl had stated that every clergyman who uttered any form of political criticism against the regime would be criminally prosecuted, arguing that "removal of these political rights" could not be enacted by the party, "but only by the state, i.e., by my decreeing that any political criticism uttered by clergymen in office" would be subject "to penal and disciplinary prosecution." Without having "to fear unrest among the population," he believed that, if violations occurred, the state could "lawfully deprive the churches of privileges and governmental subsidies."[87] This statement suggests how state officials wanted to ensure that clergymen did not create public unrest among the population. For example, on October 24, 1941, Heydrich wrote to the bureaus of the Reich SD, instructing them to avoid creating situations that encouraged resistance or turmoil within Germany. He ordered an end to attacks on the Church such as the confiscation of monasteries.[88] He also stressed that members of the Church should not in any way be led to believe that they had a right to continue working against the state. Instead, he encouraged fines be initiated against clergymen who disturbed civic peace. He also insisted that the Church was not to recover any position or property it had already lost and requested that the branches of the SD inform the central offices if and when any moves were to be made in the future. Finally, Heydrich encouraged the SD to increase their base of church informers and to work to create "unbroken chains of evidence" against the Church to be dealt with on a later date.[89] In response to Heydrich's letter and other concerns expressed by different state officials, the SD and Gestapo reduced their penal measures against Church institutions, groups, and properties and primarily limited their campaign to combating the insubordination of clergy who they believed worked directly against the state and the war effort. Realistically, by 1941, the majority of the diocesan newspapers and Church-sponsored publications had ceased to exist. In addition, the Gestapo had also banned most youth groups and parish associations, especially those that promoted social action. Practically speaking, this meant that, instead of confiscating church publications or dispersing the attendees of a parish association meeting, the Gestapo could now center its assault primarily on the actions of individual priests, especially in the areas of preaching and pastoral care.[90]

The situation of war in the Reich simply made all this essential for "victory." The SD and the Gestapo were to cease public campaigns against the Church in order to avoid unnecessary unrest among the population. They also realized that, during times of crisis, the Church normally became the institution to which people flocked for consolation and hope, especially when loved ones were fighting and dying in battle. To attack this institution, whose consolatory function was needed, would have been counterproductive. For this reason, Heydrich ordered the Gestapo and SD to combat only those people and organizations that proved a direct menace to the war effort. It is interesting to note that the move to halt incendiary attacks on the Church only revealed the Gestapo's failure to limit the humanitarian, if not pastoral, influence of the Church. Rather than attack the Church, the Gestapo and SD now regrouped and focused their efforts on collecting information on Church activities to use against it after the war.

Goebbels and other leading Nazi officials had earlier agreed that something had to be done about the contumacy of the Catholic Church toward state policies. Already in 1937, Goebbels had spoken privately with Hitler and concluded with him that the state had to work to "bend the churches and make them bow before us." According to Goebbels, this would include getting rid of celibacy, confiscating church assets, imposing age restrictions on theology students, dissolving religious communities, and depriving the churches of the authority to teach in schools. Goebbels, however, was realistic in his expectations about the length of time such a process would take to implement these extreme measures. In his diary, the propaganda minister noted that it might take "a few decades" to break the churches. But then, he cheerfully concluded, the church, like a good pet, would "eat out of our hands."[91] Though predisposed to and capable of attacking the Church and persecuting its clergy directly, Goebbels often urged moderation and caution with any issue or individual when he felt that public opinion might turn against the state or the party. Others, such as Heinrich Himmler or Martin Bormann, the chief of the party chancellery, were more inclined to act openly against the churches, even if doing so caused unrest among Catholics. In 1941, the two approaches clashed after Clemens August Graf von Galen, Bishop of Münster, preached several sermons in which he criticized the methods of the Gestapo and also challenged the state's euthanasia program against those it deemed "unworthy of life." Bormann, upon recommendation of Walter Tiessler of the Ministry of Propaganda, called for Galen's public execution by hanging. Goebbels, however, warned that the state would meet great resistance by the people of Münster and all Westphalia if they pursued a drastic course of action. Hitler ended up intervening and, siding with Goebbels, promised that Galen and the churches would ultimately have to reckon with the state once the war came to an end.[92] In turn, reckoning with churches after the war became the temporary solution of the state in its attempt to resolve problems with the Christian churches.[93] One solution envisioned and concocted by the SS, though, was actually carried out in the Warthegau, a western section of conquered Poland that the Nazi state had renamed. In this territory, state administrators fiercely restricted the freedoms of the churches and deprived them of any financial subsidies from the government. They also banned religious instruction from the schools, dissolved parish associations, instituted strict laws governing financial collections, and prohibited the existence of religious foundations and monasteries. As Ernst Helmreich concluded, in the Warthegau, the Nazi government appointed administrators to inaugurate "not a separation of Church and state, but a Church unsupported yet controlled by the state."[94]

As the war progressed, the German bishops and priests not only had to deal with increased pastoral issues of great concern to families of military personnel but also contend with continued interference of the state in the life of the Church. Increasingly, the latter issue also forced some Church leaders to grapple publicly with the larger question of the state's perpetration of human rights violations. As one might imagine, most clergymen refused to challenge the state directly, even when it was obvious to them that an apparatus of the state infringed upon an individual's natural rights. This scenario was even more evident when the issue did not revolve around specific church-related interests. Similarly, almost all of the protesters directly ignored the plight of German Jews and concerned themselves only with "Aryan" German Christians. Nevertheless, there were a few among the German hierarchy, such as Bishop Konrad von Preysing, who, in the thick of the war, still found the courage to challenge the immoral actions of the state and to publicly address its violations of human rights.

Preysing had always advocated caution among his fellow bishops and priests, even when dealing directly with the Nazi state. But he also, by his own example, encouraged a type of active connivance against the Nazi state in an effort to expose its evil, delusive nature. By the outbreak of war in 1939, two unique individuals, Monsignor Bernhard Lichtenberg, the provost of St. Hedwig, and Dr. Margarete Sommer, a staunch Catholic and advisor to Preysing on Catholics of Jewish descent, took the bishop's nonconformist stance to heart. Through both word and deed, Lichtenberg and Sommer went out of their way to remind their fellow Catholics of the Christian command to love their neighbor and of the evangelical mandate to assist Jews during their time of persecution. Their influence, coupled with Preysing's own anti-Nazi stance, led the bishop of Berlin to question publicly state policies and actions, even during time of war, which was indeed bold. Since September 1941, Preysing had also been in contact with Helmuth James Graf Moltke, one of the central figures of the Kreisau Circle resistance group, along with Jesuit fathers Alfred Delp, Lothar König, and Augustin Rösch, provincial of the Jesuit Province of Upper Germany. Introduced to Moltke through Professor Hans Peter, a political scientist and active member of the *Görres-Gesellschaft,* an organization that promoted scholarship among Catholic academics, Preysing became privy to the secret conversations of this wide-ranging resistance group that aspired, after the fall of the Third Reich, to rebuild Germany with a government and society firmly rooted in Christian principles. From 1941 until his arrest in January 1944, Moltke visited Preysing on a regular basis, confiding to him details of the development and plans of his resistance circle. Moltke also pressed Preysing to be even bolder in his sermons and public statements when challenging the Nazi state. Although Preysing listened to this committed aristocrat and sharpened his own criticism of the government in his public utterances, he still declined to become involved in the circle's plans to assassinate Hitler. For Preysing, the risks simply were too great. He feared for the Catholics in his diocese and the future of the Church in Berlin. Nevertheless, he was still willing to provide spiritual support and guidance to the circle's members.[95]

The effects of his interaction with opponents of the Nazi regime, coupled with his own abhorrence of National Socialism, soon led Preysing to take issue with the state more forthrightly. The controversy at hand was the unspoken euthanasia policy adopted by the government in fall 1941. Here, Preysing rejected the state's claim to determine who was worthy and not worthy of life. Not surprisingly, Preysing became the first German bishop to condemn the euthanasia policy of Nazi Germany.[96] On March 9, 1941, in a sermon offered in St. Hedwig's Cathedral, Preysing turned to the question of the "right to life of the individual." He pointed out to his congregation that current "theories and practice" wanted to put forward "exceptions to the sacred right to life and liberty of the innocent." Although one may put forth medical, academic, or so-called eugenic reasons, he noted, "according to God's laws no earthly power, not even the state," had the right to take innocent life.[97] In October 1941, Preysing went further than his earlier criticism of the state concerning euthanasia when he denounced the Nazi proeuthanasia propaganda film, *I Accuse.* In a dramatic letter sent to his entire diocesan clergy, Preysing boldly condemned the film, which he argued attempted to win over its audience in order to eradicate "life unworthy of life," and encouraged his listeners publicly to do the same.[98]

Later that month, Preysing learned the harsh realities of what would happen to an individual when he or she resisted the state. On October 23, 1941, the Gestapo arrested his friend and colleague, Monsignor Lichtenberg, for speaking out publicly for Jews during prayer services. Preysing immediately realized the seriousness of such an arrest. The situation also weighed heavily on his conscience. Although he had spoken with Lichtenberg about the gravity of his public pronouncements for Jews, he had not forbidden him from initiating such actions. At the same time, Preysing was even more aware of his relative separation from the other German bishops, many of whom simply refused to accept the harsh realities that faced them as Church leaders in regard to their relationship with the Nazi state. He also realized that it would be a monumental task to wean them from the imperious influence of Cardinal Bertram. Still he felt he had to make the necessary effort to speak the truth and hope that his brother bishops and fellow Catholics would listen.

In November 1941, less than a month after Lichtenberg's arrest, Preysing climbed the steps of St. Hedwig's pulpit and delivered a scathing attack against the practitioners of euthanasia. Preysing reminded his overflowing congregation that, despite what the state might argue, according to God's law there were only three justified situations for killing: in war "for the protection of the fatherland," punishment by the state of a convicted criminal, and in self-defense. "All other killing," Preysing exhorted, was a "severe sin" and incurred "great blame" whether it concerned "a child in the womb or an elderly, frail, or mentally ill person—the so-called 'unworthy life.'"[99]

Like Lichtenberg's exhortations, Preysing's words did not go unnoticed by the Gestapo and SD, who ambitiously reported on the bishop's actions. As bishop of Berlin, however, Preysing was in a much different hierarchical position than Lichtenberg. A bishop's arrest, especially that of Preysing, a leading cleric in the Reich capital, would have caused great unrest among German Catholics. Some Nazi leaders, such as Goebbels, who read the Gestapo and SD reports, realized the complexity and delicacy of the situation. By February 1942, Goebbels had already labeled Preysing a "malicious agitator" against the German war strategy and debated whether he should "order him in and read him the riot act." After weighing the pros and cons of such an action, he decided differently because he concluded "nothing would be achieved" by such action. Rather, Goebbels planned to deal with Preysing after the war.[100] Preysing refused to allow his concerns to languish and soon forced Goebbels to rethink his course of action. On March 8, 1942, Preysing ordered every priest in his diocese to read a letter to his parishioners challenging the legitimacy of the state's authority to infringe on individual rights in regard to the seizure of Church property. Earlier, the Gestapo had confiscated the Catholic seminary in Berlin, the property of St. Hedwig Hospital, and other buildings belonging to St. Hedwig's parish. In defiance, Preysing also informed his diocesan Catholics that the Gestapo had arrested four Jesuits who resided in the parish. Furthermore, he demanded to know whether the state and its court system had any evidence to indict the individuals attached to these institutions for allegedly acting against the *Volk*, state, or Reich. Preysing even characteristically admitted the futility of asking such a question because, he argued, the enemies of the Church in the state and party had already provoked these actions and continued to work toward the annihilation of Christian life in Germany "regardless of the concordat, regardless of the freedom of religious life, regardless of freedom of conscience, and regardless of national unity."[101] Once again, Preysing's action caught the attention of Goebbels, who recorded his reactions to the public letter in his diary. Upon reading his entry, one may picture Goebbels, almost cartoonish, seething in anger at the behavior of Preysing, whom the propaganda minister seemed unable to control. Nevertheless, Goebbels forced himself to keep his personal feelings to himself as he again acknowledged the precariousness of the situation. He also made it a point to contain any further actions by the party or Gestapo against the Church so as not to provide Preysing with more fuel for his fiery complaints.[102] Goebbels was quite willing to be patient, only to exact his revenge later on, after the war.

Unexposed to the direct ire of leading government and Nazi Party officials, Preysing refused to relent in his public criticisms of state policies. This time, however, the foreign press picked up on his state-antagonizing words. In June 1942, following a sermon in St. Hedwig's in which Preysing affirmed the preeminence of God's law above state law, two Swedish newspaper reporters relayed Preysing's prophetic text to their home office. Within twenty-four hours, the contents of the sermon reached London and found their way into the British press.[103] Shortly thereafter, Preysing preached yet another sermon using similar themes in which he argued that the "life of the individual, whether of an unborn child or a weak elderly person" was, according to God's law, "sacred and no power on earth" was in a position "legally to take an innocent life."[104] The latter statement once again seemed like an act of war against the state. According to Goebbels, Preysing had "once again revealed subversive theories" that set "Catholicism against us and our views. . . . With these words Bishop Preysing" spoke a language "that, if it were spoken by a normal mortal, it would make him a candidate for prison or the death penalty." Yet, Goebbels restrained himself from taking the next step and making his threats a reality. For him, there was simply too much at stake to jail a leading cleric during the war. For one, the state would lose Catholic public support. Instead, Goebbels contented himself with the thought that "someday," the state would be able to settle its accounts "with the Church."[105]

Regularly, from 1942 onward, Sommer, through her own connections and points of reference, provided Bishop Preysing with written reports that documented the plight, deportations, and murder of German Christians of Jewish descent and of German Jews. These reports included detailed information on the deportations, the conditions of life for Jews in the eastern ghettos, and the work of the *Einsatzgruppen,* the mobile killing squads that followed the German army east.[106] Although there is no documentation to suggest that these specific reports motivated Preysing to speak out against human rights violations, his knowledge of the Sommer reports clearly influenced his sermons and pastoral letters. In November 1942, Preysing preached a sermon that not only spoke about individual rights but also addressed this question specifically in relation to Christ's demand for all people to love their neighbor. Preysing exhorted his congregation to "exercise love, the love of neighbor, but also the love of the outsider." The love of neighbor offered "to us every day a welcome opportunity." The love of neighbor, Preysing explained, required "tolerance and acceptance of foreign characteristics." He insisted that no persons should be closed off from this love, even if they spoke "another language" or were "of foreign blood." Preysing affirmed that "every person" carried the "image of God in his soul" and "every person" had the "right to life and love." Continuing in this vein, Preysing asked his congregation to remember the parable of the Good Samaritan and implored his listeners to always be charitable. It was never permitted "to take away the human rights of members of foreign races, the right to freedom, the right to property, the right to an indissoluble marriage."[107] From the extant evidence, it is not clear whether Preysing was speaking in this sermon specifically about Jews or Poles or, for that matter, about any persecuted group; however, neither does the evidence exclude Jews from those whose plight Preysing mentioned. His parleys with Lichtenberg, whom the state courts had found guilty of treason and imprisoned, as well as his talks with other diocesan clergymen who were jailed or sent to concentration camps, might have tempered Preysing to be more cautious when speaking publicly. He also might not have wanted to risk arrest, which would have silenced his voice of protest altogether. Similarly, had he vacated the bishop's seat in Berlin, the Nazi state might have delayed the appointment of a new bishop indefinitely. There was also the chance that a new candidate would be more charmed by Bertram's overtures to the state than Preysing, who prophetically criticized it. At any rate, Preysing at this time was unwilling to take any conspicuous risk. Instead, he preferred to press back against the realities of Nazism from outside a prison.

In December 1942, however, Preysing brought the main issues of his June 28, 1942, sermon to a dramatic climax in his Advent pastoral letter, a document requested by the West German Bishops' Conference (Cologne, Aachen, Limburg, Mainz, Münster, Osnabrück, and Paderborn). The letter went through two rewrites and, because of its strongly worded message, was read in its totality only in the dioceses of Berlin, Limburg, and Mainz. In the diocese of Cologne, it was read in part.[108] In the letter, Preysing argued that eternal law existed "outside of man's will and was guaranteed by God." Preysing explained, among other things, that this law made a "clear and distinct division between good and evil." Then, in direct contradiction to the Nazi concept of state, he stated that, if the foundations of law were "not based outside and above the individual or the nation or even outside and above all mankind, the principles of law" would be "mutable according to man's will and according to the time, the place and the quality of the individual or the nation and thereby the notion of right" would cease to exist. "Only when the sovereign laws of God are acknowledged can human law be placed beyond arbitrary human action and become the basis of a sound national existence." He attributed these misinterpretations to eighteenth-century liberalism and argued that these errors were still being applied in the current German state. "The individual cannot and must not be permitted to be completely absorbed by the state or by the nation or by the race." Furthermore, the individual must "remain responsible for each of his deeds" because God had "endowed him with freedom and he must remain free." Therefore, "no power on earth may venture to force an individual to make declarations or to commit acts which would be against his conscience." For Preysing, this included the parents' right to choose religious instruction and training for their children and the right for couples of mixed ancestry to marry. He added that the "primeval rights enjoyed by mankind, the right to live, to exist unharmed, to be free" did not depend "upon the arbitrary dictum of governments" and could not be "taken from anyone who [was] not of our blood" or who did "not speak our language."[109]

Preysing's letter reverberated throughout his diocese, and especially in the propaganda of the allied countries. Senator James Mead (N.Y.) read portions of the letter in the U.S. Senate.[110] Preysing's words also became the focus of discussion for the U.S. National Council of Catholic Men.[111] In Germany, Goebbels noted in his diary that the "*Pfaffen* [a negative term for clerics] [were] not absent from the many who condemn us" and described how Preysing's letter aided enemy propaganda in the United States and England and within Jewish communities.[112] Although Preysing spurred discussions in Allied countries concerning the abuse of human rights, the politically repressed climate in Germany did not permit the dissemination and discussion of opposing views. On December 10, 1942, the priests of the Berlin diocese read the pastoral letter to those in attendance at Sunday Eucharist.

Preysing's concern over the lack of human rights and freedom in the Third Reich also found expression in the 1943 Decalogue letter of the Fulda bishops' conference. Preysing's letter offered words of witness to the gross infractions of human rights that individuals witnessed daily in the Third Reich. Even in his boldness—in his sermons and letters against the injustices committed against personal freedoms—Preysing, like the rest of the German episcopacy, hesitated to take on the actions of the government against European Jewry and undesirables directly. Perhaps if he had gained powerful allies among the German episcopacy, Preysing might have been willing to tackle this issue in a clearer fashion rather than seeking to make general statements against human rights abuses. Nevertheless, his voice was one of the few that spoke for the minority opinion among the episcopacy, and, it must be noted, without it Bertram's hesitancy to speak at all about human rights abuses would have prevailed.

Despite his bold words, Preysing did not encourage the faithful of his diocese to resist the state outright. Instead, he exhorted the Catholic faithful to endure their Church's turmoil in the same way that Christ bore his suffering on the cross. For example, in February 1938, at the height of measures directed against the Catholic Church following the public reading of *Mit brennender Sorge* the previous year, Preysing devoted his entire Lenten pastoral letter to the theme of suffering. In the document, Preysing compared the suffering of the Church to the suffering Christ endured during his crucifixion.[113] In his January 1940 Lenten pastoral letter, Preysing also addressed the idea of suffering by focusing on the reality of the cross of Christ. According to Preysing, those who have the courage to carry the cross will receive blessings as did Simon of Cyrene. He pointed out that "Christianity, the religion of the cross, offers no guarantee against earthly suffering."[114] On September 8, 1941, he again focused on the image of the cross in his pastoral letter, reminding Berlin Catholics that "no Christian house should be without a picture of the cross." He continued, "In the evening, the family should gather around the cross and joyfully reflect on the fact that the cross is our only and surest hope."[115] Again in February 1942, in his pastoral letter, Preysing invited Berlin Catholics to stand firm in faith and trust in God in the same way as the biblical character Job.[116]

Preysing's November 2, 1941, sermon revealed his obsession with the cross and suffering. He condemned the taking of innocent life and contrasted the Catholic worldview with the secular weltanschauung of National Socialism: "We Christians have another point of view. We know that we are on the road, that we have no permanent dwelling place here, but rather aspire for a future life; life is for us less a gift than a task; to fulfill God's will is the actual calling of humanity." He ended the statement with a quotation from Paul's letter to the Romans: "All the sufferings of this present time are not worth comparing with the glory about to be revealed to us" (Rom. 8:18).[117]

Along with other members of the German Catholic hierarchy, Preysing viewed earthly existence as nothing but a stepping-stone to eternal life. It was a time of testing, a time of turmoil that also might be filled with joy and peace—signs of the coming kingdom of God. In 1944, even in the midst of inevitable military defeat and rumors of atrocities on the eastern front, Preysing asked Berlin Catholics to turn to the mercy of God and reconsecrate their diocese and each parish to the most sacred heart of Jesus.[118] The German bishops had not yet moved to a theology that encouraged Catholics to use the gospel to confront both the social and political ills of their society. Instead, they emphasized a pietistic sharing in the sufferings of Christ. This piety, in part, helps explain why the bishops were not more forthright in their protests against the state. The German bishops' understanding of the state demonstrates how difficult it was for them to question or even resist the state. In the war years, however, it became clear to Preysing and some other members of the German hierarchy that the state had no intention of abiding by the provisions of the concordat or maintaining its Christian foundations. This knowledge sparked the makeshift pastoral letters that ensued.

Whether for pastoral or national reasons, however, the bishops, Preysing included, did not feel compelled to speak more forcefully against the persecution and deportation of Jews. What they did do, especially Preysing, was provide German Catholics with a clearly different weltanschauung than that of the Nazi Party and its minions. This Catholic worldview called on Christians to love and care for their neighbor and provided them with the means to analyze for themselves the outright anti-Christian propaganda of National Socialism. For Preysing, this weltanschauung, above all, required "tolerance and acceptance" of all people, irrespective of foreign blood.

three

Negotiating Pastoral Care

In his July 8, 1934, sermon, given shortly after the Röhm purge, Father August Froehlich made a bold, but accurate, statement: "For us there is only passive resistance. If the government demands something that does not agree with the Ten Commandments, we shout a 'No' against it and say: one must obey God more than mankind."[1] In making this statement, Froehlich walked a fine line between urging his parishioners to internalize dissent against the state and exhorting them to rebuff the state publicly when it infringed upon their religious beliefs. Of course, a Catholic was free to interpret his pronouncement in multiple ways. Perhaps this was exactly what Froehlich wanted: an open-ended response that was not locked into one form of resistance. Such a response would enable Catholics to listen to his words and assess them according to each person's political acumen.

Father Bernhard Kleineidam, parochial vicar at several parishes during the Third Reich, noted that, although he never politically opposed the Nazi state, conflicts with the state often grew out of his pastoral ministry as a youth leader. According to Kleineidam, it was a prophetic act simply to profess the Catholic faith before the world.[2] More often than not, the Gestapo saw such bold religious avowals as political acts falling outside the realm of purely religious activity and moved to suppress them. At times this civic quelling, enforced with more vigor in some regions than in others, made ministry for parish priests a great challenge. In National Socialist Germany, the Gestapo would not tolerate anyone, especially religious leaders of influence, making statements that could negatively undercut the ideology of the state. In essence, the Gestapo wanted priests to limit their sphere of influence to predictable comfort zones. That is, they did not want any priest to expand his *Seelsorge* (pastoral care) beyond the sacristy or church courtyard. In more practical terms, the Nazis expected self-effacing clerics to refrain from any criticism of the state, even when the Nazi ideological machine infringed upon the ministry of the Church. Thus, if a priest criticized Nazi propaganda for slandering the Church or its members, Gestapo agents felt they had every right to arrest him for political crimes. Not surprisingly, from the Nazis' perspective, any clerical criticism of the state was regarded as a direct attack on the state. Of course, the arrested clergyman would have rejected this appraisal of his ministry, but to no avail, and would have had to deal with the "criminal consequences" of his "aggression" in court or in the basement of some Gestapo headquarters. A tense relationship existed between some Berlin diocesan parish priests and the Gestapo. The plight of one particular priest thrust into conflict with the Gestapo and how he responded to the situation throws light upon the quandary of many priests.

In 1933, there were 260 active priests who belonged to the Berlin diocese. During the Third Reich era, the Gestapo and other apparatuses of the Nazi state either interrogated, warned, fined, arrested, imprisoned, transported to a concentration camp, or executed seventy-nine of them.[3] Other priests might have also joined their ranks, but there are no written records tracing their pastoral activity during the Third Reich. The majority of these seventy-nine priests whose activities the state recorded during the Nazi years of power did not as a whole define themselves as political opponents of the state. Instead, most of them considered themselves good, patriotic Germans who felt they had never jeopardized the authority of the state and had given challenge only when it attempted to undermine the authority and teachings of the Catholic Church. The actions of these priests, of course, would constitute *Resistenz* as defined by Martin Broszat, because their intent was to limit the encroachment of Nazi authority and ideology on their ministry. Once again, though, it must be noted that the majority of these priests would have rejected this term *(Resistenz)* to describe their defiant actions. Perhaps *Seelsorge-Resistenz,* which essentially means refusal for pastoral reasons, best captures a priest's motivation for challenging the imperatives of state or party authorities. The Gestapo, however, refused to accept this argument and viewed priests who challenged the state as politically motivated and, therefore, in league with the enemy.

Evidence of the Gestapo's successive attempts to uncover the statements of such priests surfaced in an April 1935 SD report on Catholicism in Potsdam. According to the report, Father Heribert Podalski had taught the children of his parish a new song that contained lyrics that undermined state authority. When questioned about this incident, Podalski denied any wrongdoing. He further stated that the Catholic Church had a language of its own and that nothing in the song was meant to challenge the state. Upon hearing of this incident, an SD official commented that, since "political Catholicism" knew how "to camouflage its propaganda" that worked "to undermine and to excite mistrust to a far-reaching extent," it was very difficult to build a case against any priest. To the dismay of the officials, the lack of concrete evidence in Podalski's case enabled him to escape even a warning from the Gestapo.[4]

Despite the Gestapo's fundamental mistrust of Catholic clergy in the initial years of National Socialist rule, there arose a unique parochial situation in which the Gestapo attempted to protect the rights of Father Joseph Juzek, pastor of St. John the Baptist, a parish in Stettin. This case highlights some aspects of the often unpredictable response of the Gestapo and the Nazi state to issues involving the Church. On the evening of May 9, 1934, a woman denounced for improper identification a representative of the diocese's Caritas association. As a result, the local military police found and detained the fifty-six-year-old solicitor. To gather more information regarding the lawfulness of the charitable collection, at ten in the evening, a military patrol went to the rectory of Father Juzek to search the offices in his presence. There, they confronted the priest about the "illegal" collection, searched and confiscated a number of items, and returned to their barracks. Soon thereafter, at 11:00 p.m., a second military patrol returned to the rectory and insisted that the priest accompany them to their barracks for questioning. Juzek had no choice but to comply. Unconvinced of the permit's authenticity, the military police ended their interrogation and placed Juzek into "protective custody."[5] The military police released Juzek the following afternoon, only after questioning his secretary, who convinced them of the permit's validity. Some time later, the Gestapo received news of the event and became infuriated over the "unlawfulness of this intervention." To rectify the situation, the Gestapo interviewed Father Juzek about his experience and then took measures to ensure that "such infringements would be avoided" in the future.[6] More than likely, the Gestapo was more concerned with the encroachment of the military police into regions under its jurisdiction than with the actual "illegal" detainment of Father Juzek. In any case, Juzek benefited from their intervention. On July 24, 1935, Father Juzek again received the assistance of the Gestapo when a crowd of approximately 1,000 young men between the ages of eighteen and twenty-one gathered in front of the rectory to chant and sing anti-Catholic songs. Immediately after some of these young men (in an effort to enter the residence forcefully) broke a window of the rectory, the Gestapo and local police arrived and quietly dispersed the gathering. The young men had been protesting Juzek's actions of the prior Sunday. While saying mass, Juzek had expelled four uniformed Hitler Youths from the Church because "according to their own declaration they were not Catholic, and, according to the statement of the priest, they had behaved oddly in the Church."[7]

Although the Gestapo assisted Father Juzek, more often than not their appearance signaled great problems for a clergyman. Moreover, once a priest came into conflict with the Gestapo, the latter could assign agents to monitor his activities on a regular basis in an effort to uncover a greater offense or to gather more information to use against him. In 1942, the Gestapo investigated Father Georg Klemt, pastor of Holy Cross Church in Berlin-Hohenschönhausen. The local Gestapo had previously summoned Klemt to their offices at least three times for making statements against the state. Each time, he had eluded charges or imprisonment. Finally, in 1942, while attending a farewell party for his parochial vicar, Father Bernhard Robben, Klemt led the youth present in singing several secular songs. The Gestapo immediately arrested him on suspicion that he was organizing youth groups apart from those sponsored by the state. Although they never officially charged Klemt, they kept him for three and a half weeks in the cells of the Gestapo office on Berlin's Alexanderplatz, only to release him without explanation.[8] In a similar case, Father Alois Dobczynski, pastor of Our Lady Comforter of the Afflicted in Barth-Ostsee, had repeated conflicts with the state from 1935 onward. According to the testimony of a priest friend after the war, throughout the Third Reich, Dobczynski had maintained a political outlook that was at variance with the state. Unfortunately, his activities under National Socialism cannot be traced fully.[9] What is known is that on November 29, 1940, the Gestapo summoned Dobczynski to their station and demanded that he sign a letter admitting that he had participated "in propaganda against the state." When the priest refused to comply, the Gestapo immediately arrested him and held him in "protective custody." In the ensuing days, they alleged that he had sent greetings to Polish civilian workers and invited them to his church for mass with the regular German congregation—a forbidden practice after the invasion of Poland. In the middle of January 1941, as suddenly as he had been arrested, the Gestapo released Dobczynski without any explanation.[10] These two cases illustrate a familiar pattern followed by the Gestapo. Usually by arresting a priest and holding him in detention for a brief period of time, Gestapo agents were able to quell anticipated acts of resistance by frightening the confined clergyman into submission.

Other priests received much harsher punishments than Klemt and Dobczynski, especially when they refused to learn from their past encounters with the Gestapo. An illustrative example of this pattern is found in the case of Father Albert Willimsky, pastor of Holy Rosary parish in Freisack, Brandenburg.[11] In 1935, the Potsdam Gestapo imposed against Willimsky a prohibition of residency in the district of Westhavelland. Earlier, Willimsky had been denounced for expressing his sympathy for those who had supported the status quo in the January 1935 Saar referendum. He was also accused of making "disparaging remarks" about Alfred Rosenberg and Reich youth leader Baldur von Schirach and for questioning the honorableness of the winter relief collections of an NSDAP welfare organization.[12] In a separate incident, Willimsky was also cited for not having flown the national flag at his parish on a designated day.[13] Having gathered enough evidence against him, the Potsdam Gestapo, through its district attorney's office, introduced criminal proceedings against Willimsky for violation of the law of December 20, 1934, which, in conjunction with the decree of the Reich president of March 21, 1933, prohibited treacherous attacks upon the state and the party.[14] On April 4, 1935, yielding to the residency prohibition and to avoid further conflict, the chancery office moved Willimsky to Gransee, just northeast of Freisack, and made him pastor of Assumption parish.

Unfortunately for Willimsky, his troubles did not end there. That is, the priest did not do anything to temper his clashes with the state. Indeed, if anything, he continued to provoke local police and Gestapo with his comments. For example, in August 1935, the director of the *Landjahr* for the province of Brandenburg denounced Willimsky for reading during Sunday mass in May a prohibited pastoral letter that challenged the curriculum of the *Landjahr,* for making derogatory statements against the state's leaders, and for racial teaching in his sermon. The director also denounced him for reading another letter, on a Sunday in July, that included challenges to the sterilization law.[15] For these and similar statements that created "unrest among the population," the Potsdam Gestapo prohibited Willimsky from residency in the entire region.[16]

When Vicar General Steinmann received word of the prohibition, he immediately attempted to intervene in Willimsky's behalf to contest the decision at the district governor's office in Potsdam. Steinmann assured them that Willimsky had been "informed adequately" and that his "official activity as a priest and minister would no longer offer reason for complaints."[17] Because the diocese had a shortage of priests, Steinmann did not want to lose one of his ministers. Pastorally, he was also concerned about Willimsky's safety. In his mind, the best response for Willimsky was no response, so Willimsky was told to keep quiet and obey the laws of the state. Willimsky, however, refused to see his actions as an affront to the state. In his reply to Steinmann, he stated that in May he had read the prescribed pastoral letter without any knowledge of its prohibition and only after first gaining the permission of a local police officer. He also stated that he had read the second pastoral letter in July, maintaining that Church authorities had ordered him to read it and that, to his knowledge, state authorities had not forbidden it. He added that, as an "old veteran" of the First World War, he had always said to his parishioners that a good Catholic also had to be a "true servant of the state."[18] In the eyes of the Gestapo, Willimsky was hardly an obedient citizen.

For a brief time, Willimsky heeded Steinmann's warnings and avoided further confrontation. Even the mayor of Gransee acknowledged that

Willimsky had for the better changed his attitude toward the state and that as mayor he could now support the priest's attempt to gain permission to teach religion in the public school.[19] In September 1935, the Gestapo also seemed to have agreed and lifted the residency prohibition for the area of Westhavelland.[20] A few months later, in January 1936, Willimsky reported to his brother Heinrich that he had been acquitted of all charges brought against him in relation to his previous comments. According to Willimsky, the judge had acknowledged that it was a priest's duty "to defend the faith."[21]

Willimsky's confrontational nature, however, soon brought him into conflict, this time not only with the state but also with some of his parishioners. The event that sparked his reentry into police records occurred when a Martha S. accused him of boxing a person's ears in the confessional and discussing the content of a confession from the pulpit. The Gransee pastor did not take these charges lightly and immediately wrote her a letter in which he threatened her with a lawsuit if she did not retract her statements.[22] A few days later, upon learning of more malicious attacks upon his character, he sent a similarly worded second letter.[23] Thereafter, Gustav S., Martha's husband, wrote the priest and reminded him to be careful of what he said because they "lived in the Third Reich." In his reply, Willimsky accepted Gustav's challenge and acknowledged that indeed he recognized that they were living in the Third Reich—a Reich where allegiance was "one of the highest virtues." Then he demanded that Gustav have his wife retract her statements against him. Willimsky also revealed the core of his complaint against Frau S.—that she had willingly chosen to leave her parish in Gransee, in whose boundaries she lived, to attend services at another Catholic parish. This had infuriated the pastor, who saw her action as a direct challenge to his pastoral jurisdiction. Willimsky also told Gustav that his wife had acted just like a Protestant by choosing which church to attend depending on the minister who was holding the service. For him, this behavior was entirely unacceptable and undermined the entire structure of parish boundaries and the authority of pastors.[24] There was no further correspondence between Willimsky and Martha or Gustav S. to reveal what became of the charges. The extant correspondence between them, however, shows that Willimsky also went after another parishioner, Frau L., who publicly dared to mock him and the sacrament of penance. He also threatened to report her to the police if she did not withdraw her comments.[25]

What is most interesting about both cases is the extent to which Willimsky was willing to go to protect his honor. More important, however, is that he still trusted the police and justice system to uphold his rights in Nazi Germany, even after his own run-ins with authorities. It is clear his trust came from the previous court decision in which the judge had decided in his favor and supported him in his defense of the faith. Willimsky would soon learn, in April 1936, that the courts would not always support his claims. He was found guilty of violating the Reich Flag Law of October 24, 1935, because he had failed to fly the national swastika flag over his church on November 9, 1935, the anniversary of the Munich 1923 *Putsch*. As a result, he was fined fifty Reich marks plus 2.50 Reich marks for the cost of the proceeding.[26] At the time, Willimsky denied any malicious intent for not following the provisions of the law and requested that the sentence be overturned.[27] Though the court refused to accept his objection, the chief public prosecutor's office in Berlin discontinued the proceeding and repealed the fine on the basis of an April 23, 1936, amnesty law that repealed fines and prison sentences of less than six months.[28] Once again Willimsky had escaped punishment.

In July 1936, Willimsky again challenged the state's obstruction of Catholicism when he wrote to Bernhard Rust, minister of science, education, and culture, to complain about the practices of the director of the *Landjahr* home in Alt-Lüdersdorf. After learning that Willimsky had recently read a pastoral letter that was critical of the Hitler Youth and had also preached against neopaganism, the director had refused to allow the Catholic girls under her care to attend mass. Instead, she held a service herself in lieu of the mass. When challenged, the director told Willimsky that she wished "her girls only to be educated in the National Socialist spirit." In his letter, Willimsky called the director an "instrument of Satan" who utilized "real Russian and Bolshevist methods" to run the home. He demanded that the government punish and dismiss her.[29] Nothing came of his protest; nor was Willimsky punished for his harsh accusations against the *Landjahr* director.

In September 1936, Willimsky again ran afoul with the state, only this time with the director of a different *Landjahr* home, in Löwenberg, where he regularly went to the local school to hear confessions and offer mass for the boys in the camp. During a regular visit there, Willimsky made statements to two children against the SS newspaper *Das Schwarze Korps* and the *Völkischer Beobachter* for their exaggerated coverage of the morality trials. He also allegedly declared that church persecution in Germany was much worse than Bolshevism's ill-treatment of Catholics in Spain. When questioned by the Gestapo, Willimsky readily admitted to making statements against the negative press coverage of the morality trials, but he denied comparing the church persecution in Germany with Bolshevism in Spain. He explained that he had stated that the "struggle against religious and priests" everywhere was a "harbinger and a side effect of the Bolshevist world revolution." Once again, Willimsky escaped punishment when the chief public prosecutor in Berlin accepted Willimsky's testimony and decided not to pursue the charges.[30] A local administrator, however, did take revenge on Willimsky and barred him from using the school building for any pastoral activity.[31]

Less than a year later, Willimsky was denounced for allegedly using a religious instruction class in Rauenhendorf as a forum to express his disenchantment with the press and the media's treatment of the morality trials.[32] When questioned, Willimsky admitted to making the statement about the newspapers but denied uttering any comment about the radio. According to him, he had only followed the argument of his bishop who, in a pastoral letter, had expressed concern over the morality trials and that, for this reason, he was "totally innocent" of any criminal wrongdoing.[33] For one more time, Willimsky escaped prosecution when the court dropped the charges against him because of the stipulations of the April 30, 1938, amnesty law in honor of the Austrian annexation.[34]

On October 3, 1938, however, Willimsky's luck came to an end, when the Gestapo arrested him for criticizing the government and its leaders for maligning the Catholic Church during a conversation with twenty-four-year old Christel S., a Protestant and member of the Nazi Party. The two had first met when Christel S. approached Willimsky to find out whether the train they shared was heading toward Oranienburg.[35] Despite Willimsky's bewilderment of the situation—or perhaps because he was flattered that Christel S. had approached him instead of one of the women present in the train car, something that went against the customary norm of German society—he responded volubly. Later, when they both later boarded the commuter train at Oranienburg to Gransee and sat near each other, Willimsky initiated a conversation with the young woman as they passed the concentration camp Sachsenhausen. After finding out that she was Protestant and had many misconceptions about the Catholic faith, he used the opportunity to clarify the actual nature of the morality trials of priests. In the process, he also criticized the work of Rosenberg. Later, in a sworn statement, Willimsky testified that he had spoken purely in defense of his religion and in self-defense of his own priesthood and that Christel S. had misinterpreted his words as a political attack on the state. That is, he had simply informed the woman of his belief that Christianity and National Socialism had not yet bridged the gap between them and that "religious battles" lay ahead, which he felt "had to be avoided under all circumstances."[36] In this statement, Willimsky revealed that he was not fundamentally opposed to National Socialism, but only opposed to those elements within the movement that opposed Christianity. Despite his own imprisonment, Willimsky could not clearly see the fundamental dichotomy between the two.

Despite Bishop Preysing's efforts to procure his release from prison, Willimsky remained in "protective custody" for almost seven months.[37] On May 3, 1939, the Gestapo finally ordered his release from jail, but only after he promised to sign a statement "to abstain from any political activity or propaganda hostile to the state in the future."[38] Upon his release, Bishop Preysing immediately transferred him from Gransee to

Saint Peter and Paul parish in Podejuch near Stettin. Preysing wanted to keep Willimsky out of further trouble. Despite Preysing's efforts, in August 1939, the special court of the Berlin district court found Willimsky guilty of violation of the law of December 20, 1934 and sentenced him to six months in jail. The court then credited him with time served in "protective custody."[39]

Willimsky did not last long in his new assignment. True to form, he refused to keep his comments about the situation of the Catholic Church in Germany to himself. In addition, he did not seem to understand the seriousness of the state's actions against him. Nor would he acknowledge that his actions and statements contained any political overtones. In October 1939, Otto H., a salesman in the Stettin Karstadt department store, denounced Willimsky for making derogatory comments about the war with Poland, about Minister of Propaganda Goebbels, and about the press coverage of the morality trials. During a shopping trip, Willimsky, believing he was addressing a fellow Catholic, confided in the salesman and criticized some activities of the government. When questioned, Willimsky admitted to calling into question the press coverage about the war with Poland. For example, he found it hard to believe that "tiny Poland" first attacked Germany. He denied, however, ever making any statements against Goebbels. In his defense, he argued that as a Catholic priest he was "obligated to carry out pastoral care wherever he considered it proper" and insisted that he spoke only as "a Catholic and in a purely ministerial manner."[40]

This time the Gestapo refused to listen to his line of argumentation, especially because war had broken out. The Gestapo also wanted to erase any hint of defeatism or doubt in the minds of ordinary Germans. Therefore, on October 10, 1939, the Stettin Gestapo detained Willimsky for a month.[41] By the end of the month, the Gestapo recommended that Willimsky, on account of his continued hostile stance, be placed in a concentration camp for an indefinite period.[42] The Gestapo and the minister of church affairs placed the decision in the hands of Reinhard Heydrich, head of the RSHA (*Reichssicherheitshauptamt,* Reich Security Main Office), created in 1939 as an amalgamation of the SD and the Sipo (*Sicherheitspolizei,* Security Police), the latter combining the Gestapo, the Kripo (*Kriminalpolizei,* Criminal Police), the Orpo (*Ordnungspolizei,* Order Police), and the Grepo (*Grenzpolizei,* Border Police).[43] On January 9, 1940, Heydrich ordered Willimsky's incarceration in Sachsenhausen, and on January 29, 1940, he was transported there with other new prisoners.[44] The harsh conditions and the bitter winter were too much for Willimsky, who died of pneumonia in the camp's infirmary on February 22, 1940.[45]

The case of Albert Willimsky raises many compelling issues about the estrangement between the Gestapo and parish priests. On the surface, Willimsky boldly protested against the government in defense of his faith tradition and his own priesthood. His early successes in the court system reinforced his belief that his challenges were just, even in the eyes of the state. The Gestapo eventually proved, however, that there was a limit to what it would tolerate from anyone who challenged the state ideology. Confrontational by nature, Willimsky was willing to challenge both parishioners and acquaintances in an effort to salvage the Church's moral truth, as he understood it, from the contradictions of Nazi propaganda. In the process, and without being circumspect, he apparently talked too much about unsettling moral and ecclesial issues that he wished to rectify, especially after his incarceration and while awaiting trial. Despite these "minor shortcomings," Willimsky spoke his mind and stubbornly clung to the Catholic point of view that his Nazi listeners found unbearable. Amid this confrontation with the state, Willimsky was often alone. Although he based his challenges against the government upon statements made by the bishops in pastoral letters, chancery officials cautioned the priest to avoid direct confrontation. Their main concern was to have the pastoral needs of the parish met, which would be impossible if the pastor was in jail. In three separate cases, the chancery's answer to Willimsky's difficult situation was to transfer him to a new parish. Despite these moves, Willimsky was not deterred from protesting against what he considered an injustice against the Church and the priesthood.

Similar to Willimsky, several other diocesan priests in Berlin also challenged the state's ingrained distrust of Roman Catholicism. Their cases differ from Willimsky's in several ways, however. Primarily, there was a dearth of documentary evidence with which to compile a full case study of these individuals. Unlike Willimsky, these priests did not continually defend the Church in the face of opposition. In most instances, the state simply misunderstood the priests. Sometimes, too, their parishioners, who carried personal grudges against them and wished to use the police as a vehicle of revenge, wanted to victimize them. As Robert Gellately has argued in his pioneering study, *The Gestapo and German Society,* the Gestapo did not have to have agents patrolling and infiltrating every sector of German society. Rather, members of the general populace were often willing to denounce their "neighbors" for illegal activities against the state. Many times, they based their accusations on preexisting enmities.[46]

Among the priests who faced charges was Father Paul Ernst Gediga, pastor of St. Otto Church, in Stolp, Pomerania. In 1934, he first attracted the attention of the Gestapo when, during a sermon, he encouraged the youth of his parish to defend their Catholic faith.[47] In 1935, a visitor to his church denounced him for making derogatory statements from the pulpit about the propaganda ministry, neopaganism, and Alfred Rosenberg. During his interrogation, Gediga denied making any direct criticism of the government. He conceded that he had only informed his congregation that the "propaganda ministry in the Rhineland [had] approved the performance of plays that stood in sharp contrast to Catholic views." He also refuted the claim that he had made comments against Rosenberg. Instead, he had informed his parishioners that they could purchase from the rectory a work that examined the contents of Rosenberg's *Myth of the Twentieth Century,* an anti-Semitic and antireligious work that many National Socialists viewed as a textbook of Nazi ideology.[48] For lack of concrete evidence, the state dropped its case against Father Gediga.[49]

In February 1935, Father Franz Radtke, parochial vicar of St. Boniface was denounced for preaching against sterilization.[50] There is no record of whether the Gestapo pressed charges. In the same year, several students of the newly ordained Father Gregor Rittmeyer, of St. Joseph Church in Greifswald, denounced him for allegedly encouraging his students during a religious instruction class "to leave the Hitler Youth and to join a Catholic youth group." They also claimed he had told jokes against Göring and Goebbels, had made negative comments about Schirach and Rosenberg, and had hit the students repeatedly. Although, in all probability, the reason for this denunciation originated from the final complaint, it is worthy to note that the Nazi state indirectly encouraged students to denounce authority figures and seek revenge against them, in this case the parish priest who tried to instill strict discipline in the curriculum. The Gestapo, of course, took this denunciation seriously and began an investigation of Rittmeyer. During the course of the investigation, the priest declared that he had not spoken about the Hitler Youth, but merely had asked the children to join a religious society. He also claimed to have rebuked the children for telling jokes about state leaders. He admitted to making comments about Schirach and Rosenberg, but corrected the wording of the accusation. According to Rittmeyer, he had not called them neopagans, but had explained to his students that, in contrast to Catholics, they "did not believe in a supernatural God." Finally, the priest admitted to disciplining the children mildly, according to the culturally acceptable norms of the time. The attorney general's office in Stettin accepted the priest's statement and dropped the case.[51]

Father Paul Fähnrich, pastor of St. Aloysius in Berlin, twice underwent a similar process. In December 1938, and again in January 1939, someone denounced Fähnrich for making statements hostile to the state during his sermons. The specific contents of the statements, however, were not recorded. In the first incident, Fähnrich testified on his own before the Gestapo, persuading them not to pursue any charges. In the second case, despite members of the Gestapo observing and reporting the contents of the sermon, no charges were pursued.[52] Only in 1942, when war was fully under way, did Fähnrich finally receive a warning from the Gestapo for reading a pastoral statement by Bishop Preysing that was believed to be hostile to the state.[53] The warning revealed that the Gestapo would no longer tolerate what it might have overlooked before the war began.

Caring for the Faithful

In the 1930s and 1940s, the primary pastoral task of Catholic priests was the administration of the sacraments, the principal means of salvation. For Catholic priests, pastoral care took precedence over any other concern. Pastoral activity revolved around the liturgical and social life of individual parishes. Catholics viewed their parish as a place for both worship and recreation. During the Nazi period, the parish became a haven for Catholics escaping the harsh realities of the new German state.

Father August Froehlich presiding over a committal service for one of his parishioners.

above—Bishop Konrad von Preysing seated attending a 1937 celebration of the Society of the Virgin Mary. Father Ulrich Kaiser, O.P., is on the far right in his white Dominican religious habit.

right—Monsignor Bernhard Lichtenberg preaching in St. Lambert's Church in Charlottenburg, Berlin.

Monsignor Steinmann, Bishop Schrieber, and Monsignor Adolf Strehler inspect the noontime meal at a diocesan soup kitchen for the homeless and needy.

Fathers Herbert Simoleit, Ernst Daniel, and Paul Pade in a 1942 First Communion procession at St. John the Baptist parish in Stettin.

The Church and the State

The German Catholic Church had a tempestuous relationship with the National Socialist state. Often finding it hard to distinguish between nationalism and support for National Socialism, Church leaders regularly sent mixed signals to their priests and laity in regard to the Church's official relationship with the Nazi regime and its ideology. At times this discrepancy led individual clerics to embrace Hitler's party and government.

Father Josef Roth greeting Hitler during a rally of the NSDAP in Nuremberg.

St. Hedwig's flagged with the Nazi Swastika following a 1933 celebration of the ratification of the Reich-Vatican concordat.

Joseph Goebbels, seizing the moment for propaganda, joins Monsignor Georg Banasch to inspect the remains of St. Hedwig's Cathedral following a bombing raid.

Celebrating Berlin Catholicism

Though in a religious minority in a largely Protestant area, Berlin Catholics were extremely proud of their faith. Having few religious celebrations or practices that were indigenous to Berlin, the city's Catholics created their own forms of celebration to display their faith. Liturgical rallies and popular gatherings provided the best forums for publicly proclaiming their faith. During the Nazi period, this often led Catholic churchmen to adapt Nazi Party vocabulary and gestures for Catholic purposes in an effort to reach, in particular, their younger members.

Bishop Bares, Nuncio Orsenigo, and Monsignor Steinmann bless the crowds following mass during the 32nd *Katholikentag* in the Hoppegarten, Berlin.

Nicolaus Bares preaching at St. Hedwig's during a 1934 mass to enthrone him as bishop of Berlin.

At the 1934 *Katholikentag*, Dr. Erich Klausener offering a speech in which he proclaims his love for Germany. Only a few days later, the Gestapo would murder him during the Röhm Purge.

Catholic youth parade with various societal flags during a 1933 Catholic youth rally in Neukölln Stadium.

Racing games during the 1933 Catholic youth rally.

The parish ministry that created the greatest challenge for priests was pastoral care of youth. In every way, state and party leaders attempted to wrest influence of young people from the Church and its clergy. Nazi officials viewed the baggage of past confessional hostilities among Christian denominations as detrimental to the unity of the German *Volk*. Therefore, they aimed to train all German youth in the virtues of Nazi ideology as a defense against religious sectarianism. Of course, many citizens of the new state maintained their religious affiliation and carried with them the ancient hostilities between Catholics and Protestants in Germany. This was particularly evident in youth work and in the *Landjahr* homes and camps. For example, according to a Gestapo report, in September 1934, Father Karl Anders, pastor of Holy Redeemer Church in Anklam Pomerania, complained in a letter to another pastor that officials of the youth movement had brought Catholic children from Upper Silesia to a *Landjahr* home in the predominantly Protestant area twenty-two kilometers from the church in Anklam, simply to separate and alienate them from their faith. Because the children could not easily attend mass, Anders volunteered to celebrate mass at their residence. The directors, however, most of whom were Protestant, resisted his suggestions and efforts. The Gestapo also noted that Father Franz Müller, pastor of Sacred Heart Church, in Königsberg, Neumark, attempted to stir up the Catholic children against the Protestant children in a *Landjahr* camp near his parish. Müller probably attempted to instill in the children a willingness to profess their faith amid a setting that was not open to religion in general, much less to Catholicism.

The Gestapo viewed both priests' actions as destructive to local community building and recommended that Anders and Müller receive harsh sentences to prevent similar actions from occurring in the future.[54] There is no record, however, that the Gestapo took any action against the priests following the incidents. In 1941, however, the Gestapo did charge Müller with violation of the law of December 20, 1934, for publicly criticizing the *Landjahr* program and for holding an unauthorized special collection for the Boniface Society to support Catholics who lived in largely rural Protestant areas. During the course of the trial, Müller denied making any statements against the *Landjahr* program and even praised the program for its efforts to introduce children to the countryside. He also explained the purely religious nature of the collection. More likely than not, the priest realized the seriousness of the charge during war and sought to escape punishment. It worked. On the basis of his testimony and that of a witness who supported his defense, the court acquitted Müller.[55]

Encouraging the Catholic youth to stay true to their faith created problems for several members of the Berlin clergy. This was especially true of the parochial vicars of Holy Cross parish in Frankfurt an der Oder. In October 1938, Father Hermann Johannes Bronz ran afoul of the Gestapo when he joined forces with Father Johannes Wittenbrink of Immaculate Conception Church in Berlin-Karlshorst to produce and distribute a letter directed to the youth of the diocese. Bronz and Wittenbrink described the persecution of the Church in the Nazi state. The joint letter contained such statements as "today the gospel is stamped out with force." Although the Gestapo wished to pursue charges against the priests, the 1938 amnesty law forced them to drop the proceedings.[56] One month later, however, the Gestapo got revenge when its report against Bronz, along with an evaluation against him by the Nazi party's district personnel office in Frankfurt, encouraged the district governor to withdraw Bronz's permission to teach in the schools within his parish's boundaries. The district governor's office also recommended that the provincial governor's *(Oberpräsident)* Ministry of Secondary Schools withdraw Bronz's permission to teach in the schools throughout the entire region.[57]

A similar situation arose in May 1939 in the same parish, when Father Bruno Radom's permission to deliver religious instruction in schools was revoked for his dissemination of prohibited Catholic literature to young Catholics.[58] Likewise, in 1941, the Ministry of Church Affairs denied Father Erich Klawitter, director of the diocese's Pastoral Care Office for Youth, a commission in the army chaplaincy because of his previous work in behalf of Catholic youth.[59] Apparently, in 1936, Klawitter, while assisting with mass at Holy Family Church in Berlin, exhorted the youth of the parish not to deviate from personal faith, even if public "associations were to be prohibited and religious instruction were not allowed in the schools." Although the state dropped the charges, record of the incident remained in Klawitter's Gestapo files.[60]

None of the priests described above actively chose to resist the measures of the state or even to question them. Instead, they were reacting pastorally to the limitations placed upon their ministry, especially their contact with young people. From an average priest's perspective, it was absolutely necessary to educate the youth in the tenets of the Catholic faith from childhood to adulthood. If this mandate were neglected, many priests believed, an entire generation of "illiterate" Catholics would emerge, thus endangering the future of the Church. Once the state had prohibited the activities of Catholic youth groups and limited the availability of religious instruction by withdrawing permission for priests to teach religion in the public schools, the Berlin clergy reacted forcefully by using a wide array of methods to reach the young people of their parishes. For example, in December 1940, Father Maximilian Loboda, a Polish citizen[61] ordained in 1935 for the diocese of Berlin, was convicted and fined 200 Reich marks for violation of the government decree for the protection of *Volk* and state of February 28, 1933, and for violating the 1935 decrees against denominational youth groups.[62] His crime was organizing a group of fifteen to twenty young men—ranging from fifteen to twenty-eight years of age—for a meeting. Unfortunately for Loboda, most of the members belonged to the Hitler Youth. During his meeting with them, they celebrated an "hour of faith" that included singing religious songs and speaking about religion. Afterward, Lobada also allowed the young men to play chess and checkers and to shoot his air rifles, for which he awarded prizes to the winners.[63] After his trial, Loboda appealed the decision, but the district court in Prenzlau refused to overturn it, arguing that playing "cards and board games, ping-pong, and singing secular songs" were not activities of a "purely religious nature" and, therefore, were prohibited.[64] Also in 1939, Father Johannes Lilge, pastor of the church in Schildow near Berlin, was convicted and fined 150 Reich marks for the same offense: creating a youth group with "regularly organized socials."[65]

In the previous cases involving Berlin clergy, the priests were active in their support of religion and in their challenges to the state. In each case, the priests had crossed state-mandated limits on what constituted religious activity. The Gestapo, for its part, created these shifting boundaries and adjusted them regularly to its own advantage. As a result, priests often had to discover and distinguish these state boundaries on their own. Normally, a priest had a choice to either push forth an issue or forego it. When he espoused a controversial issue, he was simply resisting the narrow limitations the state had imposed on him. In some situations, however, priests could still end up in conflict with the Gestapo, even if in their comments they did not actively challenge the state's encroachments on their faith. For example, in 1937, Father Bruno Schubert, pastor of Holy Trinity Church in Brandeburg-Havel, came into conflict with the Gestapo for caring for the spiritual needs of inmates at a nearby prison.[66] As a dedicated minister, Schubert befriended many of the religious and priests who, on account of their ongoing monetary trials, found themselves imprisoned. Schubert not only provided them with pastoral care, but also brought them food, religious items, and medicine. Inspection of the Gestapo records reveals that someone in the prison denounced him, not only for these acts of compassion, but also for illegally mailing letters for the prisoners. The Gestapo especially wanted to put an end to the latter behavior because it created a possibility for unrest among the civilian population, who, upon receiving uncensored letters that contained information about the poor conditions under which prisoners were forced to live, might have wanted to protest the situation. In response to the denunciation, the Gestapo ordered some agents to check Schubert's mail. Shortly thereafter, on April 8, 1937, a Gestapo officer searched Schubert's apartment and brought him into custody at the Gestapo station on Alexanderplatz.[67] Although charges were never filed, on May 7, after Schubert had endured crowded jail conditions and confinement to a tiny cell, his health failed and he died. The Gestapo immediately released a statement asserting that Schubert had hanged himself in his cell.[68] Family members and diocesan officials refused to believe the Gestapo's claim.[69] After the war, Bishop Preysing confided to a family member that, based upon information he had received, Schubert had died from nervous exhaustion.[70] At the time, however, the news of Schubert's death had an unsettling effect on his parishioners at Holy Trinity, causing rumors to circulate throughout the parish. In conjunction with this case, the Gestapo arrested Father Bruno Golubski, the second parochial vicar assigned to Holy Trinity, and held him in "protective custody" for one week.[71]

As is evident from the case of Father Schubert, the Gestapo would under no circumstances tolerate anyone who caused unrest among the German people. Fearing that such disturbances might only serve to underscore deeper strife in the nation and cause further civil unrest, the Gestapo forcefully suppressed statements or letters read from the pulpit. Such documents enabled bishops to inform the Catholic faithful quickly of situations they deemed anti-Christian. In addition, reading a pastoral letter or statement from the pulpit only added extra emphasis and importance to any document because the pulpit was symbolically connected to the proclamation of scripture, the Word of God.[72]

Surprisingly, in Berlin there were only a few reported cases where the Gestapo arrested and imprisoned priests for reading such documents publicly.[73] One such case took place in October 1935, when the Gestapo in Oranienburg questioned Father Walter Görlich, parochial vicar at Sacred Heart parish, and "initiated a criminal proceeding against him" at the district attorney's office in Berlin. His crime was that he had read a pastoral letter that spoke against the sterilization law during mass.[74] Interestingly enough, the majority of Berlin priests read the same pastoral letter in their churches, but the Gestapo singled out Görlich for violating the law of protection against hereditary disease.[75] The Gestapo was often selective in its enforcement of the law in an effort to exact revenge on individual priests who had previously escaped its grip. This was true for Father Görlich. Fortunately for him, the Berlin district attorney's office never pursued the case.

The one document that outraged the entire Nazi leadership was the 1937 papal encyclical *Mit brennender Sorge* ("With Burning Concern"). The document especially offended the Nazis because it was a papal encyclical, and pastors throughout the Catholic world were bound to read it, causing even more scandal for the German government. In Berlin, however, the only priests charged in connection with the "scandal" of the encyclical were those involved in its production and distribution. Such were the cases of Fathers Bernhard Hack, first parochial vicar at St. Michael parish in Berlin, and Franz Karl Heinrich Schreibmayr, parochial vicar at Holy Cross parish in Berlin-Wilmersdorf, both of whom disseminated the encyclical to parishioners. In June 1937, Schreibmayr escaped fine or imprisonment after interrogation by the Gestapo.[76] Hack was not so lucky. On May 25, 1937, the Gestapo arrested him and held him in the Alexanderplatz station for "duplicating and distributing three thousand copies of the Papal message" on March 14, 1937.[77] On June 17 and again on August 11, 1937, Bishop Preysing wrote to Minister of Church Affairs Hans Kerrl to petition for Hack's release from prison, especially because no formal charges had been issued.[78] In late September, in a rare instance, the Gestapo honored Preysing's petition for Hack's release and reported that the "complaints by Preysing have been taken care of."[79] The Berlin district attorney's office, however, still pursued criminal proceedings against Hack for violation of the December 20, 1934, law against treacherous attack upon the state and party. For unknown reasons, in March 1938, the district attorney's office dropped the charges.[80] Although both Hack and Schreibmayr purposely chose to copy and distribute the papal encyclical, their motives were purely pastoral.

Unlike Hack and Schreibmayr, who simply read statements issued by the Church hierarchy, Father Albert Coppenrath, pastor of St. Matthias Church on the Winterfeldtplatz in the Schöneberg district of Berlin, took matters into his own hands and created his own "pulpit announcements" to inform his congregation of Nazism's inconsistencies with Catholic principles and practice.[81] Both Nazi Party leaders and government officials saw Coppenrath as a thorn in the state's side, a scourge whose persistent use of pulpit announcements brought him into direct conflict with the Nazi state.[82] In fact, Berlin Gestapo agents referred to him as the "damned pig-head of Westphalia" and complained that he kept them too busy.[83] His parishioners, however, recognized Coppenrath as an affable man who had a close relationship with them.[84] They also knew he could quickly "become gruff" if expected to do something outside "the moral or traditional rules."[85] For his part, Coppenrath refused to view himself as someone who worked against his fatherland. If anything, he always considered himself to be of strong "patriotic" character, which, he explained, meant "oriented to the fatherland." Indeed, he argued, he was "national to the bone."[86]

At first, like many of his fellow Germans, Coppenrath trusted both Hitler and his government to solve the social ills that plagued Germany. On May 29, 1933, for example, he wrote to a friend that he had no difficulty with the new situation in Germany, adding, "[E]ven the grimmest Party fanatic, if he is honest, cannot deny that National Socialism has already brought a good many things to our *Volk* and fatherland."[87] Despite experiences to the contrary, Coppenrath regularly reminded his listeners that Hitler had earlier declared Christianity would form the "foundation of the moral life of our *Volk*."[88] In addition, Coppenrath portrayed himself as one who stayed out of politics altogether. He believed that for an ordained minister the practice of engaging in party politics from the pulpit could only harm his ministry and alienate his parishioners.[89] On occasion, though, he contradicted himself, as was the case on December 9, 1934, when just before the plebiscite on the Saarland Coppenrath preached in favor of the region's return to Germany because it had been "forcefully and against the will of the inhabitants separated from the German motherland."[90] Before he supported this motion, however, he explained to his congregation at all the Sunday masses that this issue of the plebiscite did not deal in "affairs of the party." Instead, he stated, it was a "national question of great significance."[91]

The event that most jolted Coppenrath's faith in the new government and forced him to become involved in a political matter was the murder of Erich Klausener, the leader of Berlin's Catholic Action. Immediately after the murder, State Secretary Koenig of the Ministry of Transportation contacted Coppenrath, who was Klausener's parish priest, and asked him to break the horrible news to Klausener's wife. In their conversation, Koenig also pointed out that the government had ruled Klausener's death a suicide. Coppenrath, infuriated over the news, delivered it to Frau Klausener and accompanied her to her husband's office. At the office door, SS guards refused the two entry; this was part of the plan to cremate Klausener's blood-stained body and prevent any investigation of his death.[92]

Even before Coppenrath had publicly commented on the murder of Klausener, the Nazi propaganda machine had created the story that the former Catholic Action leader had been connected with General Kurt von Schleicher and other "so-called traitors" of the fatherland. Knowing Klausener well, Coppenrath refused to accept such a dubious story and soon began a campaign through pulpit announcements to rehabilitate Klausener's tarnished name. On July 1, 1934, Coppenrath announced the news of Klausener's death to his parish community and stressed how deeply Klausener loved his *Volk* and his fatherland. Even though he realized he could be arrested by the Gestapo, Coppenrath ignored concerns for his own well-being. For example, he publicly stated, "No one who knew Klausener will believe this fraud!"[93] Then, on July 7, 1934, convinced of Klausener's innocence, Coppenrath presided over a requiem mass for the deceased. He was joined by his curates, Bishop Bares, the cathedral chapter, and members of Klausener's family. Afterward, they interred Klausener's ashes in the parish cemetery.[94] Then, still ignoring the advice of the Berlin chancery to act with "restraint" and "refrain from adding to the obituary" of the deceased, Coppenrath graphically described at each Sunday mass the internment of Klausener's ashes. In the course of his talks, he also made his congregation mindful of an announcement from the Vatican newspaper *L'Osservatore Romano* that discarded the state's claim of suicide. Finally, he told his congregation that the deceased's body had been cremated without the permission of the family and against the teachings of the Church.[95]

The Gestapo, of course, saw the situation through a different lens. From the Gestapo's perspective, Coppenrath's statements sowed unrest in the population and his announcements brought unwanted notoriety to the incidents of June 30.[96] Therefore, on September 5, 1934, the Gestapo called on the pastor to appear at its local office for questioning concerning his recent public statements. Interestingly enough, during this interview, the Gestapo agents were less concerned with Coppenrath's comments concerning Klausener's death and more concerned about the editorial comments in his pulpit announcements. Evidently, a Catholic Gestapo informant had reported that Coppenrath, in reference to the death of Klausener, had chosen a particular passage from an "epistle" (extraneous to the assigned biblical texts for the day) to warn his congregation "against false prophets" who came to them in sheep's clothing but inwardly were "ravenous wolves: 'you will know them by their fruits.'" Coppenrath, of course, reveled in the agents' confusion and explained that he did not "choose" this text, but that it was the text from the Gospel of Matthew 7:15–16, which was read every seventh Sunday after Pentecost.[97] Consequently, the Gestapo agents released Coppenrath, who in turn, on September 9, described (in a pulpit announcement) to his congregation at all the Sunday masses the events of the interrogation—including the misunderstanding of the gospel verse.

Coppenrath also did not relent in his desire to see Klausener's good reputation restored. Instead, a week later, on September 16, 1934, at the opening of a new meeting and recreation site for the youth of St. Matthias near Lichtenrade, Coppenrath consecrated the site "Erich-Klausener-Place." Coppenrath declared to the thousands present that day: "We name this site not for an enemy of the state, but for a man who loved his *Volk* and fatherland with a burning love. . . . We name this site not for a man who committed suicide, but for a man who lived as a faithful Catholic and died as a true Catholic. We name this site after a man whose slogan continually and always was: 'Everything for Germany—Germany for Christ!'"[98] Coppenrath saw this dedication as especially fitting because Klausener, shortly before his death and in his role as a director in the transportation ministry, had appropriated an old train car and converted it to a temporary shelter at the Lichtenrade recreation site.[99]

In December 1934, Coppenrath's campaign for Klausener intensified when he suggested to Bishop Bares that he take up a collection to construct a memorial in honor of Klausener in the St. Matthias cemetery. Bishop Bares sympathized with Coppenrath and granted this request. Bares also asked Coppenrath to prepare a statement to be read on February 10, 1935, in all diocesan parishes before the collection. Although the collection announcement circumvented the question of suicide, it did call the church's attention to Klausener's service and his faith in God.[100] In reaction to this, on February 16, 1935, Lammers, in behalf of Hitler, wrote to Bares and asked him to reconsider building the memorial to avoid provoking "immense agitation among the public."[101] For the moment, Bares heeded Lammers's "polite" warning. Later, however, he refused to allow the issue to die. Instead, Bares argued that no further action could be taken until a "complete explanation of the situation" could be obtained.[102] Bares planned to continue seeking the truth surrounding Klausener's death, but his own untimely death on March 1, 1935, prevented any further investigation.

On February 27, 1935, the Gestapo did take further action in the Klausener affair and confiscated the funds collected for the memorial, along with an additional 5,000 Reich marks from the designated diocesan bank account. In addition, Gestapo agents interrogated Coppenrath three times, on April 12, 1935, February 3, 1936, and April 7, 1936, about the collection for the Klausener memorial. Each time Coppenrath fully admitted that he had written the announcement for the collection and had also informed his congregation on numerous occasions that the Gestapo had confiscated the money. He also made the Gestapo aware that it had confiscated 5,000 Reich marks of the diocese's money that had nothing to do with the collection. Upon investigation, the Gestapo returned the surplus. Despite the Gestapo's pressure, Coppenrath remained bold in his determination to honor Klausener's name. When asked whether he would pursue the erection of the memorial, he answered, "Obviously, at least as far as it depends on me! I do not possess 5,000 [Reich marks]; since the confiscation of the collection, I have played the lottery and on the day I win 5,000 Reich marks, I will give that for the building of the memorial."[103] The Gestapo accepted his challenge and requested before the *Sondergericht*—a criminal court established to remove political opponents of the Nazi state—a proceeding against both Coppenrath and Vicar General Paul Steinmann. The court, however, refused to hear the case, citing a lack of evidence to support infringement of the law against treacherous attacks on the party and state and sent the case back to the district court of Berlin. Later, on September 30, 1937, the state attorney general proceeded with a case against both men. He charged Coppenrath with "encouraging the collection" and "writing the relevant appeal" and Steinmann with "sending the appeal to the parish offices."[104] As a result, on July 4, 1938, the court announced its decision and found Coppenrath guilty of instigating the collection on political grounds. Despite the conviction, the court suspended the case against Coppenrath because his "crime" was committed before April 30, 1938, at which time the government had proclaimed an amnesty law in honor of the annexation of Austria that nullified penalties of six months or less. Outraged that the court had found him guilty of acting from political motives, on July 12, 1938, Coppenrath protested the decision and demanded to be exonerated. The court did not grant his request.[105]

Because of his persistence in the Klausener affair, the Gestapo kept Coppenrath under almost constant surveillance. This scrutiny in turn led to numerous summonses demanding that he appear before local Gestapo authorities for questioning about a variety of issues, including not flying the swastika flag from the church on the day of the funeral of Reich Governor Loeper. This latter incident enabled Gestapo agents to interrogate him, search his rectory, and hold him in "protective custody" overnight. Thereafter, Coppenrath received a summons to appear in court. Once there, he faced charges but used the courtroom to lodge his own complaints against the Hitler Youth who had vandalized church property and demonstrated near his church during a Sunday mass. He also argued that, because of the expense, he had not purchased an additional swastika flag large enough for the church.[106] At this point, Coppenrath realized that he was certainly being arrested not only because of an offense against the flag ordinance, but also because of his pulpit announcements. In his own defense, he volunteered that his pulpit announcements were being made in response to the "scandalous attacks on Christianity and the Catholic Church." In addition, he noted that he had no "political intentions," but sought only to "safeguard legitimate interests and fulfill [his] pastoral duty."[107] This time the court sided with Coppenrath, who received only a nominal fifty–Reich mark fine for violating the flag order. The court also did not declare him hostile to the state, a finding that overjoyed the pastor.[108]

Despite his courtroom victory, Coppenrath did not escape the experience entirely unscathed. He later confided to several priest friends that the idea that he might have to go to prison for a prolonged period of time terrified him. His experience in the Alexanderplatz police station had awakened him to the horrors the state could inflict upon its "enemies."[109] In the same conversation, Coppenrath also revealed how he had questioned the German bishops' oblique response to the state following the death of Klausener. For him and many others, this was a moment of lost opportunity.[110] It should be noted that Coppenrath shared these opinions only with his closest of friends. In public, Coppenrath limited his criticism directly to pulpit announcements.

For the Gestapo, however, every announcement had the potential to disturb the peace within the state. As a result, Coppenrath's safety was always in danger. Although it is possible that Coppenrath thought to justify delivering future announcements by using the pulpit to describe his encounters with the Gestapo, he did not push his parishioners to resistance and normally reported that the Gestapo had treated him in a just manner or had not harmed him in any way.[111] In one case, after several members of his parish blocked an unidentified Gestapo agent from confiscating an edition of the weekly Church newspaper, Coppenrath even warned his congregation to never "reproach a police officer or even to take steps against him," because he carried out the action on "instruction from a higher authority."[112] After the war, Coppenrath argued that he had made such statements to protect those around him. If resistance to the encroachment of the state on church life had to be made, Coppenrath wanted to take sole responsibility.

In another sense, he did not wish to be responsible for another person's arrest and imprisonment. This fact was clear even with regard to his own curates. In one instance, for example, the Gestapo "invited" one of Coppenrath's curates to report to the local office for questioning. Before the young priest left the rectory, Coppenrath told him to place sole responsibility upon the pastor's shoulders for the content of his notices and their delivery. Coppenrath always accepted full responsibility for his announcements. After this event, Coppenrath chose to make all the pulpit announcements himself.[113]

As Coppenrath himself admitted, he was and remained throughout his life a committed nationalist.[114] He also refused to believe that, as a pastor, he did things that were "politically motivated." Instead, Coppenrath always argued that he limited himself to the pastoral sphere, questioning those actions and events that brought offense to Catholicism. Indeed, he was not afraid to mention the names of higher Nazi officials—including Goebbels, Schirach, and Rosenberg—especially if he thought their actions attacked his church. In the eyes of Nazi officials, however, Coppenrath was a troublemaker and clearly unreliable. Others, too, viewed Coppenrath's comments as "politically motivated."[115] As early as April 1934, a Berlin cabaret performer asked his audience: "What is new in politics?" He continued, "Unfortunately, I do not know what is going on since I was not in St. Matthias Church last Sunday!" The audience understood and appreciated the joking remark.[116] For Coppenrath, though, this was no laughing matter.

Although it is easy to see that Coppenrath was a strong personality who could stand on his own in the face of injustice, one should bear in mind that Coppenrath was not always alone. In fact, he received the constant support of his parishioners. For example, when he returned from his first night in jail following the flag controversy, his parishioners greeted him in written letters, by telephone, and in person with well wishes. Gifts of flowers awaited him, and financial gifts helped pay for the fifty–Reich mark fine in the days thereafter.[117] His parishioners, however, remained aware of the risks that their pastor took to inform them of the truth. As a result, they always seemed to expect the worst. As early as April 1934, when the police surrounded the church prior to an official requiem mass for a deceased envoy from Haiti, the parishioners assumed immediately that they had come to arrest Coppenrath for his pulpit announcements. Upon his departure from the rectory and while he was en route to the church, a "great crowd" of parishioners greeted Coppenrath and "implored" him to flee from the area.[118]

As the war began, Coppenrath's luck ran out. At first, he refrained from any pulpit announcements or comments on the "religious situation," because of the war. Following attacks on the Church by Rosenberg, however, Coppenrath felt compelled to speak out. In his homily on October 18, 1940, Coppenrath discussed the alleged sins of the Church in relation to the claims of some scholars. Although he admitted that there were definite "weaknesses and shortcomings" in the 2,000-year history of the Church, he noted that, in relation to "numerous families and groups, governments and rulers . . . [who] have shown such a wealth of scandals, such a full barrel of sins, of corruptibility and lies and deception and robberies and murder and immorality, that the scandals and sins in the 2,000-year history of the Church, no matter how sad and disgraceful, almost disappear in comparison."[119]

The stakes were raised when, on October 20, 1940, Coppenrath challenged Rosenberg directly. Furthermore, in his sermon of November 3, 1940, he questioned the intelligence of those who had denounced him to the Gestapo, in particular pointing to their lack of understanding of his pulpit statements.[120] As a result, on November 9, the Gestapo visited Coppenrath. The two Gestapo officers ordered the pastor to accompany them to Alexanderplatz station, where they held him in "protective custody" until his unexpected release on December 5, 1940. During this time, the Gestapo physically abused him. Before his release, the agent on duty warned him not to bring politics to the pulpit. In response, Coppenrath argued that he had never done that. As he left his cell, Coppenrath gave the Hitler salute to the master of the watch. This gesture was in all likelihood made in mockery, because he was not allowed to use the salute as a prisoner.[121] Upon his return to St. Matthias, on Sunday, December 8, Coppenrath thanked his parishioners who had prayed for him during his absence. After a brief vacation in his native Münster, Coppenrath returned, only to find an official letter prohibiting him from residing in or visiting any part of the diocese of Berlin.[122] Under threat of further arrest, Coppenrath returned to Münster, where he kept a low profile until the end of the war. His prison experience had apparently put fear in his heart.

Coppenrath and other priests persecuted by the Gestapo were proud, nationalistic German who dearly loved their country. Like thousands of other German Catholics, they wanted to be included in the revival of the German Reich, and in no way, of course, did they seek to be labeled "enemies of the Reich"—a title Bismarck gave to Catholics during the Kulturkampf. Indeed, for these clerics, Catholicism and Nazism shared many of the same values: staunch support of the family unit, antiliberalism, and disdain for Communism. In the beginning, the success of Hitler's government in combating unemployment and attacking lax morality in German society encouraged many priests to welcome the Hitler government. Hitler's March 1933 promises to the churches and the accommodations of the July 1933 concordat also enabled them to put their stamp of approval on the regime.

With the murder of Erich Klausener, its cover-up, and the ensuing false accusations against him, however, Coppenrath and other priests awakened to the harsh realities and contradictions of National Socialism. In addition, the ever-increasing advance of the state into areas previously set aside for the Church and for its members made many priests distrust the state. Aware of the dangers of saying too much, they remained careful to protest only against those violations that directly affected their church and ministry. In this sense, their protests emerged out of pastoral turmoil caused by the state. Such protests also arose as a form of self-defense from within the Church. For this reason, most clerics refused to call themselves opponents of the state and steadfastly denied enlistment in any form of political resistance. Nevertheless, by questioning and challenging the intrusiveness of the National Socialist weltanschauung into the life of the Church and its members, these priests provided Catholics with a haven from the all-encompassing claims of National Socialism over the lives of ordinary Germans. The Gestapo correctly recognized and identified such actions as disturbances against civic peace and, as a result, labeled these priests politically untrustworthy and ordered surveillance of their activities. Prior to the outbreak of war, the Gestapo allowed some priests leeway in their dissent, but when war came no dissent was tolerated.

four

Serving the Home Front

For the most part, Berlin's priests neither opposed the war nor enthusiastically welcomed it. Nevertheless, when Germany declared war, priests had to adapt themselves to the conflict and, at least provisionally, resolve within themselves any inner tensions that existed between their allegiance to Germany and their fidelity to Catholicism. Eventually, most priests were able to determine a role for themselves that balanced the uncertainties of war and patriotism with the challenges of ministry. Thus, by 1941, nineteen Berlin priests were serving as chaplains in various divisions and twenty-four as medics.[1] Of these priests, eight died in military action, along with an additional twenty-one seminarians, all of whom the government had drafted for regular military service.[2] Priests who were not in the military opted to retain their positions in parishes, institutions, and hospitals throughout the diocese. Though often nationalistic in their outlook and supportive of the German war effort, many clerics also felt compelled to ignore or directly disobey state ordinances (often created to "protect" the home front during the war) to fulfill their broader ministerial duties. These acts of disobedience placed them in direct confrontation with the Nazi state, whose brutal laws the Gestapo worked tirelessly to enforce. At no time was this confrontation highlighted more than during the war years, when Berlin's priests maneuvered between their own nationalism and the tenets of their Catholic faith in an effort to serve German Catholics and avoid any complicity in anti-Catholic activities.

Despite the pastoral limitations the state imposed upon them, many Berlin priests simply refused to allow their pastoral sphere to be narrowed. Indeed, they maneuvered to serve all Catholics in their midst. From this curious dichotomy of action, a paradigm of pastoral practice emerged that guided the clergy through some of the worst periods of the war. Concerned about the faith of their young men in battle, parish priests felt duty bound to reach out to their parishioner-soldiers with letters and care packages. Likewise, priests with large numbers of foreign slave laborers or civilian workers in their parishes took pains to provide the sacraments to their flocks. In each case, strict state laws governing communication, especially between German citizens and foreigners, forced clergymen to break the civil law to provide pastoral ministry to those they felt bound to serve. During the war, of course, the Gestapo dropped any pretenses of leniency and fully enforced these laws. In the city of Stettin, Pomerania, for example, the state executed six priests who defied laws regarding the spread of "defeatist" attitudes during war. The majority of these priests realized the risks they were undertaking by actively involving themselves in discussion groups that enabled their parishioners to speak frankly about the war in Europe.

On July 12, 1940, Hans Kerrl, the minister of church affairs, issued a decree that "prohibited the spread of religious literature by civilians in church positions."[3] Instructed by the Gestapo to issue such a decree, Kerrl worked with the secret police to prevent the spread of any literature that might advocate pacifism or relax the war effort in Germany. Priests such as Father Bernhard Hering, pastor of St. Hubert parish in Petershagen, near Berlin, ignored this prohibition. Instead, he drafted letters to thirty-six soldiers from his parish.[4] Though the letters mainly contained information about parish activities and exhortations to stay true to the faith, Hering also invited the soldiers "to cultivate a personal exchange of letters" with him. Of the thirty-six men, seven chose to correspond with Hering. In September and October 1940, Hering reciprocated, moving beyond religious issues to discuss "the relationship of Catholicism and Christianity to secular power." On discovering the exchange, the Gestapo immediately put an end to it. On November 7, 1940, the Gestapo arrested Hering, placing him in "protective custody." Hering was first held in Potsdam (November 7, 1940–February 15, 1941) and was then moved to Moabit Prison in Berlin, where he remained until his sudden release on August 18, 1941. During Hering's confinement, the Gestapo initiated proceedings against him for violating the law against treacherous acts against the state and party and for threatening the war effort. Despite the Gestapo's efforts, in October 1941 the district court of Berlin recommended dismissing the proceedings against Hering for lack of evidence that he had made statements that were "hateful, malicious or inflammatory" against the state. Instead, the court found only instances where he had spoken out against those in the *Volk* who held opinions against the Church.[5]

After the war, Hering claimed that his letter writing had no political motivation and reiterated that his missives were pastorally inspired.[6] Both during and after the war, Hering simply refused to allow anyone to label him as detrimental to the German state. In his mind, he was a good nationalistic German, one who both professed Catholicism and viewed Christianity as the foundation of the state. Hering's objections arose specifically from his concern to maintain Christian principles in the state and to exhort his parishioners who were soldiers to persevere in their faith.

Unlike Hering, who limited his actions to letter writing, Father Carl Heinz Sauer, parochial vicar of Holy Family parish in Berlin-Lichterfelde, willingly engaged in a "defeatist" action in his efforts to protect one young man's freedom to practice his faith. In 1941, Sauer ran afoul of the Gestapo for his efforts to aid eighteen-year-old Dutch conscript Abraham F., who wished to desert the Waffen-SS and flee to his native Netherlands. In September, Sauer had befriended Abraham, who originally had approached him to discuss the religious isolation he felt as the only Catholic in his company. Sauer encouraged him to attend mass and introduced him to Frau M. and her family, who years earlier had emigrated from the Netherlands to Germany. In November of the same year, Abraham's company leader punished him for attending mass in uniform, disobeying orders, and consulting a civilian doctor. The commander also threatened the young man with forced labor and placement in a concentration camp. To further terrify him, five fellow members of the SS physically beat Abraham. Fearing the worst, he fled to Frau M. and recounted the events. She, in turn, contacted Father Sauer. Convinced of the authenticity of the story, Sauer helped Abraham flee and provided him with "a coat, a jacket, and a hat" to help disguise him. Unfortunately, the fleeing soldier never reached his destination, but was arrested en route. In his testimony to the court, Sauer admitted helping Abraham escape, because, "according to his conviction, F. had been hindered in the exercise of his religious obligations." In this specific instance, Sauer's allegiance to his church and his commitment to ministry outranked his obligation to the fatherland, although, during the court proceeding, he stated that "as a priest—a German priest—[he] was to a very special degree duty bound to abide by the will of the God-appointed authority," to which he owed "obedience in accordance with divine, state, and Church law." Despite this patriotic declaration, the District Court of Berlin sentenced Sauer to three years in prison and took away his citizenship rights for three years for threatening the war effort. The court likewise sentenced Frau M. to one year in prison on similar charges.[7]

Sauer expressed no intention to harm the war effort, nor did he want Germany to lose the war. Rather, he offered to assist the young Dutchman precisely because the SS had infringed upon the young man's freedom to practice his faith. On that account, Sauer acted solely for pastoral reasons to protect the young man from an environment hostile to his faith. At the time, it was common knowledge among Germans that the SS pressed all its members officially to withdraw from their respective churches. In his own mind, Sauer possibly could have drawn a clear distinction between the SS and the German army. Priests often identified the SS as an anti-Catholic organization, whereas the army represented the German fatherland and, therefore, had to be supported. Notwithstanding Sauer's reasoning, any military unit would have viewed the young man's flight as desertion and treated it as such. As an authority figure and as a pastor, Sauer could also have just as easily influenced Frau M. to encourage the young man to stay at his post. Similarly, Sauer could have attempted to intervene in the Waffen-SS in Abraham's behalf over the religious issue, although he most likely would have had no success. Instead, Sauer took the matter into his own hands and made a conscious decision to help the young man flee the country. From Sauer's perspective, his action did not constitute treason, but was merely a courageous decision of faith to protect an individual's Catholic belief, especially because Abraham was a member of the SS.

Other priests within the Berlin diocese also put themselves in harm's way to aid Catholics who were not German. This is of particular importance, because, as the war progressed, the German army and the SS shipped thousands of war prisoners and foreign civilians to Germany to work as slave laborers for the war effort. In addition, there was also an extensive group of foreign nationals already living and working within the Berlin diocese to whom priests were appointed to care for their spiritual well-being. Sometimes German priests volunteered to minister to foreign nationals. For example, in September 1939, Father Erich Tschetschog, pastor of St. Boniface Church in Belzig, asked the state government to allow him, as a "Reich German priest with knowledge of Czech," to offer mass in the Niemegk community camp for Czech workers from the protectorate area. Tschetschog argued that the camp's distance—eleven kilometers from the church—made it impossible for the workers to attend the parish itself. According to Tschetschog, Bishop Preysing was willing to assign a priest for this purpose.[8] Eventually, on December 6, 1939, an official from the Ministry of Propaganda gave Tschetschog permission for the mass.[9]

The correspondence relating to Father Tschetschog's request gives the impression that the government was willing to work with the diocese to ensure that the pastoral needs of non-German-speaking inhabitants within the diocese were met. This case was unique, because it concerned Czech people from the German-occupied protectorate. The government, however, did not show the same openness to all pastoral initiatives for foreign citizens living (or forced to live) in Germany. This was especially true of Polish citizens, many of whom were brought by force into Germany, either as prisoners or forced laborers. After the attack on Poland in September 1939, native Poles were seen as enemies of Germany and the government. The RSHA also wanted to ensure that the Poles be treated as enemies of the state. To that end, by 1940 Germany enacted decrees to separate Polish laborers from the German civilian population. The RSHA particularly wanted to prevent the mixing of the German and Polish races and to hinder any sympathy for the Poles among the German population. One decree even required Poles to wear a "P" on their clothing, thus denoting their race and signaling the German population to avoid them.[10]

At first, neither the Ministry of Church Affairs nor Himmler placed severe restrictions on priests ministering to Poles. They simply required parishes to hold special masses for Polish civilian workers because they, along with Poles in general, were prohibited from attending any of the regular parish masses. Even though Latin was the language of the liturgy at the time, the Ministry of Church Affairs decreed that the Polish language could not be used in any part of the liturgy, including in the sermons and hymns. As the war progressed, the measures limiting the freedom of the church to care for Polish Catholics also increased. In December 1941, Bishop Preysing reported to the Ministry of Church Affairs that, in certain remote areas of his diocese, local officials were limiting the number of times a priest could hold mass for Poles to once a month. Consequently, Preysing petitioned the ministry to allow a special mass for Poles every Sunday.[11] In Pyritz, Pomerania, the local government had even boldly prohibited any special masses for the Polish population.[12] Preysing soon learned that these practices merely foreshadowed what was to come. On February 23, 1942, the Ministry of Church Affairs, in agreement with Himmler, decreed that special masses for Poles could only be held on "the first Sunday of every month and only between ten and twelve in the morning."[13] This regulation for special liturgies for Poles was almost impossible to undertake, because most parishes had their regular Sunday masses at the same time. Nevertheless, changes were made, which meant rearranging the entire mass schedule for one week each month. Naturally, doing so placed an extra burden upon the clergy and the parishioners alike.

Despite all of the regulations, extant correspondence between the diocese and the Ministry of Church Affairs revealed that communication was often unclear with regard to the diocese's ministry to Poles. The Nazis permitted some forms of ministry, but prohibited other forms. In an April 6, 1943, letter, for example, Bishop Preysing wrote to the Ministry of Church Affairs to request permission for baptisms, confessions, and funerals of Polish civilian workers. In his letter, Preysing stated that these points had not been clarified by earlier guidelines, including investigative guidelines issued by Himmler throughout 1942.[14] At this point in Nazi Germany, the Ministry of Church Affairs scarcely made a move without contacting one of Himmler's divisions for permission or advice as to how to proceed. Part of this caution was due to Kerrl's untimely death on December 14, 1941, and to the general weakness of the ministry, which never wielded a great deal of power or influence in Nazi Germany. Therefore, church affairs forwarded Preysing's letter to Himmler. On May 18, a representative of Himmler answered the inquiry and stated that baptism for a Polish child could take place only on the condition that the ceremony remain simple, that it be limited to immediate family members, that only German or Latin be used, and that Germans be excluded. Fearing the secrecy of the confessional and the freedom it allowed for discussion, Church Affairs also did not permit administering the sacrament of penance to Poles.[15] On June 5, 1943, the Ministry of Church Affairs informed Bishop Preysing of these regulations.[16]

Through the *Amtsblatt,* the Berlin diocese attempted to keep its clergy informed about these regulations, especially whether it was permissible or not to minister to Polish civilian workers. Because the guidelines issued by one of various governmental ministries were so opaque, the correspondence revealed how difficult a task this was. In addition, the transnational nature of religion only complicated the situation for the enforcers of the guidelines. The Catholic faith, for example, generated a common bond between Polish and German Catholics that could not easily be broken.[17] Thus, German Catholic clergy had a very difficult time turning Poles away from their Catholic churches, especially when they requested assistance in pastoral matters. This was especially true in the diocese for priests of Polish descent who spoke the language fluently. During the war years, these combined factors made the pastoral care of Polish civilian workers the leading cause of tension between Catholic priests and the Gestapo.

Breaches of the policy toward Polish civilian workers did not always yield the same punishment. For example, the infractions of Father Paul Sawatzke, pastor of Christ the King in Schönow, Pomerania, and of Father Willibald Jordan, pastor of St. Maria in Arnswalde-Neumark, were, in the eyes of the Gestapo, serious crimes, but, in relation to their crimes and the punishments inflicted upon other priests, the Gestapo imposed only sanctions on them. In the case of Father Sawatzke, some time in 1943 he used an interpreter during a mass for Polish civilian workers. It is unclear in the extant records how long Sawatzke continued this practice. When the Stettin Gestapo confronted him, Father Sawatzke denied any wrongdoing and attributed his "error" to a contradiction in various regulations released by Himmler the previous year.[18] The Gestapo refused to accept his explanation and officially issued him a warning.[19] Father Willibald Jordan, on the other hand, did not even receive a warning on account of his pastoral activity for the Poles. Instead, the Gestapo used the tactic of threatening him with time in a concentration camp. From 1943 though 1944, the Gestapo also monitored his mail and telephone calls.[20] These two men were exceptions to the norm, because other priests whom the Gestapo had confronted for their ministry to Poles *were* imprisoned or sent to concentration camps.

Even minor infractions of any regulation governing the ministry of Catholic priests among Poles could result in the arrest of the priest. On Monday, June 10, 1940, Father Paul Krause, pastor of St. Marian Church in Altdamm-Stettin, discovered just how real the threats of the Gestapo were when he was arrested for tolerating the presence of approximately sixty Polish war prisoners and civilian workers at his 10:00 a.m. mass. The Saturday prior to his arrest, a German guard who was supervising the prisoners had approached Krause to ask him if he could bring the prisoners to mass the following day. Krause protested, saying it would be impossible for him to hold a separate mass because he had to preside at three masses that Sunday. Allegedly without Krause's knowledge, the following day, two guards, about sixty Polish POWs, and a number of Polish civilians attended the regular Sunday mass alongside German soldiers and civilians. Surprised at their presence, Krause permitted them to remain for the mass.[21] Someone among the congregation, however, denounced the priest for allowing the Poles to worship with Germans. The Gestapo immediately arrested Krause and placed him in "protective custody." Yet, as in so many of these cases, the Gestapo suddenly released him—on August 5, 1940—without further explanation. For Krause, however, the ordeal was not over, because the state continued to file charges against him in the Stettin district court. After his trial, in January 1941, the criminal division of the Stettin district court found Krause guilty of violating the decree concerning contact with war prisoners and fined him 100 Reich marks. The judge did show some mercy and credited time served in lieu of the fine.[22] In this case, Krause did not even willingly welcome the Poles into his church, but simply—to avoid disrupting the order of mass—did not ask the guards to remove them. In 1941, in a separate but similar case, Father Georg Gretz, pastor of St. Paul Church in Dramburg, Pomerania, refused to send Polish civilian workers (all wearing a "P" on their uniforms) away from a mass at the parish's mission church in Falkenburg. As a result, on December 20, 1941, the Gestapo arrested him for permitting the Poles to attend a regular parish mass scheduled "for Germans" and placed him in Schneidemühl work camp. The state, however, never officially charged Gretz, and on March 20, 1942, the Gestapo released him.[23]

The Gestapo not only arrested five additional members of the Berlin clergy because of their ministry to Polish prisoners, but also sent them directly to concentration camps as punishment for their violations of the law. They included Father Paul Adamus, pastor of Our Lady Star of the Sea Church in Swinemünde; Father Paul Bartsch, of St. Otto Church in Cammin; and Father Adolf Nolewaika, pastor of Our Lady Queen of the Rosary Church in Demmin. Two additional pastors—August Fröhlich, of St. George in Rathenow, and Father Joseph Lenzel, of St. Mary Magdalene in Berlin-Niederschönhausen—were also sent to concentration camps and died as a result of the conditions and treatment there.

In some cases priests such as Father Nolewaika, according to his own testimony, ministered to the Polish people not only because they were fellow Catholics, but also because the clerics viewed doing so as an opportunity to resist the Nazi state.[24] For example, in 1940, Nolewaika went against state regulations by not only officiating at the wedding of a Polish bride and groom, but also using the Polish language whenever possible in the rite. Afterward, he invited the couple to breakfast at the rectory. Nolewaika was also known to go to great lengths to fulfill the pastoral needs of the Poles. This included traveling to remote villages to baptize children. These actions were nothing less than refusal to abide by the demands of Nazi officials and treat Poles as subhuman. Instead, Nolewaika showed respect for Poles and interacted with them as he would with any German Catholic. On September 20, 1940, the Gestapo decided it could no longer accept this questionable behavior and arrested him. Soon thereafter, on January 4, 1941, they sent him to Dachau, where he endured almost four and a half years of tortuous daily living. Finally, on April 26, 1945, as Allied forces were approaching, he escaped during a "death march."[25]

On March 19, 1941, the Gestapo also arrested Father Paul Adamus for his ministry to the Poles, but most especially because he spoke to them in their native Polish. Unlike Nolewaika, Adamus did not attribute any political reasons to his activity. His parochial vicar, Father Kurt Reuter, attempted to intervene in his behalf and explain to the mayor of Swinemünde that the pastor's arrest, especially during Holy Week, might cause "great unrest among the population," including among non-Catholics who greatly respected him. Despite Reuter's pleas, the Gestapo refused to release him.[26] Instead, they were more willing to risk unrest in the area than to release Adamus. On June 13, 1941, the Gestapo transported the priest to Dachau. On April 4, 1945, Adamus was released from the Nazi death camp.[27] In 1943, the Gestapo also arrested Father Paul Bartsch for his "friendly disposition" toward the Polish civilian workers.[28] Bartsch had been arrested before, in 1941, and had spent three weeks in prison for unknown reasons.[29] This time the Gestapo wanted to ensure that he would no longer be able "to encourage a bond with the Poles" among the German population. The Gestapo always viewed this type of behavior as destructive toward the war effort and as a blatant violation of measures designed to separate Germans from Poles.[30] Therefore, after two months of imprisonment, Bartsch was sent to Dachau, where he remained until his release on April 4, 1945. Although Bartsch survived Dachau, he would be murdered by Russian soldiers on March 24, 1950.[31]

The last two priests ministering to the Poles, Fathers Joseph Lenzel and August Froelich, died at Dachau. According to his parish chronicle, the murder of Erich Klausener radically changed Lenzel. From that point on, he publicly interacted with Jewish families, refused to give the Hitler salute, and extended his active ministry to Protestants who lived within his parish boundaries.[32] The Gestapo warned him several times for criticizing the Nazi weltanschauung in his sermons and for not hoisting the German flag on designated state holidays. It was, however, Lenzel's concern for Polish civilian laborers in his parish (i.e., allowing "Poles to participate in masses for Germans"), labeled a "crime" at this time, that led to his arrest and placement in "protective custody."[33] From there the Gestapo sent him to Wuhlheide labor camp. Finally, on May 8, 1942, the Gestapo ordered Lenzel transported to Dachau, where on July 3, 1942, less than two months after his arrival, he was reported dead.[34]

Father Froehlich met a similar fate. In contrast to Lenzel and the other priests who ran afoul of the Gestapo for ministering to Poles, Froehlich left behind a rich set of documents, including a collection of sermons documenting his experiences during the Third Reich. Froehlich was also an intensely patriotic German. At the beginning of the First World War, for example, he was drafted into the army and wounded twice, once while serving on the eastern front and then again while on the western front. Following the war, he spent more than a year as a prisoner of war in an English jail.[35]

When the Nazis first seized power, Froehlich was pastor of St. Paul Church in Dramburg, Pomerania. St. Paul's was a small diaspora parish of about 300 Catholics among 30,000 non-Catholics, most of whom were Protestant. Only thirty-five Catholics lived in the city itself. The rest lived in the countryside within eighty kilometers of the main church.[36] In the winter of 1934, a local NSDAP leader publicly accused Froehlich, along with another unnamed individual, of refusing to share their income with those who were "hungry and cold."

Of course, the NSDAP official was primarily angry with Froehlich for his continued refusal to participate in the Nazi Party's winter relief collection. Although the NSDAP leader did not mention Froehlich by name, it was clear to the public that he was referring to the local Catholic pastor.[37] Furious over such public defamation of his character, Froehlich immediately took the NSDAP leader to task and reminded him in a letter that article 5 of the Reich-Vatican concordat protected his freedom to exercise his spiritual ministry in the same manner that all civil servants enjoyed the protection of the state. He also reminded him that he had donated more funds from his private income to charity than his accuser had.[38] An exchange of correspondence ensued between the two men.[39] Finally, in disgust, Froehlich wrote to district leader W. and insisted that he intervene in his behalf and force the local NSDAP leader to apologize to him publicly.[40] W. immediately responded to Froehlich's request and reported that at a recent meeting of the NSDAP, the local party leader had already retracted his statement against the priest.[41] Froehlich had won a victory over the local NSDAP, but in gaining this success, he also made enemies. This, however, did not deter Froehlich from protesting against what he perceived to be unwarranted restrictions on the Catholic Church and its members' practice of their faith.

In 1935, and again in 1936, Froehlich took issue with the practices and dealings of the *Reichsarbeitsdienst* (Reich Labor Service) camp in Falkenburg. In March 1935, for example, two young men approached the priest and complained that camp leaders had refused them permission to attend mass and instead forced them to attend a Protestant service.[42] The following year, a Catholic theologian also confided to Froehlich that the same camp official had refused him permission to attend mass regularly and had caused him to feel ostracized in the camp because of his religion.[43] Seeking an explanation for these two complaints, Froehlich wrote the camp director. He based his charge on the articles of the concordat, which, he argued, protected the rights of Catholics to practice their faith freely.[44] Despite a series of letters, the director refused to answer his complaints.[45]

By 1936, Froehlich began to question openly the intentions of the state toward the Catholic Church. During an October sermon on the Feast of Christ the King, Froehlich criticized the superimposition of the Nazi ideology on traditional Catholic teaching. Froehlich proclaimed to his parishioners, "Christ is the King of all kings, the Führer of all Führer. He is our Führer in every respect. . . . There is no eternal Reich in this world. . . . We cannot say that the Führer is an emissary of God. Indeed, if an important man says: A time will come where one will confess Christ was great, but the Führer was greater. That is entirely foolishness, indeed blasphemy of God. Never should one elevate a human above God."[46] In 1937, in front of a local police officer and an SS man who were inspecting the parish youth library, Froehlich also questioned the attitude of the editors of the *SA Mann, Schwarzes Korps,* and *Der Stürmer* newspapers, who criticized the Church. He said he found "no difference between their manner of struggle against religion and the manner which the Communists and Bolsheviks have used."[47] As a result, the two state representatives denounced the priest and had him fined 400 Reich marks.[48] Froehlich immediately appealed the court's decision, arguing that he had acted in defense of his faith. He pointed out that if any of these newspapers were sent abroad, their content would scandalize Christians, who, among other things, would wonder about Germany's positive Christianity.[49] Although he was not allowed to appeal the decision, the court of lay assessors in Stargard, acting upon the 1938 amnesty law, dropped the proceedings.[50]

In 1941, Froehlich finally found himself in a situation too serious to escape by merely paying a fine. The first of ten incidents took place in 1941, when Froehlich took up the cause of Polish civilian workers who complained of mistreatment, including physical abuse, by their employers. Instead of referring the Polish workers to the state employment office for help, Froehlich personally became involved in three of the cases, and his intercession in one of the cases resulted in the suspension of a German employee from work for several days. As a result, the individual called Froehlich and expressed his anger over the priest's involvement. Naturally, the Gestapo did not take lightly Froehlich's intercession on behalf of the Polish civilian workers and consequently took him into "protective custody." From March 23, 1941, until April 8, the Gestapo kept Froehlich in their prison in Potsdam and released him only after a 500–Reich mark bond had been secured.[51] On April 15, 1941, Froehlich did something very daring. In an effort to explain his pastoral actions, he mailed the Gestapo a letter in which he described in detail his involvement with Polish workers. In the letter, he pointed out that there were 2,000 Polish people in his parish and, for that reason alone, no official could honestly say that he "took special interest in the Poles in these instances." Rather, he stated, he only associated "professionally, as a priest, with the Poles." Then he argued that if he had not looked after their needs, he would have been "more or less like the Pharisee who passed by the man who fell to the robbers" in the story of the Good Samaritan. Finally, he pointed out that as a priest he had "to tend to the spiritual and physical suffering" of all his fellow human beings.[52] In response, on May 20, 1941, the Gestapo arrested Froehlich for a last time and charged him "with not keeping enough distance from the Polish civilian workers."[53] For a brief time, he remained in the Gestapo Potsdam jail, but soon afterward he was transferred to Buchenwald and from there to Ravensbrück. Finally, on May 15, 1942, he was sent to Dachau, where he died shortly thereafter, on June 22, 1942.[54]

In all of the cases discussed here, the Gestapo confronted priests directly because of their ministry to Poles. With the possible exception of Father Nolewaika, who attributed some political motives to his actions, the priests reached out to the Polish people not because they sought to question the Nazi system or to reject their German fatherland, but primarily because Poles were fellow Catholics in need of pastoral care. In many situations, the Poles were also the ones who first approached the priests and asked to receive one of the sacraments. According to the ecclesiastic worldview of these German priests, the Poles who moved into their parish boundaries automatically became members of the parish and joined the ranks of their fellow German Catholics in the area. They also believed that it was a priest's responsibility to ensure that the sacramental needs of all parishioners were met. If a priest did not meet their spiritual needs, he would, in the end, have to answer to a higher power on the Day of Judgment.

Even when priests made the choice to engage themselves in ministering to the Poles, all in accordance with the guidelines of the Reich Führer of the SS and the Ministry of Church Affairs, the Gestapo still viewed them as suspects—individuals who could not be trusted. Although the Gestapo saw the majority of the Catholic clergy in this same light, its agents especially felt they could not trust those priests who showed kindness and compassion to "enemies" of the Reich and to "subhumans." Naturally, this increased the priests' risk of being warned, arrested, and imprisoned. In one sense, merely by making the conscious decision—

whether for pastoral or political reasons—to engage themselves in the pastoral care of a group of people whom the Nazis had labeled subhuman, priests risked going against the norms of the state. This indeed was an act of *Resistenz,* though priests themselves would most likely reject this categorization. More often than not, they would argue that their actions were performed only in the context of their sacramental ministry to Catholics, regardless of race or nationality.

Another point that must be stressed is that, in ministering to the Poles, German Catholic priests—especially those from the diocese of Berlin—did not have to cross a vast social barrier. Nazi ideology against the Poles was relatively new. German and Polish Catholics shared a faith, and for many years Polish migrant workers had traveled throughout the countryside of Brandenburg and Pomerania. In addition, many of the Berlin clergy were of Polish ancestry and spoke the language. All of these factors enabled German priests to sympathize with the Polish civilian workers and prisoners of war and to act on their behalf.

Whereas all of the priests described above clashed with the Gestapo over pastoral programs and duties, a number of more politically minded priests—in what has been called the "Stettin Affair"—did minister within the Third Reich. They believed that Hitler was fighting an unjust war of conquest and domination and could find no place for him or his rule in their hearts. It should be noted that although from the very outset of the Third Reich Gestapo officials from Stettin were hostile toward Catholic priests, it is difficult to determine whether this belligerent attitude altered the clerics' attitudes toward the Nazi regime. Their mutual suspicion, however, was abundantly evident. During the war years, this distrust became even more apparent when, over the course of a few months, the Gestapo arrested thirteen priests for participating in treasonous acts against the state. Before the Stettin Affair was over, six priests had died at the hands of the Nazis—four by guillotine, a fifth from the misery of his incarceration, and the last from injuries sustained while serving in a penal battalion.[55]

The reasons behind the Gestapo's initial action against the priests are not clear. Bombing raids during the war destroyed many of the records related to the affair. Although several secondary works have exhausted the remaining material, drawing firm conclusions about the origins of the conflict remains difficult.[56] Events seem to have begun when Franz Hofer, the Nazi district leader of Tirol, decided to pursue Father Carl Lampert, an Austrian canon lawyer and Innsbruck diocesan official. Lampert had incurred the wrath of the Innsbruck Gestapo three times before for alleged acts against the state and for creating unrest among his native population. In 1940, for example, Lampert had encouraged a Catholic women's religious community in Innsbruck to resist the state's efforts to close their convent. For this, he spent fourteen days in "protective custody." A few days after his release, and after a thorough search of his house, in which they uncovered documents hostile to the state, the Gestapo arrested him again. He spent another four weeks in prison. Finally, in June 1940, the Gestapo took Lampert into "protective custody" for a third time because he had publicly read the obituary of a priest who died in Buchenwald. This final detention caused unrest among the population. Despite the reaction of Lampert's parishioners, on August 25, 1940, the Gestapo sent him to Dachau, where he remained until August 1, 1940.[57] Because Lampert was forced to flee his homeland, Bishop Preysing assigned him to a Stettin hospital that was administrated by the Sisters of Mercy of St. Charles Borromeo. There, Lampert assisted the hospital chaplaincy and did pastoral work at St. John the Baptist Church, the largest parish in the city. For Hofer, however, Lampert remained a target. Acting on that supposition, he sent Franz Pissaritsch, a young SS candidate from Austria, to investigate Lampert's activities. Pissaritsch was also in contact with the Pomeranian Nazi district leader, Franz Reinhard Schwede-Coburg, who detested Catholics and entertained the public hope of cleansing his district of them. Schwede-Coburg planned to herald this achievement to Hitler as a future birthday present.[58] Upon his arrival in the area, Pissaritsch met with several top-ranking SS officers, including Bruno Müller and Karl Trettin. All were concerned with the activities of Father Lampert and his interaction with the Catholic clergy in the area.[59] Collectively, they were all responding not only to Hofer, but also to the state, which had issued measures after a September 22, 1941, meeting under the direction of Albert Hartl, a member of the SS and former Munich priest. At this meeting, Hartl and other Nazi officials initiated steps to weaken the Church by gathering information from pro-Nazi informers and initiating well-planned selective actions against the Church. Ernst Kaltenbrunner, the new director of the RSHA (following Heydrich's assassination in 1942), encouraged the adoption of these measures and highly recommended their implementation in Stettin. Under the name "Georg Hagen," Pissaritsch assumed the identity of an Austrian Catholic who had recently moved to the area to work as an engineer at a nearby factory.[60]

Hagen quickly befriended the clergy of the area, first approaching Father Ernst Daniel, pastor of St. John the Baptist, with the aim of becoming more involved in the parish. Daniel, in turn, directed him to his parochial vicar, Father Herbert Simoleit, who served as chaplain to some of the remaining Catholic organizations and also to the soldiers stationed in the city. In no time, Simoleit acted as a friend to Hagen. In addition, Hagen also became well acquainted with Father Lampert.[61] During the course of their friendship, Simoleit invited Hagen to a weekly gathering that he chaired every Wednesday for the young men of his parish, including some soldiers stationed in the area. Father Friedrich Lorenz, who was also a parochial vicar at St. John the Baptist, likewise on occasion attended the meetings. Assisted by a lay member of the parish, Rudolf Mandrella,

Simoleit helped lead the discussions. Over the course of the meetings, the men talked about a variety of issues, both religious and secular, including the aims of the war and the actions taken against Jews of Eastern Europe.[62] Whenever he was in attendance, Hagen actively participated in the meetings and afterwards took copious notes that were later used to incriminate the clergy.[63] Hagen portrayed himself as an opponent of the Nazi regime and, in this role, attempted to bait Lampert by divulging secrets concerning the weapons being built in the Peenemünde factory where he worked. Together with Lampert and another visiting priest, Father Vincenz Plonka, pastor of Sacred Heart Church in Wolgast, Pomerania, they listened to foreign radio broadcasts—programs that had been banned to Germans by a decree enacted at the beginning of the war.[64]

Late on the night of February 4, 1943, after having gathered enough evidence to indict the priests, the Stettin Gestapo arrived at the rectory. Sixteen Gestapo agents greeted Fathers Daniel and Lorenz at the door. A thorough search of the rectory did not produce much evidence, but the Gestapo did uncover a copy of a controversial letter by Werner Mölder.[65] Mölder, a Luftwaffe fighter ace, inspector of the German fighter pilots, and a devout Christian, had written a letter to Erich Klawitter, the director of the youth office in Berlin, praising him for standing up for the rights of Christianity.[66] For all practical purposes, the Gestapo did not need to collect any further evidence because of Hagen's thorough informing, yet the agents continued to dig. The Gestapo was also convinced that area priests, especially Lampert, who had connections in the Vatican, were involved in a spy network and somehow, even from a church tower, were broadcasting secrets to the enemy. That same evening, the Gestapo arrested Daniel, Lorenz, Simoleit, and Plonka. Later, they also arrested Father Leonhard Berger, pastor of the church in Zinnowitz, for joining the other priests during a visit while they listened to foreign radio broadcasts.

The Gestapo officers ruthlessly interrogated the priests, especially Fathers Lampert and Lorenz. Using a variety of methods, including threats against family members, the Gestapo was able to get Father Simoleit to incriminate his previous pastor, Father Alfons Maria Wachsmann, pastor of Greifswald and professor of theology at the University of Greifswald. Wachsmann, who, like Simoleit, had also conducted a weekly discussion for students at the nearby university, was also arrested, along with his two chaplains, Karl Renner of the Cologne archdiocese and Friedrich Förster. In addition, the Gestapo arrested Father Albert Hirsch, pastor of St. Peter and Paul in Louisenthal; Father Karl Böhmer, pastor of Sacred Heart in Greifenberg; Father Paul Bartsch, pastor of St. Otto in Cammin, near Stettin; Father Werner Bunge, pastor of Christ the King in Stettin; and Father Jakob Weinbacher, of the archdiocese of Vienna. The Gestapo charged most of them with either listening to foreign radio broadcasts or endeavoring to harm the war potential of Germany. They arrested Weinbacher and Bunge solely because of their friendship with Lampert. The Gestapo held all of the clerics in "protective custody" and released them only after the proceedings against Lampert had ended.[67]

In 1944, the courts sentenced Wachsmann, Lampert, Lorenz, and Simoleit to death for listening to foreign radio broadcasts and for harming the war effort of Germany. Hirsch was sentenced to four years in prison and in 1944 died while incarcerated in Gollnow prison. Berger received two and a half years in prison but chose to serve as a medic in a penal battalion. On October 25, 1944, he was killed in action. Daniel, Böhmer, Plonka, and Förster were all sentenced to prison, serving two to four years for their "crimes." Though arrested in relation with the Stettin Affair, Bartsch was sent to Dachau for ministering to Polish civilian workers.[68]

As had been the case for the priests discussed above, none of the Stettin clergy defined himself as a political resister of the state. Although the two weekly discussion groups, run by Simoleit and Wachsmann, addressed the political issues of the day, they did so only within the context of their religion. The Stettin priests also began to question the legitimacy of the war as Germany's military might began to wane. As recounted in trial testimonies, reports of atrocities committed against Jews also overshadowed their discussions and raised concern for Germany's future.[69]

Two priests who offer a different model of opposition to the German state during the Stettin affair were Lorenz and Wachsmann. During World War I, Lorenz left his novitiate to serve in the military. Twice wounded, he survived the war and returned to the seminary for his priestly education. Though his devotion to the Church took prominence in his life, he also enjoyed military life. In 1939, for example, he received permission from his religious superiors to enter the army chaplaincy, first serving in Stettin. After the war broke out, he accompanied his division into Poland and from there traveled west to Holland. He showed special sensitivity to the Polish clergy and did not hide his visits to nearby rectories. In 1941, he was devastated when the army released all religious officers from its ranks, and even asked both his provincial, Father Robert Becker, O.M.I., and his ordinary, Bishop Konrad Preysing, for permission to enlist as a regular soldier to fight for his country. Both of them refused his request, stating that the concordat expressly forbade it.[70] Thereafter, he returned to parish ministry in Stettin. As a former soldier, he was naturally curious about the war's progress. Because the Stettin priests did not trust the German radio broadcasts, especially those focusing on the war, the temptation to listen to the foreign radio reports was often too great for them to resist. Although Lorenz participated in the Wednesday discussions about the war and more than likely encouraged the young people in attendance to question the events around them, he did not view his activities as treasonous or political. In his testimony, Lorenz stressed that priests should never be politically active. For him, the conflict between the Church and the state in Nazi Germany was not politically based, "but an ideological problem."[71]

Similar to Lorenz, Father Wachsmann was a soldier in the First World War. Unlike Lorenz, he was discharged early on because of a medical condition with his feet.[72] Whereas Lorenz eschewed conflict with the Nazi regime, in the summer of 1933 Wachsmann provoked his first confrontation with the Nazis by making it difficult for SA men to attend mass. In 1934, he also attended the funeral of a Protestant professor driven to suicide by the excessive taunts and extreme pressure put on him by local Nazis. Wachsmann attended the funeral not only to support the deceased's family, but also to make a public statement against the treatment that the professor had endured. Wachsmann was the only faculty member who attended the funeral.[73] This small humanitarian act gave mixed signals to Catholics and non-Catholics alike, who understood the Church's teaching against suicide and its prohibition against Catholics attending Protestant services. It also bore witness to Catholics who recognized the deeper value of the Protestant professor's life.

Greatly influenced by Father Romano Guardini, Wachsmann also became a proponent of the new liturgical movement in Germany, that viewed liturgy not as a momentary experience of sacramental insularity, but as a broader life-giving vehicle of grace for the wider Christian community. In Greifswald, Wachsmann attempted to encourage his students at the Wednesday gatherings to experience this sense of Christian community in an environment of exploring and learning. He also used this gathering "to immunize the students against the poison of the new teaching" of National Socialism. To counter Nazi pervasiveness in all areas of life, he used the weapon of truth and the gospel of Christ.[74] In early December 1943, the *Volksgerichtshof* (People's Court), under the notorious Judge Roland Freisler, heard Wachsmann's case. Wachsmann openly admitted that he had listened to London broadcasts at least fifty times, even though "he knew it was forbidden to do so." He was not afraid to speak up during the hearing for, in many ways, he had already accepted his destiny. In particular, the court cited Wachsmann's influence over the young people who had attended his weekly gatherings, especially his "defeatist" statements that challenged the possibility of a German victory.[75] For his honesty and commitment to Christian witness, Wachsmann lost his life.

Though two very different individuals, Lorenz and Wachsmann had common destinies. Intensely patriotic and perhaps caught in a situation not entirely of his making, Lorenz, like many priests in this chapter, was divided between his love for his fatherland and his love for his church. Although on occasion he did participate in Father Simoleit's weekly discussion group, he did not consciously choose to resist the state or challenge its teachings. For him, the struggle between church and state was an ideological conflict. He refused to acknowledge any political labeling of his actions. By contrast, Wachsmann's conflicts with the Nazis began soon after they seized power. His view of the Christian community also conflicted with the exclusiveness of the National Socialist *Volksgemeinschaft*. He clearly wished to create a buffer between the disciples of Hitler and his parishioners, thereby retaining the values of the Church in the midst of a world filled with anti-Christian messages and images. Neither of the two priests desired to confront the state head on. Their own Christian witness, circumstances, and pastoral scheme to maintain their Christian values pulled them into a conflict not of their own choosing or making.

During the war years, the Gestapo became even more relentless in its pursuit of those who opposed the state. The majority of priests described here consciously went against the laws of the state in an effort to provide pastoral care to those they were duty bound to serve. In many cases, these actions constituted *Resistenz*. In the case of the Stettin priests, however, their support of discussion groups during the war, as Germany's victory appeared bleak, constituted a fundamental challenge to the war efforts of the Nazi state. Through their actions, the priests provided their parishioners and select university students with opportunities to question the state. In addition, it could be assumed that a priest such as Alfons Wachsmann actually worked to shape the consciousness of young people, exposing them to the ideological evil that was inherent in the Nazi war of conquest. Prior to their capture, it appears that these groups were even beginning to question policies concerning the treatment of Jews in Germany. This represents an important development because, from the 1920s through the 1940s, a vast gulf separated Judaism and German Roman Catholicism.

five

Jews and the Diocese of Berlin

Catholics have "a very strong dislike of Jewry."[1] In 1927, Monsignor Maximilian Kaller, pastor of St. Michael's in Berlin-Mitte and future bishop of Ermland, wrote these words to a group of lay Catholics who were connected with the "Apostolate of Prayer for the Conversion of Israel," an association dedicated to converting Jews to Catholicism. Of course, not every Catholic fit Kaller's description, but very few German Catholic leaders, whether through their actions or words, would directly challenge Kaller's statement. Behind this undercurrent of prejudice toward Jews lay centuries of anti-Semitism that characteristically portrayed Jews as a people who rejected and crucified Christ.[2] Ancient myths of blood libel also rigidly circumscribed Jews as ritual murderers of Christian children. These myths lingered in the minds of Catholics and non-Catholics alike, mirroring poisonous feelings and, more often than not, wrenching them from the fuller truth.[3] In addition, Christian scripture, especially the Gospel of John, proclaimed regularly during mass and in Catholic liturgical texts, includes certain passages and prayers that were popularly anti-Semitic.[4] As a result, it was very difficult for Catholics to reassess their oral tradition and distance themselves from this inherent form of anti-Semitism.

By the late 1920s, some Church leaders, including officials at the Vatican, issued statements that condemned anti-Semitic hatred in an effort to reform society (not, however, the Church) against an evil that they believed victimized Jews.[5] At the same time, Catholic lay and religious leaders began to distinguish between religious and secular Jews. In this regard, Church leaders and theologians argued that Catholics could tolerate religious Jews because they shared a similar outlook regarding the importance of revealed religion as the foundation of society. By contrast, Catholic leaders repudiated secular Jews, linking them to liberalism and even Bolshevism, which most Catholics considered as destructive forces within society.[6] Nevertheless, by 1930, such intermittent toleration helped advance the nomination of Georg Kareski, the leader of Berlin's Jewish community, as a Center Party candidate for the Reichstag. Ironically, then, as right-wing movements were on the rise in Germany, the Center Party launched a campaign against anti-Semitism, proclaiming it a "crime against civilization."[7]

Despite these incremental improvements in the relationship between Catholics and Jews, centuries of misunderstanding and prejudice did not go away overnight. From the time of the National Socialist takeover until the end of the war, relations between the Catholic Church and Germany's Jewish community were especially tenuous. In part, the religious atmosphere that prevailed at the time helps explain why Catholics failed to speak out in behalf of Jews, especially in their dire time of need. In addition, a wide theological gap existed between Catholics and non-Catholics, compounding the situation. Nevertheless, despite its pastoral role in Germany, the Church failed to equate persecuted Jews with victims of euthanasia or even to try to create a protective counterspace to shield the former from persecution, deportation, and execution. At best, the bishops and clergy of Berlin attempted to reach out to and provide sacramental care for Catholics of Jewish descent. After 1938, this even led indirectly to diocesan organizations assisting Jews who had *not* converted to Catholicism. The diocese, however, never made any direct attempt to rescue Jews from annihilation. Berlin, of course, under the leadership of Bishop Preysing, stood out more than most dioceses, primarily because of the courage of Monsignor Bernhard Lichtenberg and Dr. Margarete Sommer, both of whom spoke on behalf of Jews. On balance, though, the Catholic Church failed to forge a theology of rescue and fellowship that embraced all people, especially Jews. Sadly, at best, the Church could only reaffirm its sacramental charge to save all baptized Catholics and to root itself in that restrictive mission as the challenge of Nazism overflowed with a lethal anti-Semitism.

During the Weimar Republic, the Berlin diocese and many other German Catholic dioceses used Monsignor Kaller's work, *Our Lay Apostolate: What It Is and How It Should Be,* as a guidebook for participation in associations sponsored by the Church. In the section titled "Apostolate of Prayer for the Conversion of Israel," Kaller differentiated between religious and secular Jews. According to Kaller, "enlightened 'modern' Jewry . . . is actually a shameful stain on Jewish people. Stock market and business, art and theater, literature and press and, above all, politics are widely subjected to its destructive influence. This 'modern' Jewry undermines everything that is Christian and any religion and morality; it is composed of cynical egotism, sophisticated business sense and unscrupulous disdain of morality." For this reason, Kaller argued, Catholics had to defend themselves against this "Jewish danger" and overcome it "by any and all permissible means."

At the same time, however, Kaller also stressed that Catholics could never in good conscience adopt an anti-Semitism that preached "a struggle against the Jewish race" and sought "to destroy all Jews without exception or at the very least" expel them. He pointed out, for example, that the pope had condemned this form of anti-Semitism as heresy. According to Kaller, this anti-Semitism used "the Christian religion as a cloak for un-Christian feelings and political machinations." Instead, he reminded Catholics, they were obliged to love all individuals, including Jews, and had "to be resolute in rejecting and combating seduction." Interestingly enough, Kaller ended this section of his book by reminding his readers of Jesus' Jewish ancestry and by highlighting (with a quote from Deuteronomy) the fact that the Jewish people were the chosen people of God.[8]

By offering a caricature of the "modern" Jew, however, Kaller was clearly accepting the antiliberalism and antisocialism that was prevalent among German Catholics. This form of ideology identified Jews as the creators and proponents of a socialism that yearned for the removal of Christian values from public life.[9] Kaller, though, was not alone in his views. Leading members of the German hierarchy also shared his belief that Jews had an inordinate influence in the world, especially in regard to the press, and used it to propagate their socialist ideas and limit coverage of Catholic concerns. For example, on March 31, 1933, Oscar Wassermann, the director of the *Deutsche Bank* of Berlin and president of the Inter-Denominational Working Group for Peace, through the intercession of Monsignor Bernhard Lichtenberg, met with Cardinal Bertram to request the Church's intervention in a planned April 1, 1933, boycott of Jewish-owned businesses. Immediately following the meeting, Bertram wrote to his fellow German bishops to inform them of his meeting with Wassermann. In his letter, Bertram concluded that the boycott was solely an economic matter—an area of life that in his view was outside the bishops' sphere of activity. Furthermore, Bertram added, "The press that is predominantly in Jewish hands has been totally silent regarding the persecution of Catholics in various countries."[10] Here Bertram expressed his belief that it was not within the Church's own pastoral interests to commit itself to any single group outside Roman Catholicism.

Although Kaller and others attempted to explore the nature of anti-Semitism, the average Catholic could easily have misconstrued their intentions. Despite having first exhorted Catholics to respect and love religious orthodox Jews and to reject and defend themselves against the actions of "modern" Jews, further on in his presentation Kaller encouraged Catholics to pray for the salvation of Israel. In doing so, he chose language that was also critical of religious, orthodox Jews—the very same group whom he had singled out in a positive light and had contrasted with "modern" Jews. The prayer Kaller cited read "O God, . . . we plead with you to turn a compassionate gaze on the remnants of the house of

Israel, that they may acquire the knowledge of Jesus Christ, our only savior, and have a share in the precious grace of salvation. Amen. Father forgive them; for they do not know what they do!" In addition, Kaller encouraged Catholics to pray the last line of the prayer three times in succession, following the consecration of the Eucharist during the mass.[11]

In the diocese of Berlin, Kaller's text was not the only publication that might have influenced the opinion of Berlin Catholics about Jews. The textbooks used by Catholics during their childhood religious education also contained comments on Jews in reference to biblical history. Texts such as the *Kleine Schulbibel* (Little School Bible) and *Biblische Geschichte* (Bible History) identified Jews as the people who "demanded" Christ be put to death on the charge of blasphemy. These texts made it possible for Catholics at an early age to develop an aversion to their Jewish neighbors.[12] Despite the widespread use of these texts, determining the level of contempt Catholics had for Jews remains difficult. What is even more challenging is the fact that many Catholics who lived through the Nazi period afterwards denied having harbored any hostile feelings or ill will toward their Jewish neighbors. An interview with Gertraud Tietz, a Berlin Catholic who grew up in the Third Reich, illustrates this point well, and her comments offer insights into this difficult question. When asked how priests and teachers in Catholic religious education classes portrayed Jews, Tietz answered assuredly that although her teachers, mostly members of the laity, inferred that Jews had crucified Christ, they never made this issue the direct theme of a religion class, nor did they dwell on the point. Furthermore, she maintained, her teachers and priests did not directly teach her to hate Jews.[13] Rather, the handed-down assertions of her teachers (blaming Jews for Christ's death) defined, at least partially, the atmosphere in which an argument for anti-Semitism seemed reasonable.

To a greater degree, however, Kaller's understanding of "modern" Jews revealed that Catholics, despite whatever education they may have received, were already confronted with more than just traditional religious prejudices against Jews, even before the National Socialists assumed power in Germany. Kaller's notion of "modern" Jews clearly incorporated secular anti-Semitic ideas, all of which viewed Jews' influence as detrimental to a Christian-based society. In the 1930s, racial anti-Semitism, which was validated by the *Völkisch* movement and was at the core of the National Socialist weltanschauung, elevated both preexisting religious and secular prejudices against Jews to a national status.[14] In turn, according to National Socialist philosophy, blood rather than religion became the determining factor in ascertaining Jewish identity. As a result, this line of thought not only affected thousands of Jews who had already converted to Christianity, but it also challenged the view that most Catholics held of Christians who for centuries were of Jewish descent, and of Jews, whether religious or secular, who were residents of their community.

Although in its joint statements the German Catholic hierarchy never sanctioned the impulse behind the National Socialist racial weltanschauung, it also never specifically discussed the persecution of Jews in pastoral letters or public statements.[15] Instead, in 1933, at the onset of National Socialist persecution of Jews, the hierarchy expressed the belief that Jews could take care of themselves. For example, in April 1933, Cardinal Faulhaber of Munich, in a letter to Cardinal Pacelli, Vatican secretary of state, specifically made this point in reference to the April 1 boycott: "It is at this time not possible to intervene because the struggle against the Jews would at the same time become a struggle against the Catholics and because the Jews can help themselves, as the hasty breaking off of the boycott shows."[16] Indeed, at this time, the Catholic Church was too obsessed with its own problems with the new state to even consider speaking out in behalf of Jews.

Despite the Catholic Church's negligence in this area, the German Catholic hierarchy did regularly challenge the racial teaching of the National Socialists. As early as March 21, 1931, Berlin's Bishop Christian Schreiber exhorted Catholics to reject the National Socialist teaching that placed "race higher than religion."[17] Again, during a 1932 Christmas radio address, Schreiber called on Catholics to build bridges that transcended "all differences of parties, of weltanschauung, of race, and of religion."[18] Also, Schreiber's successor, Nicolaus Bares, published an article in the Berlin diocesan newspaper that emphasized that Christ, who "accepted the blood of Adam and joined our human race," enabled humanity to enjoy salvation. Bares further emphasized that "no *Volk*, no race is excluded."[19] In 1933, the German bishops assembled at Fulda voiced their anxiety over the new racial teaching and how it affected Catholics of Jewish descent. Already, for example, the Nazis had racially viewed these Catholics as Jews and, consequently, were subjecting them to discrimination under the new laws that regulated civil service and higher education.[20] According to the bishops, unity was not achieved "solely through uniformity of blood, but also through the uniformity of thought." For this reason, they continued, when the state demanded "unity" exclusively through the criteria of "race and blood," injustices were bound to impede "the Christian conscience" because it concerned people (i.e., Catholics of Jewish descent) who were "born again in Christ through the holy sacrament of baptism."[21] Despite these statements, the bishops still seemed more specifically concerned about Catholics of Jewish descent than about Jews who had not converted.

Early in the Third Reich era, the Berlin diocese also published an array of articles that challenged the Nazi racial teaching.[22] In 1932, for example, the diocesan newspaper and the *Märkische Kalender* published articles addressing the stark differences between Catholic teaching and the Nazi race-based weltanschauung.[23] Moreover, once the Nazis gained power, the Berlin diocese continued to challenge Nazi racial teaching. In 1934, for example, the diocese of Berlin encouraged its priests in the monthly *Amtsblatt* to read Max Domschke's *Glaube aus dem Blut?* (Faith from Blood?), which examined the National Socialist racial policy in light of Catholic dogmatic teaching.[24] Again in 1935, the vicar general's office of the Berlin diocese, in conjunction with other German dioceses, published a detailed academic study, *Studien zum Mythus des XX. Jahrhunderts* (Essays Concerning the Myth of the Twentieth Century), that specifically disputed the anti-Semitic and anti-Christian writings of Alfred Rosenberg, the chief ideologist of the Nazi Party.[25]

Examination of these publications today reveals why the German Catholic Church rejected Nazi racial teaching, especially when the latter came into conflict with Catholic dogma and instruction. For example, in 1932 the Berlin diocesan newspaper published essays deliberating upon the Nazi weltanschauung, under the heading "Catholic Church and National Socialism." The series of four unsigned articles specifically addressed the contradiction between Nazi racial teaching and Catholic doctrine. The second article noted "that the National Socialist's racial principle" directly contradicted "Catholic teaching on faith and morality"—specifically, the teaching that all baptized believers were equal regardless of their racial origin. Although the article admitted that Catholics could accept a "fully justified nationalism" that was based "on the communal feeling of the *Volk* united by bonds of blood and mind," it also clearly pointed out that, "if these limits of national sentiment—established by God's command"—were ignored, the result would be a "heathen nationalism" that elevated the "commonality of blood to its highest principle." Such a belief, the article continued, would be "characterized by glorification of race, overestimation of one's own *Volk*'s positive traits, and a hatred of the characteristics of other peoples." Despite these comments, the article nevertheless did not condemn the tenets of the Nazi Party platform that spelled out the criteria used for determining membership in the *Volk*. According to the article, these issues were purely political in nature and as such were not within the Church's sphere of influence. The article did, however, note that the question of who was German should be left open to interpretation.[26] Nevertheless, these concessions, though tentative and provisional, only served to undermine the unequivocal position of the Church on racism.

The third article of the series defended Christ's Jewishness and the legitimacy of the Old Testament. Though conceding that Catholics had "no reason to champion today's Jewish creed," for they knew "only one true religion, the Catholic faith," the article emphasized that Catholics could not forget that "in the Old Testament God especially chose and guided Jewry; [and] that Christ, the son of God, became man within Jewry, submitting to the divine commands of the Jewish religion and fulfilling as well as perfecting the Old Testament teaching in the Christian faith." The article concluded that Catholics who rejected the Old Testament were "in contradiction with Catholic faith."[27]

Reference to Catholicism's Old Testament lineage, which many Catholic writers and commentators made use of during the Nazi years of power, has often been viewed as a defense of the Jewish people. In point of fact, however, the majority of writers who protested the Nazi assault on Hebrew scripture did so primarily to protect Christianity's foundational link to that divinely revealed source. The clearest example of this misreading occurred in the 1933 Advent sermons of Cardinal Faulhaber in Munich. After their delivery and subsequent appearance in the Basel *National-Zeitung,* which wrongly exploited their contents to show the fallacy of the Nazi racial principle, members of the World Jewish Congress, who were meeting in Geneva, publicly endorsed Faulhaber's statements. Soon after, however, Faulhaber's secretary protested the use of the Cardinal's sermons in this fashion and declared that the cardinal "took no position on the Jewish question of today."[28] In reality, Church leaders feared aligning themselves too closely with Judaism or emerging as defenders of Jews, lest the National Socialists attack and discard Catholicism as easily as they had assailed Judaism. According to one writer for the Berlin Catholic newspaper who covered Catholicism and National Socialism, if the Nazis viewed the Church "as a danger to the state," it could lead in fact to a new Kulturkampf—one that would "exceed the Kulturkampf of the 1870s."[29]

In a 1932 *Märkischer Kalender* article, "The Error of National Socialism," "Spectator"—the pen name of an unidentified author—not only rejected the National Socialist racial weltanschauung, but also shed light on why Catholics could become enthralled with the Nazi movement. According to Spectator, the Catholic rejection of liberalism and its repudiation of the Enlightenment that promoted secularization and individualism only encouraged Catholics to move toward a more communal understanding of life. For the author, this "yearning for community," which included a search for a weltanschauung that would redefine life, led many Catholics to embrace at least the external tenets of National Socialism.

For many ordinary Germans, Spectator argued, the dire economic situation that plagued the country made the "messianism of National Socialism" appealing; however, the article continued, most people did not fully grasp the implications of the weltanschauung of the National Socialist movement, especially its *völkisch* (national) racial ideology, which was at odds with Catholic teaching.[30] To underscore this point, Spectator revealed how Rosenberg's *Myth of the Twentieth Century* had found its origin in the writings of pioneer *völkisch* authors such as Paul Lagarde and Houston Stewart Chamberlain.[31] Spectator also stated that these earlier *völkisch* works had attempted to undermine Christianity in their critique of the Old Testament, St. Paul, and the hierarchy of the Catholic Church.

For the remainder of the article, Spectator refuted Johannes Stark's work, *Nationalsozialismus und Katholische Kirche* (National Socialism and the Catholic Church), which had attempted to show the compatibility of

Nazism with the Church.[32] According to Spectator, a suitable relationship between Catholicism and National Socialism could only be possible when the party changed "its heathen unruly ways" and altered "its methods of agitation." Until then, Spectator pointed out, Catholics must heed the warning of their bishops to avoid the National Socialist movement.[33]

A final critique of Nazi ideology appeared in Max Domschke's 1934 work, *Glaube aus dem Blut?* In this work, Domschke made known the Church's position on racial research. According to Domschke, the Church did not raise any objection "to serious research into race and the maintenance of the race." The Church, he added, "has at all times been sympathetic to endeavors to keep the special character of a *Volk* as pure as possible and, by references to the *Blutsgemeinschaft* (community based upon blood ties), to deepen an awareness of *Volksgemeinschaft.*" Although Domschke stated that "no one will deny that the National Socialist state has done a great service by encouraging the forces that lie latent in blood and race," the Catholic Church opposed any attempts "to construe a contrast between Christianity and race" by declaring blood and race to have the "absolute highest worth" or by attempting to create a God (i.e., German God) who "was only a product of race." Moreover, he emphasized, the Christian belief in an eternal soul surpassed the more limited blood and race—attributes of matter—because it aspired for reunion with God in the supernatural world. Consequently, like the authors of the articles in the diocesan newspaper, Domschke insisted that on the issue of blood and race the Church was primarily concerned with how Nazi ideology affected and challenged its dogma and proclamation of revelation.[34]

Several different articles, especially those printed in diocesan publications, revealed that the Berlin diocese also raised similar concerns for the well-being of non-Aryans. The first article concerning non-Aryans appeared in the diocesan *Amtsblatt* on December 5, 1933—during the tenure of Bishop Schreiber—under the title "Care for Catholic non-Aryans." In this brief article, the anonymous author publicly informed the clergy of the work of the St. Raphael Association, whose central office was in Hamburg. The Church had founded this organization to assist Catholic non-Aryans with emigration.[35] In February 1937, under Bishop Preysing, a second article, "Catholic Non-Aryans," appeared in the same publication, offering similar information concerning the St. Raphael Association. This time, however, the article stressed that the work of the association was being conducted under the authority of the German bishops.[36] Then, on May 29, 1938, a significant article appeared in the Berlin diocesan newspaper under the title "Responsibility of Christians for Non-Christians." This article contained an excerpt from the work of Austrian theologian Michael Pfliegler, whose *The Living Christian before the Actual World* reminded Christians of their vocation to live out their baptismal call in the world by practicing good works for lapsed Christians and for non-Christians alike.[37]

Catholics, of course, were comfortable doing works of charity for those who were not of their faith. As Father Carl Sonnenschein, the prominent Catholic priest and writer during the Weimar Republic, had attested, there was no monopoly in doing works of charity. Therefore, according to Sonnenschein, any group—whether Roman Catholic, Protestant, Salvation Army, Quaker, or Jewish—that worked to alleviate its neighbors' plight must show respect for all. In Sonnenschein's view, to do so was to fulfill the second great commandment of God: love your neighbor. Sonnenschein, however, emphasized that love of neighbor was not limited to an individual's particular denomination or people, but instead was "formulated *übervölkisch* (beyond ethnic boundaries) by Christ" and, therefore, extended "over the border of denomination," as demonstrated in the story of the Good Samaritan (Luke 10:25–37).[38]

Bishop Schreiber made similar comments in his pastoral letters. For example, in August 1931, Schreiber rooted his letter in Christ's commandment to "love your neighbor as you love yourself." He encouraged the members of his diocese not only to live out their "sacred obligation of sacrificial Christian love," but also to resist surrendering to the "bitterness" and "indoctrination" of "radical groups." Instead, he exhorted Catholics to work for reconciliation between the rich and poor "through acts of Christian love."[39] Likewise, in a September 1932 pastoral letter to the members of the diocese, Schreiber discussed the unemployment situation and the lack of funds for both state and church to meet the needs of people seeking assistance. He invited Catholics to share in the sacrificial act of the Sacred Heart of Jesus and to "derive from it the impulses and actions" for their love of neighbor.[40]

The German Catholic Church took the issue of charity very seriously and prided itself in its extensive network of Caritas programs, which the bishops personally coordinated through a central bureau in Freiburg im Breisgau. Throughout Germany, Caritas was active at both the parish and diocesan levels to assist the needy. Parish Caritas organizations, for example, provided material donations such as clothing and food to the poor; supported expectant mothers and their families; administered orphanages, hospitals, and nursing homes; ran programs for alcoholics; and offered counseling in a variety of areas. In Berlin, Caritas, in conjunction with the Lutheran Mission, even sponsored facilities located in ten Berlin train stations to assist travelers and the homeless.[41]

Even though the German dioceses had firmly established Caritas programs, the question remained who would benefit from the charity. Prior to the Third Reich, Catholic religious and lay leaders primarily directed Caritas programs to meet the needs of their Catholic parishioners, although some of the programs such as the missions in train stations were meant to assist anyone in need. During the Third Reich, however, and especially after the passage of the 1935 Nuremberg laws, which deprived

Jews of German citizenship, the question of whom to assist became a serious issue. In 1938, Father Heinrich Weber, former director of the Caritas Association in the diocese of Münster and professor of pastoral theology at the University of Breslau, published a remarkable study for its time, *The Essence of Charity*. It eventually became a theoretical guidebook for the work of Caritas. In the work, Weber sought to explain how Christ's command to love God and neighbor should be practically carried out in parish life. According to Weber, "Every person, even foreigners, indeed even enemies of the *Volk* fall under the concept of 'neighbor.'" Similar to Father Sonnenschein, Father Weber referred his readers to the parable of the Good Samaritan as a practical application of this teaching.[42] Weber also reinforced this instruction when he wrote that it was "demanded by Christ that our neighbor [was] not only blood relations or friends, but every person who suffers, whether a Samaritan or a pagan or a Jew." The command of Christ to love one's neighbor superseded "all personal, societal, social, national, and religious barriers" and required that one must be willing to sacrifice one's own bodily well-being for the salvation of one's neighbor.[43] Weber emphasized, however, that one should "never place one's own salvation in jeopardy in order to love neighbor."[44]

These statements affecting Christian outreach were remarkable for 1938 Germany. In essence, Weber was challenging National Socialist ideology, especially its teaching on who should be embraced in German society. Despite these statements, Weber also made distinctions concerning the term "neighbor." He stated that, though each person was our neighbor, "not everyone" was our "neighbor to the same degree."[45] Therefore, he argued, "the union of blood, of family, tribal identity and membership in a race, the union of a household, the union of the same homeland and of friendship, the union of the same faith and the same culture" all established and gave rise "to narrower and closer partnerships."[46]

It is interesting to note that the Berlin diocesan catechism also defined neighbor in terms similar to Weber's, leading one to conclude that this understanding was generally taught and accepted. According to the catechism, a neighbor was "every human being, whether a friend or an enemy." Every person was worthy of love because each individual was "created in the image of God, saved through the blood of Christ, and called to eternal life." But, similar to Weber's work, the authors of the catechism also taught that, although one must love all people, one did not have to love all "to the same extent." Instead, one must have a greater love for those who "stand nearer to us, or those who deserve it more," such as the poor and those in distress.[47]

Although Weber and the authors of the diocesan catechism made distinctions, including one very inclusive point of difference, "to those who deserve it more," the basic teaching that all people—including Jews—were neighbors, remained. Weber concretely answered the question of who was a neighbor, notably during the Nazi years of power, but the bishops of Berlin failed to define the question more clearly. For example, in his April 1934 pastoral letter on Caritas, Bishop Bares identified the charitable recipients as the Church's "suffering children" and the "brothers and sisters" of Catholics to whom the letter had been addressed.[48] In a separate letter, dated October 24, 1934, Bares followed his annual appeal for Caritas with an invitation to Catholics to participate in the government's winter relief program; Bares urged Catholics to join in the efforts of the government to offer financial and material assistance to their *Volksgenossen* (members of the same ethnic group). He did not, however, define or stress the term "*Volksgenossen.*" Instead, he suggested such assistance should be carried out to fulfill the Christian commandment of love. In addition, toward the end of the letter, Bares suggested how beautiful it might be if everyone would "joyfully, and again in a Christian spirit of Caritas," participate in the winter relief program as both an example to their children and, more important, to relieve the "distress of their neighbors."[49] Neighbors, though, were a socially specified group.

In 1935, when Konrad von Preysing became bishop of Berlin, his public statements on Caritas continued in a similar vein as those of his predecessors. Preysing's words, however, also contained stronger exhortations to offer charity in every situation that involved a neighbor in need. For example, in his October 1938 pastoral report on the work of winter assistance, Preysing urged Berlin Catholics not only to fulfill their "obligation to the fatherland and their Christian duty" to relieve the suffering of their *Volksgenossen,* but also "to practice compassion in all difficult situations." In this action, he added, Christians fulfilled the greatest commandment: "You shall love your neighbor as you love yourself" (Gal. 5:16).[50] On May 1940, in a letter delivered on the occasion of Caritas Sunday, just after the outbreak of the Second World War and during a period of heightened discrimination and persecution of German Jews, Preysing also reminded Berlin Catholics that these acts of charity should never be limited to monthly contributions for the good works of the associations, but, instead, should include "personal assistance for your neighbor." According to Preysing, such personal involvement enabled individuals to reveal their true "love of humanity" to their families, neighborhoods, work places, and parishes; however, to see the suffering of their neighbor, Berliners needed to have their "eyes alert in order to see the hidden misery of others, and a fine ear in order to hear their secret cries."[51] Here he was suggesting that Catholics' own destiny was part of the broader destiny of all peoples.

In a November 1942 sermon preached in St. Hedwig, Preysing went a step further and announced to his congregation that they also needed to exercise this love of neighbor in a way that reflected love for "the outsider." To this end, he entreated Christians to "tolerate and to accept foreign ethnic character. . . . That is a necessary and daily demand." According to the bishop, no one should "be excluded from this love," including those who "speak another language or are of foreign blood." For, Preysing continued, "every person carries the image of God" in his or her soul and, therefore, "every person has the right to life and love." Preysing even made his point clearer when he stated that it was never permissible "to take away from members of foreign races their right to freedom, their right to property, their right to an indissoluble marriage." He also stated that no one was ever "allowed to commit atrocities" against members of a foreign race because it was not only an "injustice directly" against their own people, but also a denial of the right to life—a life that was "desired by God and determined by God." As a result, Preysing stated, "no people and no groups of people can deprive another people of their right to life."[52]

In making such pointed statements, Preysing spoke much more boldly than his fellow bishops. Although he took a risk making these statements, especially in time of war, Preysing's audience could still interpret them however they wished: for the enslaved foreign workers, for the prisoners of war, or for anyone persecuted. The use of such phrases as "every person" ensured that his words would not be limited to just one group. During the war, such ambiguity in Berlin, so public a place, was necessary in order to avoid arrest, as Monsignor Bernhard Lichtenberg would unfortunately discover in 1941 when he was arrested for the "crime" of publicly praying for persecuted Jews. Despite making such statements, Preysing's words came too late to challenge the ubiquitous force of Nazi policy. In addition, his statements in behalf of German Jews were not supported by any kind of coordinated effort or movement from within the hierarchy.[53]

Nevertheless, Preysing did live out his personal call to practice charity for all. In July 1938, he began discussions to found a relief agency specifically designed to stand beside persecuted Christians of Jewish descent.[54] Previously, the St. Raphael Association, which had been founded in 1871 to assist Catholic emigrants, had undertaken this work as part of its broader mission. On August 24, 1938, Preysing met with Wilhelm Berning, bishop of Osnabrück; Heinrich Wienken, auxiliary bishop of Meißen; and Heinrich Krone, the director of Caritas Emergency Services, to organize the foundation of the *Hilfswerk beim Bischöflichen Ordinariat Berlin* (Relief Agency of the Berlin Chancery).[55] Preysing founded the *Hilfswerk* primarily as a pastoral agency in an attempt to meet the spiritual and material needs of Christians of Jewish descent.[56] In general, Jewish relief agencies had failed to address the concerns of this particular group. Preysing entrusted the advisory responsibility of the agency to his right-hand chancery man, Monsignor Lichtenberg, who served in this capacity until his arrest in fall 1941. After this incident, and not wishing to place anyone else in harm's way, Preysing himself took over the monsignor's advisory role. The real heart of the *Hilfswerk* was Dr. Margarete Sommer, a devout Catholic laywoman who courageously risked her life to run the

Hilfswerk throughout the Nazi years. She not only endeavored to make sure that the *Hilfswerk* met the material and spiritual needs of those it assisted, but also built up a variety of contacts through which she gained extensive knowledge about the persecution, ghettoization, and murder of European Jews. At great personal danger, Sommer dauntlessly passed this information on to Preysing and his fellow bishops.[57]

In its first years, the *Hilfswerk* acquired financial subsidy and food, oversaw arrangements for emigration, and provided counsel. Later, as the threats and actions against Jews in the war years heightened during the Holocaust,[58] the agency also assisted in hiding Jews, helping Jewish families prepare for deportation, and accompanying them to deportation sites.[59] The surviving reports of the agency attest to the fact that it also assisted non-Christian Jews.[60]

It is quite significant that Preysing worked to establish the *Hilfswerk* prior to *Reichskristallnacht* (November 9–10, 1938), a pogrom against German Jews, conducted primarily by SS and SA men dressed in civilian clothes. During the night, Nazis destroyed Jewish homes, institutions, synagogues, and places of business. By the next morning, ninety-one Jews had been murdered and 191 synagogues had been either partially or completely destroyed by fire, and these were only estimates reported by Himmler's assistant, Reinhard Heydrich. Other reports indicate that the destruction and loss of life were much greater.[61] In addition, Himmler had an additional 30,000 Jews arrested and imprisoned in Dachau, Buchenwald, and Sachsenhausen. After brief internment, the SS released some of them, but others remained for months, and many never returned home at all.[62]

Despite the diocese's effort to assist Catholics of Jewish descent, one that eventually encompassed non-Catholics, the Catholic Church's rejection of the Nazi racial weltanschauung still primarily hinged on those specific ideological points that contradicted Catholic doctrine and social teaching. Nevertheless, this did not mean that the Church's particular criticism of the Nazi racial weltanschauung did not likewise lead some informed Catholics to see the error of the Nazi Party's rejection of Jews. To what extent, however, is difficult to determine. The efforts of the *Hilfswerk* do strongly reveal that, despite the increasing limitation of freedom of speech during the Nazi years of power, officials within the Berlin Catholic Church did attempt in some way to encourage Catholics to support actively at least Catholics of Jewish descent. The Berlin diocese also rejected any official acceptance or promotion of the Nazi racial ideology. The diocesan leaders, for example, clearly encouraged its clergy to reject Nazi racial teaching, especially when it directly contradicted Church doctrine. This did not, however, lead to a direct protest against the state's anti-Jewish measures.

Practically speaking and at the parish level, it should also be noted that there were very few priests who reached out to Jews or even to Catholics of Jewish descent. Clearly, a few assisted Sommer in her efforts to assist and hide Catholics of Jewish ancestry. Unfortunately, because of the secretive nature of their work, few records remain. At best, priests felt bound to provide charity for Jews in need, charity comparable to the manner in which they would meet the needs (i.e., food, clothing) of any non-Catholic. But speaking out for Jews' civil rights or against the persecution of Jews would be viewed as stepping into the political realm—an area forbidden to Catholic priests by the articles of the Reich-Vatican concordat. The few who chose this path risked crossing a thin, perilous line that separated religion from politics—a choice most priests were unwilling to make, especially in regard to helping Jews. The lack of clear guidance or statements directly in behalf of the Jewish people from the German hierarchy also offered priests little impetus to risk their lives for a group outside their religion.

Many Berlin clergy believed that, if the Church and its priests did speak out for the rights of Jews, they, too, might be considered enemies of the state. Father August Froehlich expressed this same line of reasoning in a letter to the Potsdam Gestapo, explaining his actions in behalf of Poles. Because many priests refused to comply with every demand the state made of them—such as giving the Hitler salute—some people placed them "on par with the Jews and enemies of the state."[63] According to a witness, Froehlich did, however, at times stand up for Jews or at least criticized the violence directed against them. For example, in a September 29, 1946, sermon in honor of Froehlich, an unnamed priest colleague recalled an experience he had with Froehlich. The priest recalled that "1937 was the year of 'spontaneous rage of the *Volk*.' On a summer's evening all the Jewish ice-cream parlors in Berlin were smeared with tar. I accompanied Father Froehlich to the train. Shortly before the Bahnhof Berlin-Karlshorst, a Jewish-owned ice-cream parlor had been covered with inscriptions. Fifteen to twenty people stood there speechless. Father Froehlich remained standing, observed, and with a loud voice said: 'Must one not feel ashamed that something like this is possible in Germany!' Everyone stared frightened and nodded at him. Only one informer jumped at us! 'What did you say? Who are you?' With a furious, far-reaching voice he said: 'I'll give you that information. I am Father Froehlich from Dramburg in Pomerania!' We turned and went on. The informer—presumably 'a novice of the noble race'—gazed and looked bewildered."[64]

In 1935, Father Joseph Rennoch, pastor of Sacred Heart Church in Berlin, offered similar testimony in a discussion following a lecture in his parish. Rennoch chose to read a letter from a friend who lived abroad and was concerned about the fate of the Catholic Church in Germany. The friend wrote "first the Jews were persecuted and now they persecute you Catholics." When questioned, Rennoch denied ever having received such a letter from abroad. Despite this denial, there is today enough evidence to support the existence of a similar apprehensive mentality among the German clergy.[65] They were uncomfortable with the underlying Nazi ideology.

For example, following *Reichskristallnacht,* a worker in St. Mary's Hospital, where Father Johannes Fiebig served as chaplain, denounced the priest for making several statements, including, "If one attacks and persecutes the Jews, one will also attack us."[66] Fortunately for Fiebig, the Gestapo decided that the testimony of the witness would not hold up in court and decided not to pursue the charges.[67]

Not every priest let fear limit his activities. In April 1936, Father Ulrich Kaiser, O.P., agreed to officiate in secret at the marriage of a German Catholic woman and a Protestant man of Jewish descent. Officiating in secret meant that Kaiser did not inform the city's marriage registry office. Previously, the couple, upon recommendation of a social worker, had approached Father Carl Breuer, pastor of St. Pius Church in Berlin, to perform the marriage ceremony. Breuer had agreed and even published their banns of marriage, but then had refused to go through with the ceremony until they had permission from the city marriage registry office. Unfortunately, the registry office had refused to grant them a marriage permit, allegedly because the groom did not possess German citizenship. Upon being turned down by both the marriage office and Breuer, the couple returned to the social worker seeking further assistance. She willingly continued to assist them and sent them to Father Georg Köhler, a canon lawyer, advisor in the diocesan chancery, and professor at the Berlin seminary. He, in turn, reviewed their case and put them in contact with Father Kaiser, a Dominican priest who was pastor of St. Paul Church in Berlin and superior of the local religious community. Kaiser eventually performed the wedding ceremony in private, without state permission.

Thereafter, however, someone denounced Kaiser for performing the wedding without the necessary permits. During the course of the Gestapo's investigation, Father Köhler was also questioned. For his part, Kaiser attempted to exonerate himself on the basis of article 26 of the concordat, which permitted a Church marriage over a civil marriage when a couple was in a state of emergency (i.e., illness or living in mortal sin).[68] Unfortunately for Kaiser, however, neither Father Köhler nor Father Breuer supported him with this interpretation in the court of law. In fact, Father Breuer argued that he had refused to perform the marriage because it "was the only thing that a German priest could do in this case." According to Breuer, Father Kaiser "did not handle the situation lawfully." Father Köhler testified that he believed Kaiser initially wanted permission to witness a "'marriage of conscience' that would be concluded only in the presence of a priest without witnesses, during which the Church's blessing would not be conferred, but during which, only for their peace of conscience, the couple would be told that they could consider themselves married before God and men." Without the support of his fellow priests, Kaiser was left to the mercy of the court, which showed little. On July 12, 1937, the criminal division of the Berlin district court sentenced Kaiser to three months in prison.[69]

In making his decision, Father Kaiser clearly acted out of pastoral concerns for the couple, both of whom were Christian. It would be interesting to speculate how he might have reacted if the groom had not been baptized. It is possible that Kaiser was also concerned because, although the couple was engaged, according to Church teaching they were living in a sinful situation. Furthermore, in their discussions before the ceremony, the couple might have revealed something to the priest that did not come out in the trial because of confidentiality and the seal of confession. This also might have led him to see the urgency and need to perform the marriage. With the evidence presented, however, there was no hint of pregnancy before marriage; nor does it appear the couple had been living together in "mortal sin." Because Father Köhler directed them first to Father Kaiser, he must have known that the priest would be much more pastorally sensitive than the cold Father Breuer. Yet, by making minute legalistic distinction about how Kaiser administered the rite, Köhler refused to back Kaiser fully. Köhler's lack of support for Kaiser probably revealed more of a fear of reprisal on his part than a deliberate intent to incriminate a fellow priest. Breuer, on the other hand, reveals the portrait of a cantankerous older pastor who has been in authority for too long—he had been the pastor of St. Pius since 1908—and has lost all pastoral sensitivity. His comments also reflect the intricacy of caution: he was not going to exert himself for this couple; nor was he in any way going to question a decision of the state.

Similar to Father Kaiser, Father Max Schnura, pastor of St. Thomas of Aquinas in Berlin-Charlottenburg, extended his hand to assist a Catholic of Jewish descent. In March 1942, a seventy-year-old Catholic woman of Jewish descent who had been a parishioner for more than twenty-five years needed an expensive form of cancer treatment and sought assistance from the parish Caritas funds. Schnura willingly assisted the woman and for his efforts was denounced, arrested, and held in the Alexanderplatz Gestapo station in Berlin for several months. On May 1, 1942, without trial, Schnura was then readied to be transported to Wuhlheide forced labor camp. A sympathetic prison doctor, however, intervened and prevented the transportation.[70] A few weeks later, the Gestapo released Schnura on account of his poor health, but only after a sizable bond had been paid.[71]

It is important to note that both Kaiser and Schnura were called upon to assist Christians or Catholics of Jewish descent. This assistance had nothing to do with their protest against an ordinance of the state, but rather had everything to do with a pastoral issue of the Church. From their point of view, the people they assisted were Christians or Catholics by virtue of their baptism. Unlike the officials of the state, they did not identify these individuals as Jews; instead, they saw them as members of the baptized Christian community. The state, however, refused to accept this religion-based distinction and had them arrested. Kaiser's and Schnura's actions, however, were not common. Indeed, the support for Christians of Jewish descent was never widespread among the clergy. In reality, according to the extant evidence, Monsignor Lichtenberg was the only priest in Berlin who, through his daily intercessory prayers, publicly and forcefully spoke out for Jews of whatever persuasion. If others also engaged in this activity or assisted Jews in different ways, their stories have not been recorded. Several priests of the Berlin diocese did choose to speak against Nazi racism, but even some of those who did—in their own words—either revealed an ingrained racism or denied any wrongdoing when charged.

The latter was true of Father Albrecht Kopschina, pastor of Assumption parish in Hoppenwalde, who challenged the racism of the National Socialists. In 1937, during an instruction class for confirmation, Father Kopschina told the students that when Christ exhorted his disciples to "'go into all the world and teach all people' he did not say 'with proof of Aryan ancestry.'" When questioned, however, Kopschina denied adding the editorial comment to the biblical exhortation. Still, the Stettin public prosecutor wanted to pursue the case against Kopschina for making this statement, among others, against the state.[72] The prosecutor, however, discontinued the case in 1938 because of the amnesty law.[73]

Father Johannes Seidel, first parochial vicar of Holy Cross Church in Frankfurt an der Oder, was also denounced in 1938 for speaking positively about the Old Testament and the "chosen state of the Jewish *Volk*" during a religious education class in the Friedrich Gymnasium. When confronted by the Gestapo, however, Seidel denied making the comments as such and explained that he was merely defining Jews as a people who were "chosen by God to carry divine revelation and to preserve the belief in one God." He added that he also made a "sharp division between the Jews before and after Christ" and warned against an "overemphasis on racial thought," which should "never take the place of religion."[74] Although Seidel did speak in favor of Jews as the chosen people, he was primarily referring to their role in salvation history as the forebears of Christ. His distinction between Jews before and after Christ was illustrative of how priests viewed Jews who had not accepted Christ as the Messiah. Apparently, the court agreed, because it did not find Seidel guilty of making any statements against the state and dismissed the case.[75] Father Wolfgang Lauen, parochial vicar at St. Michael in Berlin, also made similar comments about the religious divisions among Jews. In addition, according to a witness, on July 24, 1938, he spoke strongly about the sameness of all races in his sermon. During his testimony, Lauen admitted to making such statements but offered a clarification. According to him, he "stressed the identical nature of the races from the viewpoint of the Church, and that he emphasized it only in the context of religion and spiritual salvation." He also denied any hostile intent or attack against state policy and stated that he recognized "the state's right to expel a foreign race from its territory." The court accepted Lauen's explanation that "he had dealt with racial thinking only from the Church's viewpoint in his sermon" and exonerated him of all charges of violation of the law against a treacherous attack on the state and party.[76] In his sermon, Lauen followed the traditional teaching of the Church, which stated that all people, regardless of race, were through the sacrament of baptism equal in the eyes of God, although his assertion that the state had a right to expel "a foreign race from its territory" must be seen specifically in the context in which it was made. It is clear that Lauen understood the seriousness of the charges brought against him and attempted to convince the judges of his respect for the laws of the state. There is not enough evidence, however, to uncover a complete picture of Lauen's motivations for his comments, either in his sermon or during his trial. What may be concluded is that anyone who publicly challenged the racial policy in any way, however insignificant, risked being arrested by the Gestapo and thrown into prison. By making such comments from the pulpit, even in relation to the Church's teaching on salvation, Father Lauen accepted that risk and its consequences. However bold it might seem, it is also important to keep in mind that Lauen and other clerics like him were limited in the scope of their comments by their narrow view of salvation and by their reluctance to apply Church teaching to the political realm.

In 1941, the Chamber of Reich Literature, which gave authors permission to publish, refused membership to Father Kurt Willig, pastor of St. Konrad, in Berlin-Schönberg, because of earlier statements he had made in behalf of Jews.[77] According to the chamber's report, in 1934, during a sermon, Willig had stated that "Jesus was a Jew and a member of the chosen people. The 'racial fanatics' cannot change this with their theories. Our salvation lies only in the name of Jesus." Again, in 1935, during a lecture on Church history, Willig also stated that Jews were the "chosen *Volk*. No one can change that."[78] Though Willig only received a warning in these cases, the Gestapo arrested him in 1942 for producing and distributing copies of Bishop Galen's sermons against euthanasia and other literature. Eventually, the Gestapo sent him to Dachau for three years.[79]

With the exception of Monsignor Lichtenberg, the Catholic clergy did not risk their lives to save secular or religious Jews. In most cases, the priests who made statements against Nazi racial policy did so for inherently parochial reasons—to defend their own faith tradition, especially its origins, against attack. For these members of the clergy, Nazi racism denigrated the role of the Jewish people in Christian salvation history. By maligning Jews, especially those of the Hebrew scriptures, the Nazi theorists had ultimately attacked Christ who was himself a Jew. However, what did frustrate the Catholic clergy during this time was the racial teaching of the state. For the learned priests, who had studied both the Hebrew and Christian scriptures, the works of the Nazi theorists on race were not only blasphemous, but also academically preposterous. Evidence of the priests' frustration over the proliferation of such teachings in German society surfaced in the ministry of Lauen, Seidel, and other members of the German Catholic clergy. There is no other significant reason to explain why a priest would risk so much to make a polemical statement, whether in front of students or during a parish lecture, that would put him in direct conflict with the Gestapo. Often, the priest regretted his remarks, and, once in control of his feelings and fully conscious of the consequences, denied ever having made such a statement. But such statements were made and displayed an uneasiness with the regime's racist ideology.

The few kind acts by priests for persons the state racially defined as Jews were sometimes performed for the benefit of Christians of Jewish descent. But this was to be expected by virtue of the sacrament of baptism, because all priests were taught to regard these Jews as Catholic Christians. Except for the heroic efforts of the *Hilfswerk* on behalf of Catholics of Jewish descent (and, later, for religious and secular Jews) and the work and efforts of Monsignor Lichtenberg, no other priest in the recorded documents reached out to Jews in a significant way during their time of persecution, isolation, ultimate deportation, and murder. The Church's hierarchy provided no clear encouragement to act on behalf of Jews. As a people, Jews were not part of the Catholic Church. Consequently, any pastor or priest who undertook such a supportive task knew from the outset that, by initiating such an act, he could easily place himself in serious jeopardy. In view of the penalty—loss of citizenship, imprisonment, and possible execution—priests took seriously the Gestapo's well-defined racial policies. Nevertheless, not every priest feared the wrath of the Gestapo. In fact, some saw themselves as Nazi collaborators, artisans of the Nazi state, and enthusiastically embraced Nazi ideology. Though few in number, these priests actually sought to find a niche in the larger Nazi world for their own misshapen egos.

six

For the Glory of the Führer
Brown Priests

In Nazi Germany there existed a small number of priests whose primitive allegiance to and membership in the Nazi Party became a scandal to the Catholic Church.[1] The diocese of Berlin proved no exception to this phenomenon. These "brown" priests—"brown" because of the official color of Nazi uniforms—differed radically from the rest of the clergymen who had fervently shared in the first wave of national enthusiasm for Hitler when he came to power as Reich Chancellor. Their allegiance also went far beyond the traditional mode of German nationalism that the majority of Catholic priests continued to profess throughout the Third Reich. Furthermore, the Röhm purge and the murder of Erich Klausener did nothing to shake the faith and trust in Hitler of these brown priests. Instead, they continued to view Hitler as a messianic figure who was sent by God to "save" Germany from destruction. In their minds, the Catholic Church, like every institution in the German state, had to join the Nazis in their work to revitalize and awaken anew the German nation. For them, this entailed, not least of all, embracing Nazi racial doctrine and ideology. Therefore, even when many priests began to dissociate themselves from Nazism because of their disillusionment with the state's encroachment into pastoral areas (i.e., youth groups, parish associations), brown priests became, conversely, more engaged and militant in their association with the party and, shockingly, remained that way until the very end.[2]

Brown priests are important in any study of the Berlin clergy because they appear at times to have worked together as a unit to promote state and party goals within their parishes and ministries. Their writings and activities under National Socialism also reveal how Catholic National Socialists lifted traditional anti-Semitic formulas from popular Catholic sources in an effort to create a hybrid Catholic doctrine to bolster National Social-ism's racial anti-Semitism. This observation supports the recent work of David Kertzer, who has argued that the Catholic Church, through its leaders and ministers, tolerated a religious, social, and economic anti-Semitism that ultimately provided a seductive basis upon which Na-tional Socialism built its racial and annihilative anti-Semitism.[3] At the local church level, bishops (even Konrad von Preysing, who was strongly anti-Nazi) were not as greatly troubled by the anti-Semitic actions of brown priests as they were by the recalcitrant activities of these priests who refused to obey episcopal directives and remove themselves from politics. To compound the tragedy, in their attempt to work provision-ally with the state to fulfill their ecclesial mission, the bishops largely ig-nored the anti-Semitic statements of the brown priests. And although most bishops privately deplored the activities of these priests who sup-ported state policies that directly conflicted or limited church teaching and practice, the bishops' primary concern was always the protection of the institutional church from harm.

Most priests who openly supported the NSDAP received a moral wound from which they never recovered after the war. Although the membership of German Catholic clergy in Hitler's party was minimal, the force of their evil witness tainted the entire church. How a priest could predicate his faith in Christ on the moral profits of Nazism re-mains a mystery. The encouragement a priest received and the difficul-ties that ensued when he became a member must have far outweighed the exclusiveness of Christ's mandate of love. The lives and thoughts of brown priests in the diocese of Berlin will always remain within Chris-tianity's vision of moral and theological terror. How the state and Church dealt with the actions of these clergymen might make the riddle of their evil choices less mysterious, but by no means less central to the drama of this perverse period.

It is difficult to determine exactly how many brown priests there were among the ranks of National Socialism. In 1942, a British Catholic period-ical, the *Tablet,* investigated the relationship between German priests and the Nazi Party and speculated that "less than a hundred . . . openly ex-pressed their sympathy with the Party," and only half of these priests were members of the Nazi Party.[4] In 1973, Frederic Spotts estimated that there were approximately 150 Roman Catholic priests who had actually become members of the Nazi Party.[5] He based this number on American military documents indicating that "an average of five priests in each diocese, as well as some seminarians and members of orders, belonged to the Party."[6] This number is relatively small compared to the 21,461 diocesan priests, along with several thousand more religious order priests, who served the Catholics of Germany.[7] More recently, Wolfgang Dierker has estimated that there were between twenty and 200 priests who served as informants

(*Vertraunensmänner*) to the SS and Gestapo.[8] Unlike the brown priests, who professed their support for National Socialism publicly, however, the informants normally performed their duties in secret.

Despite their limited number, the brown priests made their presence known among both Catholic clergy and laity. People noticed them because they were exceptions to the norm—that is, unlike the overwhelming majority of priests, these renegades often placed their own careers and welfare above their ministry and duty to the people whom they were called to serve. As a result, they allowed radical nationalism, antiliberalism, and anti-Semitism to absorb them and determine their understanding of the world. Their acceptance of and devotion to National Socialism, however, ought not be attributed to one specific event or ideology. Instead, these clergymen, similar in nature to most National Socialists, individually turned and aligned themselves to the Nazi Party for a variety of reasons.[9] For some, the events that followed World War I and the subsequent foundation of the Weimar Republic meant a spiraling social and moral decline in German society that only National Socialism could stop.[10] Others saw membership in the NSDAP as a means to advance their careers in both the state and the Church.[11] Still others embraced Nazism primarily because of its anti-Semitism, linked to a belief that Jews were the cause of Germany's misfortune.[12] Interestingly enough, despite their allegiance to National Socialism, the majority of these priests were not entirely willing to forsake their priesthood and leave the Church. Instead, they walked a thin line between maintaining their ministerial position and serving the needs of the Nazi Party.

Regardless of a particular priest's motives for supporting National Socialism, both the Church and the state made it difficult for Catholic clergy to add their name to the NSDAP membership card index in Munich and to agitate publicly for the party. On the part of the state, Hitler himself, in the infancy of the Nazi movement, encouraged priests who were "old fighters" to delay their membership in the party or desist from explicit agitation to avoid conflicts with their own church superiors. Possibly this had more to do with Hitler's decision to keep the party and religion totally separate than with his anxiety about arousing the ire of a diocesan bishop and his chancery.[13] Even if this were Hitler's reasoning, priests assumed that he wanted to prevent conflict with diocesan officials. For example, in the fall of 1923, Hitler encouraged Dr. Lorenz Pieper, a Paderborn priest and member of the NSDAP—seven months earlier, Pieper had resigned from his assignment as assistant priest at St. Peter's Church in Hüsten to travel to Munich and agitate for the Nazi movement—to return to Paderborn to avoid any further difficulties with his bishop. Hitler allegedly stated to Pieper that he could not have a "suspended" priest working for his party.[14] In the case of Father Josef Roth of the archdiocese of Munich and Freising, sometime before 1933 Hitler had allegedly encouraged Roth not to join the party, evidently to avoid problems with Church superiors, despite the young priest's zealous enthusiasm for the movement.[15]

Until 1931, each diocese had to contend with a few Nazi priests, like Dr. Pieper or Dr. Philipp Haeuser of the Augsburg diocese, who individually agitated for National Socialism and other right-wing organizations.[16] Gradually, however, at different times in or near March 1931, the bishops separately released common pastoral guidelines for all Catholics who wanted to associate themselves with National Socialism. In the second point of the guidelines, for example, they "strongly forbade priests to work with the National Socialist movement in any manner."[17] This decree stayed in effect until March 28, 1933, when the joint German episcopacy, through the Fulda bishops' conference, issued a statement that repealed the prohibition against membership in or activity for the NSDAP.[18] This reprieve for Catholic priests who joined the Hitler movement, however, was short lived. Article 32 of the July 1933 concordat excluded priests and members of religious congregations from "membership in political parties and activity for such parties."[19] After that, the German bishops, who chose to reprimand their priests for speaking out publicly on behalf of National Socialism, regularly turned to this article to justify their rebuke. According to church affairs minister Hans Kerrl, whose assistant, Father Josef Roth, was experiencing difficulties in receiving his bishop's permission to work for the government, this reference of the bishops was a "completely inappropriate" misuse of article 32.[20] Kerrl was also not the only government official who held this opinion. A May 1940 memo from an official in the Reich Chancellory concerned itself solely with the history of the question of membership of clergy in the NSDAP. According to the memo, in December 1933, Hitler requested a new interpretation of article 32 that would not preclude membership in the NSDAP. This interpretation, at least on the part of the state, was adopted. The memo added that in 1938, a government official had determined that the NSDAP was "not a party in the sense of article 32" and, therefore, did not affect Catholic priests' membership in the Nazi Party.[21] Yet, even if Catholic priests managed to join the party and remain active members, a doubt concerning their loyalty still lingered in the minds of many fellow party members. For example, in 1939, as Roth lectured on the theme of "The Catholic Church and the Jewish Question" at a symposium sponsored by the Reich Institute for History of the New Germany, an attendee who had also lectured on the subject and was "surprised that Roth received so much applause" abruptly confronted Roth and related what an SD official had once told him—that one needed to deal with "the utmost caution" with anyone who had been "a Jesuit."[22] Many convinced National Socialists used "Jesuit" as a belittling designation for anyone who supported the interests of the Catholic Church.

For those who did so, joining and supporting the party openly often led to a great deal of difficulty with Church superiors. This barrier frequently had less to do with the nature of a priest's specific activity and more to do with his direct disobedience of the wishes of the dioceses. Kerrl realized that anyone who worked "full time or in visible ways for National Socialism" had to expect "unpleasant reprimands and punishments." Kerrl added that these conflicts, which arose from heated exchanges between priests and their Church superiors, were "indeed sometimes a burden for the party." These clashes also frequently caused the removal of a priest from his parish—the very place "among the Catholic population" where he could have promoted the aims of the movement.[23] More often than not, a priest who had previously encountered problems with his bishop and chancery because of his pro-Nazi stance received no support from the NSDAP. For example, a June 13, 1936, memo from Kerrl to Rudolf Hess, deputy to the Führer, revealed this dilemma. In his letter, Kerrl requested that Hess reply to two previous requests for a solution to disputes between priests and their superiors. According to Kerrl, the party had a "certain moral obligation to help such priests" who had actually "become victims of their National Socialist convictions."[24] On August 22, 1936, Kerrl finally received a reply from Martin Bormann, then chief of staff to Hess, who offered him no real guidance when he advised Kerrl to deal with the matter himself or, in "special cases," to turn to the Gestapo for further investigation.[25]

In 1933, in the newly established Berlin diocese, five priests—Wilhelm Knobloch, Walter Leonards, Anton Scholz, Johannes Strehl, and Karl Marco Willimsky—openly pronounced their support for the NSDAP. Leonards, Scholz, and Strehl were confirmed Nazi Party members. One additional priest, Dr. Johannes Allendorf, publicly stated that he favored the aims of the movement. An additional six priests were also active in the NSDAP: Robert Chrysostomus Conrath, Paul Arthur Drossert (Tournai, Belgium), Karl Johannes König (Paderborn), Simon Pirchegger (Graz-Seckau, Austria), Josef Roth (Munich/Freising), and Anselm Vriens, a Trappist monk from Holland. These latter priests were either members of a religious community or from outside the Berlin diocese. And although they resided in Berlin, they held no official ministerial position under the diocesan chancery. Besides these men, there were also at least four ex-priests who actively supported the Nazi Party: Albert Hartl (Munich-Freising), Friedrich Murawski (Paderborn), August Wilhelm Patin (Munich/Freising) and Sebastian Schröcker (Munich/Freising). These men had deserted their priestly ministry for the Nazi Party and lived and worked in Berlin for the Nazi state.[26]

It is quite possible—and even probable—that other priests in the Berlin diocese openly supported National Socialism. Evidence of this fact can be found in a July 1934 SD report for Potsdam. In it, an SD official states that a "small segment of Catholic pastors" was "oriented in a good German sense" and had supported "the National Socialist movement with all their energy." The SD informant also pointed out that, because these pastors did not wish to suffer any "setbacks from superiors," they did not publicly make known their support of the NSDAP.[27] Altogether, the diocese of Berlin was a fertile recruiting field for the church information service of the SD. As Wolfgang Dierker has pointed out, however, the SD did not list the identities of all their informants.[28] In June 1936, another example surfaced in the SD correspondence, this time detailing the activities of Dr. Simon Pirchegger, a diocesan priest from Graz-Seckau, Austria. In 1936, Pirchegger, after experiencing difficulties with his superiors over his pro-Nazi activity, immigrated to Berlin and shortly thereafter to Bonn to assume teaching duties at the university there.[29] Upon his arrival in Berlin, the SD stated that Pirchegger had "assembled around himself a group of twenty-five Catholic priests" who were "loyal to the National Socialist State." Only Dr. Pieper was mentioned as a member of this group. In March 1936, the SD asked these priests to promote a "yes" vote from within the Catholic population to confirm Hitler's policies (i.e., reoccupation of the Rhineland). According to the letter, at the last minute these priests "withdrew their appeal in order not to jeopardize the authority of the German bishops," who in many dioceses had issued individual statements promoting the referendum.[30] Although no additional evidence of this group's existence has surfaced, their hesitation to act jointly as a group in the face of a possible reprimand by a local bishop reveals just how segregated they were—from the party whose support they could not always count on and from their own bishops, who in the end supported the referendum anyway. As the SD official exclaimed in his letter, their "attitude indicates how ideologically weak" this group was.[31] These men were outsiders, but outsiders who were especially afraid to break with the Catholic Church. More often than not, this simply could be attributed to the fear of losing their monthly income—their only means of financial subsistence from the diocese.

In 1933, the most prominent Nazi priest in the Potsdam vicariate was Johannes Strehl who, as both an opportunist and an aspirant to higher positions, promoted himself as the first National Socialist Catholic priest appointed to be a pastor.[32] As an individual, Strehl preferred to undertake the duties of a Nazi adherent over the responsibilities of a Catholic pastor. He cared more about advancing in the National Socialist movement than about getting along in a sacramental church. Ordained in 1914, Strehl served as a parochial vicar in a variety of parishes during and after the war years. In 1931, Bishop Christian Schreiber offered Strehl his first position of leadership by appointing him the administrator of St. Ann's Church in Lichterfelde-Berlin. While serving in this relatively small community of Catholics (1,500 parishioners), Strehl received word that Father Karl Warnecke, pastor of St. Peter and Paul in Potsdam, had decided to retire.[33] Realizing the importance of the position and the opportunity to advance, Strehl began to maneuver within the Nazi Party to obtain this new position.

Utilizing his connections through his membership in the Catholic Association for National Politics[34]—a reactionary, right-wing, pro-Nazi group of Catholic professionals who promoted rapprochement between German Roman Catholicism and National Socialism—he became a favored candidate of Dr. Ernst Fromm, the district governor (*Regierungspräsident*) of Potsdam, for the position. According to a March 21, 1931 law, the state held patronage rights over certain delegated parishes, including Potsdam. On April 28, 1933, Fromm wrote to Wilhelm Kube, NSDAP district commander and provincial governor (*Oberpräsident*) of Brandenburg and Berlin, recommending Strehl for the pastorship of St. Peter and Paul.[35] Fromm described Strehl as a "pastor who will hold firm to the guidelines of the government and who will strive for the coordination of church and state."[36] Kube, who himself had been involved in party, state, and religious questions vis-à-vis Protestant churches, eagerly took up Strehl's cause to obtain for him the vacant pastorship in his district.[37]

In the meantime, on May 1, 1933, to ensure the state's support for his candidacy as pastor of St. Peter and Paul and to solidify his own support for National Socialism, Johannes Strehl joined the Nazi Party and was assigned number 2,658,955. Strehl, confident he would receive the position in Potsdam, listed "Catholic pastor" as his profession on his enrollment card.[38] By waiting until May to join the party, Strehl honored the prohibition against membership in the Nazi Party, especially for clergy, which the bishops repealed in March 1933. His membership, however, seemed a bit too opportune in relation to his candidacy for the Potsdam pastorate. In a June 1933 letter to Hitler, Georg Lossau, president of the Catholic Association for National Politics, supported this interpretation. In his letter praising Strehl, Lossau described him as one who "has openly declared his allegiance to the NSDAP since the days of the repeal of the bishops' prohibition."[39] Lossau, however, did not offer any insight or information about Strehl's pre-1933 stance toward the Nazi Party. Strehl, therefore, like so many Germans, more than likely viewed the Nazis' rise to power as an opportunity for self-advancement and joined the party to further his own goals. This is not to say, however, that Strehl did not support the aims and ideology of the movement, because his future activities clearly promoted the values of the party.

On May 5, 1933, confident that Strehl would support the aims of the Nazi Party, Kube wrote to Bishop Schreiber to present Strehl as his candidate for the position. In the letter, Kube mentioned nothing of Strehl's political orientation.[40] Several weeks later, on May 30, 1933, the Berlin chancery office appointed Strehl as pastor of the Potsdam parish.[41] Whether the diocese had any knowledge of Strehl's support of the NSDAP is unknown. There are no records to prove it; however, a recommendation from Kube, an individual known for his involvement in Protestant churches' affairs, should have sparked some interest in this question. According to a letter (sent after Strehl's appointment) from Monsignor Paul Steinmann to Cardinal Bertram, Strehl wanted in his new position to "stand by the Church with advice and action" on church and state relations.[42] Perhaps Steinmann, who himself was sympathetic to the new state in its early years and was in fact running the diocese in the absence of Bishop Schreiber, took this comment as a positive sign, especially during the time between the repeal of prohibitions against the NSDAP and the conclusion of the concordat.[43] At that time, high hopes existed in the minds of many churchmen for good working relations with the state.

Strehl lost no time planning his installation as pastor and the celebration that was to follow. On June 1, 1933, he moved to Potsdam and on June 6, 1933, wrote directly to Hitler and other government officials, inviting them later that month to his installation. In his letter, he announced to Hitler that his appointment marked the "first time in Germany that a Catholic NSDAP pastor" took office on the recommendation of the government. In addition, he pointed out that, if Hitler attended the installation and subsequent celebration, it would ensure "that Catholics and Catholic priests would no longer be slandered and suspended if they belonged to the NSDAP."[44] On the same day, Lossau also wrote to Hitler to invite him to the celebration following the installation. Lossau described Strehl as one who was loyal to the Führer and who never missed a meeting of his association.[45] Lossau must have seen this situation as an opportunity not only to support his friend Strehl, but also, more important, to help his own association gain national prominence. Despite their enthusiasm for the movement, gracious invitations, and hopes for national prominence, on June 15, Hans Lammers, the chief of the Reich chancellery, wrote to Strehl and Lossau, declining their invitations on behalf of the Reich chancellor. Clearly, Hitler was not going to use this occasion to lend any state support to the Catholic Church. The refusal of the invitation, however, did not deter the ardent zeal of Lossau and Strehl, who, together with two additional colleagues from their association, sent a telegram a few days later to the chancellor "from the first National Socialist Catholic installed as a pastor in Potsdam" and his colleagues, pledging their admiration for and loyalty to Hitler.[46]

Soon after Strehl assumed his pastorship in Potsdam, rumors began to circulate in Church circles that the government was planning to name Strehl state commissioner for the Catholic Church. On June 23, Steinmann wrote to Cardinal Bertram and stated that he had received "confidential information" concerning Strehl's possible appointment and suggested that the bishops preempt any move by the state by designating a representative of their own choosing to the Reich government.[47] On June 25, 1933, Bertram informed the metropolitan bishops of the German

Church provinces of this information and suggested the appointment of Steinmann to this position.[48] The bishops, however, did not immediately act on Bertram's suggestion; nor did the government pursue creating such a position.[49] Bertram's suggestion, however, reflected the bishops' disapproval of someone not of their liking.

Unfortunately, there is not much known about Strehl's activities as pastor of St. Peter and Paul. It is known, however, that he could be relentless in his support of the state and the Nazi Party. For example, in January 1934, Strehl, from his pulpit during Sunday mass, refused to read the mandated pastoral letter concerning marriage that contained a new paragraph against sterilization. Instead, Strehl informed the Potsdam Gestapo of the mandated reading of the pastoral letter and denounced Steinmann, Dr. Georg Köhler, Monsignor Bernard Lichtenberg, and Monsignor Georg Banasch—all diocesan chancery officials—for their part in preparing and disseminating the document to be read.[50] For their part, the Potsdam Gestapo forwarded both Strehl's letter and a copy of the pastoral letter to headquarters in Berlin, which in turn sent the information with a cover letter to Lammers in the Reich chancellery. In the cover letter, a Gestapo official noted that Strehl always spoke "in exemplary ways in favor of harmonious cooperation of the Catholic Church with National Socialism."[51]

In August 1935, in a separate incident, Strehl even brought charges against his own parishioners who allegedly defamed his character. Evidently, Strehl had taken a liking to alcohol and was known to enjoy drinking in the local taverns. Cornelius M. and Otto E. accused Strehl of drinking so much one night that he collapsed outside a tavern and was unable to preside at Sunday mass the following day. On a different occasion, they again alleged that Strehl had consumed so much alcohol that he had to be helped home by two SA men. These rumors had enough credence in the city for an artist to create a caricature of Strehl drinking beer at the local tavern with the caption reading, "That is the drunken Catholic pastor of Potsdam." This cartoon was later published in a city newsletter. During the subsequent trial that convicted Strehl's accusers and sent them both to jail, albeit for two months and one month, respectively, local Catholics raised the liturgical question as to whether Strehl, by drinking beer so late, had also broken the mandated fast period for a priest about to celebrate mass. At the time, this was a serious issue among Catholics. The *Potsdamer Beobachter,* which reported the story, minimized the liturgical concerns of Catholics and, while upholding the character of Strehl, condemned Strehl's accusers. According to the author of the article, Strehl was attacked because he was "a National Socialist, and that identity did not suit the Center Party Catholics in Potsdam."[52]

On March 31, 1936, Strehl, at forty-eight years of age, suddenly resigned from his Potsdam pastorship. It is unclear whether the new Bishop of Berlin, Konrad Preysing, known for his anti-Nazi stance, forced

Strehl to resign (as he did other brown priests) or whether Strehl resigned for health reasons (i.e., alcoholism). On May 15, 1937, Preysing
subsequently appointed Strehl chaplain of a nursing home run by the
Grey Sisters in Berlin-Spandau, a position he held until the end of the
war. Again, it is unclear whether this was a state appointment or an assignment delegated by the diocese. In either case, Strehl no longer had
influence over a large congregation.[53]

The process that prevailed in the Berlin diocese to replace Strehl and
provide a candidate acceptable to both the state and the Church offers an
insight into how a local bishop could still control the appointment of candidates for a parish pastorship (though with state approval) and how
widespread the lack of communication was among government bureaus.
On April 15, 1936, Dr. Johannes Allendorf—a decorated veteran of World
War I, recipient of a doctorate from the University of Freiburg, former
counselor and secretary to the bishop, and, at the time, pastor of St.
Joseph in Berlin-Tegel—sent his application directly to Kube. Allendorf enclosed a brief curriculum vitae listing three Nazi Party members as referees
and concluded his letter with "Heil Hitler."[54] The use of the Hitler greeting
did not necessarily signify an individual's allegiance to Nazism, but Allendorf could have used it to win over Kube's support for his candidacy for
the Potsdam position. The testimonies of the witnesses, however, presented Allendorf in a different light.

In the extant correspondence concerning Allendorf's application, two
of the three listed referees wrote a recommendation for the priest. The ear-
liest reply came from Herr F., a teacher who related how in 1931 Allendorf, as secretary to the bishop, helped to establish a relationship between
the Theater of Youth, an organization sympathetic to National Socialism,
and the Berlin diocesan chancery, despite resistance from within the diocese. Furthermore, he declared that Allendorf was a "genuine and honest
supporter of the new Germany" who, after Hitler's appointment as Chancellor, flew the swastika from his parish buildings and declared himself
"faithful to the government," again despite resistance from a number of
his parishioners.[55] Dr. Z., a school administrator, was much more reserved
in his response. According to Dr. Z., Allendorf was a Catholic priest who
sincerely made "an effort to bring his religious views in harmony with the
völkische events of our time." Allendorf, he continued, was of the opinion
that the Führer saw "in both Christian denominations important factors
for the preservation of German ethnicity." Dr. Z. also found that Allendorf
worked for unity between church and state and conveyed an extraordi-
nary show of respect for the Protestants in his community.[56]

Though these responses reveal that Allendorf supported the early efforts of the new state to unify the nation and strengthen Germany, they
do not conclusively reveal the portrait of an individual who completely
supported National Socialism. Because of his voluntary military service

and experience in the war, Allendorf's nationalism is understandable. His support of the state while the Nazis continued to persecute Catholic priests and religious and to encroach on the activities of the Church, however, eventually leads one to conclude that Allendorf was more sympathetic to the new government than to his church.

Despite his application for the position and his enthusiasm, Allendorf was not the government's first candidate. For example, in May 1936, the SD, in its attempt to promote candidates, did not even consider Allendorf. Instead, it suggested Anton Scholz, pastor of Holy Family Church in Strasburg/Uckermark, who, according to an SD report, was already active as an informant to the SD Section East on church matters. It was the SD's hope that Scholz would continue providing the "extraordinarily valuable material" that, up to that point, "was supplied by Strehl."[57] For unexplained reasons, however, the SD did not immediately pursue Scholz's candidacy.

Instead, on June 2, 1936, Kube forwarded to Fromm a copy of Preysing's three nominations for the Potsdam pastorship. It included the names of Johannes Wittenbrink, Alfons Wachsmann, and Johannes Allendorf.[58] It is clear from the contents of this letter that Allendorf had been in consultation with Preysing concerning filling the vacant pastorship. A few days later, on June 6, Kube suggested a fourth name for the candidacy, Paul Arthur Drossert, a priest from Tournai, Belgium, who in 1927 had been released of his diocesan duties and was living privately in Potsdam. In 1932, apparently on the order of the Berlin chancery, Drossert had lost his residency in the St. Joseph House with the Sisters of Charity of St. Charles Borromaeus because of his pro-National Socialist talks and, more specifically, for signing an appeal for Hitler that appeared in *Der Angriff* and the *Völkischer Beobachter*.[59] Kube admitted that it seemed "hardly possible to achieve the candidacy of Father Drossert." With this in mind, Kube focused on choosing a candidate from among the three presented by Preysing. It is interesting that, in his correspondence with Fromm, Kube showed evidence that he wanted a man who was not only loyal to the party and the state, but also would be qualified to fulfill his pastoral duties in the parish.[60] By the middle of July, Kube had determined that Wittenbrink was "politically unreliable" and Wachsmann was "politically questionable," even though he was a known member of the National Socialist People's Welfare organization, an NSDAP charity that promoted its racial ideology.[61]

In August 1936, Scholz's name, with the endorsement of the SD leadership, surfaced in the discussion. The SD informed the Kurmark district leadership of the Nazi Party that Scholz should be made pastor of the Potsdam parish, if only temporarily. Immediately after that communication, an official from the district leadership wrote Fromm of their concerns about Scholz, who, because of his political views, had already been "repeatedly transferred." Instead, they wanted to appoint a pastor like Strehl, who, in addition to supporting his faith and his church, would "fight with full conviction and fervor for the movement and Adolf Hitler."[62] In the same month, Scholz himself sent in an application for the position.[63] It was followed shortly by a letter to Fromm from the local Nazi Party in Zossen, where Scholz had once served as pastor. In his letter, Fromm advocated the candidacy of Scholz for pastor of St. Peter and Paul.[64] In the midst of these suggestions over party-political matters, Kube was forced to resign from his position as *Oberpräsident* and was succeeded in August by Emil Stürtz. Despite this change of power, on August 29 Fromm decided in favor of Allendorf for the position and informed Stürtz of his choice.[65] At the same time, Fromm wrote to the NSDAP in Zossen to inform them that it was too late to add Scholz to the list of candidates.[66] On September 1, 1936, Stürtz accepted this recommendation and informed Bishop Preysing of his choice.[67]

Little is known about Allendorf's tenure as pastor of St. Peter and Paul. It is clear that he did not encounter any problems with the state or the party. Allendorf clearly was a strongly patriotic German who supported the new government. The portrait that Nazi Party members painted of him was also positive; however, his inclusion on the list of candidates by Preysing, a noted anti-Nazi, prompts a second look at Allendorf, an appraisal that cannot be made until further information detailing his life becomes available. This is likewise true of Wilhelm Knobloch, pastor of St. Anthony Church in Potsdam-Babelsberg, who, because of his activity for the Nazi Party, was forced into retirement by Bishop Preysing on February 6, 1939.[68] Although material on Knobloch is scarce, it appears that he volunteered to conduct research at the division for race research in the Ministry of Interior. According to his 1937 application, he wished to devote two hours a day to researching and writing the history of his family. A 1937 note, however, alludes to the fact that Knobloch was conducting research beyond the scope of his particular family. It is possible that he used his volunteer service to investigate the family histories of his own parishioners!

In 1939, Bishop Preysing also had to confront Father Walter Leonards, pastor (since December 1930) of St. Mary Magdalene Church in Prenzlau-Uckermark, a vicariate of Eberswalde, and force him into retirement because of his pro-Nazi journalistic stands.[69] Until 1936, Leonards appears to have had no notorious conflicts with superiors over his pro–National Socialist stance. In a 1930 article that he penned concerning Catholicism in Treptow-Pomerania, where he served as parochial vicar from 1925 to 1930, Leonards appeared content with his Church when he attested proudly to the struggle of Roman Catholicism to take root in the predominantly Protestant area.[70] In 1936, however, Leonards came into conflict with the Berlin chancery when Monsignor Lichtenberg questioned him about adding new lyrics to traditional hymns and using them during mass. Lichtenberg alleged that Leonards had altered the words of the Gloria, changing

"Praise and Honor to God in the highest, and peace to the people on earth" to "We pray for our Führer; he is Your image on earth." Lichtenberg asked him to clarify who had issued the required Church approval for the alteration of lyrics.[71] Leonards's response has not been found.

According to Father Walter Adolph, who worked in the Berlin chancery and left written recollections of his experiences under National Socialism, Leonards became active as a journalist for a Netherlands Press Bureau. Netherlands Trappist Father Anselm Vriens, pastor for Flemish and Dutch Catholics in Berlin, ran this pro-Nazi agency. Vriens's aim was to disseminate propaganda disguised as official press reports. His intent was also to present a pro-Nazi picture of Church-state relations and minimize or suppress any existing conflicts. Though Leonards was now a member of the Berlin diocese, he had originally been a Trappist and in 1910 was ordained a priest in Holland. He met Vriens during his early years in the priesthood, before World War I. At the onset of war, he returned to Germany to serve as a military chaplain and, subsequently, remained in Berlin as a diocesan priest.[72]

On December 9, 1937, Leonards wrote a commentary on a pastoral letter of Preysing that did not truly represent the more critical words of the bishop and then sent it to news agencies throughout the world. In the same month, after Preysing learned of Leonards's involvement with the Nazis and his commentaries in the press bureau, he threatened him with suspension if he wrote for the agency again.[73] Evidently, Leonards did not heed Preysing's warning, and on July 1, 1939, the bishop placed him into forced retirement.[74]

Leonards did not accept this forced retirement graciously and, as a result, increased his efforts in behalf of the Nazi Party. During this time, he was even given credit for spreading hateful propaganda against the bishops in articles he did not author. For example, in 1939–1940, several of the German bishops attributed to Leonards a series of newsletters critical of the episcopacy and their stance vis-à-vis the state. Published under the name "Catholic Pastors' Emergency League," these newsletters were later found to be the work of the Gestapo, which had unsuccessfully attempted to raise the ire of Catholics against their bishops.[75] On April 1, 1940, Leonards joined the NSDAP, listed his profession as an editor, and became member number 8,011,773.[76] Leonards's name also appeared in a card index of the Reich Security main office, where he was identified as a "retired priest" and "present employee of the German army."[77] After the war, Leonards resumed his pastoral ministry, first in the archdiocese of Paderborn and then in the diocese of Trier. In making application for parish ministry in both dioceses, Leonards failed to mention his efforts on behalf of National Socialism. Upon inquiry into Leonards's personal character by the Trier chancery, the dioceses of Berlin and Paderborn approved his resumption of ministry in Trier and failed to mention his NSDAP activities. Both, however, did state concerns over his pastoral conduct. The Berlin vicar general reported that the diocese had to remove Leonards from office because of his misappropriation of parish funds. Similarly, Paderborn noted that Leonards had a difficult time working with the pastor in his present parish in Rudersdorf. Evidently, the diocese of Trier had a great shortage of priests, significant enough to employ Leonards. Therefore, on April 12, 1950, the Trier vicar general, Heinrich von Meurers, assigned him to a small parish in Sevenich. Meurers, however, would soon regret this decision. From 1950 until his death on July 23, 1965, Leonards regularly caused headaches for diocesan officials by involving himself in local politics and creating disharmony among parishioners.[78]

Bishop Preysing was not always able to act against the Nazi priests in his diocese. For example, in 1937, Father Anton Scholz, who had also applied for the vacant Potsdam pastorship, received a state appointment as prison chaplain in Brandenburg-Görden that did not meet with Preysing's approval.[79] Scholz had always been a problem for the diocese. Despite his love of and dedication to ministry, Scholz was also known in the diocese for his difficult personality.[80] There is no evidence, however, to suggest that his difficulty with superiors led him to join the party. His personality, though, led Scholz to be regularly transferred, serving as a parochial vicar in a variety of parishes before finally being appointed, in 1928, pastor of Immaculate Conception Church (1,100 parishioners) in Zossen. He held this position until 1935, when difficulties again arose. This time, the controversy was in relation to his activities for the Nazi Party. Bishop Preysing, who had just arrived in the diocese, gave him one last chance and appointed him administrator of the tiny parish of Holy Family (260 parishioners) in Strasburg-Uckermark.[81] Preysing seemed to think relegating Scholz to this small, insignificant parish would keep him out of trouble. Instead, Scholz maintained contact with members of the Nazi Party from his former parish in Zossen and actively applied for positions in larger parishes.[82]

Scholz's involvement with the NSDAP began even before 1933. Since 1931, he had been a member of the SA, and on March 1, 1933, he joined the NSDAP, before the repeal of the German bishops' prohibition.[83] He made no secret of his allegiance to National Socialism, that he had served as an informant on church affairs for the SD, or that he had promoted good relations between the state and the Catholic Church.[84] In November 1933, Scholz even sent the chancery office his own review of a recent novel, *Imperator mundi*, which was pro-Nazi in content. In his review, Scholz pointed out that the author encouraged her readers "to slip off their alien, materialistic shell and see the swastika in its internal essence as the sign of the triumphant love of God." With this statement, Scholz surprised even Vicar General Steinmann, who normally was open to the new state. Steinmann replied, "This word from the mouth of a Catholic priest will widely arouse astonishment, because not the swastika, but the cross of the savior is the symbol of salvation."[85] Steinmann's comments revealed that, despite any political leanings, he was not about to compromise theology and the teachings of the Church to accommodate the new ideology of National Socialism. Scholz, who embraced the movement early on, had already decided that National Socialism provided him with the answer to life-threatening problems within German society.

In May 1945, following the collapse of Nazi Germany, Scholz lost his position as prison chaplain in Brandenburg-Görden. Preysing refused to offer him another ministry assignment; however, Father Albrecht Jochmann, the pastor of Holy Trinity Church in Brandenburg-Havel and vicar of the Potsdam vicariate, allowed Scholz to remain in Brandenburg-Görden and to assist with parish ministry in the area.[86] Jochmann was unusually kind to Scholz and in August 1945 wrote to Preysing, testifying to Scholz's ministry on behalf of the prisoners of the Third Reich, many of whom he had accompanied to their executions.[87]

After the war, Scholz could not understand why the Berlin chancery office and bishop would not assign him to another parish. He also refused to take any responsibility for his past actions of promoting the Nazi Party. In a June 1950 letter to the Berlin chancery, Scholz expressed his disbelief over his situation: "The fact, that I since . . . 1929 belonged to the diocese of Berlin, that I lost my position without personal guilt in 1945, and that I have been waiting for a new position while in a difficult situation for five full years and that I am already 59 years old, and that not only all my classmates and many younger priests but even some of my former students hold distinguished Church positions, it appears legitimate to venture once again to request the honorable chancery for a parish."[88] In November 1950 and March 1951, Scholz again attempted to obtain a pastorship, and again he failed.[89] Finally, in April 1951, after Bishop Preysing's death in December 1950, Vicar General Dr. Maximilian Prange appointed Scholz administrator of the parish in Birkenwerder (1,800 parishioners) under the direct supervision of the Father Franz Kaiser, the pastor of the central Church in Berlin-Hermsdorf, Our Lady of Grace.[90] On October 1, 1957, Scholz retired with pay from full-time ministry. Then in 1961, he left the German Democratic Republic with official permission and moved to Bavaria, in the Federal Republic of Germany, to live with his sister. On December 21, 1980, after many years in retirement, the cantankerous Anton Scholz died at the ripe old age of eighty-nine.[91]

Although Strehl, Leonards, and Scholz joined the NSDAP, apparently for a variety of reasons—opportunism, antiliberalism, nationalism, alienation from the Church, and insubordination with Church superiors—the extent of their commitment remains unclear. Each one, however, saw in Nazism a way to acquire benefits in a distressing time. Each one also adapted various aspects of its ideology, including its anti-Semitism, about which none expressed any misgivings. In the cases of two other brown priests, Karl König and Josef Roth, who both came from dioceses outside Berlin, evidence of their commitment to Nazism is more apparent. Indeed, their writings alone reveal to us what led them to align themselves with National Socialism: an adamant anti-Semitism and belief that Nazism would solve the perceived ills that plagued Germany at the demise of the Weimar Republic.

In 1926, following his early retirement from his pastoral duties in the diocese of Paderborn, König first moved to Cologne and then to Berlin.[92] König was frustrated with the state of German society and culture and had convinced himself that Germany was spiraling downward into ruin and destruction. He attributed this descent to the 1918 revolution, the institution of a liberal democratic government, political Catholicism, Bolshevism, and Jews. In National Socialism, König saw the saving force that would rescue Germany from moral and political ruin and restore it to greatness.[93] König also believed that Hitler and his party could rid the nation of those liberal elements that attacked the core of German society. To this end, König made a private pledge to direct all his energy to help the state combat those forces that he perceived were against it. To fulfill this undertaking, he joined the NSDAP[94] and, under the title "Chronicle of the Center," provided the Reich chancellery and other government agencies with regular reports detailing the events in the German Catholic Church that he considered political and harmful to the Nazi state.[95] These reports were also used by the SD to gather information against the Church.[96]

Although a contemporary described him as an "unsavory figure" who openly expressed his glee over the government's persecution of elements in the Catholic Church he believed acted against the state,[97] König continually argued that no one, including the state, was persecuting the Catholic Church. Instead, he pointed out that never in its history was the Church more "involved in the welfare of the human soul than today in Germany." He argued that the state attacked only those people and groups that were harmful to Germany. König also stated proudly that the Führer had smashed everything that was "evil in Germany, the terrible literature, the terrible theater, the terrible art, the terrible parties, and the terrible government and laws."[98]

In his analysis of the situation, König continually lumped together Jews, Free Masons, and the Jesuits as groups that had concentrated their "attack against our Führer and against his *Volk*."[99] According to his ramblings, Jews had influenced and infiltrated the former Catholic Center Party, which he still saw as a force working to harm Germany. He argued that German Catholics could be brought in line with the Nazi state only when "the Lord God, the Führer and his comrades as well as the German *Volk*" could unconditionally rely on a faithful German Catholic bishop, "Church newspapers and the Center press were banned," "the Jesuits were expelled from the schools," and, finally, "Catholics would agree to leave a

Church whenever a Center-influenced priest spoke against the state or party." Furthermore, he believed that Germany knew how to solve its Jewish question: through force, terror, and intimidation. He then listed a series of headlines from newspapers throughout the world detailing attacks and terror against Jews in Germany.[100]

König also introduced these sentiments into his sermons and speeches. In an October 1935 talk to a Nazi Party gathering in Rottach-Egern, he spoke against the "baneful connection of the Center with the SPD, Jews, and the other powers of disbelief and subversion."[101] Again, on March 8, 1936, in Bad Nauheim, König attacked Jews and Bolsheviks in a sermon in which he compared the transfiguration of Christ to the revitalization of Germany under Hitler.[102]

König greatly overestimated the importance of the information he provided the government and firmly believed that it affected the course of Nazi policy and church-state relations. In March 1938, this led him to write to the Paderborn chancery, informing the staff that he had arranged for the repeal of prohibition against the diocesan newspaper. A chancery official noted at the bottom of the letter that this "was not achieved through König's mediation" and added that there actually was "no known case where König intervened with the state or party office with any trace of success."[103] König, however, never let the doubt of diocesan officials deter him. Instead, he regularly wrote to state and party officials, dropping names of important people who he believed greatly appreciated his efforts in behalf of the state.[104] He also used every public occasion possible to let people know whom he knew. To this end, in December 1935, he informed a newspaper in Bad Nauheim, where he had a speaking engagement, that Minister-President Hermann Göring had sent him a signed picture in recognition of his efforts for the state. He vainly detailed similar information in newsletters he would send out to friends and acquaintances.[105]

Both the Paderborn and Berlin dioceses made attempts to control König's actions, but with little success. On November 12, 1935, he received a letter from the Paderborn chancery that demanded he stop making speaking appearances at political rallies. On November 16, König sharply answered the rebuke and assured the chancery that his words were always "purely of a pastoral nature." He also described himself as a "priest-private man" who did not speak from an official ministerial position. In December, the chancery wrote an even sharper letter back to König, again demanding he refrain from speaking at political rallies. The diocesan official also rejected his creation of the term "priest-private man" as detrimental to the priesthood. As a result, König refused to follow the requests of his diocesan superiors, who gave up their inquiry the following year.[106] In June 1938, the Berlin chancery tried to encourage the city government to withdraw an offer it had made to König to teach Catholic religious instruction at two schools in Berlin-Schöneberg. According to the chancery,

König possessed neither the required approval of the local ordinary nor the consent of his diocesan bishop in Paderborn to teach religion.[107] The chancery also informed Church Affairs Minister Kerrl of the situation.[108] At the same time, the Paderborn chancery office told König that he did not have the required permission to teach religious education.[109] König, of course, ignored the concerns of his superiors and, with the city government's permission, accepted the new teaching posts.

Living away from his local ordinary, König was impossible to control. He simply refused to obey the directives of his superiors and often collided with them in an endless correspondence that never fully resolved the issue central to his concern. As a result, König devoted his full energy to serving the Nazi movement and its goals. His special task in this mission was to provide Nazi officials with information to further limit the activity of the Catholic Church. For this, the Nazi officials rewarded him with praise. The more he was praised, the more his hatred toward certain elements in Catholicism and in German society grew. In many ways, through these actions, König formed his own notion of the Church, one that incorporated the ideology of National Socialism and attributed salvation to Hitler and the Nazi Party. On February 18, 1939, however, death suddenly put a stop to König's fanatical efforts to aid National Socialism.[110]

Josef Roth was even more fanatical than König in his devotion to National Socialism, his loathing of the Versailles Treaty and the Weimar Republic, and his anti-Semitism.[111] Roth had served voluntarily in World War I. As with many soldiers, defeat and its humiliating aftermath left a lasting impression upon him. Roth also saw a great weakness in German society and somehow attributed all his country's ills to the permeating influence of Jews in every aspect of German life. As early as 1923, as a parochial vicar, Roth published a vile anti-Semitic tract titled "Catholicism and the Jewish Question." In it he argued that people had to leave their "catacomb anti-Semitism" and embrace a radical anti-Semitism that would lead to the removal of Jews from any influence in public life. Such an expulsion would rid society of their "enjoyment," take away their "rights as citizens," exclude them "from all state offices," refuse them "licenses for any trade and industry," and prohibit any Jewish "literary and propaganda activity." According to Roth, it was permissible for a Catholic to adopt racial anti-Semitism because Jews had transmitted immorality—that which the Catholic must resist—through their blood. Therefore, for Roth, the Christian command to love one's neighbor excluded Jews as neighbors because, from the beginning, every Jew was "already a latent danger for the Christian religion and morality," and for that reason, "the Jewish race on account of its demoralizing influence inherent in its nature" had to be "eliminated from the public life of our religion and our *Volk*."[112] Cardinal Faulhaber reprimanded Roth for publishing such a tract without Church approval but, at the same time, did not issue a compensatory letter condemning Roth's racism. Of course, Roth learned his lesson after the cardinal's rebuke and subsequently only published under pseudonyms. It is interesting to note that in response to the cardinal's letter Roth did as he would always do, respond with a letter pledging fidelity, disclaiming any wrongdoing, and promising obedience to the Church in the future.[113]

In 1934, Roth, who had already been campaigning for the Nazi Party before its seizure of power, joined the SA and more publicly aligned himself with the NSDAP.[114] In the same year, he began teaching religion at the National Socialist Leadership School, in Feldafing.[115] Soon thereafter, in August 1935, Hans Kerrl invited him to join the newly established Ministry of Church Affairs. To accept this position, he asked Cardinal Faulhaber to grant him time off from his regular diocesan duties. Although at first Faulhaber denied the request, with the encouragement of his chancery, whose officials believed Roth's assignment could prove useful for the diocese, Faulhaber relented and granted Roth permission to move to Berlin and assume the new position.[116] In light of the venomousness of Roth's anti-Semitic tract, today this seems astonishing. Perhaps the chancery thought that Roth's anti-Semitism was the norm for German priests or merely common to his class. In 1936, upon receiving a more permanent position as head of the Catholic division, Roth requested an extension through the Berlin chancery for permission to continue his work in the Ministry of Church Affairs.[117] This time Faulhaber was not as agreeable and denied Roth's request after the chaplain admitted that he had not regularly presided at daily mass.[118] At that time Faulhaber was also privy to information coming from another brown priest, Abbott Alban Schachleiter, who had advised the cardinal (through a chancery official) not to give approval to Roth's new position because of his disloyalty to Rome, his careerism, and his advocacy for a German National Church.[119] (Roth's anti-Semitism, it seems, was not even taken into account.) Though Schachleiter supported Hitler fully, he refused to support anything that went against his understanding of official Church teaching. Faulhaber also suspected that Roth had been publishing and working against the Church, but did not have evidence to support his suspicions.[120]

In the Ministry of Church Affairs, Roth worked against what he considered political Catholicism and the encroachment of the Catholic Church into the domain of the state. He viewed the Reich concordat as an outdated agreement concluded by a state in its infancy and, in his own words, strove "to sabotage, to undermine, and to work for the annulment of the concordat through my entire professional activity."[121] Not only had the laws of the new National Socialist state subsumed the concordat, but in 1935, under the pseudonym of Walter Berg, Roth published an article in which he argued that the Church itself had grown so ancient and ineffective the National Socialist revolution needed to supplant it.[122]

For Roth, Christianity not only was restrictively obsolete and lacking in significance but also was permeated by what he perceived as the enervating effects of Judaism. As early as 1923, Roth had presented an image of Christ as a "heroic strongman," calling upon people not to mourn but to be strong in spirit.[123] In his essay on Roth, Raimund Baumgärtner said the cleric wanted Christianity to reclaim more manly virtues and ideals, which, he believed, with Christianity's stress on charity and good work, had become effeminate. In this vein, Roth argued that masculine Christian virtues "rebel against institutions and endeavors that do not fight suffering with all their might, but only offer good words and support to those who suffer."[124]

By 1940, Roth had come to the conclusion that Christianity could not be saved from the distorting influences of Judaism. In a 1940 lecture at the Reich Institute for the History of New Germany, which was also published in the same year, Roth again addressed the issue of the "Catholic Church and the Jewish Question." According to Roth, Judaism permeated the Church to its core. This included hundreds of years of Jesuit overtures to allow Jews into its ranks. Despite a history of anti-Jewish Church law, the Church now had lost the battle against Judaism and was preaching tolerance. "The Catholic Church," he concluded, "will never come to a clear and determined struggle against Judaism and will never become an ally in the national ideological struggle because it would have to give up its own mission and its own spiritual substance."[125]

In 1940, Roth turned his back on the Church not only because of its alleged Jewishness, but also, according to remaining fragments of his diary, because of his own struggle with celibacy. Somehow, despite his own involvement in state measures against the Catholic Church and notwithstanding his sanctioning of the arrest of individual Catholic priests, Roth never withdrew from the Catholic priesthood. In 1939–1941, his own vow of celibacy was questioned, however, when he entered into a relationship with a recently divorced woman, Käthe S. According to Roth's diary entries and the recorded testimony of his fellow employee, Dr. Sebastian Schröcker, Roth endured a pang of conscience in deciding whether to marry the woman. Käthe seemed to make his decision even harder, for though she professed her love for Roth, she constantly returned to live with her former husband for short periods. Roth's diary fragments revealed that the situation tore at his conscience and confused him.[126] Before he had the chance to resolve the matter—or create more problems for his own church—Roth, on August 20, 1941, drowned while vacationing in Tattenberg am Inn, in Tirol.[127]

Brown priests supported National Socialism for a variety of reasons: patriotism, anti-Semitism, antiliberalism, anti-Bolshevism, and opportunism. Although these men had different reasons for joining and supporting the Nazi Party, one characteristic united them: alienation from their faith tradition. That is, for many reasons, including the ones mentioned above, they no longer saw their church and faith tradition as the sole means of salvation. Whether consciously or otherwise, they also imposed a messianic role on Adolf Hitler and the Nazi Party, believing that their Führer could offer them and their country the means to a better society, happiness, and life. In turn, they allowed Nazism to become the all-important guiding factor in their lives. Despite this factor, all of them, at least externally, were unable to sever ties with their religious tradition. Catholicism had a grip on them. For many, this hold could be attributed to their need for a monthly subsidy from the diocese to subsist. Others, such as Scholz and even König, however, held fast to their priesthood and continued to identify themselves as members of the Roman Catholic clergy. Ministry, especially in Scholz's case, was of prime importance, even though it was tainted by Nazi ideology. Indeed, these Nazi priests were anomalies who distorted their own perception of Catholicism to accommodate and serve National Socialism and its annihilative leadership.

Perhaps not all of the brown priests were outright anti-Semites like König and Roth, but anyone who belonged to the NSDAP long enough would have been forced to embrace some form of anti-Semitism. This was not a very difficult task at the time, because their own faith tradition had a long, perplexing history of anti-Semitism, especially in its biblical and theological rendering of the crucifixion. Not every priest, however, embraced this anti-Semitism or allowed it to direct his life's choices. Unfortunately, very few priests in Germany spoke out for their Jewish neighbors. One exceptional Berlin cleric, however, was not afraid to risk his life to advocate for Jews.

seven

The Unique Path of
Bernhard Lichtenberg

In his willingness to challenge the policies of the Nazi state in a profound and consistent manner, Monsignor Bernhard Lichtenberg far outstripped the rest of the clergy in his diocese. Not only did he embody the backbone of *Resistenz* by charting in his homilies a way for others to defend the Church against encroachment by the state, he also publicly protested these intrusions at the expense of his health and safety. Throughout his priestly ministry, Bernhard Lichtenberg—monsignor, pastor, politician, and spokesperson for the oppressed—consistently highlighted two themes in his preaching. First, he championed the idea that our "human life is a spiritual struggle on earth" for which the Catholic, through education in the faith, must make a personal decision to submit "to the will of God, and live according to God's law and the Church's law." Second, Lichtenberg exhorted his various congregations to follow Christ's words echoed throughout the New Testament—to love their neighbor, especially in everyday life situations.[1]

Lichtenberg's case is extremely important in any discussion of Catholic resistance among Catholic lower clergy because, although he stayed within the parameters and limitations of traditional Catholic theology and teaching, Lichtenberg still found the courage and wherewithal in this tradition to move beyond the constructed world of German Catholicism and to pray publicly for all persecuted Jews. It must also be kept in mind that Lichtenberg was not a proponent of any new theology or movement within the Church. Instead, he found his theological base in the ancient traditions and spirituality of the Catholic Church.[2] Thus, for Lichtenberg, faith was fundamental; everything in the world had to be viewed through a Catholic prism. Thus, in a 1931 article in the Berlin diocese's *Märkischer*

Kalender, an annually published collection of articles on Catholic life in
Berlin, Lichtenberg attempted to awaken the dormant faith of Berlin
Catholics by focusing on stories of recent converts. Writing a brief commentary on the spiritual lives of these converts, Lichtenberg revealed a
highly motivated Catholic faith. For example, in one instance Lichtenberg discussed the case of a Jewish man who first experienced an intellectual attraction to Catholicism through the study of philosophy, canon
law, and theology. Lichtenberg reported that following the gentleman's
conversion to Catholicism, many of his fellow Jews "viewed him as a
renegade." According to Lichtenberg, this did not bother the man because he knew that his "devout Jewish ancestors who now rested in the
peace of God could give thanks to their creator that God had taken the
blindfold from the eyes of their descendants."[3] Lichtenberg ended the article by lamenting the fact that so many Catholics in Berlin could easily
discard their "holy Catholic faith like a worn-out shoe." This was especially hard for him in light of the attested "fervent longing" of non-
Catholics for the Catholic faith and, most of all, because cradle Catholics
would have nothing to say on the last day when God would demand of
them "an account" of their stewardship.[4]

This is just one example reflecting the importance, uniqueness, and
centrality of the Catholic faith for Lichtenberg. Whereas today Lichtenberg's comments may appear insensitive and even anti-Semitic, a Catholic
in the 1930s would deem them acceptable and a normal form of discourse. The mission of the Catholic Church was to save souls, and the
Church taught that one accomplished this specifically through baptism
into the Catholic Church. Nevertheless, Lichtenberg's comment concerning the man's "devout Jewish ancestors who now rested in the peace of
God" reveals a sensitivity to Jews that was not easily found among
Catholic priests or laity of that time.

Despite his willingness to reflect sensitivity to issues outside of Catholicism, Lichtenberg always placed his own religious tradition before all others. Indeed, he believed it was his duty to defend his faith publicly whenever it was attacked or questioned in any way. For example, following a
confrontation over the sacrament of Penance, Lichtenberg wrote to a
Protestant minister, stating that although he recognized Jesus' command
to do to others what one would want done to oneself, he also followed another mandate of Christ: "Who recognizes me before humans, him will I
also recognize before my father, who is in heaven." To this end, Lichtenberg publicly defended his faith according to his priestly responsibility as
a "custodian of a community."[5]

Lichtenberg, the second of five children, learned his devout allegiance
to Catholicism from his parents, August and Emilie, who themselves had
withstood the onslaught of the Kulturkampf in the predominantly Protestant city of Ohlau, some 30 kilometers southeast of Breslau.[6] They were

among the Catholic minority population in this region who fought against the anti-Catholic legislation of Bismarck by supporting the Center Party. Also, both August and Bernard's uncle Alfred Hubrich held positions in the Center Party, the latter serving twenty-five years as a representative in the Reichstag.[7] As a result, Bernhard's family instilled in him a mixture of Catholic piety and political Catholicism, both of which encouraged him to defend his faith. Bernhard's Catholicism, however, was not a narrowly defined regional Catholicism. Instead, both before and after his ordination, Lichtenberg had the opportunity to travel throughout Germany and other European countries, as well as the United States, to witness the practice of the Catholic faith abroad and to absorb other cultures and traditions.[8]

On June 21, 1899, after completing his theological studies in Innsbruck and Breslau, Lichtenberg was ordained by Cardinal Georg Kopp for the diocese of Breslau.[9] Immediately afterward, Lichtenberg celebrated his first mass in his home parish at Ohlau. On this occasion, the Lichtenberg family asked a priest friend to offer the homily. The guest preacher, Father Eymmer, prophetically declared, "A priest remains a priest even when in chains and shackles." In fact, Eymmer was referring to his own experiences during the Kulturkampf, in which the police had arrested him while he presided at the altar. Ironically, this statement would also hold true for Lichtenberg in years to come. It was also not surprising that, on the day of Lichtenberg's ordination, the entire Lichtenberg family, along with the rest of the local congregation, processed through the city of Ohlau to celebrate the occasion, the first of its kind to be held since the Kulturkampf.[10]

In August 1900, Cardinal Kopp transferred Lichtenberg to St. Mauritius in Friedrichsberg-Lichtenberg, on the outskirts of Berlin, to minister to Catholics in the growing metropolis.[11] There he discovered his love for pastoral ministry under the guidance of Father Nikolaus Kuborn, who would befriend the young priest. This friendship would last until Kuborn's death.[12] During his next four assignments, Bernhard put the pastoral skills he learned under Kuborn into practice: as parochial vicar in Charlottenburg, Sacred Heart Church (1902); as parochial vicar in Berlin, St. Michael (1903); as pastor in Friedrichsfelde-Karlshorst (1905); and as pastor in Pankow (1910).[13] In 1905, Lichtenberg founded the parish in Friedrichsfelde and on May 20, 1907, in characteristic fashion, organized the first *Corpus Christi* procession in the parish since the Reformation. He announced it in the Catholic newspaper *Germania*.[14] In 1906, Lichtenberg also organized and supervised the building of the Friedrichsfelde rectory, which contained the church in a double room of the house.[15] Soon, in 1913, when he received the appointment as pastor of Heart of Jesus parish in Charlottenburg, Lichtenberg would oversee a larger building project. The parish of more than 6,500 Catholics had a church with only 467 seats.[16] Lichtenberg accepted the challenge and began a campaign to seek funds for the building project that led him to preach in Catholic churches throughout Germany. Lichtenberg also had to maneuver around a group of developers who feared the loss of property value and the influx of a Catholic working class into the area.[17] Despite the difficulty of the task, on October 3, 1937, several years after Lichtenberg had left the parish, Bishop Preysing consecrated the completed new church that Lichtenberg had worked so hard to build.[18] In the early years of his priesthood, Lichtenberg entered each new project with great energy, whether it was urban ministry, building up new parish communities, or raising funds to erect new churches. Moreover, he was greatly loved and respected by his parishioners, a large number of whom were of Polish heritage. Lichtenberg gained their trust, especially by making such statements as the following (to his new congregation in Charlottenburg): "I was sent here by the bishop neither to Germanize nor to Polonize, but to be a pastor."[19]

Lichtenberg's openness did not mean that he was free of nationalism. During the Great War, he proudly served his country; however, he did so as a Catholic priest who was called to serve all Catholics, regardless of national background. Therefore, as chaplain to soldiers stationed in Charlottenburg, he ministered to both Germans and to foreign prisoners of war.[20] In 1917, in his capacity as army chaplain, the Reich war press office sent him on a trip to the Eastern front. For his efforts in this mission, he was awarded the Service Medal of the Red Cross.[21] On December 21, 1921, after the war, a Berlin City Councilor forced Lichtenberg to explain his war record in light of his current statements promoting peace. Tired of Lichtenberg's preaching of "love of neighbor," the councilor publicly accused him of hypocrisy for blessing weapons used in war. Before Berlin city council, Lichtenberg, himself a representative for the Catholic Center Party, stood up and answered his accuser: "I was a part-time military chaplain with the Elisabeth regiment during the war and I can recall that I addressed soldiers at least thirty times; however, if I gave a blessing, I did not bless the weapons, but only the soldiers."[22] Though Lichtenberg was a proud German, he was also a Catholic priest whose faith always superseded all other concerns.

After the war, Lichtenberg joined many German Catholics in supporting the work of the Peace Association of German Catholics and its leading member, Father Franziskus Maria Stratmann, O.P.[23] In 1931, for example, in connection with the peace work of this group, Goebbels's newspaper, *Der Angriff,* viciously attacked Lichtenberg and Stratmann for sponsoring a private showing of the film *All Quiet on the Western Front* to the members of the Peace Association.[24] In November 1931, Lichtenberg also served as the main preacher at the association's eighth national convention. In his homily, he stressed the "necessity of the peace movement and of prayer" as the association's most important tasks. Before he ended, he rooted his message in the core of Catholic belief, declaring that "the world will come to peace when it acknowledges Christ as its King."[25] On September 6, 1933, after the Nazi seizure of power that would lead to the prohibition of the Peace Association and the detention of its chair, Father Stratmann, Lichtenberg asked the German episcopacy to take "the Peace Association and its chairman under its wings."[26]

Lichtenberg's support for the peace movement did not mean he would quietly veer away from a fight, especially if he believed his cause to be just. In his activity for the Center Party, Lichtenberg regularly found himself compelled to speak out boldly for the rights of the Church, especially for protection of denominational religious education.[27] He followed one basic principle: "Where there is only one single Catholic child—there will also be Catholic religious instruction."[28] Similarly, Lichtenberg also fought for the Church's ethical and moral teachings to be upheld in the public sphere. In 1929, during a regional assembly meeting in Charlottenburg, Lichtenberg spoke against both the building of an air- and sunbath in Jungfernheide Park and against the development of a childbirth and sex information center.[29] Lichtenberg argued that the "bath" had nothing to do with medicine. Instead, he argued, it would only promote nudism and a nudist culture. Lichtenberg feared that the proponents of air- and sun-baths were led "not only by medical motivations, but by party-political, anti-Church tendencies."[30] Lichtenberg attacked the idea of a childbirth and sex information center because it promoted abortion and contraception, two issues that the Catholic Church had always challenged. He argued that the "*Volk* must not be educated to use contraception in order to be spared abortion, just as the devil should not be allowed to be exorcised through Beelzebub; but the people should be taught self-control, absolute sexual abstinence before or outside of marriage and reasonable abstinence in marriage."[31]

Lichtenberg was not content with merely campaigning against any form of planned parenthood. Rather, he linked his comments to the declining birthrate in Germany and, thereby, revealed a side of himself that today would be considered racist. In his statement, for example, he argued that recent statistics showed that Germans were "a dying *Volk.*" He continued, "The white race begins to die because of its culture. In the world there are two-thirds colored people and only one-third white. The colored race increases two times as quickly as the white race. One can deduce already approximately the time when the white race will disappear from the earth. So contraception works disastrously for an entire *Volk* and makes it a slave to foreign *Völker.*"[32] Lichtenberg made such statements in an attempt to uphold the traditional teaching of the Church that was later expressed by Pope Pius XI in the encyclical *Casti Connubii* (*On Human Marriage*, 1931). In that encyclical, the pope spoke out against contraception and declared that sex in marriage was primarily for procreation.[33]

Lichtenberg's arguments became problematic when he chose to utilize language found in writings on eugenics—a movement that was prevalent not only in Europe but also in the United States.[34] The comment, nevertheless, may be seen in light of the work of Hermann Muckermann, a former Jesuit and social ethicist, whose own writing on eugenics during the Third Reich was questionable. Donald Dietrich, however, concluded that, prior to 1933, Muckermann had "insisted that no conflict need arise between racial hygiene and Catholicism as long as racial hygiene was applied to the human species as a whole with all of its races without differentiating between inferior and superior races."[35] In this regard, Lichtenberg never veered in the direction of a negative and racist (*völkisch*) philosophy. Nor did he demean one race while glorifying the Germanic, Nordic race. Instead, he concerned himself with the "white" race in general. Part of his concern at that time also lay in the general anxiety among people throughout Europe who wanted to rebuild the European population after suffering tremendous losses in World War I. Nevertheless, the use of any argument based on race invites misunderstanding and suggests more deviant racial theories, such as those found in the *völkisch* camp.[36] Despite the taint of racism, there is no evidence that Lichtenberg reverted to this line of thinking.

In his public career, Lichtenberg would again make a statement that today appears controversial. On December 10, 1935, in a letter to Hitler, Lichtenberg made a questionable statement protesting a new edition of a nineteenth-century anti-Catholic tract, *Der Pfaffenspiegel*, written by Otto von Corvin-Wiersbitzki, and repudiated another work, *What the Christian Does Not Know about Christianity*, by E. K. Heidemann.[37] In his request for a prohibition of these works, Lichtenberg stated that the newest research had determined that Corvin was "of non-Aryan background."[38] In his letter, Lichtenberg did not elaborate on this point. Nevertheless, Lichtenberg has been criticized for these comments.[39] Such judgments, however, are premature because other comments on the work, such as the February 28, 1937, pulpit proclamation against *Der Pfaffenspiegel* in the archdiocese of Munich and Freising, were more critical of Jews. For example, point 2 of the proclamation read, "Otto von Corvin-Wierzbitzki, who compiled this book . . . from writing that is hostile to the Church, was an adventurer and revolutionary, . . . a Free Mason and a hater of Germans, a friend of Jews and of Marxists and Communists. Jews do good business with his books, Marxists and Communists consider it a quick promotional material to disseminate their corrupting ideas."[40] In his letter, Lichtenberg did not link Jews with Communists; nor did he identify them as distributors of anti-Church propaganda. In addition, it was common among the German Catholics of Lichtenberg's day to group secular Jews with liberals and even Communists and to see them all as working against the endeavors of the Catholic Church. Much of this stems from the belief that, during the Weimar Republic, Jews made up a large percentage of the Social Democratic and Communist parties—parties considered hostile to the Catholic Church.[41] In this regard, in 1937, Lichtenberg could simply have been pointing out the irony of the situation to Hitler: that the Nazis, who had persecuted and vilified Jewish people, chose to utilize a book by a "so-called" Jewish author to attack the Catholic Church—a denomination within Christianity that Hitler earlier had argued would form a basis for the Third Reich.

Despite these comments, the majority of Lichtenberg's statements regarding Jews and other persecuted groups were favorable. Whether he focused his criticism on contraception or on a more politically charged matter, Lichtenberg was never afraid to raise his voice to confront any issue that contradicted Church teaching, infringed on the rights of the Church, or was incompatible with his conscience. This critical posture included events outside of Germany. For example, on May 11, 1928, Lichtenberg wrote to the Mexican Ambassador in Berlin, protesting the persecution of the Catholic Church in that country.[42] Lichtenberg, however, did not limit his protest to written letters. He also put his words into action. In November 1929, the Ludendorff Tannenberg Association, a nationalistic, anti-Semitic, anti-Catholic group under the leadership of General Erich Ludendorff, held an open meeting in the Hohenzollern Festival Hall. That evening, a Mr. Ziegler made a speech entitled the "History and Aims of the Jesuit Order," and a Mr. Ullert presented "Why Does Ludendorff Fight against Rome?"[43]

Upon hearing of the open invitation of the association, Lichtenberg invited a group of men from his parish to attend the event with him. As soon as Litchenberg entered the room, an official of the Ludendorff Association recognized him and invited him to sit on the stage with the speakers. He accepted the invitation. After listening to one of the speakers for a period of time, Lichtenberg grew tired of the repeated insults "against the Jews, against the Jesuits and against the Church" and especially the mockery of the Host, in which the "White Pope" was allegedly adored. He rose and took over the floor from the speaker, answering each claim, point by point. By the end of the evening, the majority of the association's members had left the hall while the remaining Catholics broke out in song, proclaiming their fidelity to the Church.[44] On November 13, 1929, immediately following this event, Lichtenberg wrote Reich President Hindenburg not only about the Charlottenburg meeting but also about the need to prohibit the distribution of *The Secrets of the Jesuit Quest for Power and Its End,* a book written by General Ludendorff and his wife, Mathilde Spiess Ludendorff.[45] Three days later, Dr. Meissner, the chief of the presidential chancellery, replied to Lichtenberg's letter and stated that there was nothing the Reich president could do to relieve the situation or stop the book from being distributed.[46]

Lichtenberg maintained his fighting spirit as the Nazis rose to power. In October 1931, as a chancery official, Lichtenberg took responsibility for enforcing the diocesan prohibition against the distribution of the sacraments to members of the NSDAP. Despite his bishop's hesitancy, Lichtenberg took a hard-line interpretation.

Once Hitler came into power, Lichtenberg had to face even greater problems and choices. One such case arose in March 1933, upon the announcement of an official government boycott of shops and businesses owned by German Jews that was to take place on April 1. When approached by Oscar Wassermann, director of Deutsche Bank in Berlin and president of the Inter-Denominational Working Group for Peace, for a letter to see Cardinal Bertram (so that Wassermann could request the Church's intervention in the boycott), Lichtenberg answered in the affirmative. Bertram, however, viewed the issue as outside the Catholic Church's sphere of concern and refused to encourage his fellow bishops to intervene.[47] Again in November of the same year, Lichtenberg supported another effort to assist "non-Aryans"; however, this group—the Reich Association of Christian German Citizens of Non-Aryan or Not Purely Aryan Descent—as its title suggested, limited itself to the concerns of Jews who had converted to Christianity.[48] Nevertheless, Lichtenberg spoke at the group's gathering of November 3 and declared that "the Catholic Church sees in every baptized person a completely worthy member of the mystical body of Christ."[49]

Lichtenberg's actions did not go unnoticed; nor did his past history as a Center Party representative place him in a positive light in the eyes of the Nazi government. In the summer of 1933, in conjunction with the July 5, 1933, disbandment of the Center Party, the Gestapo conducted a search of Lichtenberg's home. Afterward, it interrogated him and issued a warning.[50] Nevertheless, this action did not deter his fighting spirit, or convince him to keep his opinions to himself. Instead, it appears that the search and interrogation only deepened his opposition to the Nazi regime.

Lichtenberg's resolute stance against Nazism revealed itself especially in connection with his role as a diocesan chancery official. In his notes of June 24–26, 1936, on diocesan business, Father Walter Adolph recorded that there was a difference of opinion among the chancery officials concerning how to deal with the state. Adolph noted: "Father [Paul] Weber and Father [Georg] Köhler were therefore directly and indirectly always antagonists of Father [Heinrich] Heufers and Lichtenberg, who, for the most part, saw the difficulties of the Church in the light of fundamental considerations and, accordingly, supported the sharpest defense measures in all areas."[51] Adolph attributed Weber's and Köhler's more reticent maneuvers in church-state affairs to their friendship with Father Eduard Gehrmann, S.V.D., who served from 1930 to 1945 as personal secretary to the Vatican Nuncio to Germany, Cesare Orsenigo.[52] Both Gehrmann and

Orsenigo were quite sympathetic to National Socialism. Adolph observed that the Vatican embassy, through the nuncio and his staff, "played a key role in the Berlin chancery."[53] Lichtenberg, however, did not let the reservations of his fellow priests affect his own judgment. On his own, he took a more confrontational posture against the regime.

On July 14, 1933, the Reich cabinet passed not only the Reich-Vatican concordat but also the Law for the Prevention of Hereditary Diseased Offspring, which legalized compulsory sterilization of anyone who suffered from hereditary disease, physical deformity, or alcoholism.[54] The Reich government, however, did not immediately promulgate the new sterilization law that was to go into effect the following year. Instead, it chose to wait eleven days until the Vatican signed the concordat on July 20, 1933, because the law was in direct contradiction to Catholic teaching.[55] It seems clear that the government anticipated opposition from the churches. The Fulda bishops' conference delegated Bishop Wilhelm Berning of Osnabrück and Bishop Conrad Gröber of Freising, both of whom were more open than their fellow bishops to the Nazi state in the early years of Nazi rule, to make known to the state the concerns of the Catholic Church over this issue. On November 3, 1933, they met with Dr. Rudolf Buttmann, director of cultural policy in the interior ministry, along with ten other Reich officials, and sought a compromise with the law.[56] They were able to obtain only two concessions. The first exempted from sterilization individuals who fell into one of the categories stated above but only if they would voluntarily "commit themselves to an institution, or who were already confined." The second exempted Catholic physicians "from having to perform or assist in the operations if they found this objectionable on grounds of conscience."[57]

On January 1, 1934, with the noted changes, the law went into effect. Because it created a great deal of confusion among the Catholic laity and because Rome objected to the law's contents, the German episcopacy decided to add a paragraph against sterilization to the annual pastoral letter on the sanctity of marriage. On the second Sunday following the Feast of the Epiphany, the priests of Germany read this summary of *Casti Connubii* from their pulpits. In Berlin, Lichtenberg helped coordinate the pulpit message, which read, "The promulgated principles of Christian moral law apply to believers with respect to the question of sterilization. According to the directives of the Holy Father we remind you that: you are not allowed to have yourself sterilized nor to order sterilizations for another person. That is the teaching of the Catholic Church."[58] On January 13, 1933, a day prior to the reading of the statement, Walter Conrad of the Ministry of Interior, after consultation with Wilhelm Frick, the interior minister, approached Lichtenberg and requested that he negotiate a more "moderate formulation" of the planned statement. After a period of silence, Lichtenberg replied, "Why is confrontation on both sides always postponed? It will certainly come!" Conrad found Lichtenberg resistant to his overtures and—worse—with an "iron will to fight." Finally, Lichtenberg gave way and promised to talk with Cardinal Bertram; however, three hours later, the monsignor called him back and relayed that "the wording" would remain "intact."[59]

This is not to suggest that every priest agreed with the resoluteness of Lichtenberg or with the Church's stance on the new sterilization law. The example of Father Johannes Strehl, pastor of St. Peter and St. Paul Church in Potsdam, who wrote to the Gestapo on January 15, 1934, denouncing Lichtenberg and other chancery officials for their role in ordering the addition of the paragraph on sterilization to the pastoral letter is testimony to this fact. Fortunately for Lichtenberg and his colleagues, nothing directly resulted from Strehl's denunciation, although the sterilization controversy was hardly over. Furthermore, a great deal of correspondence ensued between the Reich government, the German bishops, and the Holy See over this issue. Nevertheless, despite the reiteration of the Church's position against sterilization in this correspondence, the Nazi government, until its demise, continued its policy of forced sterilization.[60]

On July 7, 1935, Frick went public in Münster with his threats against the Catholic Church for its continued opposition to the sterilization law. He stated that the Reich government was not going "to tolerate such sabotage of the Reich law," which was "binding for everyone in the state, including the members of the Catholic Church."[61] A week later, on July 15, *L'Osservatore Romano* published an article questioning the validity of the concordat in light of these accusations and in view of the recent activity of the German state against Catholic institutions and organizations. The article questioned the right of the state to require a Catholic to follow a law "even if it contradict[ed] divine law." *L'Osservatore Romano* also reiterated article 32 of the concordat, which upheld the right of priests and religious to teach the dogmatic and moral principles of the Church that, therefore, challenged the tenets of the sterilization law.[62]

Most dioceses published the *L'Osservatore Romano* article in their *Amtsblatt* and ordered it read from the pulpit.[63] In Berlin, Lichtenberg took the responsibility of ordering the article to be read from the pulpit on Sunday, July 21, 1935.[64] An SA man, Werner B., attested that in his church, St. Paul, Berlin-Moabit, the priest read the article, which Werner B. mistakenly attributed to Lichtenberg, and then "dramatically" ended the proclamation with the Lord's Prayer "for peace between state and church."[65]

Three days after the article was read in the majority of Catholic churches, Heydrich sent a letter to Hans Kerrl, the minister of church affairs, requesting that charges be brought against Lichtenberg for violating the law against treacherous attacks on state and party.[66] Kerrl never pursued charges against Lichtenberg, but the controversy over reading the July 1935 article did not end there. Lichtenberg received reports that several parishes did not follow his order to read the article on the assigned date.[67] Refusing to ignore this fact, Lichtenberg immediately ordered the reading of the article at all masses (on Sunday, July 28), in those parishes where it had not been done. He threatened to suspend priests who refused to comply and stated, "Personal differences of opinion must certainly stand back, making way for the strictest of discipline, particularly in this dangerous time."[68]

The same month that the *L'Osservatore Romano* article appeared, Father Walter Adolph, in his role as editor of the Catholic newspaper of the Berlin diocese, received a report detailing the horrors that took place in the concentration camp of Esterwegen.[69] Specifically, the report detailed the use of corporal punishment in the camp and the actions of the guards who conducted "totally uncontrolled" beatings of prisoners in the guards' barracks. It also questioned the events surrounding the killing of both Social Democrat and Communist prisoners. In addition, it spoke not only of the guards who had confiscated and destroyed rosaries, Bibles, and prayer books belonging to camp prisoners but also of the conditions experienced by Jewish prisoners, who suffered more than the other inmates and were forced to transport manure and clean out toilet waste with their hands.[70] Adolph passed the report on to Lichtenberg in the Berlin chancery. The contents of the report greatly disturbed Lichtenberg, who felt the diocese had to act. Consequently, he took full responsibility for presenting the report to the government, placing his own name at the top and addressing it to the Prussian Ministry of Interior with a request for "inspection and remedies." This was an especially dangerous move, because the plain and explicit contents of the report condemned the concentration camp. Determined that the report be placed in the right hands so that action could be taken to alleviate the situation, Lichtenberg did not send the letter by post. Instead, he delivered it in person to the Prussian interior ministry and asked to speak directly with Göring, who refused his request. Instead, a lower official met with Lichtenberg and received the report. Although Lichtenberg never received a response, Göring's ministry nevertheless took the protest seriously.[71]

On September 27, 1935, after an investigation into the claims of the report on Esterwegen, the Prussian Gestapo reported their findings to Göring.[72] Naturally, the Gestapo disagreed with the contents of the report and upheld the concentration camp system. Theodor Eicke, SS inspector of concentration camps, took the report as a personal affront and as an attack on his "camps." Then he personally answered it with a letter that attacked not only Lichtenberg but also the work of the Catholic Church in general. To Eicke, as to many convinced National Socialists, the Catholic Church was a force that continued to work in all directions against the state. Eicke even requested preventive detention for Lichtenberg for violating the law against treacherous attacks on the state and party so that,

while in detention, Lichtenberg could "for himself witness in camp Esterwegen the order and cleanliness and therefore be encouraged to introduce
this order as a model for his Church affairs."[73] For undisclosed reasons,
however, the courts decided not to pursue any action against Lichtenberg.

Giving the Esterwegen report to the Gestapo revealed Lichtenberg's
growing concern for non-Catholics and his fight against the state's infringement on human rights. Recently, Terry Parssinen made the assertion
that, in September 1938, Lichtenberg had grown so weary of the state's illegal actions that he met with a group of high-ranking German military
officers who were contemplating a stand against Hitler's drive toward
war and were advocating tyrannicide. Parssinen relied on evidence
from a very questionable witness, so it is uncertain whether this meeting ever took place. Though Lichtenberg detested Hitler, his party, and
state, there is no other evidence to corroborate that the monsignor ever
espoused murder.[74] Instead, Lichtenberg preferred to make his protests
public through legal means. For example, in November 1938, immediately following the events of *Reichskristallnacht,* in St. Hedwig Cathedral, Lichtenberg ascended the steps leading to the pulpit and, from
there, in a bold and clear voice, publicly proclaimed, "We know what
happened yesterday. We do not know what tomorrow holds. However,
we have experienced what happened today. Outside, the synagogue
burns. That is also a house of God."[75] After making this prophetic statement, Lichtenberg began to pray daily for both Jews and Christians of
Jewish descent, as well as imprisoned priests and religious persons during the services held in the cathedral. He continued to pray this same
prayer publicly for them until his arrest in 1941.

Lichtenberg not only prayed publicly for Jews and Christians of Jewish
descent but also worked actively in their behalf as advisor to the *Hilfswerk
beim Bischöflichen Ordinariat Berlin* (Relief Agency of the Berlin
Chancery).[76] In this role, Lichtenberg often wrote letters of recommendation to help both Christians of Jewish descent and Jews secure employment, often in Church institutions.[77] Lichtenberg also concerned himself
with the measures taken against Jews. For example, on September 6, 1940,
he wrote to the Reich Air Defense Association of Berlin to protest a December 14, 1939, decree against segregating air raid shelters. When he did
not receive a favorable answer, he wrote a second draft, calling for a direct
repeal of the decree. It is unclear from the evidence whether Lichtenberg
ever sent the draft.[78]

During the same period that Lichtenberg concerned himself with the
plight of Christians of Jewish descent and Jews, he also received a visit
from a woman who believed that the state had murdered her son as part
of its euthanasia program. Authorized officially by Hitler in an order back-
dated September 1, 1939, and called *Aktion T-4,* the program was designed
to rid the state of all "life unworthy of life." This designation included the

institutionalized, handicapped, and so-called asocials. [79] The woman's thirty-eight-year-old son had been institutionalized for eighteen years but, on his mother's request, had received permission to leave the institution and live with her. Before institutional officials made the final arrangements, they transferred him to another institution that the mother described as "only a collecting place for those 'sentenced to death.'" There, she believed, someone had murdered her son and burned his body before informing her that her son had died from "lip boils and meningitis."[80]

By 1941, rumors about the *T-4* program were circulating throughout Germany. On August 3, 1941, Bishop Clemens von Galen of Münster clearly and forcefully spoke out against euthanasia during a sermon delivered in St. Lambert's Church in Münster.[81] On August 26, 1941, Lichtenberg, encouraged by Galen's words and the mother's concerns, and outraged at the attack on life through the euthanasia program, chose to write a letter of protest directly to Reich Führer physician, Dr. Leonardo Conti. Lichtenberg not only accused Conti of direct involvement in the murders but also questioned their legality. He described to Conti the story of the mother and her son, repeating the familiar story known to thousands of families who had received notice that a family member had died in an institution. He then demanded that Conti account for the crimes" that state workers "committed by your order or with your approval," which challenged the "Lord over life and death to bring revenge upon the German people."[82] Lichtenberg also sent copies of the letter to the Reich chancellery, the Ministry of Interior, and the Gestapo. Because a response to his inquiry would have infringed upon the presumed secrecy of the *Aktion T-4* program, Lichtenberg never received a reply.

The prayers for persecuted Jews and prisoners and the letter of protest against euthanasia sent to Conti are only two of many examples of Lichtenberg's entanglement with the state. On November 4, 1940, Lichtenberg further revealed his rejection of the Nazi weltanschauung in a private correspondence with Karl Adam, a professor of theology at the University of Tübingen and priest of the diocese of Rottenburg.[83] The heart of this combative correspondence pertained to a lecture Adam had given at Aachen. On December 10, 1939, according to Aachen diocesan records, Adam spoke to more than 1,000 people in a lecture entitled "The Spiritual Situation of German Catholicism."[84] Adam attempted to encourage German Roman Catholicism to respond to the signs of the times, namely, to what was "positive" in National Socialism, to prevent Christianity from disintegrating within the Third Reich. In part, Adam did this in an attempt to check the influence of the German Faith Movement, a neopagan group that was attempting to form a third major religion in Germany, led by Wilhelm Hauer and favored by Nazi Party ideologist Alfred Rosenberg, among others.[85] The Nazi state favored this movement. Adam also feared that the state might disassociate itself from Catholicism because of the constant antagonisms between the two. Adam argued that "we in our German fatherland have before us a widespread, a weary, withered Christianity, a Christianity so barren, weak, and empty that one is allowed to speak of death throes of Christianity, and that into this vacuum can pour a new weltanschauung, a non-Christian and anti-Christian faith movement without encountering serious resistance."[86]

Thus, while criticizing neopaganism, Adam also sought to show how Christianity and National Socialism could be compatible. This, of course, was not Adam's first foray into this area. Previously, he had discussed this latent compatibility on two separate occasions. First, in 1933, when he published an article, "German Ethnicity and Catholic Christianity," in *Theologische Quartalschrift,* in which he discussed the question of race and specifically addressed the relationship of National Socialism to nationalism and Christianity.[87] He did so again, in 1934, in Stuttgart, at which time he criticized the German Faith Movement and, by focusing on the concept of *Volksgemeinschaft,* attempted to create a bridge between Christianity and National Socialism.[88]

Adam discovered that the National Socialist ideology concerning the formation of a community of people had a direct link to neo-Romanticism, *Lebensphilosophie,* a philosophy of life, and to the new theology of Catholic systematic theologians.[89] These ideas fostered an "organic view of reality in which all parts were seen within a whole." In a similar vein, Adam believed that Roman Catholicism also aspired "for the union of all of its members in a fellowship transcending national boundaries."[90] In this context, *Lebensphilosophie,* espoused by Adam, which included aspects of the National Socialist weltanschauung (and was itself grounded in racist ideology and imbued with the new theology of Roman Catholicism that searched for language to express the bond of community experienced in the sacramental life of the Church) could give birth in some cases to a problematic and even racist theology.

In 1933, Adam found meaning in the community ideology of National Socialism and chose to use it to restate the ideals and mission of the Church. In many instances, he adopted the vocabulary of National Socialism and incorporated terms such as blood (*Blut*), soil (*Boden*), and ethnicity (*Volkstum*) into his theological writing. Of course, in 1933 and early 1934, Adam might not have thoroughly contemplated the impact of embracing such ideas. At that time, the potential terror and horrors of Nazism were not evident to most of the German population. By 1939, however, Adam's continued overtures to National Socialism were neither understandable nor explicable. Despite his concern over the fate of Christianity, one wonders how Adam could fail to note with alarm the Nazi movement's measures against the Catholic Church, including the arrest and imprisonment of many clergy, religious, and laity. It is also alarming that he was not appalled by *Reichskristallnacht* and the persecution of Catholics of Jewish descent, Jews, and other undesirables.

In 1939, neither event seemed to have vexed Adam. Instead, he was determined to reveal the Germanness of Catholicism. Adam argued that there was a German *Ethos* that offered a "particular moral outlook toward German reality." For Adam, this *Ethos* was rooted in a human nature that was substantial and, therefore, could exist in itself. Adam argued that, for Germans, this human nature was a subsistent German nature upon which the accidental Christian character—a gift from God—was added to the human estate. According to him, Germans were not simply "Christians and Catholics as such, but German Christians, German Catholics. This 'German factor' is not something that is merely an external addition to our existence as Christians, . . . but the reverse is the case: it is our *natura germanica* which constitutes the substantial, permanent, underlying factor and Christian existence as a special gift from God is added to this original and primeval nature as an 'accident.'"[91] Therefore, he argued, for German Catholics there was "no other home than our own German *Volksgemeinschaft.*"

German blood also was and remained "the substantial carrier of our Christian reality." And "the very same German blood" tied Catholics together with all of those who were not of our belief, "to an insoluble community of blood *[Blutgemeinschaft].*"[92] Here, race became a central linking factor for Adam. Likewise, Adam tried to create a theoretical tie between German Catholics and Protestants. This was essential for him, because he believed Catholics were captive to the past and were isolated from full participation in German cultural life and, consequently, treated as second-class Germans.[93] To rectify this situation and to include German Catholics equally in the cultural and intellectual life of Germany, Adam called for the participation of German Catholic seminarians in military service, the "school of manliness." He also called for a greater incorporation of German culture into Catholic theology, the use of the German language in the liturgy, and the promotion of German Catholic saints, churches, chapels, and places of pilgrimage.[94]

Though Adam only meant to address the specific audience present in Aachen, reports and copies of the lecture soon began to circulate throughout Germany. To quell false statements about the content of his lecture, Adam himself even allowed the editor of the *Kolpingsblatt* to publish excerpts.[95] Soon after the lecture, Joseph Joos, editor of the *Westdeutsche Arbeiter-Zeitung,* a member of the Catholic Workers' Movement and former Center Party representative, received a copy of the report on Adam's talk and disseminated its contents to the entire German episcopacy. This report did not portray Adam's comments in a favorable light.[96]

In June 1940, Freiherr Leopold von Nagel, a retired government official and German Catholic, who was also a National Socialist, sent a letter challenging the report passed on by Joos. Nagel attempted to use the contents of Adam's lecture as a rallying cry for "peace between the Church and the

National Socialist–oriented state." To this end, he implored the bishops to put an end to the criticism of Adam.[97] Some time between June and November 1940, Nagel personally brought his concerns regarding Adam's lecture to the chancery of the Berlin diocese. There he met and discussed the issue with Lichtenberg. In the meeting, Nagel not only praised Adam but also pointed out to Lichtenberg that the Gestapo would be investigating those individuals who criticized the Aachen lecture. Following their meeting, Nagel also provided Lichtenberg with a complete transcript of the lecture. Although Lichtenberg was familiar with the lecture and troubled by the reports he had read concerning it, this was the first time he had seen a complete transcript of the address. On November 4, 1940, upon reading the text of Adam's lecture, Lichtenberg became outraged over its contents and, after consulting with a priest friend, wrote directly to the Tübingen theologian with his personal criticism.

Lichtenberg began by pointing out that although Adam had stated at the introduction to his lecture that he wished to provide a clear and explicit explanation of the present situation of German Catholicism, he offered only a "fatal vagueness."[98] Lichtenberg then forcefully challenged Adam's notion that the highest earthly task of German Catholics was their service to the Reich: "A new formulation of our highest earthly tasks! Up to now the old formulation was contained in the answer to the first catechism question: 'Why are you on earth?' . . . Up to now the answer was: 'In order to fulfill the will of God and to become blessed through this activity.'"[99] Lichtenberg recognized that a citizen of a state must acknowledge the right of the state to govern and act as a servant of God for the good of its citizens, but he qualified this point when he asked, "And how is it in the cases in which the secular authority is not 'God's helper for your own good'?" In these cases, Lichtenberg responded, "One must obey God more than man."[100]

Likewise, Lichtenberg challenged Adam's tendency to place the National Socialist weltanschauung and Christianity's revealed truth on the same level. He pointed out that the National Socialists, specifically Adolf Hitler, understood Christianity not as the objective revealed truth but as a mere weltanschauung. He quoted directly from *Mein Kampf* and showed that Hitler had argued that this Christian worldview could only be broken and replaced by a new weltanschauung—namely, National Socialism.[101]

Lichtenberg also criticized Adam's portrayal of German Catholicism as weary, wilted, and unfruitful. Although Lichtenberg understood that Adam had been reacting to the impact of the German Faith Movement and the Nazi weltanschauung as promoted by Rosenberg in German society, he asserted that Adam's use of the term *weltanschauung* reflected the very same Nazi influence. Thus, Lichtenberg charged, in utilizing *weltanschauung* in this fashion, Adam blatantly denied "the fact that the representatives of the new weltanschauung suppress Christian, dogmatic Catholicism and promote a non-Christian and anti-Christian weltanschauung." Lichtenberg then specifically asked Adam: "Is not the *Myth of the Twentieth Century* by Rosenberg favored by the National Socialist weltanschauung? If this *Myth* is a private work, then it is a private work that was imbedded in the cornerstone of the Brown House in Munich and whose author was awarded a 100,000–Reich mark prize by the Führer of the party."[102]

Finally, Lichtenberg rejected how Adam had attempted to intertwine nationalism with German Catholicism, to the point of exalting "German nature." Lichtenberg pointed out that, despite Adam's technical argument, "German nature does not properly speaking exist as 'German nature in itself.'" He added that fixation with national thinking in the Catholic Church could "even be the beginning of a national Church."[103] Lichtenberg reminded Adam that no matter what nation a people belonged to, the teaching and discipline of the Catholic Church remained the same. In addition, he rejected Adam's endorsement of military service for seminarians during peacetime and discarded the emphasis he placed on use of the German language in liturgy.[104] Lichtenberg ended his letter by revealing that he had chosen to write this letter of protest primarily because Adam's lecture had "found approval" with individuals such as Nagel. Lichtenberg also remarked that although the Gestapo might investigate those who criticized Adam's lecture, this threat would not deter him as a "Catholic priest and a German man" to speak his opinion. Nor would it prevent him from writing and taking responsibility for doing so before the Gestapo.[105]

On November 23, 1940, Adam answered his critic in a letter that reflected both his indignation and condescension. Adam referred to Lichtenberg's letter as "irritable" and took every opportunity in his reply to highlight Lichtenberg's failure to understand the themes of the lecture. Adam pointed out that his lecture was not meant for the "larger German public," but only for the audience of "purely mature Catholics." If he had realized that the contents of his lecture would be circulated throughout Germany, he would "have formulated everything with more care in order to prevent malicious misinterpretation." Adam stressed that he had nothing to do with the actions or letter of Nagel.[106]

After these opening comments, Adam addressed Lichtenberg's criticisms in language that revealed, more clearly than ever, his support of the Nazi state. First, Adam agreed with Lichtenberg that fulfilling God's will was correctly the highest task of humankind. Indeed, Adam emphatically stated, "this will is to be fulfilled on earth. . . . The highest earthly worth remains for me—and for those who do not want to be unfaithful to their German blood—the unity of the German *Volk* in the new Reich." Adam then stressed that, even if many officials in the Reich government "engage in anti-Christian Church politics, its 'authority' nevertheless remains my authority that I am obligated 'in conscience' to obey." For Adam, this was an "active obedience," because the people of Germany stood today "in a

'*Volksgemeinschaft,*' of which ancient cultures had no knowledge." Adam then added that "whoever sabotages this *Volksgemeinschaft* directly or indirectly is to me neither a German nor a Christian."[107]

In passing, Adam conceded Lichtenberg's point that "'wherever state authority is not God's accomplice for the good,' one must certainly obey God more than man."[108] Adam, however, questioned what was meant by the term *good* and concluded, "Who can establish with certainty . . . whether the authority here and now is not 'God's accomplice?'" He continued, "How do we know, for example, with certainty that the dissolution of monasteries or schools, etc., is against the will of God? Was the ancient Church not a Church of martyrs without state-legitimated religious instruction, without monasteries, without a Cathedral Chapter and theological departments?"[109] Adam believed that, even an encroachment and attack on Christianity by officials or groups within the government would not justify or authorize Christians in any way "to assume an attitude of resentment against the authority."[110]

After replying to many minute points Lichtenberg had raised, Adam stated, "I am saddened, not because your misinterpretations affect me personally, but because they show me that in the very place in which our leading prelates ought to have their finger on the pulse of time as nowhere else—in the nation's capital—the driving ideas of my lecture are not understood, [and] that even there they do not see, or do not want to see, what German Catholicism is in need of if it is to be in the near future not merely a sanctuary for senile and yellowed human beings, but a viable asset of creative and strong human beings."[111]

Despite Adam's interpretation of Lichtenberg's response, if anyone understood where the Church should bear up against National Socialism, it was Lichtenberg. On November 30, 1940, after receiving Adam's reply, Lichtenberg immediately wrote back to the theologian. He conceded that he may have misinterpreted parts of Adam's letter, but he still stressed that, despite Adam's objections, the theologian did promote a new weltanschauung that was grounded in the realm of politics. Lichtenberg also refuted Adam's previous comment in a letter of May 28, which is no longer extant, in which Adam stated that the "greatest depths of the national movement" were affected "by the Holy Spirit, who moves where he desires."[112] Lichtenberg found that "Karl Adam not only defends, in speech and writing, the justification for a German weltanschauung and a German ethos, but also expresses his conviction that the ultimate depths of the national movement have been touched by the Holy Spirit, which arrives where it wishes to."[113]

The diverse responses by both Adam and Lichtenberg reveal the depth of reaction to the National Socialist state, even at a time when most clerics perceived that the Nazis were working against the Church. What Lichtenberg might have lacked in theological sophistication, he made up for in the genuineness of his response to Adam's lecture and in his desire not only to protect the Catholic Church but also to point out the impossibility of creating a bridge between the National Socialist weltanschauung and Catholic Church teaching. Adam, on the other hand, had allowed himself to be so influenced by the National Socialist milieu that he could not properly discern between what he should accept from the movement's ideology and what he should reject. Perhaps, too, Adam was an opportunist who wished to impress the state with his theological overtures in an effort to retain his teaching chair at Tübingen.

Unlike Adam, Lichtenberg kept his distance from Nazism. Luckily for him, too, his correspondence with Adam did not bring him in direct confrontation with the machinery of the National Socialist state. On the other hand, his anti-Nazi stance and his continued intercessions for the persecuted Jews did. In the fall of 1941, the state finally acted against him. On Friday, August 29, 1941, two Protestant students, Ilse Herbell and Lieselotte Schmachtenberg, decided to enter St. Hedwig Cathedral to view the architecture there. At the time, Lichtenberg was presiding over the daily evening prayer service. While admiring the building, the young women heard Lichtenberg pray for Jews.[114] Upset by the prayer, they immediately left the cathedral. In days that followed, after mulling over what they had heard, they shared their experience with a friend, Jutta Hanke, who encouraged them to report the information to the police. Eventually, Hanke's father, an official in the SS, learned of Lichtenberg's prayers and denounced him.[115]

On October 23, 1941, after several interrogations of Herbell and Schmachtenberg, the Gestapo searched Lichtenberg's home and arrested him, "on account of hostile activity against the state."[116] During the search of his home, Gestapo officers found a copy of *Mein Kampf* with Lichtenberg's annotations and a declaration Lichtenberg had written and planned to read from the pulpit the upcoming Sunday. In the declaration, Lichtenberg reacted against a recently published pamphlet that Goebbels's propaganda office had distributed throughout the Reich in an effort to stir hatred against Jews.[117] In the declaration Lichtenberg wrote, "An anonymous smear sheet against the Jews is being distributed to Berlin houses. This pamphlet states that every German who supports Jews with an ostensibly false sentimentality, be it only through friendly obligingness, practices treason against his *Volk*. Let us not be misled by this un-Christian way of thinking but follow the strict command of Jesus Christ: 'You shall love your neighbor as you love yourself.'"[118]

Both the declaration and the annotated copy of *Mein Kampf* angered the Gestapo officials and fueled their desire to undo the monsignor as they questioned him. Lichtenberg, however, held his own. He declared that, because the weltanschauung of the state, as portrayed in *Mein Kampf,* stood in contrast to Christianity, he must refuse it "as a Catholic priest . . . and also refuse it de facto." In addition, Lichtenberg argued that as a Catholic priest he could not say "yes and Amen to every decree and measure that comes from the government."[119] To underscore his disagreement, he cited his letter to Dr. Conti against euthanasia, but he also pointed out other practices of the National Socialist government with which he could not agree, such as the "elimination of religious instruction from the schools, [the] struggle against the crucifix, prohibition of the sacraments, secularization of marriage, deliberate killing of life allegedly unworthy of life, [and] persecution of the Jews."[120] In regard to the latter, he earlier in the interrogation had stated, "I spiritually oppose the deportation with all its consequences, because it goes against the chief rule of Christianity: 'You should love your neighbor as you love yourself,' and I consider the Jews also my neighbor who have immortally created souls after the image and likeness of God."[121]

During the same interrogation, Lichtenberg also admitted to praying regularly for "the severely harassed non-Aryan Christians, for the Jews, for prisoners in the concentration camps, particularly for the imprisoned priests and religious, especially for the priests of our diocese, for those with lack of faith, for those who despair and attempt suicide, for the millions of nameless and stateless refugees, for the fighters, wounded and dying soldiers on both sides, for the bombed-out cities in allied and enemy land, etc., and also the passage from the general Church prayers for the fatherland, and leaders of the *Volk*."[122] There was also a question as to whether Lichtenberg had prayed for the Bolsheviks. The witnesses remembered him mentioning them in his prayer; however, they admitted that the prayer for Jews greatly distracted their attention.[123] Lichtenberg stated that, although he had not prayed for Bolsheviks, he would have no objections to including a prayer in his daily intercessions "in order to heal their madness."[124]

In further interrogations, Lichtenberg continued in the same vein. When questioned, Lichtenberg supported Clemens von Galen, bishop of Münster, in his condemnation of euthanasia.[125] According to the extant documents, this statement alone was sufficient grounds for arrest and prosecution, because many Nazis considered Galen a traitor to Germany who should be punished.[126] Lichtenberg, however, went further, especially in his answers to questions relating to the notations found in his copy of *Mein Kampf*. Lichtenberg stated that "Hitler is not an infallible prophet. . . . I do not consider Hitler as a prophet sent by God."[127] At the very end of the interrogation that treated Hitler's work, Lichtenberg concluded, "I state with steadfast conviction that the National Socialist ideology is incompatible with the teaching and commands of the Catholic Church."[128] His argument followed the judgment he had made during an earlier interrogation session, when he stated that "if the tendency of the government's decrees and measures goes against the revealed teachings of Christianity and, therefore, goes against my priestly conscience, I must follow my conscience and accept all the consequences that personally arise to me from it."[129]

Lichtenberg had to bear all the consequences of his statements against the policies of the Nazi state. On March 21, 1942, the state district attorney's office in the district court of Berlin charged the already imprisoned Lichtenberg with violation of the pulpit law and the law against treacherous attack on the state and party. This charge stemmed specifically from Lichtenberg's intercessory prayers for Jews and for his written and planned pulpit declaration against the propaganda ministry's anti-Semitic pamphlet. When questioned, Lichtenberg admitted that he had prayed for Jews and had written the declaration and planned to read it in St. Hedwig.[130] For these offenses, the court found Lichtenberg guilty and sentenced him to a two-year prison term.[131] Since October 1941, Lichtenberg had already been imprisoned in Moabit-Berlin pretrial detention center. Now a formal sentence confirmed his captivity and the state transferred him to Tegel Prison.

Lichtenberg's local ordinary, Konrad von Preysing, did not let him suffer these ordeals alone. Instead he kept in regular contact with the monsignor and interceded for him on several occasions.[132] Preysing also kept Pope Pius XII regularly informed about the events surrounding Lichtenberg's arrest, trial, and imprisonment. On October 25, 1941, Preysing wrote to the Pope, informing him of Lichtenberg's arrest for praying for "arrested Jews." They exchanged correspondence over Lichtenberg's plight on several occasions.[133] The pope's nuncio in Germany, Cesare Orsenigo, also worked through the German foreign office to intercede in Lichtenberg's behalf.[134]

Preysing also prayed publicly during a sermon for his imprisoned priest.[135] In addition, Preysing concerned himself greatly with Lichtenberg's "already very shattered health" and even informed the pope about his anxiety over this issue.[136] This was a legitimate concern for Preysing, because Lichtenberg's health had been failing since 1939. In 1941, a doctor noted in a medical certificate that Lichtenberg suffered from a "weak heart muscle, coronary sclerosis and angina" and therefore must "painstakingly" guard himself "against any excitement and overexertion and inappropriate diet."[137] The meager diet and poor living conditions in both Moabit and Tegel only worsened his situation. On November 4, 1941, citing Lichtenberg's failing health, Preysing requested his release from pretrial custody.[138] This request was not granted. Undaunted, Preysing continued to express his concern throughout Lichtenberg's imprisonment. The bishop also visited Lichtenberg and requested that he be allowed to offer him supplementary food.[139] In addition to attempting to assist with Lichtenberg's material needs, Preysing interceded on behalf of Lichtenberg's spiritual needs. On February 17, 1942, Preysing requested permission for Lichtenberg to celebrate the sacrament of the mass in his cell and for himself to bring the needed items from St. Hedwig for the Eucharist.[140]

Before the Gestapo released Lichtenberg from Tegel prison, Preysing visited him to discuss the future. Previously, the Gestapo had approached Preysing and stated that if Lichtenberg would remain silent and accept a prohibition on preaching during wartime, they would allow him freedom upon his release from prison. Preysing told Lichtenberg that he would grant permission for him to abide by such a prohibition. Lichtenberg, however, refused to "surrender to such a promise" and stated, "What better can happen to a person than to die for his holy Catholic faith? Today, I am ready, in fact this hour, to die for it!"[141] Though Lichtenberg realized how weak and frail he was, he returned to the suggestion he had first made during an October 1941 interrogation: he requested that Preysing allow him to accompany the deported Jews and Christians of Jewish descent to Litzmannstadt to serve as a pastoral minister to the people there. Preysing, however, attempted to dissuade him from such an undertaking because of his health. Nevertheless, Lichtenberg pressed onward.[142]

On October 22, 1943, Lichtenberg finally received his release papers from Tegel prison. In his prison file an official noted that, although Lichtenberg was a "worn-out man," he was still an "obstinate, stubborn man."[143] Clearly, he had not lost his will to fight, because he had previously vowed to "fulfill the will of God and remain true to my priestly calling to my last breath" upon his release from prison.[144] Lichtenberg's time in prison, however, left him "severely ill" and weak, according to a certificate of the prison's doctor.[145] Even if he had any fight left in him, the Gestapo saw to it that he would not be free to exercise it in public. Immediately upon his release, Gestapo officials brought him to Wuhlheide, a work camp. There, according to a constable in the police command, Lichtenberg was belittled, forced into a garbage room by a SS man along with a Kapo prisoner, and most probably beaten. In addition, the SS man left him in the garbage room for two days.[146] Finally, on October 28, 1943, the Reich Main Security Administration removed Lichtenberg from the work camp and sent him to a concentration camp on the grounds of public safety.[147] On November 3, 1943, Lichtenberg was transported to Hof, a town on the border of Thuringia and Bavaria, which served as a collecting point for prisoners. He was taken there to await transportation to Dachau concentration camp. While in the former convent of Klarissen that then served as a jail, Lichtenberg became increasingly ill and was transferred to the state hospital nearby. Understanding the seriousness of the situation, a compassionate Catholic doctor called the local parish in Hof, and Father Gehringer came to the hospital and administered the last rites. At 6:00 p.m. on Friday, November 5, 1943, Bernhard Lichtenberg died.[148]

Through his life and ministry and especially by his conscious choice to face imprisonment and ultimately death for the sake of his faith, Bernhard Lichtenberg chose the path of thousands of martyrs before him, both Christian and non-Christian, who chose to stand up for their beliefs and for those who had no one to defend them. Lichtenberg alone understood that the true nature of his faith's command to love neighbor reached beyond religious borders. He was able to come to this conclusion and make the choices he did make from within the traditions of his own Berlin Catholic milieu. His early career as a priest-politician reveals that he was truly a child of his age, resorting to cultural and religious prejudices implicit in his remarks concerning Protestants, birth control, and Jews. Lichtenberg was also not a proponent of any new theological movement. Rather, he was rooted in the traditional Catholic piety and faith tradition. Coming from this particular perspective, Lichtenberg, nevertheless, was acutely aware of the destructive onslaught of Nazism against Christian morality and chose to alert people to its ravage and desolation. In choosing a path that would ultimately lead to his death, Lichtenberg consciously decided to give witness to his faith. His willingness to be deported to a ghetto to minister to Catholics of Jewish descent and to Jews also revealed internal growth and a conscious decision on his part to accept death as a consequence of his earlier actions in behalf of others, whether Christian or not. In the history of modern Catholicism in Nazi Germany, Bernhard Lichtenberg was truly an exception.

Conclusion

During the turbulent years of Hitler's rule, German Catholicism did not escape the evils of Nazism unscathed. Ruthless Nazi officials with unlimited state power compelled both ordained and lay members of the Church to find their place among the loyal ranks of fellow German compatriots. As a result, German Catholics had to weigh, among other things, the disparity between the spiritual inadequacy of National Socialism and the questionable legitimacy of its extreme nationalism. Amid the flurry of events surrounding 1933 and the popular outcry for a revitalized state economy, which legal authorities had not only addressed but a charismatic chancellor and Führer had launched, German Catholics had to make some hard choices, both personal and political.

In this work, I have focused on one group of clerics, the priests of the Berlin diocese, in an effort to examine the peculiarities of their pastoral choices in relation to the Nazi state and the effects these choices had on the spiritual well-being of their parishioners. On a daily basis, these pastoral operants had to deal with both a diverse parish population and a plethora of Nazi officials who increasingly restricted their local ministry. The complexities of these priests' lives and their own outright rejection of, ambivalence toward, or acceptance of the Nazi state directly affected the lives of their active parishioners, who heard them preach, teach, and evaluate the complex relationship of the Catholic faith to the ever-changing political world in which they lived and worshipped.

It is not scientifically possible to gauge the effectiveness of the words and actions of the priests who challenged some aspect or law of the state. We know, for example, that no major protest against the state flowed from the sermons of a priest in the Berlin diocese or from the letters of a bishop.

What no one can adequately appraise, however, is the effect of one priest's injunction to love one's neighbor, for example, immediately after an event as monstrous as *Reichskristallnacht*. Might the priest's remark have roused a believer to view the act of desecration differently? Perhaps his words might also have provoked some other listeners to inquire about the welfare of Jewish neighbors. Or, using another example, possibly the arrest and imprisonment of a clergyman (like Bernhard Lichtenberg) might have moved a mother to rethink an earlier decision she made to let her child participate in a Hitler Youth rally. Indeed, these conjectural examples are but minor refractions, overt forms of *Resistenz* alongside the underlying terror of National Socialism. Yet, by encouraging their parishioners (by word and deed, whether directly or indirectly) to examine the state critically, these priests provided their parishioners with a counter-worldview quite antithetical to National Socialism. Unfortunately, it was not always a worldview free of extreme nationalism or anti-Semitism. Nevertheless, such clerical acts of *Resistenz* provided an alternative space for Catholics to challenge the all-pervasive momentum of Nazism and its fatal ideology.

One of the greatest satisfactions of a priest is to have his words accepted eagerly by his parishioners. As noted above, Berlin Catholics were not—as a whole—practitioners of their faith. Mass attendance was unusually low because of the transient nature of many single Catholics in the German metropolis and the larger number of working-class Catholics who did not always have the time to meet their religious obligations fully. In addition, the diasporic nature of the diocese made it difficult for many Catholics to worship on a regular basis. Still, the priests of Berlin did their best to break down these barriers and reach out to their parishioners. They would visit homes, produce newsletters, and encourage other Catholics to invite their neighbors to join them at mass and parish functions. Priests worked hard at promoting their faith because for them there was no other more dynamic reality in the world. For an ordained priest, the Church and the parish were the center of the universe.

In the 1930s and 1940s, Catholic priests the world over saw themselves as primarily sacramental ministers, specifically serving members of their parishes. In the seminary, theology professors taught future priests to view themselves as God's special instruments through which Christ would mediate and dispense divine grace in the sacraments. The seminary professors who trained Berlin's future priests also taught their charges to focus primarily on internal issues that directly affected their Church—not on extraneous side issues such as national or international politics. Indeed, despite the nationwide presence of the Catholic Center Party and the active involvement of civic-minded priests within the party, seminary faculty saw no reason to encourage future priests to engage in the affairs of the state—except when the government or some other organization directly threatened the rights of the Church. In other words, future priests were to focus their energies on the liberties of the eternal hereafter and not on the restrictions of the temporary present.

Priests were also taught to accept suffering in the spirit of the saints and, in the event of persecution, to elect martyrdom. Even the staunch anti-Nazi Konrad von Preysing emphasized this type of spirituality in his writing, especially during the war. Thus, by granting the Catholic Church the exclusive right to procure guarantees for the exercise and protection of its divine mission (while, at the same time, allowing the state—by making provisions for it—to curtail any activities that it deemed outside the Church's spiritual realm), the Reich-Vatican concordat solidified a unique understanding of Church as a society complete in itself, an understanding that made its communal existence for others (i.e., non-Catholics) less central to its sacramental mission for Catholics. Such a belief also elevated the clergy of the Catholic Church to a very lofty but narrow position of moral influence and power. For believing and practicing Catholics, this, in effect, meant that the parish priest held their very salvation in his hands. Finally, anything that challenged this exclusive system of beliefs, including National Socialist ideology, was anathema.

Mindful of this, I have shown that the very existence of the Catholic Church and the perpetuation of its inner and outer ecclesiastical life in Germany constituted a formidable pattern of resistance against the Nazi state. The clergy not only provided pastoral ministry to the faithful, but their particular social presence also acted as an interior countermeasure to the pervasive hegemony of Nazi doctrine. This form of resistance was all the more menacing when seen in light of Nazi racist politics and, more specifically, when overshadowed by the edicts of the minister of propaganda, Joseph Goebbels, who challenged every German citizen to dedicate himself or herself totally to the Nazi state and ideology.

One of the pivotal factors that weakened the resistance of the Berlin Church to National Socialism, however, was the lack of consistent leadership. The hesitance of Bishop Schreiber to condemn National Socialism early on and his subsequent illness and untimely death during the Nazi seizure of power created a provisional void in episcopal leadership that Monsignor Steinmann failed to fill adequately. Later, Bishop Bares, Schreiber's successor, failed to fill this gap by neglecting in his short time as bishop to provide the kind of spiritual leadership or resolve needed to challenge National Socialism. Finally, in 1935, when Preysing arrived in Berlin, the Nazis were already firmly in power. Nevertheless, it was up to him to negotiate a path that not only protected the rights of the Church but also challenged the state when it either encroached upon the Church's rights or engaged in immoral actions. Preysing did his utmost to lead the priests of his diocese boldly, but he received little support from the members of the Fulda bishops' conference.

Though well informed of the political situation between the Church and state, the bishops normally left parish priests alone to make their own decisions in their local relations with state officials. Likewise, as Susan Zuccotti has noted in her work on the Vatican and the Holocaust, both Pius XI and Pius XII also provided bishops and priests with few specific guidelines.[1] Instead, priests on a daily basis were left alone to negotiate with Nazi officials and with the harsh realities of the state. As in any human situation, some priests were bolder and more courageous than others in upholding and sustaining their Christian faith and speaking out against moral injustices. A few, however, failed miserably in this task, and some even openly embraced National Socialism.

The real failure of the period is not to be found in the response of committed individuals but rather in the institution itself, the Church, which was unable to enlarge its communal mission and view itself as a church for others, especially for Jews. Tragically, the Church would not and could not formally make this shift a historical reality or possibility until the 1960s, when Vatican II issued *Nostra Aetate,* which called for recognition of Judaism and the rejection of all forms of anti-Semitism.[2] Nevertheless, even during the Third Reich, there were still unique individuals such as Bernhard Lichtenberg who saw the evils of National Socialism and, in highly motivated ways, followed both the commands of his Church and the encouragement of his bishop to love his neighbor, even at the expense of his own life. Unfortunately, during the National Socialist rule, far too few individuals were willing to embrace the ramifications of this teaching of love and to risk their lives for the survival of others.

Notes

Introduction

1. In 1946, Pope Pius XII would name Konrad von Preysing a cardinal of the Catholic Church. Therefore, because this work deals primarily with the years 1933–1945, I use the term *bishop* in reference to Preysing's rank within the hierarchy.

2. Joseph Goebbels in March 1938 to Austrian Artists, *Reichspost*, 90 (March 30, 1938), cited in Anzeneder and Kupfer, "Kirchenkampf im Erzbistum Bamberg," 151.

3. Volk, "Der Widerstand der katholischen Kirche," 126.

4. Dietrich, "Catholic Resistance in the Third Reich," 182.

5. Broszat, "Resistenz und Widerstand," 698.

6. Drapac, "Religion in a Dechristianized World," 389–416; and *War and Religion*.

7. Dirks, "Katholischen zwischen Anpassung und Widerstand," 141–42; Hehl, *Nationalsozialistische Herrschaft*, 41; and Hürten, "Katholische Kirche und Widerstand," 187.

8. Hehl, *Nationalsozialistische Herrschaft*, 41.

9. Lönne, "Motive des katholischen Widerstandes," 178; and Löwenthal, "Widerstand im totalen Staat," 627.

10. Ruhm von Oppen, "Laity and Churches in the Third Reich," 38.

11. Hellwig, "A Catholic Scholar's Journey through the Twentieth Century," 73. A special word of thanks to Robert A. Krieg for this reference.

12. Breuer, "Kirche und Fremde unter dem Hakenkreuz," 183–93; "Kirchliche Opposition im NS-Staat," 297–313; and *Verordneter Wandel?*

13. Breuer, "Kirche und Fremde unter dem Hakenkreuz," 184.

14. See Conway, *The Nazi Persecution of the Churches*; Denzler, *Widerstand oder Anpassung?* Denzler and Fabricius, *Christen und Nationalsozialisten*; Lewy, *The Catholic Church and Nazi Germany*; and Scholder, *The Churches and the Third Reich*, vols. 1 and 2. Denzler's newest work, *Widerstand ist nicht das richtige Wort*, attempts to correct this issue.

15. Lease, "Denunciation as a Tool of Ecclesiastical Control," 819; and "The History of 'Religious' Consciousness," 463 and 468.

16. Schmiechen-Ackermann, "Katholische Diaspora zwischen Rückzug und Selbstbehauptung in der NS-Zeit," 465.

17. Krose, ed., *Kirchliches Handbuch für das katholische Deutschland,* 19:176.

18. See Fandel, *Konfession und Nationalsozialismus;* and Kershaw, *Popular Opinion and Political Dissent in the Third Reich.*

19. Interview with Father Heribert Rosal, Berlin, November 14, 1996, in which he stressed how fundamental ministry was for the priest. In an interview, Father Johannes Piotrowski, Berlin, November 21, 1996, also emphasized the importance of ministry and contact with the congregation for the priest. See also Spicer, "Selective Resistance," 71–88.

1: Initial Encounters

1. *Märkische Volks-Zeitung,* June 22, 1931.

2. Ibid., June 24, 1931.

3. Kirk, *The Longman Companion to Nazi Germany,* 22.

4. Pastoral Directives of Bishop Schreiber of Berlin Concerning National Socialism, March 21, 1931, in Klein, *Berolinen Canonizationis Servi Dei Bernardi Lichtenberg: Sacerdotis Saecularis in Odium Fidei, Uti Fertur, Interfecti* (1875–1943), 2:39–41.

5. *Ecclesiastica,* October 25, 1930, 421–27.

6. Noakes and Pridham, eds., *Nazism A History in Documents* 1:16.

7. Höhle, *Die Gründung des Bistums Berlin,* 217–18.

8. *8 Uhr Abendblatt,* October 4, 1930.

9. *Montag-Morgen,* October 13, 1930.

10. *La Croix,* October 21, 1930, and *Germania,* October 23, 1930.

11. *Ecclesiastica,* April 4, 1931, 138–39 (reprinted from Cologne's *Lokalanzeiger,* March 21, 1931).

12. *Westdeutscher Beobachter,* March 17, 1931.

13. *Ecclesiastica,* April 4, 1931, 138–39.

14. Koß, "Christian Schreiber," 93.

15. See Schreiber's speech before the Catholic *Volkshochschule* in Berlin: "Die Not der Zeit und die Sendung der Kirche," *Germania,* October 31, 1931, and "Katholische Caritashilfe für den Winter 1932/33," September 15, 1932, *Amtsblatt des Bischöflichen Ordinariats Berlin,* September 24, 1932, 82.

16. Koß, "Christian Schreiber," 93–94; and "Bischof Christian Schreiber, der KV und die NSDAP," 50–52.

17. *Berlin Börsen-Courier,* March 25, 1931, BArch B R5101, 21675, f. 3.

18. Pastoral Directives of Bishop Schreiber of Berlin Concerning National Socialism, March 21, 1931, in Klein, *Berolinen Canonizationis,* 2:39.

19. Pastoral Directives of the Bishop of Berlin concerning National Socialism, March 21, 1931, in Klein, *Berolinen Canonizationis,* 2:40.

20. For a discussion of the Catholic clergy's involvement in politics see, Anderson, *Windthorst: A Political Biography;* Blackbourn, *Class, Religion and Local Politics in Wilhelmine Germany;* Ross, *Beleaguered Tower* and *The Failure of Bismarck's Kulturkampf;* Sperber, *Popular Catholicism in Nineteenth Century Germany;* Sun, *Before the Enemy Is within Our Walls;* Webersinn, "Prälat Karl Ulitzka," 146–205.

21. Stockums, *Das Priestertum,* English translation: *The Priesthood,* 5, 8, 22. On the faculty of theology at the University of Breslau, see Kleineidam, *Die katholisch-theologische Fakultät.*

22. Schubert, *Grundzüge der Pastoraltheologie,* III, 147, 176–77.

23. *Germania,* November 15, 1930.

24. Helen Radtke, August 6, 1934, Abel essay 250, in Heineman, ed., *A Third Reich Reader,* 87–88.

25. Bräutigam to Schreiber, September 11, 1931; Lichtenberg/Chancery to Bräutigam, n.d.; Bräutigam to Lichtenberg/Chancery, October 4, 1931, in Klein, *Berolinen Canonizationis,* 2:50–52.

26. *Katholisches Kirchenblatt für das Bistum Berlin,* July 24, 1932 in DAB VI/1 Gretz, n.f.

27. The German hierarchy was not alone in its fear of Communism. This was a widespread fear among most Roman Catholic churchmen resulting from the persecution and suppression of the Catholic Church in the Soviet Union. The situation of the Church in Mexico and Spain also compounded these fears. On the Vatican and Communism, see Graham, *The Vatican and Communism during World War II,* and Kent, *The Lonely Cold War of Pope Pius XII.* On the situation of the Church in the Soviet Union, Mexico, and Spain, see Holmes, *The Papacy in the Modern World,* especially 77–117, and Rhodes, *The Vatican in the Age of the Dictators.*

28. *Germania,* April 6, 1930.

29. Ibid., December 25, 1932.

30. Ibid., January 7, 1930.

31. Hürten, *Deutsche Katholiken,* 57.

32. Stehlin, *Weimar and the Vatican,* 47.

33. Gordon, *Voluptuous Panic,* 1–8; and Eckardt and Gilman, *Bertolt Brecht's Berlin.*

34. Hucko, ed., *The Democratic Tradition,* 175.

35. Bengsch, *Bistum Berlin,* 95.

36. Hürten, *Deutsche Katholiken,* 145.

37. Höhle, *Die Gründung des Bistums Berlin,* 127, and Sonnenschein, "Volksmission," (originally printed March 21, 1926), 31.

38. Sonnenschein, "Großstadt" (originally published September 5, 1926), 84–85, 87.

39. Sonnenschein, "Der Katholizismus," 427; and Eschenburg, *Die improvisierte Demokratie,* 129.

40. Rauterkus, "Zur Charakteristik des Berliner Katholizismus," 30.

41. Klausener, "Haben wir Berliner Katholiken Grund zum Optimismus?" 24–25.

42. Rauterkus, "Zur Charakteristik des Berliner Katholizismus," 29–30.

43. Lampe, "Pfarrseelsorge in Berlin," 37.

44. Krose, ed., *Kirchliches Handbuch,* 19:176, 310.

45. *Schematismus des Bistums Berlin für das Jahr 1933,* 3, 67–95.

46. Kaller, *Unser Laienapostolat,* 29.

47. Ibid., 28.

48. Simon, "Katholische Schulen," 369.

49. In 1933, the Diocese of Meißen ranked the lowest in Germany for Sunday mass attendance. Among a Catholic population of 205,473, only 27.07 of 100 attended Sunday mass on a regular basis. Krose, ed., *Kirchliches Handbuch,* 20:250.

50. Krose, ed., *Kirchliches Handbuch,* 20:250 and 21:285–86.

51. Puchowski, "Die katholische Aktion," 120.

52. Sonnenschein, "Predigt im Dom" (originally preached on August 7, 1927), 9–10.

53. Kaller, *Unser Laienapostolat,* 31–32.

54. Ibid., 34–35.

55. *Katholisches Kirchenblatt für das Bistum Berlin,* January 8, 1933. This Catholic weekly contained the report from the *Tägliche Rundschau.*

56. *Germania,* January 21, 1931.

57. The March 13, 1932, Reich presidential election proved an exception to the rule. During the election campaign, Schreiber allowed the diocesan newspaper to publish a statement signed by various Catholic Associations that endorsed the reelection of Reich President Hindenburg. See *Katholisches Kirchenblatt für das Bistum Berlin,* March 13, 1932.

58. *Germania,* July 15 1932.

59. Ibid., March 11, 1933.

60. *Katholisches Kirchenblatt für das Bistum Berlin,* February 26, 1933, and *Amtsblatt des Bischöflichen Ordinariats Berlin,* February 22, 1933, 7.

61. *Germania,* March 22, 1933.

62. Volk, *Das Reichskonkordat vom 20. Juli 1933,* 70–71.

63. Domarus, *Hitler Reden und Proklamationen* I, 232–33 and 236.

64. Memorandum of Diego von Bergen, German Ambassador to the Holy See, March 16, 1933, in Nicolaisen, *Dokumente zur Kirchenpolitik,* 1:14–20.

65. Volk, *Das Reichskonkordat vom 20. Juli 1933,* 70, 74–75. In an interview, Father Johannes Piotrowski (b. 1912), who lived through this period and was ordained in 1936, twice emphatically stressed the importance of the events surrounding the day at Potsdam in church-state relations. Interview, Berlin, November 21, 1996.

66. *Amtsblatt des Bischöflichen Ordinariats Berlin,* April 1, 1933, 23; Mikat, "Zur Kundgebung der Fuldaer Bischofskonferenz," 209–35; and Volk, "Zur Kundgebung des deutschen Episkopats," 431–56.

67. *Katholisches Kirchenblatt für das Bistum Berlin,* April 2, 1933.

68. *Germania,* March 28, 1933.

69. Schreiber, *Instruktion für den hochwürdigen Klerus betreffend seelsorgliches Verhalten zu Anhängern des Nationalsozialismus,* in DAB VI/20, n.f.

70. The Berlin clergy were civil servants in that they received their salaries from the German state. See *Amtsblatt des Bischöflichen Ordinariats Berlin,* September 22, 1933, 73–74.

71. *Amtsblatt des Bischöflichen Ordinariats Berlin,* April 27, 1933, 27.

72. Broszat, *The Hitler State.*

73. Strehler, *Christian Schreiber,* 92–93.

74. Notes for the pastoral letter of the German Bishops, n.d., in Müller, *Katholische Kirche und Nationalsozialismus,* 150–52; and Stasiewski, ed., *Akten deutscher Bischöfe,* 1:196–210, 230–37.

75. Joint Pastoral Letter of the German Bishops, Vigil of Pentecost 1933, DAB VI/20, n.f.

76. Golombek, *Die politische Vorgeschichte des Preußenkonkordats.*

77. Bertram to Pacelli, September 2, 1933, Volk, *Kirchliche Akten,* 237–42.

78. *Pastoralblatt des Bistums Eichstätt,* June 27, 1933, insert; and *Würzburger Diözesan Blatt,* July 6, 1933, insert.

79. Samerski, "Der geistliche Konsultor der deutschen Botschaft," 261–78.

80. Reifferscheid, *Das Bistum Ermland,* 49.

81. *Germania,* August 21, 1933.

82. *Kreuz Zeitung,* October 5, 1933, BArch B R5101 21675, f. 194.

83. Protocol Concerning the Oath of the Bishop of Berlin, January 31, 1934, BArch B R5101 21806, ff. 102–3.

84. *Germania,* February 12, 1934.

85. Ibid., September 2, 1934.

86. Bares, *Im Lichte der Ewigkeit,* 181–82, 185–87.

87. Volk, *Das Reichskonkordat,* 169–200.

88. Bares, *Im Lichte der Ewigkeit,* 189.

2: Guiding the Flock

1. Adolph, *Erich Klausener,* 104–8.

2. For an account of the murders see Gallo, *The Night of the Long Knives.*

3. Noakes and Pridham, eds. *Nazism: A History in Documents,* 1:182.

4. The Cathedral Chapter (*Domkapitel*) consisted of a group of priests of the diocese, each called a cathedral capitulant (*Domkapitular*), who shared the legislative power of the bishop and therefore, in this capacity, acted as advisers to the bishop. A cathedral provost (*Dompropst*), who was also a member of the diocesan clergy, led the Cathedral Chapter. In certain issues of great importance, the Cathedral Chapter had to give its consent to the bishop. Upon the death or removal of the bishop, the Cathedral Chapter would also elect a candidate for bishop and present this nomination to the Holy See. This hierarchical structure is primarily found in European dioceses.

5. This point concerns canons 1240, sect. 1, n. 3, and 2350, sect. 2, in the 1917 code. On the question of suicide in canon law see Eichmann, *Lehrbuch des Kirchenrechts,* 2:21, 49, 428.

6. Bares to Hitler, July 12, 1934, Stasiewski, ed., *Akten deutscher Bischöfe,* 1:753–54.

7. *Katholisches Kirchenblatt für das Bistum Berlin,* July 15, 1934.

8. Lageberichte Prussia, July 1934, GStAPK I Rep. 90 Annex P Lageberichte Prov. Brandenburg 2,2, f. 215; Lageberichte Potsdam, September 1934, GStAPK I Rep. 90 Annex P Lageberichte Prov. Brandenburg 2,5, f. 115.

9. Horn, "The Struggle for Catholic Youth," 564.

10. Rempel, *Hitler's Children,* 107–11.

11. Silverman, *Hitler's Economy,* 175–99.

12. *Germania,* October 23, 1934.

13. Lewy, *The Catholic Church and Nazi Germany,* 182–201; Pauly, "Zur Kirchenpolitik des Gauleiters J. Bürckel," 414–53; and Scholder, *The Churches and the Third Reich,* 2:285–91.

14. *Katholisches Kirchenblatt für das Bistum Berlin,* January 6, 1935.

15. Fischer, *Nicolaus Bares,* 164–70.

16. Clauss, "Paul Steinmann," in *Die Bischöfe der deutschsprachigen Länder,* 738.

17. Preysing to the Fulda bishops' conference, May 31, 1933, Stasiewski, ed., *Akten deutscher Bischöfe,* 1:238.

18. Preysing to Pacelli, July 3, 1933, Volk, *Kirchliche Akten,* 110–11.

19. Knauft, *Konrad von Preysing Anwalt des Rechts,* 59–60.

20. Brinckmann had been a member of the NSDAP until he ran into problems with local party authorities concerning his work with youth, refusal to fly the swastika, and comments with regard to *Reichskristallnacht.* See Hehl et al., *Priester unter Hitler's Terror,* 1:705–6.

21. Detten to Lammers, June 5, 1935; Notes, June 22, 1935, and July 4, 1935; Detten to Funk, July 4, 1935, BArch B R43 II/175, ff. 555–75; Detten to Funk, July 6, 1935, BArch B R5101 21806, ff. 174–75.

22. Rust to Orsenigo, June 4, 1935, in Albrecht, ed., *Der Notenwechsel zwischen dem heiligen Stuhl,* 3:97–98, esp. n. 1.

23. On the family background of Preysing, see Knauft, *Konrad von Preysing Anwalt des Rechts,* 18–29.

24. Knauft, *Konrad von Preysing Anwalt des Rechts,* 32–33.

25. Preysing to Pacelli, June 4, 1935; Pacelli to Preysing, June 27, 1935; Preysing to Pacelli, July 6, 1935, in Adolph, *Kardinal Preysing und zwei Diktaturen,* 23–24.

26. See, for example, Cornwell, *Hitler's Pope.*

27. Adolph, *Geheime Aufzeichnungen,* 73.

28. On the Law for the Prevention of Hereditary Diseased Offspring, see Noakes and Pridham, eds., *Nazism: A History in Documents,* 1:457–58; and Richter, *Katholizismus und Eugenik in der Weimarer Republik und im Dritten Reich.*

29. German translation published in *Amtsblatt des Bischöflichen Ordinariats Berlin,* July 20, 1935, 59–61. English translation printed in *Catholic Mind* 33 (September 8, 1935), 324.

30. *Amtsblatt des Bischöflichen Ordinariats Berlin,* July 20, 1935, 61.

31. Berlin Gestapo to all Gestapo Bureaus, May 27, 1935, BLHA Pr. Br. Rep. 2A Regierung Potsdam I Pol. 3034, f. 6.

32. BLHA Pr. Br. Rep. 2A Regierung Potsdam I Pol. 3034, ff. 242–54.

33. "Draft for Publication in the Press," July 1935, in GStAPK I/HA Rep. 90 Nr. 2387, ff. 100–105.

34. Minister of Justice to Chief Public Prosecutors, July 20, 1935, GStAPK I/HA Rep. 90 Nr. 2387, f. 141.

35. Provincial Governor to State Councilors, Police Presidents, Mayors in Brandenburg, Wittenberge and Rathenow, and Police Officials in Eberswalde, July 28, 1935, BLHA Pr. Br. Rep. 2A Regierung Potsdam I Po. 3034, f. 258.

36. *Amtsblatt des Bischöflichen Ordinariats Berlin,* August 14, 1935, 64–66.

37. Minister of Justice to Kerrl, September 19, 1935, BArch B R5101 22268, ff. 44–45.

38. Kerrl to Provincial Governor, September 5, 1935, BLHA Pr. Br. Rep. 2A I Pol. 3034, f. 269.

39. Ibid., March 12, 1936, GStAPK I/HA Rep. 90 2387, ff. 361–63.

40. *Amtsblatt des Bischöflichen Ordinariats Berlin,* September 4, 1935, pp. 75–76.

41. Kerrl to Bishops in the Reich, April 9, 1936, in *Amtsblatt des Bischöflichen Ordinariats Berlin,* May 12, 1936, 61.

42. *Amtsblatt des Bischöflichen Ordinariats Berlin,* May 12, 1936, 61.

43. Mariaux, *The Persecution of the Catholic Church,* 295–97; Hoffmann and Janssen, *Die Wahrheit über die Ordensdevisenprozesse;* and Rapp, *Die Devisenprozesse gegen katholische Ordensangehörige.*

44. Hockerts, *Die Sittlichkeitsprozesse,* 4.

45. Ibid., 48, 63–67.

46. Ibid., 35.

47. Ibid., 56.

48. *Amtsblatt des Bischöflichen Ordinariats Berlin,* June 18, 1936, 73–74.

49. Ibid., October 2, 1936, 119–20.

50. See "Fulda Bishops' Letter for Removal of the Restrictions on the Church," issued August 20, 1936 and translated and printed in *Catholic Mind,* November 22, 1936, 457. German text printed in *Amtsblatt des Bischöflichen Ordinariats Berlin,* August 27, 1936.

51. Besier, "Anti-Bolshevism and Antisemitism," 450–51.

52. *Amtsblatt des Bischöflichen Ordinariats Berlin,* October 16, 1936, 123–25.

53. Ibid., January 1, 1937, 1–6.

54. Albrecht, ed., *Die Notenwechsel zwischen dem hl. Stuhl,* 1:403.

55. Harrigan, "Nazi Germany and the Holy See," 195.

56. Pacelli to Bertram, December 21, 1936, in Adolph, *Kardinal Preysing und zwei Diktatiren,* 72–73.

57. Albrecht, ed., *Der Notenwechsel zwischen dem hl. Stuhl,* 1:402–3; Martini, "Il Card. Faulhaber e L'Enciclica di Pio XI," 421–32, "Il Cardinale Faulhaber e L'Enciclica *Mit brennender Sorge,*" 303–20, and "Il Cardinale Pacelli e l'Enciclica contro Il Nazional-sozialismo," 12–13; Schneider, "Kardinal Faulhaber und die Enzyklika *Mit brennender Sorge,*" 226–22, and "*Mit brennender Sorge*—die Enzyklika Pius' XI," 102–13.

58. Adolph, *Kardinal Preysing und zwei Diktatoren,* 73–79.

59. Adolph, *Geheime Aufzeichnungen,* 58–59, 77.

60. Radio Communication of Heydrich to all Stapo Bureaus, March 21, 1937, 12:30 a.m., in Adolph, *Kardinal Preysing und zwei Diktatoren,* 79–80.

61. Bischöfliches Ordinariat Berlin, ed., *Hirtenworte in ernster Zeit,* 15–16.

62. Trippen, "Leben und Überleben im Dritten Reich," 1586.

63. Preysing to Pastoral Offices of the Berlin Diocese, March 19, 1937, DAB VI/20, n.f.

64. Quotation from Robert d'Harcourt, member of the Académie Française and visitor to Germany, who heard the encyclical read during Palm Sunday mass. See Leiber, "*Mit brennender Sorge,*" 417–26.

65. Kerrl to German Bishops, March 23, 1937, in Adolph, *Kardinal Preysing und zwei Diktaturen,* 81.

66. All citations to *Mit brennender Sorge* refer to the English translation of the encyclical found in Carlen, ed., *The Papal Encyclicals, 1903–1939,* 525–35.

67. Documents pertaining to the response of both the Church and the state following the public reading of *Mit brennender Sorge* may be found in Hirt, ed., *Mit brennender Sorge.*

68. Kerrl to Goebbels, June 18, 1937, BArch B R5101 21678, f. 293.

69. Pastoral Letter of Preysing, July 9, 1937, DAB VI/20, n.f.

70. Pastoral Letter of Preysing concerning *Mit brennender Sorge,* November 30, 1937, DAB VI/20, n.f. Quote from *Mit brennender Sorge* translation taken from Carlen, ed., *The Papal Encyclicals, 1903–1939,* 534.

71. Schwarz, *Die große Lüge des politischen Katholizismus.* According to Roman Bleistein, Dieter Schwarz was a pen name for Albert Hartl (1904–1982), a former priest of the archdiocese of Munich and Freising. See Bleistein, "'Überläufer im Sold

der Kirchenfeinde,'" The papers of Sebastian Schröcker, formerly a priest of the Munich-Freising archdiocese and official in the Ministry of Church Affairs, confirm this point, BArch K, Schröcker Nachlass 1516.

72. Preysing to Clergy of Berlin, February 3, 1939, in Bischöfliches Ordinariat Berlin, *Dokumente aus dem Kampf*, 59–91.

73. Kerrl to Preysing, January 26, 1939, BArch B R5101 21679, f. 29.

74. Kerrl to Foreign Office, n.d., BArch B R5101 21679, f. 63.

75. Leugers, *Gegen eine Mauer bischöflichen Schweigens*, 84–93; and Adam, *Die Auseinandersetzungen des Bischofs Konrad von Preysing*, 68–69.

76. Adolph, *Geheime Aufzeichnungen*, 252–53.

77. Preysing to Berlin Clergy, March 31, 1938, in Bischöfliches Ordinariat Berlin, *Dokumente aus dem Kampf*, 36.

78. See Adolph, *Geheime Aufzeichnungen*, 271–72.

79. *St. Petrus-Kalender für das Bistum Berlin*, 1939, n.p.

80. "Zum Geburtstag des Führers," in *Würzburger Diözesan-Blatt*, April 5, 1939, 53, which was to be read on *Weißer Sonntag*, the first Sunday following Easter, and "Zum 50. Geburtstag des Führers," in *St. Willibalds-Bote*, April 16, 1939.

81. Preysing's moderation on the war question is seen in sharp contrast to the positions of many other Catholic Church leaders. See Zahn, *German Catholics and Hitler's Wars;* Missalla, *Für Volk und Vaterland,* and *Für Gott, Führer und Vaterland;* Repgen, "Die deutschen Bischöfe und der Zweite Weltkrieg," 411–52; Smolinsky, "Das katholische Rußlandbild in Deutschland," 323–55; and Ziegler, "Haben die deutschen Bischöfe im Dritten Reich versagt?" 497–524.

82. Prange to all Pastoral Offices in the Diocese of Berlin, September 1, 1939, DAB VI/20, n.f.

83. Bertram to Hitler, April 10, 1940, in Volk, ed., *Akten deutscher Bischöfe,* 5:47–48.

84. Leugers, *Gegen eine Mauer bischöflichen Schweigens*, 87–106.

85. Diary entry of August 22, 1942, in Fröhlich, ed., *Die Tagebücher von Joseph Goebbels* part 2, 5:383–84.

86. For example, in 1937 in all the German dioceses, 4,540 priests had confrontations with the Gestapo and left written records. In 1936, 2,176 priests had confrontations; in 1938 there were 3,912; and in 1941 there were 4,188. For complete statistics (nationwide and by individual diocese) on actions against members of the Catholic clergy, see Hehl, *Priester unter Hitlers Terror,* 1:121–54, esp. 121–42.

87. Kerrl to Ley, February 17, 1940, BArch B NS 8 183, ff. 26–27.

88. The confiscation of monasteries never became a central issue for the diocese of Berlin. On the confiscation of property owned by religious communities, see Harrison, "The Nazi Dissolution of the Monasteries," 323–55, and Helmreich, *The German Churches under Hitler,* 358–61. On August 1, 1941, the Gestapo did confiscate the Berlin seminary in Grünau. On the confiscation and other difficulties with the Gestapo regarding Berlin seminaries, see Brühe, ed., *Priester Werden in Berlin,* and the materials in BArch B R5101 22531 and SAPMO-BArch D Z/B1 505.

89. Heydrich to SD Bureaus, October 24, 1941, in BArch B R58 266, ff. 75–76.

90. Hürten, "Endlösung für den Katholizismus?" 536.

91. Goebbels diary entry, May 12, 1937, in Fröhlich, ed., *Die Tagebücher von Joseph Goebbels* part 1, 3:143. See also Hockerts, "Die Goebbels-Tagebücher," 379; and Hürten, "Endlösung für den Katholizismus?" 541.

92. Burleigh, *Death and Deliverance,* 178; and Helmreich, *The German Churches under Hitler,* 360.

93. Hitler, Berlin, December 13, 1941, in Hitler, *Monologe im Führerhauptquartier,* 150. Also see the references in Goebbels's diaries discussed in Hockerts, "Die Goebbels-Tagebücher," 382; and Hürten, "Endlösung für den Katholizismus?" 538.

94. Helmreich, *The German Churches under Hitler,* 340–43. On the churches in the Warthegau, also see Stasiewski, "Die Kirchenpolitik der Nationalsozialisten im Warthegau," 46–74.

95. Knauft, *Konrad von Preysing Anwalt des Rechts,* 199–203; and van Roon, *German Resistance to Hitler,* 126–40.

96. Kitchen, *Nazi Germany at War,* 231. Normally, historians have credited Clemens August Graf von Galen, bishop of Münster, as the first Catholic prelate to speak against the Nazi policy of euthanasia. On contrasting opinions on Galen's actions, see Juropka, ed., *Clemens August Graf von Galen: Neue Forschungen,* and Griech-Polelle, *Bishop von Galen.*

97. Sermon on the Occasion of the *Papstkrönungsfeier,* March 9, 1941, DAB VI/20, n.f.

98. Information for the clergy of Berlin on the film "I Accuse," October 1941, in Bischöfliches Ordinariat Berlin, *Dokumente aus dem Kampf,* 104–6.

99. Sermon of the Bishop of Berlin in St. Hedwig's Cathedral, November 2, 1941, DAB VI/20, n.f.

100. Goebbels diary entry, February 21, 1942, in Fröhlich, ed., *Die Tagebücher von Joseph Goebbels,* part 2, 3:351.

101. Pastoral Letter of the Bishop of Berlin, March 3, 1942, read on March 8, 1942, DAB VI/20, n.f.

102. Goebbels diary entry, March 11, 1942, in Fröhlich, ed., *Die Tagebücher von Joseph Goebbels,* part 2, 3:454–55.

103. Ibid., part 2, 5:54. See also *Times* (London), June 30, 1942, and July 1, 1942, and *New York Times,* June 30, 1942.

104. Sermon of the Bishop of Berlin in St. Hedwig's Cathedral on the occasion of the Silver Jubilee of the Ordination to Bishop of Pope Pius XII, June 28, 1942, DAB VI/20, n.f.

105. Goebbels diary entry, July 13, 1942, in Fröhlich, ed., *Die Tagebücher von Joseph Goebbels,* part 2, 5:112.

106. Reports of Sommer, February 14, 1942, and November 5, 1943, in Volk, ed., *Akten deutscher Bischöfe,* 5:675–78 and 817–23.

107. Sermon of the Bishop of Berlin in St. Hedwig's on *Totensonntag,* November 15, 1942, DAB VI/20, n.f.

108. See the comments in Volk, ed., *Akten deutscher Bischöfe,* 5:959, n. 1.

109. Advent Pastoral Letter of Bishop Preysing, December 12, 1942, English translation in *Catholic Mind,* February 1943, 1–5. Original German text in DAB VI/20, n.f.

110. January 21, 1943, in *Congressional Record—Senate,* January 6, 1943–March 11, 1943, vol. 89, part 1: 266–68

111. "N. C. C. M. Statements Praise Pastoral Letter of Bishop of Berlin," in *Catholic Action* 25 (1943), p. 22.

112. Goebbels diary entry, January 27, 1943, in Fröhlich, ed., *Die Tagebücher von Joseph Goebbels,* part 2, 7:204–5.

113. Lenten Pastoral Letter of the Bishop of Berlin, February 13, 1938, read February 20, 1938, DAB VI/20, n.f.

114. Lenten Pastoral Letter of the Bishop of Berlin, January 28, 1940, read February 4, 1940, *Amtsblatt des Bischöflichen Ordinariats Berlin,* January 30, 1940, 9-12.

115. Pastoral Letter of the Bishop of Berlin, September 8, 1941, read September 14, 1941, DAB VI/20, n.f.

116. Lenten Pastoral Letter of the Bishop of Berlin, February 1, 1942, read February 15, 1942, *Amtsblatt des Bischöflichen Ordinariats Berlin,* February 7, 1942; 14-16.

117. Sermon of the Bishop of Berlin in St. Hedwig, November 2, 1941, DAB VI/20, n.f.

118. Pastoral Letter of Preysing for the Solemn Renewal of the Consecration of the Diocese to the Most Sacred Heart of Jesus, May 26, 1944; June 18, 1944; *Amtsblatt des Bischöflichen Ordinariats Berlin,* August 15, 1944, 42-43.

3: Negotiating Pastoral Care

1. Sermon given in Dramburg and Sponbrügge (*Landjahrheim*), July 8, 1934, DAB V/8 Nachlaß Froehlich, n.f.

2. Interview with Father Bernhard Kleineidam, January 8, 1997. Also see Kleineidam, *Tagebucheines Diasporapriester.*

3. In the statistical work *Priester unter Hitlers Terror,* Hehl et al. record the activities of numerous religious and diocesan priests from other dioceses who served in the diocese of Berlin. For the purpose of this chapter, only those priests who were actual members of the diocese have been included (with the addition of eight Berlin priests who were not found in Hehl's work). Hehl et al., *Priester unter Hitlers Terror,* 1:471-88.

4. Lagebericht April 1935, GStAPK I Rep. 90 P Lageberichte Provinz Brandenburg 2,5 Potsdam, f. 70.

5. The Gestapo regularly enforced a pre-World War I law that the Nazi state had strengthened through a series of decrees in 1933, which enabled it to arrest and confine an individual and put him or her into "protective custody" (*Schutzhaft*) "for an unlimited period and gave the prisoner no legal recourse." For a discussion of this practice see Dressen, "Protective Custody," 735-37.

6. Gestapo Berlin to Göring, GStAPK I Rep. 90P Nr. 54 Heft I, f. 52.

7. Lageberichte Stettin July 1933, August 5, 1935, in Thévoz et al., *Pommern 1934/35,* 2:116.

8. DAB VI/1 Klemt, Questionnaire, n.f.

9. The only account of Dobczynski's actions appeared in Lagebericht Stettin, July 1935, August 5, 1935, in Thévoz et al., *Pommern 1934/35,* 2:116.

10. Questionnaire, DAB, VI/1 Dobczynski, n.f.

11. On the background of Willimsky's life and a brief summary of his activities in the Third Reich, see Pruß, "Pfarrer Albert Willimsky," 117-21; and Kühn, *Blutzeugen des Bistums Berlin,* 160-64.

12. Record of telephone conversation between District Governor Potsdam and Lichtenberg, March 20, 1935, BLHA Pr. Br. Rep. 2A Pol. 3034, f. 237.

13. Gestapo Potsdam to Gestapo Berlin, February 27, 1935, BLHA Pr. Br. Rep. 2A I Pol. 3034, f. 234.

14. Gestapo Potsdam to Gestapo Berlin, March 29, 1935, BLHA Pr. Br. Rep. 2A I Pol. 3034, f. 236R.

15. *Landjahr* Director Province Brandenburg to the District Governor Potsdam, August 7, 1935, BLHA Pr. Br. Rep. 2A II Gen. 287, n.f.

16. Gestapo Potsdam to Gestapo Berlin, August 23, 1935, BLHA Pr. Br. Rep. 2A I Pol. 3034, n.f.

17. Steinmann to District Governor Potsdam, August 26, 1935, BLHA Pr. Br. Rep. 2A Gen. 287, n.f.

18. Willimsky to Berlin Chancery, August 26, 1935, BLHA Pr. Br. Rep. 2A Gen. 287, n.f.

19. District Administrator to Gestapo Potsdam, January 16, 1936, BLHA Pr. Br. Rep. 2A II Gen. 287, n.f.

20. Gestapo Potsdam to County Administrators, n.d., BLHA Pr. Br. Rep. 2A I Pol. 3034, f. 278.

21. Willimsky to Heinrich Willimsky, January 1, 1936, BArch B R 58 2522, f. 181.

22. Willimsky to Martha S., January 25, 1936, BArch B R58 2522, f. 178.

23. Ibid., January 28, 1936, BArch B R58 2522, f. 179.

24. Willimsky to Gustav S., February 2, 1936, BArch B R58 2522, f. 183.

25. Willimsky to Frau L., April 29, 1937, BArch B R58 2522, f. 182.

26. District Court Gransee, Summary of Punishment, April 24, 1936, BArch B R58 2522, f. 187. Willimsky later testified that he was fined 10000 Reich marks for not flagging the church with the swastika; however, the former document is a record of the actual amount of the verdict and fine directly from the court. For Willimsky's testimony, see Protocol of Inquiry, November 15, 1937, BLHA Pr. Br. Rep. 2A I. Pol. 3034, ff. 317–18.

27. Willimsky to District Court Gransee, April 27, 1936, Barch B R58 2522, f. 188.

28. Chief Public Prosecutor Berlin to Minister of Justice, December 20, 1934, BArch B R5101 22247, n.f.

29. Willimsky to Rust, July 7, 1936, BArch B R58 2522, f. 172.

30. Chief Public prosecutor Berlin to Minister of Justice, December 17, 1936, BArch B R5101 22247, ff. 12–13.

31. County Administrator to Willimsky, September 26, 1936, BArch B R58 2522, f. 193

32. District Governor Potsdam to Kerrl, December 22, 1937 with attached letter from Walter D. to Goebbels, June 21, 1937, f. 50, BArch B R5101 22247, f. 50.

33. Protocol of Inquiry, Gransee, November 15, 1937, BLHA Pr. Br. Rep. 2A I Pol. 3032, ff. 317–18.

34. District Governor Potsdam to Kerrl, BArch B R5101 22247, f. 52.

35. Chief Public Prosecutor Potsdam to Minister of Justice, October 17, 1938, BArch B R5101 22247, f. 137.

36. Willimsky to Examining Magistrate of the District Court Potsdam, October 27, 1938, BArch B R58 2522, f. 170.

37. Preysing to Chief Public Prosecutor Berlin, December 21, 1938, BArch B R58 2522, f. 152.

38. On May 11, 1939, Willimsky signed the statement. Gestapo Concluding Report on Willimsky, October 31, 1939, BArch B R58 2522, f. 116.

39. Special Court Berlin Decision, August 3, 1939, BArch B R58 2522, f. 153.

40. Interrogation of Willimsky by Gestapo Stettin, October 20, 1939, BArch B R58 2522, ff. 111, 113 R.

41. Gestapo Stettin Remarks, November 3, 1939, BArch B R58 2522, f. 118.

42. Gestapo Concluding Report on Willimsky, October 31, 1939, BArch B R58 2522, f. 116 R.

43. Roth to RSHA, Telegram, November 21, 1939, and Roth to RSHA, Telegram, December 12, 1939, BArch B R58 2522, ff. 128, 130.

44. Heydrich to Gestapo Stettin, January 9, 1940, and Gestapo Stettin to Commandant of Sachsenhausen, January 27, 1940, BArch B R58 2522, ff. 204, 207.

45. Gestapo Stettin Telegram, February 20, 1940, BArch B R58 2522, f. 211.

46. Gellately, *The Gestapo and German Society,* esp. 129–58.

47. *Lagebericht* Köslin, October 1934, November 3, 1934; Thévoz et al., *Pommern 1934/35,* 2:162.

48. Rosenberg, *Der Mythus.*

49. Attorney General (*Oberstaatsanwalt*) to Minister of Justice, August 23, 1935, BArch B R5101 22277, n.f. At the end of the war, the Russians held Gediga prisoner in a camp in Graudenz, from which he never returned. On this point, see DAB VI/1 Gediga, *Die Pommersche Zeitung,* June 3, 1995, n.f.

50. Report, Ministry Associations, February 3, 1935, BArch B R5101 22169, f. 104.

51. Attorney General Stettin to Minister of Justice, September 30, 1935, BArch B R5101 22277, f. 47.

52. Parish Chronicle of St. Aloysius, DAB VI/1 Fähnrich, f. 30.

53. Ibid., f. 46.

54. Lagebericht September 1934, October 4, 1934, in Thévoz et al., *Pommern 1934/35,* 2:42–43, 45.

55. Judgment of the Special Court of the District Court Eger, May 23, 1941, BArch B R5101 22267, ff. 22–24.

56. District Personnel Bureau to District Governor Frankfurt/Oder, October 10, 1938, BArch B R5101 22247, f. 107.

57. District Governor Frankfurt/Oder to Rust, November 24, 1938, BArch B R5101 22247, f. 106.

58. Rust to Kerrl, May 26, 1939, with copy of letter from Provisional Governor of Brandenburg to Rust, April 27, 1939, and letter of Gestapo Frankfurt/Oder to Provincial Governor's Ministry of Secondary Schools, BArch B R5101 22247, ff. 158–59.

59. Kerrl to *Oberkommando* of the army, December 28, 1943, BArch B R5101 22301, f. 44.

60. Gestapo Berlin to Kerrl, February 27, 1941, BArch B R5101 2248, f. 29.

61. Kerrl to Preysing, December 8, 1937, BArch B R5101 22530, f. 13.

62. Decision, District Court Eberswalde, June 5, 1941, for the session of March 17, 1941, BArch B R5101 22248, f. 46.

63. Attorney General Prenzlau to Minister of Justice, December 23, 1940, BArch B R5101 22248, f. 43.

64. Criminal Division of the District Court in Prenzlau, June 5, 1941, from the session of March 17, 1941, BArch B R5101, 22248, f. 47

65. District Court Summary of Punishment, April 4, 1939, BArch B R5101 22247, f. 130.

66. Dolata, *Chronik einer Jugend,* 24.

67. Josef Nowak states that Schubert was transported to Sachsenhausen and died shortly after arriving at the concentration camp. I have found, however, no evidence to support this statement. See Nowak, "Der Devisenprozeß Dr. Seelmeyer," 515–16; and Hehl, *Priester unter Hitlers Terror,* 1:485.

68. Johannes (unnamed) to Chancery, May 6, 1974, DAB I/5 Schubert, Bruno, n.f.

69. Martha A. to Chancery, February 11, 1947, DAB I/5 Schubert, Bruno, n.f.

70. Preysing to Martha A., April 14, 1947, DAB I/5 Schubert, Bruno, n.f.

71. Adolph, *Geheime Aufzeichnungen,* 163.

72. Barthels, *Zeitnahe Seelsorge.* Barthels (1907–1990) was a priest of the Würzburg diocese.

73. The Gestapo may have summoned a number of priests to question them, but it did not take formal steps against them. These summonses were not recorded in the extant records, but often only in questionnaires filled out by the priests after the war. For example, see the questionnaire of Father Georg Klemt, who reported having been questioned by the Gestapo "three or four times" and warned for criticism of the Nazi weltanschauung. Questionnaire, DAB VI/1 Klemt, n.f.

74. Gestapo Potsdam to District Governor Potsdam, February 12, 1936, BLHA Pr. Br. Rep. 2A I Pol. 3034, f. 32.

75. Gestapo Potsdam to District Governor Potsdam, March 20, 1936, BLHA Pr. Br. Rep. 2A I Pol. 3034, f. 37.

76. Lebenslauf Karte, DAB VI/1 Schreibmayr, n.f.

77. Preysing to Kerrl, August 11, 1937, and Gestapo Berlin to Kerrl, September 15, 1937, BArch B R5101 22247, ff. 29, 31.

78. Preysing to Kerrl, June 17, 1937, and Preysing to Kerrl, August 11, 1937, BArch B R5101 22247, ff. 28–29.

79. Gestapo Berlin to Kerrl, September 27, 1937, BArch B R5101 22247, f. 39.

80. Adolph, *Geheime Aufzeichnungen,* 236.

81. Coppenrath was a priest of the Münster diocese. It was the specific wish of the founder of the parish, Dr. Matthias Aulike, who came from Münster, that a diocesan priest from his home region would serve as pastor of the parish. Coppenrath, *Der westfälische Dickkopf,* 24.

82. Roth to Reich Minister of Justice, August 25, 1937, BArch B R3001 III g17 558/38.

83. Coppenrath, *Der westfälische Dickkopf,* 13.

84. Coppenrath would make almost "eight to ten house visits" daily in order to know his parishioners well. *St. Petrus Kalende,* 1962, 53.

85. Jauch, "Albert Coppenrath," 97.

86. Coppenrath, *Der westfälische Dickkopf,* 17.

87. Ibid., 25.

88. Ibid., 29 and 34.

89. Ibid., 24–25.

90. Ibid., 62.

91. Ibid.

92. Ibid., 42–43, 46.

93. Ibid., 43–45.

94. Adolph, *Sie sind nicht vergessen,* 176.

95. Coppenrath, *Der westfälische Dickkopf*, 47–50.

96. Coppenrath's announcements brought enough notoriety so that detractors created a pamphlet to attack Klausener, Coppenrath, and the "political Catholicism" alive on *Winterfeldtplatz*. See "Aus der 'Erich-Klausener'—Matthiaskirche am *Winterfeldtplatz* zu Berlin," BHStAM StK 7256, n.f.

97. Coppenrath, *Der westfälische Dickkopf*, 59.

98. Ibid., 60. See also the Lagebericht September 1934, GStA I Rep. 90 Annex P, Lagebericht Prov. Brandenburg, Berlin 2, 2, f. 185.

99. Coppenrath, *Der westfälische Dickkopf*, 59.

100. Lagebericht, February 1935, BArch B R43/II/175, f. 289.

101. Lammers to Bares, February 16, 1935, BArch B R43/II/175, ff. 283–84; 291–92.

102. Coppenrath, *Der westfälische Dickkopf*, 64.

103. Ibid., 72.

104. Ibid., 73.

105. Criminal Case, February 6, 1940, DAB VI/1 Coppenrath, n.f.

106. *Germania*, 1935, newspaper clipping, DAB, VI/1 Coppenrath, n.f.

107. Coppenrath, *Der westfälische Dickkopf*, 101. Even after the war, Coppenrath continued to argue that he never acted from political motives, but solely for pastoral reasons. See Questionnaire, DAB VI/1 Coppenrath, n.f.

108. Coppenrath, *Der westfälische Dickkopf*, 101.

109. Adolph, *Geheime Aufzeichnungen*, 236.

110. Ibid., 235–36.

111. Coppenrath, *Der westfälische Dickkopf*, 102.

112. Ibid., 88.

113. Ibid., 40, 79–80.

114. Ibid., 5.

115. This was true of Father Karl König (1876–1939), a Paderborn priest who resided in Berlin and was an ardent supporter of National Socialism. In May 1935, König denounced Coppenrath to the Reich chancellery for making a pulpit announcement concerning the confiscation of the Katholisches Kirchenblatt für das Bistum Berlin by the Berlin Gestapo. König to Reich Chancellery, May 5, 1935, BArch B R43 II/163a, f. 164–67.

116. Coppenrath, *Der westfälische Dickkopf*, 28.

117. Ibid., 102. See also the 1937 case, Attorney General to Minister of Justice, August 7, 1937, BArch B R3001 III g17 555/38, f. 17.

118. Coppenrath, *Der westfälische Dickkopf*, 35.

119. Ibid., 168.

120. Ibid., 170–71.

121. Ibid., 192–93.

122. Ibid., 200.

4: Serving the Home Front

1. *Schematismus des Bistums Berlin 1941*, 144–46.

2. *Schematismus des Bistums Berlin 1947*, 168.

3. Kerrl to Church Authorities, July 12, 1940, in Volk, ed., *Akten deutscher Bischöfe*, 5:73–74.

4. War Letter of St. Hubert Berlin, Christmas 1939, Number 4, DAB VI/1 Hering, n.f.

5. District Attorney Berlin to Minister of Justice, October 11, 1941, BArch B R5101 22248, ff. 98 R-99, 100. In 1942, the district governor of Potsdam ordered Hering's permission to teach in the schools revoked, most likely as a result of the above incident. District President Potsdam to Kerrl, September 23, 1942, BArch B R5101 22248, f. 107.

6. Questionnaire, Hering, DAB VI/1 Hering, n.f.

7. District Court Berlin, Criminal Proceeding, sitting of July 7, 1942, BArch B R5101 22248, ff. 124–27.

8. Tschetschog to Stinnes of the O.B.R., September 24, 1939, BArch B R5101 22384, f. 257.

9. Ministry of Propaganda to Kerrl, December 6, 1939, BArch B R5101 22384, f. 256. On December 27, 1939, Kerrl reported the granting of permission for the mass in Czech at the Niemegk camp. See Kerrl to Preysing, December 27, 1939, BArch B R5101 22384, f. 258.

10. Körner, "Katholische Kirche und Polnische Zwangsarbeiter," 130.

11. Preysing to Ministry of Church Affairs, December 5, 1941, BArch B R5101 21690, f. 229.

12. Preysing to Ministry of Church Affairs, May 18, 1942, BArch B R5101 21691, f. 18. In July 1942, the ministry finally answered Preysing and assured him that the local government would be required to lift its ban for a special mass for the Poles according to the stipulations of the decree of February 23, 1942. See Ministry of Church Affairs to Preysing, July 31, 1942, BArch B R5101 21691, f. 19.

13. Preysing to Kerrl, May 18, 1942, BArch B R5101 21691, f. 18.

14. Preysing to Ministry of Church Affairs, April 6, 1943, BArch B R5101 21691, f. 180.

15. Himmler to Ministry of Church Affairs, May 18, 1943, BArch B R5101 21691, f. 191. The SS and the Gestapo had a longstanding hatred and distrust for the sacrament of penance. See Padberg, "Reinhard Heydrich und das Beichtgeheimnis," 289–96.

16. Ministry of Church Affairs to Preysing, June 5, 1943, BArch B R5101 21691, f. 182.

17. On this point, see Körner, "Katholische Kirche und Polnische Zwangsarbeiter," 128–42, and Delaney, "Racial Values vs. Religious Values," 271–94.

18. Gestapo Berlin to Ministry of Church Affairs, November 2, 1943, BArch B R5101 21692, f. 27.

19. Ministry of Church Affairs to Preysing, November 12, 1943, BArch B R5101 21692, f. 27 R.

20. Karte, DAB VI/1 Jordan, n.f., and Hehl, *Priester unter Hitlers Terror*, 1:477.

21. Attorney General Stettin to District Court Criminal Division Stettin, November 1, 1940, BArch B, R5101 22277, f. 90.

22. District Court Stettin Criminal Division Decision, January 9, 1941, BArch B R5101 22277, ff. 93–95.

23. Questionnaire, DAB VI/1 Gretz, n.f.

24. Questionnaire, DAB VI/1 Nolweika, n.f.

25. *Petrusblatt* 43/1985, in DAB VI/1 Nolweika, n.f.

26. Reuter to Mayor of Swinemünde, April 2, 1941, DAB VI/1 Adamus, n.f.

27. Questionnaire, DAB VI/1 Adamus, n.f.

28. Report, June 4, 1943, in Boberach, ed., *Berichte des SD*, 833. See also Questionnaire, DAB VI/1 Bartsch, n.f.

29. Margarete Sommer to Berlin Chancery, October 14, 1946, DAB VI/1 Bartsch, n.f.

30. Report, June 4, 1943, in Boberach, ed., *Berichte des SD*, 833.

31. Karte, DAB VI/1 Bartsch, n.f.

32. Pruß, "Pfarrer Joseph Lenzel," 103, and Kühn, *Blutzeugen des Bistums Berlin*, 170.

33. Bericht, January 19, 1942, in Boberach, ed., *Berichte des SD*, 610.

34. Wittschier, "Joseph Lenzel," 551–52, in DAB VI/1 Lenzel, n.f.

35. Lange, "Pfarrer August Froehlich," 94.

36. Froehlich's biographer, Josef Mörsdorf, asserted that there were 600 Catholics living in Damburg at the time; however, the Berlin *Schematismus* stated that there were only 300. See Mörsdorf, *August Froehlich: Pfarrer von Rathenow,* 13, and *Schematismus des Bistums Berlin 1933,* 62.

37. Undated newspaper clipping, DAB, V/8 Nachlaß Froehlich, n.f.

38. Froehlich to Herr B., January 17, 1934, DAB V/8 Nachlaß Froehlich, n.f.

39. Herr B. to Froehlich, January 22, 1934, and Froehlich to Herr B., January 24, 1934, DAB V/8 Nachlaß Froehlich, n.f.

40. Froehlich to Herr W., February 9, 1934, DAB V/8 Nachlaß Froehlich, n.f.

41. Herr W. to Froehlich, February 10, 1934, DAB V/8 Nachlaß Froehlich, n.f.

42. Froehlich to Reichsarbeitsdienst Falkenburg, March 26, 1935, DAB V/8 Nachlaß Froehlich, n.f.

43. Ibid., June 29, 1936, DAB V/8 Nachlaß Froehlich, n.f.

44. Ibid., April 8, 1935 and June 29, 1936, DAB V/8 Nachlaß Froehlich, n.f.

45. See the correspondence between Froehlich and the Reichsarbeitsdienst Falkenburg, DAB V/8 Nachlaß Froehlich, n.f.

46. Sermon, Dramburg and Polzin, October 25, 1936, DAB V/8 Nachlaß Froehlich, n.f.

47. Attorney General to Minister of Justice, December 2, 1937, DAB V/8 Nachlaß Froehlich, n.f.

48. Summary of Punishment, District Court Dramburg, February 7, 1938, DAB V/8 Nachlaß Froehlich, n.f.

49. Froehlich to District Court Dramburg, February 17, 1938, DAB V/8 Nachlaß Froehlich, n.f.

50. Attorney General to Minister of Justice, June 18, 1938, BArch B R5101 22277, f. 74.

51. Lange, "Pfarrer August Froehlich," 97.

52. Froehlich to Gestapo Potsdam, April 15, 1941, DAB V/8 Nachlaß Froehlich, n.f.

53. Klara K. to Himmler, July 17, 1941, DAB V/8 Nachlaß Froehlich, n.f.

54. Hehl, *Priester unter Hitlers Terror,* 1:475.

55. See Fischer, *Antifaschistisches Erbe-Mythos oder Auftrag?* 70–83, and "Der Fall Stettin," 122–30; Herberhold, *A. M. Wachsmann;* Klosterkamp, *Kind und Opfer;* Knauft, *Fall Stettin;* Kühn, *Blutzeugen des Bistums Berlin,* 45–87; Pruß, "Kuratus Leonard Berger," 91–94, "Pfarrer Albert Hirsch," 98–100, "Kaplan Herbert Simoleit,"

110–13, and "Pfarrer Dr. Alfons Maria Wachsmann," 114–17; and Walser, *Carl Lampert* and *Dreimal zum Tod verurteilt.*

56. See Knauft, *Fall Stettin;* and Klosterkamp, *Kind und Opfer.*

57. Reich War Tribunal, September 22, 1944, DAB V/71–4 Stettin, n.f.

58. Klosterkamp, *Kind und Opfer,* 69.

59. Knauft, *Fall Stettin,* 16.

60. Ibid., 16–18; and Klosterkamp, *Kind und Opfer,* 69, 78–79.

61. Daniel Report 1943, DAB V/71–4 Stettin, ff. 4–5.

62. Prosecutor of the Supreme Military Tribunal Torgau, November 11, 1943, DAB V/71–4 Stettin, n.f.

63. The notes were destroyed during the war.

64. Knauft, *Fall Stettin,* 23.

65. Daniel Report, DAB V/71–4 Stettin, f. 2.

66. The British produced a forged Mölder letter, which attacked the Nazi government, and dropped it over Germany. See the commentary in Knauft, *Fall Stettin,* 26–27.

67. Daniel Report, DAB V/71–4 Stettin, ff. 5–13.

68. Knauft, *Fall Stettin,* 49.

69. Reich Supreme War Tribunal Torgau, September 22, 1944, session of September 2–4, 1944, VHA Reichskriegsgericht, 2(I), Geh. Kdos. 1943–45, Friedrich Lorenz, n.f.

70. Klosterkamp, *Kind und Opfer,* 24, 49, 53.

71. Ibid., 108.

72. Pruß, "Pfarrer Dr. Alfons Maria Wachsmann," 115.

73. Herberhold, *A. M. Wachsmann,* 71 and 75.

74. Ibid., 77.

75. Volksgerichtshot Decision, December 3/4, 1943, BArch B R60 I 102, n.f.

5: Jews and the Diocese of Berlin

1. Kaller, *Unser Laienapostolat,* 264. On June 14, 1927, work had received the Church's imprimatur through Vicar General Tilmann. Pages 9 and 10 contain testimonies from leading Church figures throughout Germany, praising the first edition of the book. In their statements, they reveal how widespread was the use of this work by Catholic associations throughout Germany.

2. Among the extensive literature on the subject of anti-Semitism in the Christian churches see especially: Banki and Pawlikowski, eds., *Ethics in the Shadow of the Holocaust;* Baum, *Is the New Testament Anti-Semitic?* and *Christian Theology after Auschwitz;* Bergen, "Catholics, Protestants, and Antisemitism," 329–48; Carroll, *Constantine's Sword;* Dietrich, *God and Humanity in Auschwitz;* Flannery, *The Anguish of the Jews;* Greive, *Theologie und Ideologie;* Hürten, *Deutsche Katholiken,* 425–40; Kertzer, *The Popes against the Jews;* Littell, *The Crucifixion of the Jews;* Reuther, *Faith and Fratricide;* Tal, *Christians and Jews in Germany.*

3. For the origins of such myths see Hsia, *The Myth of Ritual Murder: Jews and Magic in Reformation Germany.*

4. See Crossan, *Who Killed Jesus?*

5. For a discussion of anti-Semitism in the Catholic Church in the 1920s and 1930s see Phayer, *The Catholic Church and the Holocaust,* 1–19, here 1–2; and Passelecq and Suchecky, *The Hidden Encyclical,* 96–100.

6. For example, see Gundlach, "Antisemitismus," 505–6.

7. Lill, "German Catholicism's Attitude towards the Jews," 154, 161–62.

8. Kaller, *Unser Laienapostolat,* 264–65.

9. On this point see Dietrich, *Catholic Citizens in the Third Reich,* 233–36; Hürten, "Judenhaß—Schuld der Christen?" 1500.

10. Here Bertram referred to the persecution of Catholics, especially in Mexico and Russia. See Bertram to German Bishops, March 31, 1933, in Stasiewski, ed., *Akten deutscher Bischöfe,* 1:42–43. On Bertram's comment see Brandl, "Katholische Kirche und Juden im Dritten Reich," 9.

11. Kaller, *Unser Laienapostolat,* 266–67.

12. The *Biblische Geschichte* reads: "The Jews demand the death of Christ on account of blasphemy." Then the author used the traditional passages from the Gospel of John in which Jews demand that Pilate crucify Christ. See Bischöflichen Ordinariat zu Berlin, *Biblische Geschichte,* 235–36. See also Bischöfliches Ordinariat zu Berlin, *Kleine Schulbibel,* 76–77.

13. Interview with Frau Gertraud Tietz, Berlin, December 19, 1996. Alfons Heck, who grew up in the Mosel Valley of the Rhineland during the Third Reich, confirmed Teitz's statement when he recorded in his memoirs: "All Catholic children knew that the Jews had killed Christ, which seemed worse than being a Protestant." See Heck, *A Child of Hitler,* 14.

14. The Völkisch movement incorporated a wide variety of right-wing groups, the majority founded after the First World War and whose weltanschauung incorporated an extreme nationalism, a rabid anti-Semitism, and often a strong anti-Catholicism. On the origin and thought of the Völkisch movement see Hermand, *Völkisch Utopias and National Socialism;* Mosse, *The Crisis of German Ideology* and *Toward the Final Solution;* Perry, "Racial Nationalism and the Rise of Modern Antisemitism," 241–67; Puscher, *Die völkische Bewegung;* Puscher, *Handbuch zur Völkischen Bewegung;* Scholder, *The Churches and the Third Reich* 1:74–87; Stackelberg, *Idealism Debased;* and Stern, *The Politics of Cultural Despair.* The centrality of the racial principle in the National Socialist weltanschauung is discussed in Burleigh and Wippermann, *The Racial State.*

15. This tragic fact has been noted in numerous works and articles. See especially Friedländer, *Nazi Germany and the Jews,* 42–44 and 46–49; Lewy, *The Catholic Church and Nazi Germany,* 274–84; Phayer, *The Catholic Church and the Holocaust;* and Tinnemann, "The German Catholic Bishops and the Jewish Question," 55–85.

16. Faulhaber to Pacelli, April 10, 1933, in Stasiewski, ed., *Akten deutscher Bischöfe,* 1:54.

17. Bishop of Berlin, Berlin, March 21, 1931, in Klein, *Berolinen Canonizationis,* 2:39.

18. *Germania,* December 25, 1932.

19. Ibid., December 25, 1934.

20. See the texts of the following laws: Law for the Restoration of the Professional Civil Service, April 7, 1933; Law Regarding Admission to the Bar, April 7, 1933; and Law against the Overcrowding of German Schools and Institutions of Higher Learning, April 25, 1933, are found in Dawidowicz, *A Holocaust Reader,* 38–43.

21. Joint Pastoral Letter of the German Bishops, Vigil of Pentecost 1933, DAB VI/20, n.f.

22. Many of these articles had a far-reaching impact. For example, on August 8, 1935, the *Neue Zürcher Zeitung* published excerpts from an article in the *Katholisches Kirchenblatt für das Bistum Berlin* from the summer of 1935 that stressed Pope Pius XI's emphasis on the universality of the Church that incorporated all races. See *Neue Zürcher Zeitung*, August 8, 1935, BArch B NS 43 131, n.f.

23. See *Katholisches Kirchenblatt für das Bistum Berlin*, June 5, 1932, June 12, 1932, June 19, 1932, and June 26, 1934; and Spectator, "Der Irrtum des Nationalsozialismus," 99–106.

24. See Domschke, *Glaube aus dem Blut?*. The Berlin diocese chancery along with the Catholic publishing house of Germania sponsored the publication of Domschke's work that dealt with questions of "race and religion." On June 7, 1934, the Berlin *Amtsblatt* included an article that encouraged the clergy to read the work and distribute it to their congregations. See *Amtsblatt des Bischöflichen Ordinariats Berlin*, June 7, 1934, 53. Other dioceses joined suit in promoting the title. For example, the diocese of Eichstätt in Bavaria also made its clergy aware of the title and urged them to distribute it to their parishioners. See DAE Kreuz und Hakenkreuz I, n.f.

25. Bishop Bares recommended that his clergy read and disseminate the contents of the works critical of Rosenberg's philosophy. See foreword of Bares in *Studien zum Mythus des XX. Jahrhunderts*, iii, and *Katholisches Kirchenblatt für das Bistum Berlin*, April 21, 1935.

26. *Katholisches Kirchenblatt für das Bistum Berlin*, June 12, 1932.

27. Ibid., June 19, 1932.

28. The sermons may be found in Faulhaber, *Judentum, Christentum, Germanentum*. For a discussion of the events surrounding the 1933 Advent sermons see Gallin, "The Cardinal and the State," 385–404; and Hamerow, "Cardinal Faulhaber and the Third Reich," 145–68, and *On the Road to the Wolf's Lair*, 131–45.

29. *Katholisches Kirchenblatt für das Bistum Berlin*, June 5, 1932.

30. Spectator, "Der Irrtum des Nationalsozialismus," 100–101.

31. On Lagarde, see Lougee, *Paul de Lagarde*, and Stern, *The Politics of Cultural Despair*, 3–94. On Chamberlain, see Field, *Evangelist of Race*.

32. See Stark, *Nationalsozialismus und Katholische Kirche*.

33. Spectator, "Der Irrtum des Nationalsozialismus," 106.

34. Domschke, *Glaube aus dem Blut?* 24–26.

35. *Amtsblatt des Bischöflichen Ordinariats Berlin*, December 5, 1933, 106–7.

36. Ibid., February 4, 1937, 23.

37. See Pfliegler, *Der lebendige Christ vor der wirklichen Welt*.

38. Sonnenschein, "Caritaspflicht" (originally printed September 11, 1927), 87.

39. Schreiber, "Hirtenbrief zur Caritas Opferwoche," in *Amtsblatt des Bischöflichen Ordinariats Berlin*, August 18, 1931, 81–82.

40. Schreiber, "Katholische Caritashilfe für den Winter 1932/33," in *Amtsblatt des Bischöflichen Ordinariats Berlin*, September 24, 1932, 82.

41. Caritasverband für das Bistum Berlin, *Caritas-Arbeit im Bistum Berlin 1938*, 7.

42. Weber, *Das Wesen der Caritas*, 68.

43. Ibid., 146. In this passage, Weber quotes from a text of the Tübingen theologian Karl Adam, *Glaube und Liebe*.

44. Weber, *Das Wesen der Caritas*, 77.

45. Ibid., 152.

46. Ibid., 155.

47. Fürstbischöfliches Ordinariat zu Breslau, *Katholische Katechismus,* 49.

48. Bares, "Hirtenwort anläßlich der Caritas-Sammlung," in *Amtsblatt des Bischöflichen Ordinariats Berlin,* April 17, 1934, 24.

49. *Germania,* October 29, 1934.

50. *Amtsblatt des Bischöflichen Ordinariats Berlin,* October 10, 1938, 71.

51. Ibid., May 28, 1940, 46.

52. Sermon of Preysing, November 15, 1942, DAB V/16, n.f. The Fulda bishops' conference made similar statements in a joint pastoral letter of September 1943 (read in Berlin in two parts: Sundays, September 19 and 26, 1943) and a joint pastoral statement of August 19, 1943 (read on Sunday, August 29, 1943). See *Hirtenbrief der deutschen Bischöfe über die Zehn Gebote,* September 1943, (Version specific to Berlin) DAB VI/20, n.f.; and *Hirtenwort des deutschen Episkopats,* in Volk, ed., *Akten deutscher Bischöfe,* 6:178–84. For a discussion of the development of the latter letter and statement by the German bishops see Leugers, *Gegen eine Mauer bischöflichen Schweigens,* 260–93; Volk, "Die Fuldaer Bischofskonferenz, 56–82, "Episkopat und Kirchenkampf im Zweiten Weltkrieg. 1," 83–97, and "Episkopat und Kirchenkampf im Zweiten Weltkrieg. 2," 98–113.

53. On this point, see Phayer, *The Catholic Church and the Holocaust.*

54. General Vicar Prange to Caritasverband for Berlin, July 7, 1938, DAB I/1–104.

55. On the efforts of the Berlin *Hilfswerk* see Knauft, "Einsatz für verfolgte Juden," 591–603, and *Unter Einsatz des Lebens;* Phayer, *Protestant and Catholic Women in Nazi Germany,* 204–24; Reutter, *Die Hilfstätigkeit katholischer Organisationen,* 163–65, 278–83, 287–89, and *Katholische Kirche als Fluchthelfer im Dritten Reich,* 105–16; *St. Hedwigblatt,* Berlin, October 16, 1988, 331–32, and November 13, 1988, 363, 367; Vuletić, *Christen Jüdischer Herkunft im Dritten Reich.*

56. Adolph, *Kardinal Preysing und zwei Diktaturen,* 178.

57. From September 1941, Dr. Margarete Sommer (1893–1965) ran the *Hilfswerk* and also served as an advisor to Bishop Preysing on Jewish issues. On Sommer's work, see Herzberg, *Dienst am Höheren Gesetz;* Oleschinski, "Daß das Menschen waren, nicht Steine," 395–416; Phayer, "Margarete Sommer, Berlin Catholics, and Germany's Jews," 112–20, and "The Catholic Resistance Circle in Berlin," 216–29; and Phayer and Fleischner, *Cries in the Night,* 14–41.

58. On August 23, 1941, Himmler issued a decree that "ordered the emigration of Jews be stopped immediately." Between October 16 and November 4, 1941, the first deportations of Jews from the Reich to Lodz began. See Yahil, *The Holocaust,* 293–94.

59. Phayer, *Protestant and Catholic Women in Nazi Germany,* 214–15.

60. Hilfswerk reports: April 1, 1939, to March 31, 1940; April 1, 1940, to March 31, 1941, DAB I/1–104, n.f.

61. Kaplan, *Between Dignity and Despair,* 123. Kaplan stated that more than 100 Jews lost their lives, "not counting the camp deaths or suicides occurring shortly thereafter." Yahil reported that the number of destroyed synagogues was "about double those figures." Yahil, *The Holocaust,* 111.

62. Kaplan, *Between Dignity and Despair,* 121–25; Noakes and Pridham, eds., *Nazism: A History in Documents,* 1:553–58; Schultheis, *Die Reichskristallnacht in Deutschland;* Yahil, *The Holocaust,* 109–14.

63. Froehlich to Potsdam Gestapo, April 15, 1941, DAB V/8 Nachlaß Froehlich, n.f.

64. Sermon, Berlin-Neukölln, September 29, 1946, DAB V/8 Nachlaß Froehlich, n.f.

65. Chief Public Prosecutor Berlin to Minister of Justice, April 19, 1936, BArch B R5101 22247, f. 122.

66. Gestapo Report, November 21, 1938, BArch B R5101 22247, f. 109.

67. Gestapo Berlin to Kerrl, February 2, 1939, BArch B R5101 22247, f. 111.

68. Chief Public Prosecutor Berlin to Minister of Justice, April 21, 1936, BArch B R5101 22247, ff. 84–87.

69. District Court Berlin, Criminal Case Decision, July 12, 1937, BArch B R5101 22247, ff. 102–3. This incident made national news and was reported in *Germania,* July 13, 1937.

70. Schnura to District Office Charlottenburg, March 18, 1946, DAB VI/1 Schnura, n.f.

71. Hehl, *Priester unter Hitlers Terror,* 1:485.

72. Minister of Justice to Kerrl, August 5, 1937, BArch B R5101 22277, f. 65.

73. Lagebericht, May 1938, SAPMO-BArch D Z/B1 1652 Akt 5, f. 127.

74. Chief State Prosecutor to Minister of Justice, February 13, 1938, BArch B R3001 IIIg17 1322/38, ff. 1–3.

75. Chief State Prosecutor to Minister of Justice, February 13, 1938, BArch B R3001 III g17 1322–38, f. 4 R.

76. Special Court of the District Court Berlin, July 18, 1939, BArch B R5101 22247, f. 172.

77. President of the Chamber of Reich Literature, October 10, 1940, BArch B R5101 22248, n.f.

78. Gestapo to Kerrl, January 12, 1941, BArch B 22248 R5101, f. 26.

79. Report, March 11, 1942, in Boberach, ed., *Berichte des SD,* 626; and Hehl, *Priester unter Hitler Terror,* 1:488.

6: For the Glory of the Führer

1. These pioneering comprehensive studies first mentioned the existence of brown priests: Conway, *The Nazi Persecution of the Churches,* 133, 169, 406–7; Dietrich, *Catholic Citizens in the Third Reich,* 55; Hetzer, *Kirchenkampf in Augsburg,* 35–36; Lewy, *The Catholic Church and Nazi Germany,* 6–7, 10, 101, 155, 272; May, *Kirchenkampf oder Katholikenverfolgung?* 308–9; Natterer, *Der Bayerische Klerus,* 283–95; and Scholder, *The Churches and the Third Reich,* 1:135, 2:228.

2. Wagener, "Unterdrückungs und Verfolgungsmaßnahmen gegen Priester," 56.

3. Kertzer, *The Popes against the Jews.*

4. *Tablet,* "Catholic Priests and the Nazi Party," 17.

5. My own research supports Spotts's estimations.

6. In his analysis, however, Spotts dedicated only one paragraph to Catholic Nazi priests and seven pages to Protestants pastors who made similar choices in regard to the party. This contrast revealed his clear lack of access to sources to undertake a full analysis of the Catholic clergy sympathetic to National Socialism. Spotts, *The Churches and Politics in Germany,* 109.

7. The Catholic statistical yearbook for Germany indicated that in 1933 there were 16,887 priests in parish ministry, with an additional 4,574 priests who served as chaplains and teachers or were in retirement. This does not include the numerous religious priests stationed throughout the German dioceses in varied ministries. Krose, ed., *Kirchliches Handbuch*, 19:n.p., statistical foldout.

8. Dierker, *Himmlers Glaubenskrieger*, 369.

9. Childers, *The Nazi Voter*, 262–69.

10. May, *Kirchenkampf oder Katholikenverfolgung?* 309.

11. For example, see the November 21, 1935, letter from Kerrl to Goebbels, in which Kerrl warned him of priests who only wished "to use the party as a screen" after difficulties with Church superiors concerning nonpolitical issues. Kerrl to Goebbels, November 21, 1935, BArch B R5101 22314, n.f. On this point, see *Tablet*, "German Priest and the Nazi Party," 18–19; and Fandel, *Konfession und Nationalsozialismus*, 467–68.

12. Greive, *Theologie und Ideologie*, 41, 76; and Breuning, *Die Vision des Reiches*, 21.

13. On this point of separation of the Nazi Party and religion, see Scholder, *The Churches and the Third Reich*, 1:88–98.

14. Tröster, "'. . . die besondere Eigenart des Herrn Dr. Pieper!'" 54.

15. Brandl, "Josef Roth," 743. On Roth also see Baumgärtner, "Vom Kaplan zum Ministerialrat," 221–34; Bleistein, "'Überläufer im Sold der Kirchenfeinde,'" 71–109; and Kreutzer, *Das Reichskirchenministerium*, 161–82.

16. On Häuser, see Blümel, *Dr. Theol. Philipp Häuser*; *Landkreis Schwabmünchen*, 94–96; 448–51; Hetzer, *Kirchenkampf in Augsburg*, 35–36; Lenski, "Pfarrer Dr. Philipp Häuser"; and Pötzl and Wüst, eds., *Bobingen und seine Geschichte*, 922.

17. Schreiber to Berlin Clergy, March 21, 1931, in Klein, *Berolinen Canonizationis*, 2:40.

18. Kundgebung der Fuldaer Bischofskonferenz, March 28, 1933, in *Amtsblatt des Bischöflichen Ordinariats Berlin*, April 1, 1933, 23.

19. Kupper, *Staatliche Akten*, 273.

20. Kerrl to Goebbels, November 21, 1935, BArch B R5101 22314, n.f. On Roth's concerns see Roth to Heß, December 13, 1935, BArch B R5101 22268, f. 84.

21. Note, May 1940, BArch B R43 II/155, ff. 72–73.

22. Baumgärtner, "Vom Kaplan zum Ministerialrat," 234.

23. Kerrl to Goebbels, November 21, 1935, BArch B R5101 22314, n.f.

24. Kerrl to Heß, June 13, 1936, BArch B R5101 22268, f. 128.

25. Bormann to Kerrl, August 22, 1936, BArch B R5101 22268, f. 135.

26. On the exploits of these individuals, see Alvarez, *Spies in the Vatican*; Alvarez and Graham, *Nothing Sacred*; Boberach, "Organe der nationalsozialistischen Kirchenpolitik," 305–31; Dierker, *Himmlers Glaubenskrieger*; Graham, "Documenti di Guerra da Mosca," 542–50; Kreutzer, *Das Reichskirchenministerium*, 182–86; Patin, *Beiträge zur Geschichte*; Sereny, *Into That Darkness*; and Stehle, *Graue Eminenzen*, 152–59.

27. Lagebericht July 1934, GStAPK I/Rep. P Lageberichte Provinz Brandenburg 2,5 Potsdam, f. 144.

28. Dierker, *Himmlers Glaubenskrieger*, 370–71.

29. On May 1, 1932, Pirchegger joined the NSDAP and was assigned number 901,259. Pirchegger Karte, BArch, NS-Akt, PBU. On Pirchegger, see Hofmüller, *Steirische Priester*, 93–101.

30. On the 1936 referendum and the German bishops, see Lewy, *The Catholic Church and Nazi Germany,* 201–5; and also Stasiewski, ed., *Akten deutscher Bischöfe,* 3:299–303, 310.

31. SD Berlin to SD-Section East Berlin, June 28, 1936, SAPMO-BArch D Z/B1 1691, f. 757.

32. Strehl to Hitler, June 6, 1933, BArch B R43 II/174, f. 31.

33. On the history of Catholics in Potsdam, see Allendorff, "Katholisches Leben in Potsdam," 260–92; on Strehl, see ibid., 289.

34. There is very little information on the *Katholische Vereinigung für nationale Politik.* According to Guenter Lewy, it was founded "as early as 1920" in Berlin to achieve "a synthesis between right-wing radicalism and Catholicism." Their publication, *Der Rütlischwur,* is not to be found in the German library system, nor was it located in my archival research. According to an October 1, 1997, correspondence with Lewy, it might have been among the collection he used that belonged to the late Father Franz Rödel in Jetzendorf. See Lewy, *The Catholic Church and Nazi Germany,* 6. Father Robert Chrysostomus Conrath was also a member of this group in Berlin and participated in pro-Nazi activity during the first years of power of the NSDAP. On Conrath, see Conrath, "Der Studentenseelsorger in Berlin," 57–59, and Groothuis, *Im Dienste einer überstaatlichen Macht,* 459–63.

35. On Wilhelm Kube see Adamy and Hübener, "Provinz Mark Brandenburg," 11–31, and Weiß, "Wilhelm Kube," 285–87.

36. Fromm to Kube, April 28, 1933, BLHA Pr. Br. Rep. 2A Regierung Potsdam II Pdm. 525, n.f.

37. On Kube's activity in regard to the German Protestant denominations and the German Christians, see Scholder, *The Churches and the Third Reich,* 1:197–209, 287–90.

38. Strehl Karte, NS-Akt, BArch B, PBU.

39. Lossau to Hitler, June 6, 1933, BArch B R 43 II/174, f. 34.

40. Kube to Schreiber, May 5, 1933, BLHA Pr. Br. Rep. 2A Regierung Potsdam II Pdm. 525, n.f.

41. Strehl-Lebenslauf, BDA VI/1 Johannes Strehl, n.f. There is a discrepancy concerning the exact date of Strehl's appointment. The 1936 diocesan *Schematismus* for Berlin recorded the date of the appointment as May 25, 1933; however, in a letter to Hitler dated June 6, 1933, Strehl stated that Bishop Schreiber appointed him on May 30, 1933. See Strehl to Hitler, June 6, 1933, BArch B, R43 II/174, f. 31.

42. Steinmann to Bertram, June 23, 1933, in Stasiewski, ed., *Akten deutscher Bischöfe,* 1:255.

43. See his comments in the *Kreuz Zeitung,* October 5, 1933, BArch B R5101 21675, f. 194.

44. Strehl to Hitler, June 6, 1933, BArch B R43 II/174, f. 32.

45. Lossau to Hitler, June 6, 1933, BArch B R43 II/174, f. 34.

46. Lossau, Strehl, Wilhelm Keller, and Dr. Müller to Hitler, June 21, 1933, BArch B R43 II/174, f. 41.

47. Steinmann to Bertram, 23 June 1933, in Stasiewski, ed., *Akten deutscher Bischöfe,* 1:255. In a 1947 written recollection, Konrad Gröber (1872–1948), Archbishop of Freiburg, also recounted hearing this rumor concerning the appointment of Strehl as state commissioner for Catholic Church affairs and the opposition of the Berlin bishop to this appointment. Darstellung Gröbers, 1947, in Volk, ed., *Kirchliche Akten,* 319.

48. Bertram to Faulhaber, Gröber, Hauck, Klein, and Schulte, June 25, 1933, Stasiewski, ed., *Akten deutscher Bischöfe,* 1:253–54.

49. In 1935, a Church Information Bureau of the episcopal administrative authorities in Berlin was achieved under the direction of Monsignor Dr. Georg Banasch (1888–1960), a chancery official. This bureau was created to assist communication between diocesan chanceries, to formulate public statements for the bishops, and to inform the diocesan chanceries of State activity that affected the Catholic Church. In November 1935, the Gestapo arrested Banasch and confiscated records of the bureau. In March 1936, Banasch was finally released from custody and did not return to his work at the bureau. Father Heinrich Heufers provisionally took over the bureau. Finally, on August 20, 1936, the Fulda conference dissolved the bureau in an effort to separate any future endeavors of this nature from attachment to a particular diocese. In December 1936, in its place, the bishops established the commissioner's bureau of the Fulda bishops' conference, and soon thereafter Cardinal Bertram appointed Monsignor Heinrich Wienken, priest of the Münster diocese and, in 1937, auxiliary bishop of Meißen, as its director. On the Information Bureau and Wienken, see Höllen, *Heinrich Wienken,* 54–69.

50. Strehl to Gestapo Potsdam, January 15, 1934, BArch B R43 II/174, f. 193.

51. Gestapo Berlin to Lammers, February 3, 1934, BArch B R43 II/174, f. 192.

52. *Potsdamer Beobachter,* August 24, 1935, in BArch B R5101 22384, n.f.

53. See *Schematismus des Bistums Berlin* 1937, 129, and 1938, 41, 120. After the war, Strehl went into full retirement and lived in Königshausen über Schwabmünchen in Bavaria until his death on May 18, 1951. See *Schematismus des Bistums Berlin* 1947, 158; Bischöfliches Ordinariat Berlin, *Zum Gedächtnis,* 19.

54. Allendorf to Kube, April 15, 1936, BLHA Pr. Br. Rep. 2A II Pdm. 525, n.f.

55. F. to Fromm, April 24, 1936, BLHA Pr. Br. Rep. 2A II Pdm. 525, n.f.

56. Dr. Z. to Fromm, May 5, 1936, BLHA Pr. Br. Rep. 2A II Pdm. 525, n.f.

57. SD Report to C., May 9, 1936, SAPMO-BArch D Z/B1 1691, f. 813.

58. Kube to Fromm, June 2, 1936, BLHA Pr. Br. Rep. 2A II Pdm. 525, n.f.

59. From the "Chronik des St. Josephshauses, II," 1932, 58–59, DAB VI/1 Paul Drossert. His signature on the appeal for Hitler during the time when the German bishops had prohibited activity for the Nazi Party led the chancery to publish a denouncement of him in the April 17, 1932, edition of the *Katholisches Kirchenblatt für das Bistum Berlin.* The Berlin chancery ordered Drossert to move into St. Hedwig's Hospital and take up residency there. There is very little documentary evidence on Drossert, making his fate unclear until 1937, when he became a chaplain for the German Wehrmacht. In 1941, he was promoted to a supervisory position and also undertook prison chaplaincy in Torgau. Sometime after the war, he incardinated into the Berlin diocese and assisted with parish ministry in Zossen and Gatow. He died on January 24, 1969, and was buried in the cemetery of St. Hedwig.

60. Kube to Fromm, June 6, 1936, BLHA Pr. Br. Rep. 2A II Pdm. 525, n.f.

61. Gauleiter Pomerania to Fromm, 15 July 1936; Gauleitung Groß-Berlin Personalamt to Fromm, July 20, 1936; BLHA Pr. Br. Rep. 2A II Pdm. 525, n.f.

62. Kreisleiter Gauleitung Kurmark to Fromm, August 21, 1936, BLHA Pr. Br. Re. II 2a Pdm. 525, n.f.

63. Scholz's application mentioned in Fromm to Stürtz, August 29, 1936, BLHA Pr. Br. Rep. 2A II Pdm. 525, n.f.

64. Ortsgruppe NSDAP Zossen to Fromm, August 28, 1936, BLHA Pr. Br. Rep. 2A II Pdm. 525, n.f.

65. Fromm to Stürtz, August 29, 1936, BLHA Pr. Br. Rep. 2A II Pdm. 525, n.f.

66. Fromm to Ortsgruppe NSDAP Zossen, n.d., BLHA Pr. Br. Rep. 2A II Pdm. 525, n.f.

67. Stürtz to Preysing, September 1, 1936, BLHA Pr. Br. Rep. 2A II Pdm. 525, n.f.

68. *Schematismus des Bistums Berlin* 1939, 123.

69. Placed into retirement on July 1, 1939; *Schematismus des Bistums Berlin* 1941, 107, 142.

70. Leonards, "Treptow an der Rega," 134, 144–49, in DAB VI/1 Walter Leonards, n.f.

71. Lichtenberg to Leonards, March 21, 1936, in Klein, *Berolinen Canonizationis,* 2:101–2

72. For additional information on Leonards, see *Domkapitular Schäfer,* May 9, 1955, BAT, Abt. 88, Nr. 112, Walter Leonards, n.f. On Vriens and the Netherlands Press Bureau, see Hürten, ed., *Deutsche Briefe, 1934–1938,* 1:330–31 and 2:923–24, 930–31, 1026; and Volk, ed., *Akten Kardinal Michael von Faulhabers,* 2:340, n. 4.

73. Adolph, *Geheime Aufzeichnungen,* 163, 202.

74. *Schematismus des Bistums Berlin* 1947, 114. In 1950, upon receiving an inquiry into Leonards's character, the Berlin vicar general wrote to the Trier vicar general and informed him that the Berlin diocese had retired Leonards because of financial improprieties with parish funds. It is interesting that the letter makes no mention of Leonards's efforts on behalf of the Nazi state. See Vicar General Berlin to Vicar General Trier, June 19, 1950, BAT, Abt. 88, Nr. 112, Walter Leonards, n.f.

75. See Volk, ed., *Akten Kardinal Michael von Faulhabers,* 2:618, n. 2, and 652, n. 4. Also see Lewy, *The Catholic Church and Nazi Germany,* 254. Copies of the eight newsletters of the kath. Pfarrer-Notbund may be found in DAE Bischöfe und Klerus 1933–45, n.f. and Kreuz und Hakenkreuz 1 (Pfarrer Kraus), Documents 30, 31; also see Kölker to Rosenberg, December 19, 1939, BArch B NS43 110, n.f.

76. Walter Leonards Karte, NSDAP Akt, BArch B, PBU.

77. BArch B R58 1581, n.f.

78. See the correspondence in BAT, Abt. 88, Nr. 112, Walter Leonards, n.f.

79. Helms to Kerrl, August 3, 1937; Kerrl to Helms, August 12, 1937, BArch B R5101 22384, n.f.

80. Kreisleiter Gauleitung Kurmark to Fromm, August 21, 1936, BLHA Pr. Br. Rep. 2A II Pdm. 525, n.f.; Testimony of Father Albrecht Jochmann to Preysing, August 11, 1945; Father Scherer of Oberösterreich to Preysing, March 6, 1946; Schühly, S.J., to Ordinariat Berlin, April 29, 1955, DAB I/5, n.f.

81. *Schematismus des Bistums Berlin* 1937, 69, 117.

82. Ortsgruppe NSDAP Zossen to Fromm, August 28, 1936, BLHA Pr. Br. Rep. 2A II Pdm. 525, n.f.

83. SA number 100,361; NSDAP number 1,545,459. Anton Scholz Karte; SA-Akt, BArch B, PBU.

84. DDR Ministerium für Staatssicherheit to Bezirksverwaltung Frankfurt/Oder, September 20, 1960, SAPMO-BArch D Z/B1 1691, n.f.

85. Steinmann to Scholz, November 27, 1933, BLHA Pr. Br. Rep. 2A II Pdm. 525, n.f.

86. Scholz to Chancery Berlin, June 12, 1950, DAB I/5 Scholz, n.f.

87. Jochmann to Preysing, August 11, 1945, DAB I/5 Scholz, n.f.

88. Scholz to Berlin Chancery, June 12, 1950, DAB I/5 Scholz, n.f.

89. Ibid., November 11, 1950; Scholz to Berlin Chancery, March 15, 1951; DAB I/5 Scholz, n.f.

90. Prange to Scholz, March 28, 1951, DAB I/5 Scholz, n.f.

91. Lebenslauf Scholz, DAB I/5 Scholz, n.f.

92. The documentary evidence does not offer any insight into why König, in 1926, left his pastoral duties in the diocese and retired from active ministry shortly thereafter. König Lebenslauf, EAP, Sammlung zum Karl König.

93. Undated (after 1939) obituary for König, EAP, Sammlung zu Karl König. Also see König to Lammers, March 15, 1935, BArch B R43 II/1636, ff.11–12

94. Although I was unable to locate König's NSDAP membership card or NS-file, contemporary articles from Nazi publications regularly describe him as a member of the party. For example, see *Schwarze Korps,* March 2, 1939.

95. König Easter Letter, Easter 1934, BHStAM StK 7255, n.f.

96. SD to Ziegler, June 19, 1936, SAPMO-BArch D, Z/B1 1691, f. 709.

97. Here, Adolph referred specifically to König's behavior in a courtroom during a currency trial procedure. See Adolph, *Geheime Aufzeichnungen,* 163.

98. König to Lammers, July 4, 1935, BArch B R43 II 1636a, ff. 122–23.

99. König to Lammers, July 25, 1935, BArch B, R43 II/1636a, f. 41.

100. König to Lammers, August 9, 1935, BArch B, R43 II/1636a, ff. 2–4.

101. *Tegernseer Zeitung,* October 18, 1935 in EAP, Sammlung zu Karl König, n.f.

102. The content of this sermon carried even more weight in light of the fact that it was the day after the retaking of the Rheinland and the German Day for Remembrance for Fallen Heroes. Sermon, March 8, 1936, EAP, Sammlung zu Karl König, n.f.

103. König to Simon, March 7, 1938, EAP Sammlung zu Karl König, n.f.

104. For example, see König to Röhm, May 20, 1934, BArch B, R43 II/1636, ff. 114–15; König to Lammers, Pentecost 1934, BArch B, R43 II/1636, n.f.; König to Runte, May 12, 1936, BHStAM StK 7257, n.f.

105. König newsletter, 21 April 1936, EAP, Sammlung zu Karl König, n.f. An unnamed friend even planned to write a biography of König's exploits in the Third Reich entitled '*Pfarrer König, was wollen Sie?' Christliches, nationales und sozialistisches Leben und Wirken eines katholischen Pfarrers.* According to inquiries, König's friend never wrote this book. Unnamed to König, April 24, 1936, EAP, Sammlung zu Karl König.

106. See the following letters: Gierse to König, November 12, 1935; König to Gierse, November 16, 1935; Gierse to König, December 17, 1935; König to Gierse, January 13, 1936; consecutively printed. See BHStAM StK 7257, n.f.

107. Lichtenberg to Stadtpräsidenten Abt. für höheres Schulwesen Berlin, June 18, 1938, BArch B, R5101 22341, f. 166.

108. Lichtenberg to Kerrl, June 18, 1938, BArch B R5101 22341, f. 165.

109. Prange to König, July 16, 1938, BArch B R5101 22341, f. 170.

110. Göring to Klein, February 22, 1939, EAP, Sammlung zu Karl König, n.f.

111. Roth was a rabid anti-Semite who, during his career in the Ministry of Church Affairs, would regularly refer to a colleague in the Protestant Division of the ministry who he believed had Jewish blood as "Jude" (Jew) anytime he encountered him in the corridors of the ministry building. Recollection of Dr. Sebastian Schröcker, BArch K, Roth Nachlaß 898, n.f.

112. Roth, *Katholizismus und Judenfrage*, 2, 5, 10.

113. Bleistein, "Überläufer im Sold der Kirchenfeind," 74–75.

114. Roth joined the SA on April 1, 1934, and was assigned number 287,274. Roth, SA-Akt, BArch B PUB, n.f.

115. Brandl, "Josef Roth," 742.

116. See the series of correspondence between Faulhaber, Munich chancery and Roth in AEM Nachlaß Faulhaber 7269, n.f.

117. Steinmann to Neuhäusler, April 23, 1936, AEM Nachlaß Faulhaber 7269, n.f.

118. Roth to Faulhaber, May 17, 1936; Faulhaber to Roth, May 28, 1936, AEM, Nachlaß Faulhaber 7269, n.f.

119. Report of Neuhäusler, August 28, 1935, AEM Nachlaß Faulhaber 5539, n.f. On Schachleiter, see the pro-Nazi contemporary work by Engelhard, *Abt Schachleiter*, which was published at great expense during the war. For a critical analysis of Schachleiter's activities in Nazi Germany utilizing a wealth of sources, see Bleistein, "Abt Alban Schachleiter OSB," 170–87.

120. These concerns are expressed in the questions Faulhaber posed to Roth before he decided to suspend his approval. See Faulhaber to Roth, May 7, 1936, AEM, Nachlaß Faulhaber 7269, n.f.

121. Persönliche Erinnerungen, BArch K, Roth Nachlaß 898.

122. See Berg, "Die Kirche ist alt geworden," 125–127.

123. Sermon of Roth, during the Memorial Mass for the German Day in Nuremberg on September 4, 1923, *Bayern und Reich* 1 (1923), BArch K Roth Nachlaß 898, n.f. On July 29, 1941, similar images of Christ were presented by Father Philipp Häuser during his funeral eulogy for Roth. See AEM Nachlaß Faulhaber 7269.

124. Baumgärtner, "Vom Kaplan zum Ministerialrat," 227. Compare these to the images of a "manly church" of the Protestant German Christians. See Bergen, *Twisted Cross*, 61–81.

125. Roth, "Die katholische Kirche und die Judenfrage," 175.

126. BArch K Roth Nachlaß 898, n.f.

127. Roth Obituary, AEM Nachlaß Faulhaber 7269.

7: The Unique Path of Bernhard Lichtenberg

1. Erb, *Bernhard Lichtenberg*, 18.

2. Klein, "Bernhard Lichtenberg und die Berliner Blutzeugen," 1703.

3. Lichtenberg, "Was können die Katholiken von den Konvertiten lernen?" 105.

4. Ibid., 106.

5. Ogiermann, *Bis zum letztem Atemzug*, 38.

6. Ibid., 11.

7. Klein, "Bernhard Lichtenberg und die Berliner Blutzeugen," 1701.

8. Erb, *Bernhard Lichtenberg*, 13; and Klein, *Seliger Bernhard Lichtenberg*, 9–10. Lichtenberg took part in the September 9–13, 1908, International Eucharistic Congress in London and the 1926 Eucharistic World Congress in Chicago.

9. Lichtenberg studied at the Faculty of Theology at the Leopold-Franzens University, Innsbruck (April–July 1895), and then at the Faculty of Catholic-Theology at the Königlichen University of Breslau (October 1895–October 1898). Kock, *Er widerstand*, 216.

10. Erb, *Bernhard Lichtenberg,* 13.

11. Ibid., 14; Klein, "Bernhard Lichtenberg und die Berliner Blutzeugen," 1703.

12. Erb, *Bernhard Lichtenberg,* 15–16; Klein, "Bernhard Lichtenberg und die Berliner Blutzeugen," 1704.

13. Höhle, *Die Gründung des Bistums Berlin,* 107.

14. Kock, *Er widerstand,* 63.

15. Erb, *Bernhard Lichtenberg,* 17.

16. Ibid., 21.

17. Klein, "Bernhard Lichtenberg und die Berliner Blutzeugen," 1705–1706.

18. *Amtlicher Führer durch das Bistum Berlin 1938,* 38.

19. Erb, *Bernhard Lichtenberg,* 24.

20. Kock, *Er widerstand,* 79.

21. Ogiermann, "Bernhard Lichtenberg," 280.

22. Kock, *Er widerstand,* 80. In 1919, following the turbulent war and revolution, it was not surprising that Lichtenberg and other priests entered the representative ranks of the Center Party to protect the Church's rights in the new Weimar government. Until his appointment to the Cathedral of St. Hedwig in 1931, Lichtenberg served as a representative of the Center Party in the district assembly in Charlottenburg and intermittently in the Berlin assembly. In addition, he remained a member of the party until its dissolution in 1933. For a discussion on Lichtenberg's involvement in politics, see Klein, "Bernhard Lichtenberg und die Berliner Blutzeugen," 1707.

23. On Father Stratmann and the Friedenbund deutscher Katholiken, see Stratmann, *In der Verbannung.*

24. *Der Angriff,* June 26, 1931, Mann. *Prozeß Bernhard Lichtenberg,* 19–21.

25. *Germania,* November 10, 1931.

26. Klein *Berolinen Canonizationis Servi Dei Bernardi Lichtenberg: Sacerdotis Saecularis in Odium Fidei, Uti Fertur, Interfecti (1875–1943),* 1:71–72.

27. Lichtenberg had "very thick skin" and never allowed people's comments to stop him from expressing his views. He was also willing to place his life in jeopardy to speak the truth. In a November 1918 meeting in north Berlin in the *Pharus* Hall, Lichtenberg served as the main speaker and discussion leader. Several individuals in the audience disagreed with his views and shouted "Beat the *Pfaffen* dead!" Lichtenberg ignored them and, although someone offered him a relatively secret means of leaving the hall once the meeting had ended, chose to exit with the crowd. Luckily, no one harmed him, but instead, the crowd "made way for him." See Ogiermann, *Bis zum letzten Atemzug,* 38–39.

28. Erb, *Bernhard Lichtenberg,* 23.

29. During the Weimar Republic, there was a growing interest in the human physique, nudism, family planning, and birth control. On these topics see Toepfer, *Empire of Ectasy;* Grossmann, *Reforming Sex;* and Usborne, *The Politics of the Body.*

30. Klein, *Berolinen Canonizationis,* 1:26.

31. Klein, *Berolinen Canonizationis,* 2:28.

32. Ibid., 27. In the same article Lichtenberg had written concerning the air and sunbath: "The air and sunbath in the Volkspark will degenerate into the nudist movement, like the gymnastic and sports week of 1925 in the festival hall of our city hall, where naked girls appeared covered only with narrow aprons, dancing in the manner of the Laban System, that recalls in its savagery an African black-dance." On the Laban Movement, see Toepfer, *Empire of Ecstasy,* 99–107. The quote

recalls the predominant attitude of superiority that the so-called white Europeans had over the so-called black Africans and so-called yellow Asians. The works of Weindling, *Health, Race and German Politics,* and Adas, *Machines as the Measure of Men,* help place the quote and held belief in historical perspective.

33. Pius XI, "Casti Connubii," in Carlen, ed., *The Papal Encyclicals 1903-1939,* 391-414.

34. On the connection between German and American eugenic racism see Kühl, *The Nazi Connection.*

35. Dietrich, "Nazi Eugenics," 52.

36. Dietrich, "A Catholic's Adaptation to German Eugenics," 77-78.

37. In 1845, Corvin published an "anti-Church pamphlet *Historical Monuments of Christian Fanaticism* (since 1869 published under the title *Pfaffenspiegel*), in Klein 1992a, 76, n. 1. Lichtenberg claimed that Corvin had plagiarized the work from known anti-Church writers "Weber, Ammann, Theiner, and Münch." Lichtenberg to Hitler, December 10, 1935, BArch B R43/II/175, f. 677. See also Klein 1992b, 100-101.

38. Lichtenberg to Hitler, BArch B R43/II/175, f. 677.

39. Lewy, *The Catholic Church and Nazi Germany,* 278. On Lichtenberg specifically Lewy wrote: "Even Provost Lichtenberg, a man who later paid with his life for trying to help the Jews, found it necessary in 1935 to address a personal letter to Hitler in which he protested the use of the book and pointed out that Corvin, according to the latest research, was not of Aryan descent." On Lewy's biases see Volk, "Zwischen Geschichtsschreibung und Hochhuthprosa," 225-347. Volk wrote: "Lewy has decided in favor of the absolute moralist. Therefore, the accuser of the compromise-willing Church pays little heed to the old question asked by historians regarding the tangible possibility of carrying out ethical exigencies" (340).

40. Chancery of the Archdiocese of Munich and Freising to the Honorable Sites of Ministry of the Archdiocese, February 25, 1937, in Neuhäusler, *Kreuz und Hakenkreuz,* 350.

41. Besier, "Anti-Bolshevism and Antisemitism," 447-56; Dietrich, *Catholic Citizens in the Third Reich,* 235; Hannot, *Die Judenfrage in der katholischen Tagespresse,* 176-79; Heitzer, "Deutscher Katholizismus und Bolschewismusgefahr," 355-87; and Mazura, *Zentrumspartei und Judenfrage,* 171-79.

42. Lichtenberg to Ambassador of Mexico in Berlin, May 11, 1928, in Klein, *Berolinen Canonizationis,* 2:24.

43. Lichtenberg to Hindenburg, November 13, 1929, in Klein, *Berolinen Canonizationis,* 2:32.

44. Ogiermann, *Bis zum letzten Atemzug,* 40.

45. Lichtenberg to Hindenburg, November 13, 1929, in Klein, *Berolinen Canonizationis,* 2:32-33.

46. Meissner to Lichtenberg, November 16, 1929, in Klein, *Berolinen Canonizationis,* 2:33-34.

47. Bertram offered four reasons for his hesitation to protest or interfere: "1. the fact that this concerns an economic struggle with an interest group that has no close bond with the Church; 2. that the step appears as an interference in an area that hardly touches on an area of activity of the episcopacy; the bishops, however, have good reason to confine themselves to their own area of activity; 3. that the steps will likely be unsuccessful because the arguments for and against are sufficiently known by sources in influential positions without our input; therefore, 4. the tactical consideration that this step, which will not remain in confidence in

closed groups, would surely find its most incorrect interpretation in the widest circles of all Germany, which in view of the extremely difficult and gloomy overall situation can in no way be a matter of indifference." He then added, "In passing it may be mentioned that the press that is predominantly in Jewish hands has been totally silent in view of the persecution of Catholics in various countries." Bertram to German Bishops, March 31, 1933, in Klein, *Berolinen Canonizationis*, 2:64–65; and Matheson, ed., *The Third Reich and the Christian Churches*, 11; Müller, *Katholische Kirche und Nationalsozialismus*, 98–99; Stasiewski, ed., *Akten deutscher Bischöfe*, 1:42–43, n. 3.

48. On the Reichsverband, see Röhm and Thierfelder, "Zwischen den Stühlen," 332–60.

49. *Mitteilungsblatt des Reichsverbandes christlicher-deutscher Staatsbürger nicht arischer oder nicht rein arischer Abstammung*, November 2/10, 1933, in Klein, *Berolinen Canonizationis*, 2:69.

50. Klein, *Berolinen Canonizationis*, 1:70.

51. Adolph, *Geheime Aufzeichnungen*, 29; Klein, *Berolinen Canonizationis*, 2:102; and Kock, *Er widerstand*, 96–97.

52. From 1925–1929, Gehrmann had also served as personal secretary to Nuncio Eugenio Pacelli. On Gehrmann's life, see Preuschoff, *Pater Eduard Gehrmann*, and Kraus, "Der Sekretär zweier Nuntien," 167–95. Gehrmann is the priest Michael Phayer refers to as Nuncio Cesare Orsenigo's "priest assistant" and "member of the Nazi party." See Phayer, *The Catholic Church and the Holocaust*, 45. According to an October 28, 1945 letter from Leiber to Preysing, Gehrmann was a member of the NSDAP, DAB V/16–4.

53. Adolph, *Geheime Aufzeichnungen*, 9.

54. Noakes and Pridham, eds., *Nazism: A History in Documents*, 1:457–58.

55. Pius XI, "Casti Connubii," in Carlen, ed., *The Papal Encyclicals 1903–1939*, 391–414. See p. 401, par. 68, of the encyclical for the section on sterilization.

56. Peters, "The Catholic Church and the Reich," 42. See also Friedlander, *The Origins of Nazi Genocide*; Klee, *Euthanasie im NS-Staat*, 36–38; Lewy, *The Catholic Church and Nazi Germany*, 258–63; Nowak, *"Euthanasie" und Sterilisierung*, 111–19; Richter, *Katholizismus und Eugenik*.

57. Peters, "The Catholic Church and the Reich," 46.

58. Steinmann to Pastors and Parochial Vicars of the Diocese of Berlin, January 12, 1934, BArch B R43 II/174, f. 194.

59. Diary of Walter Conrad, January 13, 1934, in Conrad, *Kirchenkampf*, 39, and Klein, *Berolinen Canonizationis*, 2:69–70.

60. See the correspondence between Frick, Bertram, and Faulhaber in Stasiewski, ed., *Akten deutscher Bischöfe*, 1:535–39, 585–89, 653–56, and Albrecht, ed., *Der Notenwechsel*, 1:60–61, 96–98.

61. *Amtsblatt des Bischöflichen Ordinariats Berlin*, July 20, 1935, 59–60, translation into German of an article from *L'Osservatore Romano* on questions regarding the Reich-Vatican concordat of 1933.

62. *Amtsblatt des Bischöflichen Ordinariats Berlin*, July 20, 1935, 59–61.

63. Minister of Justice to Kerrl, September 19, 1935, BArch B R5101 22268, ff. 44–45.

64. *Amtsblatt des Bischöflichen Ordinariats Berlin*, July 20, 1935, p. 61. Reportage of the reading from the pulpit found in GStA I/Rep. 90 P Lageberichte Prov. Brandenberg 2, 1, July 1935, f. 231.

65. Werner B. to SA Group Berlin-Brandenburg, July 21, 1935, BArch B R5101 21676, f. 246.

66. Heydrich to Kerrl, July 24, 1935, BArch B R5101 21676, f. 181.

67. A Gestapo V-Mann report attached to Heydrich's letter to Kerrl of July 24, 1935, confirmed that among the twenty-nine parishes and chapels listed, the priests in seven of them did not read the letter. The twenty-nine parishes listed represented only a portion of the entire diocese of Berlin. See BArch B R5101 21676, ff. 185–86.

68. Quoted in Kock, *Er widerstand,* 97.

69. On the history of the report see Adolph, *Sie sind nicht vergessen,* 216, n. 11.

70. Lichtenberg to Ministry of Interior, July 18, 1935, in Klein 1992b, 82–84.

71. Adolph, *Sie sind nicht vergessen,* 209.

72. Berlin Gestapo to Göring, September 27, 1935, in Klein, *Berolinen Canonizationis,* 2:97–100.

73. Berlin Gestapo to Göring, September 27, 1935, in Klein, *Berolinen Canonizationis,* 2:100.

74. Parsinnen relied on an interview with "Dr. Schultze" (December 5, 1969) found among the Deutsch Papers housed in the United States Army War College, Carlisle, Pennsylvania. Schultze's account cannot stand on its own without further corroboration. See Parssinen, *The Oster Conspiracy,* 95 and 210, n. 31. Dr. Erich Schultze (1901–1981) was a member of the NSDAP since 1932/1933 and a soldier in the Wehrmacht who in 1942 was court-martialed and sentenced to one year in prison for unauthorized use of rank and for unauthorized wearing of a military decoration. It was in Berlin-Tegel Prison that he came into contact with Lichtenberg. After the war, on June 12, 1961, Landgericht München I sentenced him to a year and two months for fraud. See Klein to Spicer, August 19, 2003, copy in possession of the author.

75. Mann, *Prozeß Bernhard Lichtenberg,* 9.

76. Knauft, "Einsatz für verfolgte Juden," 592.

77. See, for example, Letter Of Recommendation of Lichtenberg for the Catholic Non-Aryan Kühnauer, May 14, 1940, and similar letter for Non-Aryan Simonstein, September 23, 1940, in Klein, *Berolinen Canonizationis,* 2:124–26.

78. Reich Air Defense Association Group Berlin I/Linden to Lichtenberg, September 14, 1940, and draft of a letter from Lichtenberg to Reich Air Defense Association Group Berlin I/Linden, September 23, 1940, in Klein, *Berolinen Canonizationis,* 2:124–25.

79. On *Aktion T-4* and euthanasia in Nazi Germany, see Aly, Chroust, and Pross, *Cleansing the Fatherland;* Burleigh and Wippermann, *The Racial State,* 136–82; Burleigh, *Death and Deliverance;* Friedlander, *The Origins of Nazi Genocide;* Kater, *Doctors under Hitler;* Klee, ed., *Dokumente zur Euthanasie;* and Klee, *Euthanasia im NS-Staat.*

80. Lichtenberg to Conti, August 26, 1941, in Klein, *Berolinen Canonizationis,* 2:151.

81. The homily is printed in Löffler, ed., *Bischof Clemens August Graf von Galen,* 2:874–83.

82. Lichtenberg to Conti, August 26, 1941, in Klein, *Berolinen Canonizationis,* 2:150–51.

83. For an analysis of the Lichtenberg-Adam confrontation, see Spicer, "Last Years of a Resister," 248–70.

84. Kreidler, "Karl Adam und der Nationalsozialismus," 136–37; and Krieg, *Karl Adam,* 133–35.

85. On the German Faith movement see Nanko, *Die Deutsche Glaubensbewegung;* and Scholder, *The Churches and the Third Reich,* 1:451–53, 2:98–102. On Hauer, see Dierks, *Jakob Wilhelm Hauer,* and Scott-Craig and Davies, eds., *Germany's New Religion,* 27–84.

86. Adam, *Die geistige Lage des deutschen Katholizismus,* December 10, 1939, BArch B NS43 20, ff. 231R-232.

87. Adam, "Deutsches Volkstum," 40–63. Adam never published the second part of the article; however, a draft, "Deutsches Volkstum und katholisches Christentum, Fortsetzung," may be found in Diözesanarchiv Rottenburg, N67, Karl Adam, Nr. 34, n.f.

88. Adam, "Vom gottmenschlichen Erlöser," 111–45. Originally printed in two parts in *Deutsches Volksblatt* (Stuttgart) "Christus und das deutsche Volk," 86 (January 23, 1934), and "Die Erlösungstat Jesu Christi," January 24, 1934. Also see Kreidler, "Karl Adam und der Nationalsozialismus," 132–33, and Krieg, *Karl Adam,* 123–26, for an analysis of the lecture. The concept of Volksgemeinschaft tied directly into Adam's understanding of community within the Church. On this point, see Adam to Pirchen, July 4, 1940, UAE, Flugblatt Sammlung, Number 196, and Scherzberg, *Kirchenreform mit Hilfe des Nationalsozialismus.*

89. See Krieg, *Karl Adam,* 159–78, for a discussion of theology and neo-Romanticism.

90. Krieg, *Karl Adam,* 9.

91. Adam, *Die geistige Lage,* BArch B NS43 20, ff. 238R–239.

92. Ibid., f. 240R.

93. Ibid., f. 239R.

94. Ibid., ff. 240R–241R.

95. See Schulte to Orsenigo, September 27, 1940, in Volk, ed., *Akten deutscher Bischöfe,* 5:75, and Note of Sebastian concerning a Conversation with Bornewasser, November 8, 1940, in Volk, ed., *Akten deutscher Bischöfe,* 5:252. In the latter, Sebastian noted that Cardinal Bertram had declared to President Hürth of the *Kolpingsblatt* that if the newspaper continued to print things in a similar vein concerning Adam's comments, he would close down the newspaper.

96. Aretz, *Katholische Arbeiterbewegung,* 225; and Joos, *Am Räderwerk der Zeit,* 155–57.

97. Nagel to Cardinals, Archbishops and Bishops of Germany, June 4, 1940, BArch B R5101. (Specific folder undetermined. Copy in the possession of the author.)

98. Lichtenberg to Adam, November 4, 1940, in Klein, *Berolinen Canonizationis,* 2:126.

99. Ibid., 126–27.

100. Ibid., 127.

101. Ibid., 127–29. Lichtenberg quoted from *Mein Kampf,* chap. 5, "Philosophy and Organization." See Hitler, *Mein Kampf,* 454–55.

102. Lichtenberg to Adam, November 4, 1940, in Klein, *Berolinen Canonizationis,* 2:133.

103. Ibid., 135.

104. Ibid., 136.

105. Ibid., 137.

106. Adam to Lichtenberg, November 23, 1940, in Klein, *Berolinen Canonizationis,* 2:138.

107. Ibid., 138–39.

108. Ibid., 139.

109. Ibid.

110. Ibid.

111. Ibid., 142.

112. Lichtenberg to Adam, November 30, 1940, in Klein, *Berolinen Canonizationis,* 2:144.

113. Ibid., 146.

114. *Protokoll,* September, 29, 1941, in Mann, *Prozeß Bernhard Lichtenberg,* 44–45. The young women's names are specified in Note of the Gestapo Concerning Interrogation of the Witnesses, October 6, 1941, in Klein, *Berolinen Canonizationis,* 2:156.

115. See Klein, *Berolinen Canonizationis,* 1:83, n. 6, for a discussion of the evidence and testimony that support the fact that Hanke's father denounced Lichtenberg. At first, the reason for Lichtenberg's arrest and preventive detention was not even clear to the Ministry of Church Affairs, which sent a letter of inquiry to the Ministry of Interior over this question. Church affairs questioned whether the Gestapo arrested Lichtenberg for his "scandalous" letter to Dr. Conti against the euthanasia program. See Kerrl to Frick, October 31, 1941, in Klein, *Berolinen Canonizationis,* 2:178.

116. Arrest Order, Gestapo—Berlin, October 23, 1941, in Klein, *Berolinen Canonizationis,* 2:159.

117. *Wenn Du dieses Zeichen siehst . . . Jude,* an anonymous anti-Semitic pamphlet, October 1941, in Klein, *Berolinen Canonizationis,* 2:157–58

118. Pulpit declaration, October 1943, in Klein, *Berolinen Canonizationis,* 2:160–61.

119. Interrogation of Lichtenberg by the Gestapo, October 25, 1941, in Klein, *Berolinen Canonizationis,* 2:165–66.

120. Ibid., 167.

121. Ibid., 166

122. Interrogation of Lichtenberg, October 25, 1941, in Klein, *Berolinen Canonizationis,* 2:168.

123. *Protokoll,* September 29, 1941, in Mann, *Prozeß Bernhard Lichtenberg,* 45.

124. Interrogation of Lichtenberg, October 25, 1941, in Klein, *Berolinen Canonizationis,* 2:168.

125. Ibid., 171.

126. See Ministry of Propaganda to Berndt, November 10, 1941, in Klein, *Berolinen Canonizationis,* 2:193.

127. Interrogation of Lichtenberg, October 30, 1941, in Klein, *Berolinen Canonizationis,* 2:177.

128. Ibid., 177–78.

129. Interrogation of Lichtenberg by the Gestapo, October 25, 1941, in Klein, *Berolinen Canonizationis,* 2:165–66.

130. Attorney General Berlin to Special Tribunal Berlin, March 21, 1942, BArch B R5101 23335, ff. 53–56. A letter from the SD to Kerrl, confirms that the charge related to the "intercessions for Jews and prisoners." SD to Kerrl, November 24, 1941, BArch B R5101 23335, ff. 48–49.

131. Court Decision, May 22, 1942, BArch B R5101 23335, ff. 59–65.

132. Preysing visited Lichtenberg on five separate occasions: December 9, 1941; May 4, 1942; November 4, 1942; March 21, 1943; and September 29, 1943. See Klein, *Berolinen Canonizationis,* 1:41–46

133. See, especially, Pius XII to Preysing, April 20, 1943: "It gives us . . . solace to hear, that Catholics, specifically Berlin Catholics, have shown the so-called non-Aryans so great a love in their distress, and we say in this connection a special word of fatherly appreciation as well as intimate sympathy to the imprisoned Monsignor Lichtenberg." Mann, *Prozeß Bernhard Lichtenberg*, 105. Also see Pius XII to Preysing, March 21, 1944, in Klein, *Berolinen Canonizationis*, 2:330.

134. Note of Ernst Freiherr von Weizsäcker, State Secretary in the Foreign Office, March 10, 1942, in Mann, *Prozeß Bernhard Lichtenberg*, 87. The foreign office seemed to be concerned about the nuncio's involvement in the Lichtenberg affair and informed Weizäcker of this possibility. See Dr. Haidlen, Vatican Advisor in the Foreign Office to Weizäcker, November 11, 1941, in Klein, *Berolinen Canonizationis*, 2:194.

135. Preysing, Sermon in St. Hedwig, November 2, 1941, in Klein, *Berolinen Canonizationis*, 2:182.

136. Preysing to Pius XII, October 25, 1941, in Klein, *Berolinen Canonizationis*, 2:169.

137. Klein, "Bernhard Lichtenberg und die Berliner Blutzeugen," 1711.

138. Preysing to Gestapo, Berlin, November 4, 1941, in Klein, *Berolinen Canonizationis*, 2:187–88.

139. Preysing to Director of Tegel Prison, March 22, 1943, in Mann, *Prozeß Bernhard Lichtenberg*, 104. This was a great concern because Lichtenberg's weight had gone from 188 pounds on October 23, 1941, to 124 pounds on March 7, 1943.

140. Preysing to Attorney General Berlin, February 17, 1942, in Mann, *Prozeß Bernhard Lichtenberg*, 85.

141. Report of Preysing, October 1943, in Mann, *Prozeß Bernhard Lichtenberg*, 111.

142. See Interrogation of Lichtenberg by the Gestapo, October 25, 1941, in Klein, *Berolinen Canonizationis*, 2:166; and Report of Preysing, October 1943, in Mann, *Prozeß Bernhard Lichtenberg*, 112.

143. Exit Form of Tegel Prison, October 22, 1943, in Mann, *Prozeß Bernhard Lichtenberg*, 90.

144. Ibid.

145. Doctor's Certificate, October 1943, in Mann, *Prozeß Bernhard Lichtenberg*, 113.

146. Ogiermann, *Bis zum letzten Atemzug*, 276–78.

147. Gestapo, Berlin, October 28, 1943, in Mann, *Prozeß Bernhard Lichtenberg*, 114.

148. Erb, *Bernhard Lichtenberg*, 63–65.

Conclusion

1. Zuccotti, *Under His Very Windows*, 311–12.
2. Abbott, ed., *The Documents of Vatican II*, 656–71.

Works Cited

Archival Sources

Archiv des Erzbistums München und Freising (AEM)
        Nachlaß Michael Kardinal Faulhaber

Bayerisches Hauptstaatsarchiv, München (BHStAM)
        Staatskanzlei (StK)

Bistumsarchiv Trier (BAT)
  Abt. 88, Nr. 112   Walter Leonards

Brandenburgisches Landeshauptarchiv (BLHA)
        Pr. Br. Rep. 2A Regierung Potsdam I Pol.
        Pr. Br. Rep. 2A Regierung Potsdam II Pdm.
        Pr. Br. Rep. 2A Regierung Potsdam II Gen.

Bundesarchiv, Koblenz (BArch K)
  Nachlaß 898   Josef Roth
  Nachlaß 1516   Sebastian Schröcker

Bundesarchiv, Abteilungen Lichterfelde, Berlin (BArch B)
  NS 8   Kanzlei Rosenberg
  NS 43   Dienstellen Rosenberg
                 Personenbezogene Unterlagen aus der NS-Zeit (PBU)
  R 3001   Reichministerium für Justiz
  R 43   Reichskanzlei
  R 5101   Reichsministerium für kirchliche Angelegenheiten
  R 58   Reichssicherheitshauptamt
  R 60   Volksgerichtshof und Oberreichsanwalt beim Volksgerichtshof

Bundesarchiv, Zwischenarchiv, Dahlwitz-Hoppegarten (SAPMO-BArch D)
Z/BI

Diözesanarchiv Berlin (DAB)
I/I-104	Hilfswerk beim Bischöflichen Ordinariat Berlin
I/5	Personen A–Z
V/8	Nachlaß August Froehlich
V/16	Nachlaß Preysing
V/38	Nachlaß Reinhold Stahl
V/71-4	Fall Stettin
VI/1	Personen A–Z
VI/20	Ergänzungsdokumentation Bischöfliches Ordinariat Berlin 1929–1945

Diözesanarchiv Eichstätt (DAE)
Kreuz und Hakenkreuz
Kreuz und Hakenkreuz: Sammlung von Pfarrer Johannes Kraus

Diözesanarchiv Rottenburg-Stuttgart
N67   Nachlaß Karl Adam

Erzbistumsarchiv Paderborn (EAP)
Sammlung zum Pfarrer Karl König

Geheimes Staatsarchiv Preussischer Kulturbesitz, Berlin (GStTAPK)
I HA Rep. 90   Preußisches Staatsministerium, Dahlemer Teil
I Rep. 90 Annex P Geheime Staatspolizei

Universitätsbibliothek-Archiv Eichstätt (UAE)
Flugblatt Sammlung

Vojensky historicky Archiv, Prague (VHA)
Reichskriegsgericht

Interviews

Pfarrer i.R. Bernhard Kleineidam, Berlin, January 8, 1997
Pfarrer i.R. Johannes Piotrowski, Berlin, November 21, 1996
Pfarrer i.R. Kanonikus Heribert Rosal, Berlin, November 14, 1996
Frau Gertraud Tietz, Berlin, December 19, 1996
Pater Richard Wagner, S.J., Berlin, December 10, 1996

Contemporary Newspapers, Newsletters, and Journals

8 Uhr Abendblatt
Amtsblatt des Bischöflichen Ordinariats Berlin
Der Angriff
Berlin Börsen-Courier

Catholic Action
Catholic Mind
La Croix
Ecclesiastica
Germania: Zeitung für das deutsche Volk
Katholisches Kirchenblatt für das Bistum Berlin
Kreuz Zeitung
Märkische Volks-Zeitung
Montag-Morgen
Neue Zürcher Zeitung
New York Times
L'Osservatore Romano
Pastoralblatt des Bistums Eichstätt
Schwarze Korps
St. Hedwigsblatt
St. Petrus Kalender für das Bistum Berlin
St. Willibalds-Bote
Tegernseer Zeitung
Times (London)
Völkischer Beobachter
Westdeutscher Beobachter
Würzburger Diözesan-Blatt

Published Works

Abbott, Walter M., S.J., ed. *The Documents of Vatican II*. Piscataway, N.J.: New Century, 1966.

Adam, Karl. "Deutsches Volkstum und katholisches Christentum." *Theologische Quartalschrift* 114 (1933), 40–63.

———. *Glaube und Liebe*. Regensburg: Josef Habbel, 1927.

———. "Vom gottmenschlichen Erlöser." In *Glaubenstage und Glaubenswallfahrten 1934*. Edited by Zentralkomitee der Generalversammlungen der deutschen Katholiken. Paderborn: Bonifacius, 1935. 11–24.

Adam, Stephan. *Die Auseinandersetzungen des Bischofs Konrad von Preysing mit dem Nationalsozialismus in den Jahren 1933–1945*. St. Ottilien: EOS, 1996.

Adamy, Kurt, and Kristina Hübener. "Provinz Mark Brandenburg-Gau Kurmark. Eine verwaltungsgeschichtliche Skizze." In *Verfolgung Alltag Widerstand. Brandenburg in der NS-Zeit: Studien und Dokumente*. Edited by Dietrich Eichholtz. Berlin: Volk & Welt, 1993. 11–31.

Adas, Michael. *Machines as the Measure of Men: Science, Technology, and Ideologies of Western Dominance*. Ithaca, N.Y.: Cornell University Press, 1989.

Adolph, Walter. *Erich Klausener*. Berlin: Morus, 1955.

———. *Geheime Aufzeichnungen aus dem Nationalsozialistischen Kirchenkampf, 1935–1943*. Mainz: Matthias-Grünewald, 1980.

———. *Kardinal Preysing und zwei Diktaturen: Sein Widerstand gegen die totalitäre Macht*. Berlin: Morus, 1971.

———. *Der Notenwechsel zwischen dem Heiligen Stuhl und der deutschen Reichsregierung. III. Der Notenwechsel und die Demarchen des Nuntius Orsenigo*

1933–1945. Mainz: Matthias-Grünewald, 1980.

———. *Sie sind nicht vergessen: Gestalten aus der jüngsten deutschen Kirchengeschichte.* Berlin: Bischöfliches Ordinariat Berlin, 1972.

Albrecht, Dieter, ed. *Der Notenwechsel zwischen dem Heiligen Stuhl und der deutschen Reichsregierung. I. Von der Ratifizierung des Reichskonkordats bis zur Enzyklika "Mit brennender Sorge."* Mainz: Matthias-Grünewald, 1965.

Allendorf, Johannes. "Katholisches Leben in Potsdam im Wandel der Jahrhunderte." *Archiv für schlesische Kirchengeschichte* 19 (1961), 260–92.

Alvarez, David. *Spies in the Vatican: Espionage and Intrigue from Napoleon to the Holocaust.* Lawrence: University Press of Kansas, 2000.

Alvarez, David, and Robert A. Graham, S.J. *Nothing Sacred: Nazi Espionage against the Vatican, 1939–1945.* London: Frank Cass, 1997.

Aly, Götz, Peter Chroust, and Christian Pross. *Cleansing the Fatherland: Nazi Medicine and Racial Hygiene.* Translated by Belinda Cooper. Baltimore: Johns Hopkins University Press, 1994.

Anderson, Margaret Lavinia. *Windthorst: A Political Biography.* Oxford: Clarendon Press, 1981.

Anzeneder, Helmut, and Karl Kupfer. "Kirchenkampf im Erzbistum Bamberg aus der Sicht zweier Zeitzeugen: Anmerkungen zu Thomas Breuers 'Verordneter Wandel'? Der Widerstreit zwischen nationalsozialistischem Herrschaftsanspruch und traditionaler Lebenswelt im Erzbistum Bamberg." *Zeitschrift für Bayerische Kirchengeschichte* 65 (1996), 150–66.

Aretz, Jürgen. *Katholische Arbeiterbewegung und Nationalsozialismus.* Mainz: Matthias-Grünewald, 1982.

Banki, Judith H., and John T. Pawlikowski, O.S.M., eds. *Ethics in the Shadow of the Holocaust: Christian and Jewish Perspectives.* Franklin, Wis.: Sheed & Ward, 2001.

Bares, Nicolaus. *Im Lichte der Ewigkeit: Ausgewählte Hirtenworte, Predigten, Ansprachen, Briefe.* Edited by Norbert Fischer. Kevelaer: Butzon und Bercker, 1936.

Barthels, Karl. *Zeitnahe Seelsorge: Entwurf einer Prinzipienlehre.* Wien: Herder, 1940.

Baum, Gregory. *Christian Theology after Auschwitz.* London: Council of Christians and Jews, 1976.

———. *Is the New Testament Anti-Semitic? A Re-evaluation of the New Testament.* Glen Rock, N.J.: Paulist Press, 1965.

Baumgärtner, Raimund. "Vom Kaplan zum Ministerialrat Joseph Roth—eine nationalsozialistische Karriere." In *Politik—Bildung—Religion: Hans Maier zum 65. Geburtstag.* Edited by Theo Stammen, Heinrich Oberreuter, and Paul Mikat. Paderborn: Ferdinand Schöningh, 1996. 221–34.

Bengsch, Hubert. *Bistum Berlin: 1000 Jahre christlicher Glaube zwischen Elbe und Oder.* Berlin: Stapp, 1985.

Berg, Walter [Josef Roth]. "Die Kirche ist alt geworden." *Deutscher Glaube* 3 (1935), 125–27.

Bergen, Doris L. "Catholics, Protestants, and Antisemitism in Nazi Germany." *Central European History* 27 (1994), 329–48.

———. *Twisted Cross: The German Christian Movement in the Third Reich.* Chapel Hill: University of North Carolina Press, 1996.

Besier, Gerhard. "Anti-Bolshevism and Antisemitism: The Catholic Church in Germany and National Socialist Ideology 1936–37." *Journal of Ecclesiastical History* 43 (1992), 447–56.

Bischöfliches Ordinariat Berlin. *Zum Gedächtnis der verstorbenen Priester im Bistum Berlin,* 1986.

Bischöfliches Ordinariat zu Berlin, ed. *Biblische Geschichte für das Bistum Berlin.* Berlin: Herder, n.d.

———. *Dokumente aus den Kampf dem katholische Kirche im Bistum Berlin gegen den Nationalsozialismus.* Berlin: Moris, 1946.

———. *Hirtenworte in ernster Zeit: Kundgebungen des Bischofs von Berlin Konrad Kardinal von Preysing.* Berlin: Morus, 1947.

———. *Kleine Schulbibel für das Bistum Berlin.* Freiburg: Herder, n.d.

Blackbourn, David. *Class, Religion and Local Politics in Wilhelmine Germany: The Centre Party in Württemberg before 1914.* New Haven, Conn.: Yale University Press, 1980.

Bleistein, Roman. "Abt Alban Schachleiter, OSB: Zwischen Kirchentreue und Hitlerkult." *Historisches Jahrbuch* 115 (1995), 170–87.

———. "'Überläufer im Sold der Kirchenfeinde' Josef Roth und Albert Hartl: Priesterkarrieren im Dritten Reich." *Beiträge zur Altbayerischen Kirchengeschichte* 42 (1996), 71–109.

Blümel, Jutta. *Dr. Theol. Philipp Haeuser, ein Pfarrer im Nationalsozialismus.* Zulassungsarbeit, Universität Augsburg, n.d.

Boberach, Heinz. "Organe der nationalsozialistischen Kirchenpolitik: Kompetenzverteilung und Karrieren in Reich und Ländern." In *Staat und Parteien: Festschrift für Rudolf Morsey zum 65. Geburtstag.* Edited by Karl Dietrich Bracher, Paul Mikat, Konrad Repgen, Martin Schumacher, and Hans-Peter Schwarz. Berlin: Duncker & Humblot, 1992. 305–31.

———, ed. *Berichte des SD und der Gestapo über Kirchen und Kirchenvolk in Deutschland, 1934–1944.* Mainz: Matthias-Grünewald, 1971.

Brandl, Ludwig. "Josef Roth." *Biographisch-Bibliographisches Kirchenlexikon.* Vol. 8. Edited by Friedrich Wilhelm Bautz. Herzberg: Traugott Bautz, 1994. 742–44.

———. "Katholische Kirche und Juden im Dritten Reich." *Klerusblatt* 77 (1997), 9–14.

Breuer, Thomas. "Kirche und Fremde unter dem Hakenkreuz: Zur Frage nach dem Selbstverständnis der katholischen Kirche in der NS-Zeit." In *Die Fremden.* Edited by Otto Fuchs. Düsseldorf: Patmos, 1988. 183–93.

———. "Kirchliche Opposition im NS-Staat: Eine Basisperspektive." In *Kirchen in der Diktatur.* Edited by Günther Heydemann and Lothar Kettenacker. Göttingen: Vandenhoeck und Ruprecht, 1993. 297–313.

———. *Verordneter Wandel? Der Widerstreit zwischen nationalsozialistischem Herrschaftsanspruch und traditionaler Lebenswelt im Erzbistum Bamberg.* Mainz: Matthias-Grünewald, 1992.

Breuning, Klaus. *Die Vision des Reiches: Deutscher Katholizismus zwischen Demokratie und Diktatur, 1929–1934.* Munich: Max Hueber, 1969.

Broszat, Martin. *The Hitler State: The Foundation and Development of the Internal Structure of the Third Reich.* Translated by John W. Hiden. London: Longman, 1981.

———. "Resistenz und Widerstand: Eine Zwischenbilanz des Forschungsprojekts." In *Bayern in der NS-Zeit IV: Herrschaft und Gesellschaft im Konflikt.* Edited by Martin Broszat, Elke Fröhlich, and Anton Grossmann. Munich: R. Oldenbourg, 1981. 693–709.

Brühe, Matthias, ed. *Priester Werden in Berlin: Eine kleine Festschrift anläßlich des 25 jährigen Bestehens des Priesterseminars in Berlin-Zehlendorf.* Berlin: Enka, 1992.

Burleigh, Michael. *Death and Deliverance: "Euthanasia" in Germany, 1900–1945*. Cambridge: Cambridge University Press, 1995.

Burleigh, Michael, and Wolfgang Wippermann. *The Racial State: Germany, 1933–1945*. Cambridge: Cambridge University Press, 1992.

Caritas-Arbeit im Bistum Berlin 1938.

Carlen, Claudia, ed. *The Papal Encyclicals, 1903–1939*. Wilmington, N.C.: McGrath, 1981.

Carroll, James. *Constantine's Sword: The Church and the Jews: A History*. New York: Houghton Mifflin, 2001.

Childers, Thomas. *The Nazi Voter: The Social Foundations of Fascism in Germany, 1919–1933*. Chapel Hill, N.C.: University of North Carolina Press, 1988.

Clauss, Manfred. "Paul Steinmann, 1871–1937." In *Die Bischöfe der deutschsprachigen Länder 1785/1803 bis 1945: Ein biographisches Lexikon*. Edited by Erwin Gatz. Berlin: Duncker & Humblot, 1983.

Congressional Record—Senate. January 6, 1934–March 11, 1943. Vol. 89, pt. 1.

Conrad, Walter. *Kirchenkampf*. Berlin: Wedding, 1947.

Conrath, Chrysostomus, O.P. "Der Studentenseelsorger in Berlin." In *Das katholische Berlin*. Edited by Heinrich Bachmann. Munich: Hanns Eder, 1929. 57–59.

Conway, John S. *The Nazi Persecution of the Churches, 1933–45*. New York: Basic Books, 1968.

Coppenrath, Albert. *Der westfälische Dickkopf am Winterfeldplatz: Meine Kanzelvermeldungen und Erlebnisse im Dritten Reich*. 2nd ed. Cologne: J. P. Bachem, 1948.

Cornwell, John. *Hitler's Pope: The Secret History of Pius XII*. New York: Viking, 1999.

Corvin, Otto von. *Der Pfaffenspiegel: Historische Denkmale des Fanatismus in der römisch-katholischen Kirche*. Berlin: E. Bartels, n.d.

Crossan, John Dominic. *Who Killed Jesus? Exposing the Roots of Anti-Semitism in the Gospel Story of the Death of Jesus*. New York: HarperCollins, 1995.

Dawidowicz, Lucy S. *A Holocaust Reader*. Orange, N.J.: Behrman House, 1976.

Delaney, John J. "Racial Values vs. Religious Values: Clerical Opposition to Nazi Anti-Polish Racial Policy." *Church History* 70 (2001), 271–94.

Denzler, Georg. *Widerstand ist nicht das richtige Wort: Katholische Priester, Bischöfe und Theologen im Dritten Reich*. Zürich: Pendo, 2003.

———. *Widerstand oder Anpassung? Katholische Kirche und Drittes Reich*. Munich: Piper, 1984.

Denzler, Georg, and Volker Fabricius. *Christen und Nationalsozialisten*. 2 vols. Frankfurt: Fischer, 1993.

Dierker, Wolfgang. *Himmlers Glaubenskrieger: Der Sicherheitsdienst der SS und seine Religionspolitik, 1933–1941*. Paderborn: Ferdinand Schöningh, 2002.

Dierks, Margarete. *Jakob Wilhelm Hauer, 1881–1962: Leben-Werk-Wirkung*. Heidelberg: L. Schneider, 1986.

Dietrich, Donald J. *Catholic Citizens in the Third Reich: Psycho-Social Principles and Moral Reasoning*. New Brunswick, N.J., Transaction, 1988.

———. "Catholic Resistance in the Third Reich." *Holocaust and Genocide Studies* 3 (1988), 171–86.

———. "A Catholic's Adaptation to German Eugenics from World War I to 1933: Hermann Muckermann, S.J." *Hispana Sacra* 42 (1991), 71–82.

God and Humanity in Auschwitz: Jewish-Christian Relations and Sanctioned Murder. New Brunswick, N.J.: Transaction, 1995.

———. "Nazi Eugenics: Adaptation and Resistance among German Catholic Intellectual Leaders." In *Medicine, Ethics, and the Third Reich: Historical and Contemporary Issues*. Edited by John J. Michalczyk. Kansas City, Mo.: Sheed and Ward, 1994. 50–63.

Dirks, Walter. "Katholiken zwischen Anpassung und Widerstand." In *Widerstand und Verweigerung in Deutschland 1933 bis 1945*. Edited by Richard Löwenthal and Patrik von zur Mühlen. Bonn: J. H. W. Dietz, 1982. 140–42.

Dolata, Walter. *Chronik einer Jugend: Katholische Jugend im Bistum Berlin, 1936–1949*. Hildesheim: Bernward, 1988.

Domarus, Max. *Hitler Reden und Proklamationen, 1932–1945: Kommentiert von einem deutsche Zeitgenossen*. Vol. 1, first half. Munich: Süddeutscher-Verlag, 1965.

Domschke, Max. *Glaube aus dem Blut? Die heidnisch-religiösen Strömungen der Gegenwart und das Christentum*. Berlin: Germania, 1934.

Drapac, Vesna. "Religion in a Dechristianized World: French Catholic Responses to War and Occupation." *Journal of European Studies* 26 (1996), 389–416.

———. *War and Religion: Catholics in the Churches of Occupied Paris*. Washington, D.C.: Catholic University of America Press, 1998.

Dressen, Willy. "Protective Custody." In *The Encyclopedia of the Third Reich*. Edited by Christian Zentner and Friedemann Bedürftig, translated by Amy Hackett. New York: DaCapo Press, 1997. 735–37.

Eckardt, Wolf von, and Sander L. Gilman. *Bertolt Brecht's Berlin: A Scrapbook of the Twenties*. Garden City, N.Y.: Anchor Press/Doubleday, 1975.

Eichmann, Eduard. *Lehrbuch des Kirchenrechts auf Grund des Codex Iuris Canonici*. 2 vols. 3rd ed. Paderborn: Ferdinand Schöningh, 1929.

Engelhard, Gildis. *Abt Schachleiter der deutsche Kämpfer*. Munich, 1941.

Erb, Alfons. *Bernhard Lichtenberg: Dompropst von St. Hedwig zu Berlin*. 4th ed. Berlin: Morus, 1947.

Eschenburg, Theodor. *Die improvisierte Demokratie: Gesammelte Aufsätze zur Weimarer Republik*. Munich: R. Piper, 1964.

Fandel, Thomas. *Konfession und Nationalsozialismus: Evangelische und katholische Pfarrer in der Pfalz, 1930–1939*. Paderborn: Ferdinand Schöningh, 1997.

Faulhaber, Michael. *Judentum Christentum Germanentum: Adventspredigten gehalten in St. Michael zu München 1933*. Munich: Huber, n.d.

Field, Geoffrey G. *Evangelist of Race: The Germanic Vision of Houston Stewart Chamberlain*. New York: Columbia University Press, 1981.

Fischer, Gerhard. *Antifaschistisches Erbe-Mythos oder Auftrag? Lehren aus dem Widerstand von Christen in Deutschland*. Berlin: Union, 1986.

Fischer, Karl. "Der Fall Stettin." In *Christlicher Widerstand gegen den Faschismus*. Edited by Wilhelm Bondzio. Berlin: Union, 1956. 122–30.

Fischer, Norbert. *Nicolaus Bares, Bischof von Berlin*. Revelaer: Butzon and Bercker, 1937.

Flannery, Edward H. *The Anguish of the Jews: Twenty-Three Centuries of Antisemitism*. Rev. ed. Mahwah, N.J.: Paulist Press, 1985.

Friedlander, Henry. *The Origins of Nazi Genocide: From Euthanasia to the Final Solution*. Chapel Hill: University of North Carolina Press, 1995.

Friedländer, Saul. *Nazi Germany and the Jews*. Vol. 1: *The Years of Persecution, 1933–1939*. New York: Harper Collins, 1997.

Fröhlich, Elke, ed. *Die Tagebücher von Joseph Goebbels sämtliche Fragmente*. Part 1, vols. 1 and 3. Munich: K. G. Saur, 1987.

———. *Die Tagebücher von Joseph Goebbels sämtliche Fragmente.* Part 2, vols. 3, 5, and 7. Munich: K.G. Saur, 1993/1994.

Fürstbischöfliches Ordinariat zu Breslau, ed. *Katholischer Katechismus für das Bistum Breslau.* Breslau: Nischkowsky, 1925.

Gallin, Mary Alice, O.S.U. "The Cardinal and the State: Faulhaber and the Third Reich." *Journal of Church and State* 12 (1970), 385–404.

Gallo, Max. *The Night of the Long Knives.* New York: Da Capo, 1997.

Gellately, Robert. *Backing Hitler: Consent and Coercion in Nazi Germany.* New York: Oxford University Press, 2001.

Golombek, Dieter. *Die politische Vorgeschichte des Preußenkonkordats 1929.* Mainz: Matthias-Grünewald, 1970.

Gordon, Mel. *Voluptuous Panic: The Erotic World of Weimar Berlin.* Venice, Calif.: Feral House, 2000.

Graham, Robert A., S.J. "Documenti di Guerra da Mosca: Spionaggio Nazista Anti-vaticano." *La Civilta Cattolica* 144 (1993), 542–50.

———. *The Vatican and Communism during World War II: What Really Happened?* San Francisco: Ignatius, 1996.

Greive, Hermann. *Theologie und Ideologie: Katholizismus und Judentum in Deutschland und Österreich, 1918–1935.* Heidelberg: Lampert Schneider, 1969.

Griech-Polelle, Beth A. *Bishop von Galen: German Catholicism and National Socialism.* New Haven, Conn.: Yale University Press, 2002.

Groothuis, Rainer Maria. *Im Dienste einer überstaatlichen Macht: Die deutschen Dominikaner unter der NS-Diktatur.* Münster: Regensberg, 2002.

Grossmann, Anita. *Reforming Sex: The German Movement for Birth Control and Abortion Reform, 1920–1950.* New York: Oxford University Press, 1995.

Gundlach, Gustav. "Antisemitismus." In *Lexikon für Theologie und Kirche.* Edited by Michael Buchberger. Freiburg: Herder, 1930. 504–5.

Hamerow, Theodore S. "Cardinal Faulhaber and the Third Reich." In *From the Berlin Museum to the Berlin Wall: Essays on the Cultural and Political History of Modern Germany.* Edited by David Wetzel. Westport, Conn.: Praeger, 1996. 145–68.

———. *On the Road to the Wolf's Lair: German Resistance to Hitler.* Cambridge, Mass.: Harvard University Press, 1997.

Hannot, Walter. *Die Judenfrage in der Katholischen Tagespresse Deutschlands und Österreichs, 1923–1933.* Mainz: Matthias-Grünewald, 1990.

Harrigan, William M. "Nazi Germany and the Holy See, 1933–1936: The Historical Background of *Mit brennender Sorge.*" *Catholic Historical Review* 47 (1961), 164–98.

Harrison, E. D. R. "The Nazi Dissolution of the Monasteries: A Case Study." *English Historical Review* 109 (1994), 323–55.

Heck, Alfons. *A Child of Hitler: Germany in the Days when God Wore a Swastika.* Phoenix: Renaissance House, 2001.

Hehl, Ulrich von. *Nationalsozialistische Herrschaft.* Munich: R. Oldenbourg, 1996.

Hehl, Ulrich von, Christoph Kösters, Petra Stenz-Maur, and Elisabeth Zimmermann. *Priester unter Hitlers Terror eine Biographische und Statistische Erhebung.* 2 vols. 3rd ed. Paderborn: Ferdinand Schöningh, 1996.

Heineman, John L., ed. and trans. "A Third Reich Reader: A Collection of Primary Sources." Unpublished manuscript, 1995.

Heitzer, Horst W. "Deutscher Katholizismus und 'Bolschewismusgefahr' bis 1933." *Historisches Jahrbuch* 113 (1993), 355–87.

Hellwig, Monika K. "A Catholic Scholar's Journey through the Twentieth Century." In *Faith and the Intellectual Life: Marianist Award Lectures*. Edited by James L. Heft. Notre Dame, Ind.: University of Notre Dame Press, 1996. 71–85.

Helmreich, Ernst Christian. *The German Churches under Hitler: Background, Struggle, and Epilogue*. Detroit: Wayne State University Press, 1980.

Herberhold, Franz. *A. M. Wachsmann: Ein Opfer des Faschismus*. Leipzig: St. Benno, 1963.

Hermand, Jost. *Völkisch Utopias and National Socialism*. Bloomington: Indiana University Press, 1992.

Herzberg, Heinrich. *Diest am höheren Gesetz. Dr. Margarete Sommer und das "Hilfswerk beim Bischöflichen Ordinariat Berlin."* Berlin: Servis, 2000.

Hetzer, Gerhard. *Kirchenkampf in Augsburg, 1933–1945: Konflikte zwischen Staat, Einheitspartei und christlichen Kirchen, dargestellt am Beispiel einer deutschen Stadt*. Augsburg: Hieronymous Mühlberger, 1982.

Hirt, Simon, ed. *Mit brennender Sorge: Das päpstliche Rundschreiben gegen den Nationalsozialismus und seine Folgen in Deutschland*. Freiburg: Herder, 1946.

Hitler, Adolf. *Adolf Hitler: Monologe im Führerhauptquartier, 1941–1944*. Edited by Werner Jochmann. Munich: Orbis, 2000.

———. *Mein Kampf*. Translated by Ralph Manheim. Boston: Houghton Mifflin, 1971.

Hockerts, Hans Günter. "Die Goebbels-Tagebücher 1932–1941. Eine neue Hauptquelle zur Erforschung der nationalsozialistischen Kirchenpolitik." In *Politik und Konfession. Festschrift für Konrad Repgen zum 60. Geburtstag*. Berlin: Duncker und Humblot, 1983. 359–92.

———. *Die Sittlichkeitsprozesse gegen katholische Ordensangehörige und Priester, 1936/1937: Eine Studie zur nationalsozialistischen Herrschaftstechnik und zum Kirchenkampf*. Mainz: Matthias-Grünewald, 1971.

Hoffmann, Ernst, and Hubert Janssen. *Die Wahrheit über die Ordensdevisenprozesse, 1935/36*. Bielefeld: Hausknecht, 1967.

Hofmüller, Harold Anton. *Steirische Priester befürworten den Nationalsozialismus und den Anschluss an das Deutsche Reich Adolf Hitlers*. Graz: Diplomarbeit, Universität Graz, 1997.

Höhle, Michael. *Die Gründung des Bistums Berlin, 1930*. Paderborn: Ferdinand Schöningh, 1996.

Höllen, Martin. *Heinrich Wienken der "Unpolitische" Kirchenpolitiker*. Mainz: Matthias-Grünewald, 1981.

Holmes, J. Derek. *The Papacy in the Modern World*. New York: Crossroad, 1981.

Horn, Daniel. "The Struggle for Catholic Youth in Hitler's Germany: An Assessment." *Catholic Historical Review* 65 (1979), 561–82.

Hsia, R. Po-chia. *The Myth of Ritual Murder: Jews and Magic in Reformation Germany*. New Haven, Conn.: Yale University Press, 1988.

Hucko, Elmar M. ed. *The Democratic Tradition: Four German Constitutions*. New York: Berg, 1987.

Hürten, Heinz. *Deutsche Katholiken, 1918–1945*. Paderborn: Ferdinand Schöningh, 1992.

———. "'Endlösung' für den Katholizismus? Das nationalsozialistische Regime und seine Zukunftspläne gegenüber der Kirche." *Stimmen der Zeit* 203 (1985), 534–46.

———. "Judenhaß-Schuld der Christen? Kirche und Antisemitismus im Wandel der Jahrhunderte." In *Wie im Himmel so auf Erden. 90. Deutscher Katholikentag*

vom 23. bis 27. Mai 1990 in Berlin. Vol. 2: *Dokumentation.* Paderborn: Bonifatius, 1990. 1495–1506.

———. "Katholische Kirche und Widerstand." In *Widerstand gegen den Nationalsozialismus.* Edited by Peter Steinbach and Johannes Tuchel. Berlin: Akademie,
1994. 182–92.

Hürten, Heinz, ed. *Deutsche Briefe, 1934–1938: Ein Blatt der katholischen Emigration.*
2 vols. Mainz: Matthias-Grünewald, 1969.

Jauch, Ernst Alfred. "Albert Coppenrath (1883–1960)." In *Miterbauer des Bistums
Berlin: 50 Jahre Geschichte in Charakterbildern.* Edited by Wolfgang Knauft.
Berlin: Morus, 1979.

Joos, Joseph. *Am Räderwerk der Zeit: Erinnerungen aus der katholiken und sozialen Bewegung und Politik.* Augsburg: Winfried-Werk, 1951.

Juropka, Joachim, ed. *Clemens August Graf von Galen: Neue Forschungen zum Leben
und Wirken des Bischofs von Münster.* 2nd ed. Münster: Regensberg, 1993.

Kaller, Maximilian. *Unser Laienapostolat: Was es ist und wie es sein soll.* Leutesdorf am
Rhein: Johannesbund, 1927.

Kaplan, Marion A. *Between Dignity and Despair: Jewish Life in Nazi Germany.* New
York: Oxford University Press, 1998.

Kater, Michael H. *Doctors under Hitler.* Chapel Hill: University of North Carolina
Press, 1989.

Kent, Peter C. *The Lonely Cold War of Pope Pius XII: The Roman Catholic Church and
the Division of Europe, 1943–1950.* Montreal: McGill-Queen's University Press,
2002.

Kershaw, Ian. *Popular Opinion and Political Dissent in the Third Reich, Bavaria,
1933–1945.* Oxford: Oxford University Press, 1987.

Kertzer, David I. *The Popes against the Jews: The Vatican's Role in the Rise of Modern
Anti-Semitism.* New York: Knopf, 2001.

Kirk, Tim. *The Longman Companion to Nazi Germany.* London: Longman, 1995.

Kitchen, Martin. *Nazi Germany at War.* New York: Longman, 1995.

Klausener, Erich. "Haben wir Berliner Katholiken Grund zum Optimismus?"
Märkischer Kalender 1931. 24–31.

Klee, Ernst. *"Euthanasie" im NS-Staat: Die "Vernichtung lebensunwerten Lebens."*
Frankfurt: Fischer, 1994.

———, ed. *Dokumente zur "Euthanasie."* Frankfurt: Fischer, 1986.

Klein, Gotthard. "Bernhard Lichtenberg und die Berliner Blutzeugen, 1933–1945." In
*Wie im Himmel so auf Erden. 90. Deutscher Katholikentag vom 23. bis 27 Mai 1990
in Berlin.* Vol. 2: *Dokumentation.* Paderborn: Bonifatius, 1990. 1691–1721.

———. *Berolinen Canonizationis Servi Dei Bernardi Lichtenberg: Sacerdotis Saecularis in
Odium Fidei, Uti Fertur, Interfecti (1875–1943).* Vol. 1: *Informatio.* Rome: Congregation de Causis Sanctorum, 1992.

———. *Berolinen Canonizationis Servi Dei Bernardi Lichtenberg: Sacerdotis Saecularis in
Odium Fidei, Uti Fertur, Interfecti (1875–1943).* Vol. 2: *Summarium—Documenta.*
Rome: Congregation de Causis Sanctorum, 1992.

———. *Seliger Bernhard Lichtenberg.* Regensburg: Schnell und Steiner, 1997.

Kleineidam, Bernhard. *Tagebuch eines Diasporapriesters: Lebenserinnerungen,
1922–1978.* Berlin, 1985.

Kleineidam, Erich. *Die katholisch-theologische Fakultät der Universität Breslau,
1811–1945.* Cologne: Weinand, 1961.

Klosterkamp, Thomas, O.M.I. *Kind und Opfer Seiner Zeit: Pater Friedrich Lorenz, OMI, Ein Lebensbild.* Rome, 1994.

Knauft, Wolfgang. "Einsatz für verfolgte Juden, 1938–1945: Das Hilfswerk beim Bischöflichen Ordinariat Berlin." *Stimmen der Zeit* 206 (1988), 591–603.

———. *"Fall Stettin" ferngesteuert.* Berlin: Bischöfliches Ordinariat Berlin, 1994.

———. *Konrad von Preysing Anwalt des Rechts: Der erste Berliner Kardinal und seine Zeit.* Berlin: Morus, 1998.

———. *Unter Einsatz des Lebens: Das Hilfswerk beim Bischöflichen Ordinariat Berlin für katholische "Nichtarier," 1938–1945.* Berlin: Bischöfliches Ordinariat Berlin, 1988.

Kock, Erich. *Er widerstand: Bernhard Lichtenberg.* Berlin: Morus, 1996.

Körner, Hans-Michael. "Katholische Kirche und polnische Zwangsarbeiter, 1939–1945." *Historisches Jahrbuch* 112 (1992), 128–42.

Koß, Siegfried. "Bischof Christian Schreiber, der KV und die NSDAP." *Grotenburg-Lusaten-Echo* 26 (April 1992), 50–52.

———. "Christian Schrieber." In *Biographisches Lexikon des KV.* Vol. 1. Edited by Siegfried Koß and Wolfgang Löhr. Schernfeld: SH-Verlag, 1994.

Kraus, Johann, S.V.D. "Der Sekretär zweier Nuntien Pater Eduard Gehrmann SVD." In *In Verbo Tuo: Festschrift zum 50jährige Bestehen des Missionspriesterseminars St. Augustin bei Siegburg, Reinl., 1913–1963.* Steyl: Steyler-Verlag, 1963. 167–95.

Kreidler, Hans. "Karl Adam und der Nationalsozialismus." *Rottenburger Jahrbuch für Kirchengeschichte* 2 (1983), 129–40.

Kreutzer, Heike. *Das Reichskirchenministerium im Gefüge der nationalsozialistischen Herrschaft.* Düsseldorf: Droste, 2000.

Krieg, Robert Anthony. *Catholic Theologians in Nazi Germany.* New York: Continuum, 2004.

———. *Karl Adam: Catholicism in German Culture.* Notre Dame, Ind.: University of Notre Dame Press, 1992.

Krose, Hermann A., S.J., ed. *Kirchliches Handbuch für das katholische Deutschland.* Freiburg: Herder, 1908–1940

Kühl, Stefan. *The Nazi Connection: Eugenics, American Racism, and German National Socialism.* New York: Oxford University Press, 1994.

Kühn, Heinz R. *Blutzeugen des Bistums Berlin.* Berlin: Morus, 1950.

Kupper, Alfons, ed. *Staatliche Akten über die Reichskonkordatsverhandlungen 1933.* Mainz: Matthias-Grünewald, 1969.

Lampe, Heinrich. "Pfarrseelsorge in Berlin." In *Das Katholische Berlin.* Edited by Heinrich Bachmann. Munich: Hanns Eder, 1929. 37–41.

Landkreis Schwabmünchen: Landschaft, Geschichte, Wirtschaft, Kultur. 2nd ed. Augsburg: Landkreis Schwabmünchen, 1975.

Lange, Gerhard. "Pfarrer August Froehlich." In *Zeugen für Christus: Das deutsche Martyrologium des 20. Jahrhunderts.* Vol. 1. Edited by Helmut Moll. Paderborn: Ferdinand Schöningh, 1999. 94–97.

Lease, Gary. "Denunciation as a Tool of Ecclesiastical Control: The Case of Roman Catholic Modernism." *Journal of Modern History* 68 (1996), 819–30.

———. "The History of 'Religious' Consciousness and the Diffusion of Culture: Strategies for Surviving Dissolution." *Historical Reflections* 20 (1994), 453–79.

Leiber, Robert, S.J. "Mit brennender Sorge: März 1937–März 1962." *Stimmen der Zeit* 87 (1961/62), 417–26.

Lenski, Reinhold. "Pfarrer Dr. Philipp Häuser (1876–1960): Ein Kämpfer für den Nationalsozialismus." Unpublished lecture, 14th Scholarly Meeting of Local Historians in the Administrative District of Schwaben, November 29–30, 2002, Irsee.

Leonards, Walter. "Treptow an der Rega (Pommern)." *Schlesische Bonifatiusverins Blatt* 71 (1930), 134, 144–49.

Leugers, Antonia. *Gegen eine Mauer bischöflichen Schweigens. Der Ausschuß für Ordensangelegenheiten und seine Widerstandskonzeption 1941 bis 1945.* Frankfurt: Josef Knecht, 1996.

Lewy, Guenther. *The Catholic Church and Nazi Germany.* New York: McGraw-Hill, 1964.

Lichtenberg, Bernhard. "Was können die Katholiken von den Konvertiten lernen?" *Märkischer Kalender 1931*, 103–6.

Lill, Rudolf. "German Catholicism's Attitude towards the Jews in the Weimar Republic." In *Judaism and Christianity under Impact of National Socialism, 1919–1945.* Edited by Otto Dov Kulka and Paul R. Mendes-Flohr. Jerusalem: Historical Society of Israel and the Zalman Shazar Center for Jewish History, 1987. 151–68.

Littell, Franklin H. *The Crucifixion of the Jews.* Reprint edition. Macon, Ga.: Mercer University Press, 1986.

Löffler, Peter, ed. *Bischof Clemens August Graf von Galen Akten, Briefe und Predigten, 1933–1946.* 2 vols. Mainz: Matthias-Grünewald, 1988.

Lönne, Karl-Egon. "Motive des katholischen Widerstandes gegen das Dritte Reich." In *Vom Widerstand lernen: Von der Bekennenden Kirche bis zum 20. Juli 1944.* Edited by Regina Claussen and Siegfried Schwarz. Bonn: Bouvier, 1986. 167–81.

Lougee, Robert W. *Paul de Lagarde, 1827–1891: A Study of Radical Conservatism in Germany.* Cambridge, Mass.: Harvard University Press, 1962.

Löwenthal, Richard. "Widerstand im totalen Staat." In *Nationalsozialistische Diktatur, 1933–1945: Eine Bilanz.* Edited by Karl Dietrich Bracher, Manfred Funke, and Hans-Adolf Jacobsen. Ulm: Franz Spiegel, 1986. 618–32.

Mann, H. G. *Prozeß Bernhard Lichtenberg: Ein Leben in Dokumenten.* Morus: Berlin, 1977.

Mariaux, Walter, S.J. *Persecution of the Catholic Church in the Third Reich.* London: Burns Oates, 1940.

Martini, Angelo, S.J. "Il Card. Faulhaber e L'Enciclica di Pio XI contro il Nazismo." *La Civiltá Cattolica* 115 (1964), 421–32.

———. "Il Cardinale Faulhaber e L'Enciclica *Mit brennender Sorge.*" *Archivum Historiae Pontificiae* 2 (1964), 303–20.

———. "Il Cardinale Pacelli e l'Enciclica contro Il Nazionalsozialismo." *L'Osservatore della Domenica* 26 (June 28, 1964), 12–13.

Matheson, Peter, ed. *The Third Reich and the Christian Churches.* Edinburg: T. and T. Clark, 1981.

May, Georg. *Kirchenkampf oder Katholikenverfolgung? Ein Beitrag zu dem gegenseitigen Verhältnis von Nationalsozialismus und christlichen Bekenntnissen.* Stein am Rhein: Christiana, 1991.

Mazura, Uwe. *Zentrumspartei und Judenfrage, 1870/71–1933: Verfassungsstaat und Minderheitenschutz.* Mainz: Matthias-Grünewlad, 1994.

Mikat, Paul. "Zur Kundgebung der Fuldaer Bischofskonferenz über die national-sozialistische Bewegung vom 28. März 1933." *Jahrbuch des Instituts für christliche Sozialwissenschaften der Westfälischen Wilhelms-Universität Münster* 3 (1962), 209–35.

Missalla, Heinrich. *Für Gott, Führer und Vaterland: Die Verstrickung der katholischen Seelsorge in Hitlers Krieg.* Munich: Kösel, 1999.

———. *Für Volk und Vaterland: Die kirchliche Kriegshilfe im Zweiten Weltkrieg.* Königstein: Athenäum, 1978.

Mörsdorf, Josef. *August Froehlich: Pfarrer von Rathenow.* Berlin: Morus, 1947.

Mosse, George L. *The Crisis of German Ideology.* New York: Grosset & Dunlap, 1964.

———. *Toward the Final Solution: A History of European Racism.* Madison: University of Wisconsin Press, 1985.

Müller, Hans. *Katholische Kirche und Nationalsozialismus: Dokumente, 1930–1935.* Munich: Nymphenburg, 1963.

Nanko, Ulrich. *Die Deutsche Glaubensbewegung: Eine historische und soziologische Untersuchung.* Marburg: Diagonal, 1993.

Natterer, Alois. *Der bayerische Klerus in der Zeit dreier Revolutionen 1918, 1933, 1945: 25 Jahre Klerusverband, 1920–1945.* Eichstätt: Brönner, 1946.

Neuhäusler, Johann. *Kreuz und Hakenkreuz: Der Kampf des Nationalsozialismus gegen die katholische Kirche und der kirchliche Widerstand.* 2nd ed. Munich: Katholische Kirche Bayerns, 1946.

Nicolaisen, Carsten, ed. *Dokumente zur Kirchenpolitik des Dritten Reiches.* Vol. 1: *Das Jahr 1933.* Munich: Chr. Kaiser, 1975.

Noakes, J., and G. Pridham, eds. *Nazism: A History in Documents and Eyewitness Accounts, 1919–1945.* 2 vols. New York: Schocken Books, 1984/1988.

Nowak, Josef. "Der Devisenprozeß Dr. Seelmeyer: Ein Generalvikar ging unschuldig ins Zuchthaus." In *Das Bistum Hildesheim, 1933–1945: Eine Dokumentation.* Edited by Hermann Engfer. Hildesheim: August Lax, 1971.

Nowak, Kurt. *"Euthanasie" und Sterilisierung im "Dritten Reich": Die Konfrontation der evangelischen und katholischen Kirche mit dem Gesetz zur Verhütung erbkranken Nachwuchses und der "Euthanasie"—Aktion.* 3rd ed. Göttingen: Vandenhoeck & Ruprecht, 1984.

Ogiermann, Otto, S.J. *Bis zum letzten Atemzug: Der Prozeß gegen Bernhard Lichtenberg, Dompropst an St. Hedwig in Berlin.* Leipzig: St. Benno, 1968.

Oleschinski, Brigitte. "'Daß das Menschen waren, nicht Steine': Hilfsnetze katholischer Frauen für verfolgte Juden im Dritten Reich." *Zeitgeschichte* 17 (1990), 395–416.

Padberg, Rudolf. "Richard Heydrich und das Beichtgeheimnis." In *Das Erzbistum Paderborn in der Zeit des Nationalsozialismus: Beiträge zur regionalen Kirchengeschichte, 1933–1945.* Edited by Ulrich Wagener. Paderborn: Bonifatius, 1993. 289–96.

Parssinen, Terry. *The Oster Conspiracy of 1938.* New York: Harper Collins, 2003.

Passelecq, Georges, and Bernhard Suchecky. *The Hidden Encyclical of Pius XI.* Translated by Steven Rendell. New York: Harcourt Brace, 1997.

Patin, Wilhelm. *Beiträge zur Geschichte der Deutsch-Vatikanischen Beziehungen in den letzten Jahrzehnten.* Berlin: Nordland, 1942.

Pauly, Ferdinand. "Zur Kirchenpolitik des Gauleiters J. Bürkel im Saargebiet (März–August 1935)." *Rheinische Vierteljahrsblatter* 35 (1971), 414–53.

Perry, Marvin. "Racial Nationalism and the Rise of Modern Antisemitism." In *Jewish-Christian Encounters over the Centuries*. Edited by Marvin Perry and Frederick M. Schweitzer. New York: Peter Lang, 1994. 241–67.

Peters, Richard A. "The Catholic Church and the Reich Sterilization Law of 1933." *North Dakota Quarterly* 43 (1975), 38–50.

Pfliegler, Michael. *Der lebendige Christ vor der wirklichen Welt*. Vienna: Tyrolia, 1937.

Phayer, Michael. *The Catholic Church and the Holocaust, 1930–1965*. Bloomington: Indiana University Press, 2000.

———. "The Catholic Resistance Circle in Berlin and German Catholic Bishops during the Holocaust." *Holocaust and Genocide Studies* 7 (1993), 216–29.

———. "Margarete Sommer, Berlin Catholics and Germany's Jews, 1939–1945." In *Remembering for the Future. Vol. 1: Working Papers and Addenda*. Edited by Yehuda Bauer. Oxford: Pergamon Press, 1989. 112–20.

———. *Protestant and Catholic Women in Nazi Germany*. Detroit: Wayne State University Press, 1990.

Phayer, Michael, and Eva Fleischner. *Cries in the Night: Women Who Challenged the Holocaust*. Kansas City, Mo.: Sheed & Ward, 1997.

Pötzl, Walter, and Wolfgang Wüst, eds. *Bobingen und seine Geschichte*. Stadt Bobingen, n.d.

Preuschoff, Hans. *Pater Eduard Gehrmann SVD (1888–1960): Diener der Kirche in zwei Diktaturen*. Münster: Historischen Vereins für Ermland, 1984.

Pruß, Ursula. "Kaplan Herbert Simoleit." In *Zeugen für Christus: Das deutsche Martyrologium des 20. Jahrhunderts*. Vol. 1. Edited by Helmut Moll. Paderborn: Ferdinand Schöningh, 1999. 110–13.

———. "Kuratus Leonard Berger." In *Zeugen für Christus: Das deutsche Martyrologium des 20. Jahrhunderts*. Vol. 1. Edited by Helmut Moll. Paderborn: Ferdinand Schöningh, 1999. 91–94.

———. "Pfarrer Albert Hirsch." In *Zeugen für Christus: Das deutsche Martyrologium des 20. Jahrhunderts*. Vol. 1. Edited by Helmut Moll. Paderborn: Ferdinand Schöningh, 1999. 98–100.

———. "Pfarrer Albert Willimsky." In *Zeugen für Christus: Das deutsche Martyrologium des 20. Jahrhunderts*. Vol. 1. Edited by Helmut Moll. Paderborn: Ferdinand Schöningh, 1999. 117–21.

———. "Pfarrer Dr. Alfons Maria Wachsmann." In *Zeugen für Christus: Das deutsche Martyrologium des 20. Jahrhunderts*. Vol. 1. Edited by Helmut Moll. Paderborn: Ferdinand Schöningh, 1999. 114–17.

———. "Pfarrer Joseph Lenzel." In *Zeugen für Christus: Das deutsche Martyrologium des 20. Jahrhunderts*. Vol. 1. Edited by Helmut Moll. Paderborn: Ferdinand Schöningh, 1999. 101–4.

Puchowski, Georg. "Die katholische Aktion." In *Das Katholische Berlin*. Edited by Heinrich Bachmann. Munich: Hanns Eder, 1929. 37–41.

Puscher, Uwe. *Die völkische Bewegung im wilhelminischen Kaiserreich: Sprache-Rasse-Religion*. Darmstadt: Wissenschaftliche Buchgesellschaft, 2001.

Puscher, Uwe, and Justus H. Ulbricht, eds. *Handbuch zur Völkischen Bewegung, 1871–1918*. Munich: K. G. Saur, 1996.

Rapp, Petra Madeleine. *Die Devisenprozesse gegen katholische Ordensangehörige und Geistliche im Dritten Reich: Eine Untersuchung zum Konflikt deutscher Orden und Klöster in wirtschaftlicher Notlage, totalitärer Machtausübung des nationalsozialistischen Regimes und im Kirchenkampf 1935/36*. Bonn: Universität Bonn, 1981.

Rauterkus, Franz. "Zur Charakteristik des Berliner Katholizismus." In *Märkischer Kalender für die Diözese Berlin 1931*, 29–31.

Reifferscheid, Gerhard. *Das Bistum Ermland und das Dritte Reich*. Cologne: Bohlau, 1975.

Rempel, Gerhard. *Hitler's Children: The Hitler Youth and the SS*. Chapel Hill: University of North Carolina Press, 1989.

Repgen, Konrad. "Die deutschen Bischöfe und der zweite Weltkrieg." *Historisches Jahrbuch* 115 (1995), 411–52.

Reuther, Rosemary Radford. *Faith and Fratricide: The Theological Roots of anti-Semitism*. Reprint edition. Eugene, Ore.: Wipf and Stock, 1997.

Reutter, Lutz-Eugen. *Die Hilfstätigkeit katholischer Organisationen und kirchlicher Stellen für die im nationalsozialistischen Deutschland Verfolgten*. Hamburg: Universität Hamburg, 1969.

———. *Katholische Kirche als Fluchthelfer im Dritten Reich: Die Betreuung von Auswanderern durch den St. Raphaels-Verein*. Recklinghausen-Hamburg: Paulus, 1971.

Rhodes, Anthony. *The Vatican in the Age of the Dictators (1922–1945)*. New York: Holt, Rinehart and Winston, 1973.

Richter, Ingrid. *Katholizismus und Eugenik in der Weimarer Republik und im Dritten Reich: Zwischen Sittlichkeitsreform und Rassenhygiene*. Paderborn: Ferdinand Schöningh, 2001.

Röhm, Eberhard, and Jörg Thierfelder. "'Zwischen den Stühlen': Zur 'judenchristlichen' Selbsthilfe im Dritten Reich." *Zeitschrift für Kirchengeschichte* 103 (1992), 332–360.

Rosenberg, Alfred. *Der Mythus des XX. Jahrhunderts: Eine Wertung der seelisch-geistigen Gestaltenkämpfe unserer Zeit*. 211th ed. Munich: Hoheneichen, 1943.

Ross, Ronald J. *Beleaguered Tower: The Dilemma of Political Catholicism in Wilhelmine Germany*. Notre Dame, Ind.: University of Notre Dame Press, 1976.

———. *The Failure of Bismarck's Kulturkampf: Catholicism and State Power in Imperial Germany, 1871–1887*. Washington, D.C.: Catholic University of America Press, 1998.

Roth, Josef. "Die katholische Kirche und die Judenfrage." *Forschungen zur Judenfrage*. IV. Hamberg: Hanseatische, 1940. 163–76.

———. *Katholizismus und Judenfrage*. Munich: Franz Eher, 1923.

Ruhm von Oppen, Beate. "Laity and Churches in the Third Reich." In *The Moral Imperative: New Essays on the Ethics of Resistance in National Socialist Germany, 1933–1945*. Edited by Andrew Chandler. Boulder, Col.: Westview Press, 1998. 35–45.

Samerski, Stefan. "Der geistliche Konsultor der deutschen Botschaft beim Heiligen Stuhl während der Weimarer Republik." *Römische Quartalschrift für christliche Altertumskunde und Kirchengeschichte* 86 (1991), 261–78.

Schematismus des Bistums Berlin 1930–1941, 1947.

Scherzberg, Lucia. *Kirchenreform mit Hilfe des Nationalsozialismus. Karl Adam als kontextueller Theologe*. Darmstadt: Wissenschaftliche Buchgesellschaft, 2001.

Schmiechen-Ackermann, Detlef. "Katholische Diaspora zwischen Rückzug und Selbstbehauptung in der NS-Zeit." *Geschichte in Wissenschaft und Unterricht* 49 (1998), 462–76.

Schneider, Burkhart, S.J. "Kardinal Faulhaber und die Enzyklika *Mit brennender Sorge*." *Stimmen der Zeit* 175 (1964–1965), 226–22.

———. "*Mit brennender Sorge*—die Enzyklika Pius' XI. gegen den Nationalsozialismus (1937)." In *Das Wort der Päpste*. Edited by Wilhelm Sandfuchs. Würzburg: Echter, 1965. 102–13.

Scholder, Klaus. *The Churches and the Third Reich.* Vol 1: *Preliminary History and the Time of Illusions, 1918–1934.* Translated by John Bowden. Philadelphia: Fortress, 1988.

———. *The Churches and the Third Reich.* Vol. 2: *The Year of Disillusionment: 1934 Barmen and Rome.* Translated by John Bowden. Philadelphia: Fortress, 1988.

Schubert, Franz. *Grundzüge der Pastoraltheologie. III. Theorie der Seelsorge oder Pastorale Hodegetik.* Graz und Leipzig: Ulrich Mosers, 1935.

Schultheis, Herbert. *Die Reichkristallnacht in Deutschland nach Augenzeugenberichten.* Bad Neustadt a. d. Saale: Rotter, 1985.

Schwarz, Dieter [Albert Hartl]. *Die große Lüge des politischen Katholizismus.* Berlin: Franz Eher, 1938.

Scott-Craig, T. S. K., and R. E. Davies, eds. and trans. *Germany's New Religion: The German Faith Movement.* New York: Abingdon, 1937.

Sereny, Gitta. *Into That Darkness: An Examination of Conscience.* New York: Vintage, 1983.

Silverman, Dan P. *Hitler's Economy: Nazi Work Creation Programs, 1933–1936.* Cambridge, Mass.: Harvard University Press, 1998.

Simon, Werner. "Katholische Schulen, Religionsunterricht und Katechese in Berlin im ausgehenden 19. und beginnenden 20. Jahrhundert." In *Seelsorge und Diakonie in Berlin: Beiträge zum Verhältnis von Kirche und Großstadt im 19. und beginnenden 20. Jahrhundert.* Edited by Kasper Elm and Hans-Dietrich Loock. Berlin: Walter de Gruyter, 1990. 341–84.

Smolinsky, Heribert. "Das katholische Rußlandbild in Deutschland nach dem Ersten Weltkrieg und im 'Dritten Reich.'" In *Das Rußlandbild im Dritten Reich.* 2nd ed. Edited by Hans-Erich Volkmann. Cologne: Böhlau, 1994. 323–55.

Sonnenschein, Carl. "Caritaspflicht." In *Notizen aus den Weltstadt-Betrachtungen.* Vol. 2. Edited by Maria Grote. Frankfurt: Josef Knecht, 1951. 81–89.

———. "Großstadt." In *Den Menschen Recht verschaffen.* Edited by Werner Krebber. Würzburg: Echter, 1996. 83–88.

———. "Der Katholizismus." In *Volk und Reich der Deutschen.* Vol. 1. Edited by Bernhard Harms. Berlin: Reimer Hobbing, 1929. 407–28.

———. "Predigt im Dom." In *Notizen-Weltstadtbetrachtungen.* Vol. 8. Berlin: Germania, 1929. 8–12.

———. "Volksmission." In *Notizen-Weltstadtbetrachtungen.* Vol. 4. Berlin: Germania, 1928. 29–32.

Spectator. "Irrtum des Nationalsozialismus." *Märkischer Kalender 1932,* 99–106.

Sperber, Jonathan. *Popular Catholicism in Nineteenth-Century Germany.* Princeton, N.J.: Princeton University Press, 1984.

Spicer, Kevin, C.S.C. "Last Years of a Resister in the Diocese of Berlin: Bernhard Lichtenberg's Conflict with Karl Adam and His Fateful Imprisonment." *Church History* 70 (2001), 248–70.

———. "Selective Resistance: The German Catholic Church's Response to National Socialism." In *Confronting the Holocaust: A Mandate for the 21st Century.* Part 2. Edited by Stephen C. Feinstein et al. Lanham, Md.: University Press of America, 1998. 71–88.

Spotts, Frederic. *The Churches and Politics in Germany.* Middletown, Conn.: Wesleyan University Press, 1973.

Stackelberg, Roderick. *Idealism Debased: From Völkisch Ideology to National Socialism.* Kent, Ohio: Kent State University Press, 1981.

Stark, Johannes. *Nationalsozialismus und Katholische Kirche.* Munich: Franz Eher, 1931.

Stasiewski, Bernhard. "Die Kirchenpolitik der Nationalsozialisten im Warthegau 1939–1945." *Vierteljahrshefte für Zeitgeschichte* 7 (1959), 46–74.

————, ed. *Akten deutscher Bischöfe über die Lage der Kirche, 1933–1945.* Vol. 1: *1933–1934.* Mainz: Matthias-Grünewald, 1968.

————, ed. *Akten deutscher Bischöfe über die Lage der Kirche, 1933–1945.* Vol. 3: *1935–1936.* Mainz: Matthias-Grünewald, 1980.

Stehle, Hansjakob. *Graue Eminenzen, Dunkle Existenzen. Geheimgeschichten aus vatikanischen und anderen Hinterhöfen.* Düsseldorf: Patmos, 1998.

Stehlin, Stewart A. *Weimar and the Vatican, 1919–1933: German-Vatican Diplomatic Relations in the Interwar Years.* Princeton, N.J.: Princeton University Press, 1983.

Stockums, Wilhelm. *Das Priestertum: Gedanken und Erwägungen für Theologen und Priester.* Freiburg: Herder, 1934.

————. *The Priesthood.* Translated by Joseph W. Grundner. St. Louis: Herder, 1942.

Stratmann, Franziskus Maria. *In der Verbannung: Tagebuchblätter 1940 bis 1947.* Frankfurt am Main: Europäische Verlaganstalt, 1962.

Strehler, Adolf. *Christian Schreiber, Das Lebensbild eines Volksbischofs.* Berlin: Germania, 1933.

Stern, Fritz. *The Politics of Cultural Despair: A Study on the Rise of the Germanic Ideology.* Berkeley: University of California Press, 1974.

Studien zum Mythus des XX. Jahrhunderts mit Nachtrag: "Paulus und das Urchristentum." Cologne: J. P. Bachem, 1935.

Sun, Raymond Chien. *Before the Enemy Is within Our Walls: Catholic Workers in Cologne, 1885–1912: A Social, Cultural and Political History.* Boston: Humanities Press, 1999.

Tablet. "German Priest and the Nazi Party." Reprinted in *Catholic Mind* 40 (January 8, 1942), 17–24.

Tal, Uriel. *Christians and Jews in Germany: Religion, Politics, and Ideology in the Second Reich, 1870–1914.* Translated by Jonathan Jacobs. Ithaca, N.Y.: Cornell University Press, 1975.

Thévoz, Robert, Hans Branig, and Cécile Lowenthal-Hensel. *Pommern 1934/35 im Speigel von Gestapo-Lageberichten und Sachakten.* 2 vols. Berlin: Grote, 1974.

Tinnemann, Ethel Mary. "The German Catholic Bishops and the Jewish Question: Explanation and Judgement." *Holocaust Studies Annual* 2 (1984), 55–85.

Toepfer, Karl. *Empire of Ectasy: Nudity and Movement in German Body Culture, 1910–1935.* Berkeley: University of California Press, 1997.

Trippen, Norbert. "Leben und Überleben im Dritten Reich: Kirche und Katholizismus in der Zeit des Nationalsozialismus." In *Wie im Himmel so auf Erden. 90: Deutscher Katholikentag vom 23. bis 27. Mai 1990 in Berlin.* Vol. 2: *Dokumentation.* Paderborn: Bonifatius, 1990. 1581–1593.

Tröster, Werner. "'...die besondere Eigenart des Herrn Dr. Pieper!' Dr. Lorenz Pieper, Priester der Erzdiözese Paderborn, Mitglied der NSDAP Nr. 9740." In *Das Erzbistum Paderborn in der Zeit des Nationalsozialismus. Beiträge zur regionalen Kirchengeschichte 1933–1945.* Edited by Ulrich Wagener. Paderborn: Bonifatius, 1993. 45–91.

Usborne, Cornelie. *The Politics of the Body in Weimar Germany: Women's Reproductive Rights and Duties.* Ann Arbor: University of Michigan Press, 1992.

van Roon, Ger. *German Resistance to Hitler: Count von Moltke and the Kreisau Circle.* Translated by Peter Ludlow. London: Van Nostrand Reinhold, 1971.

Volk, Ludwig, S.J. "Episkopat und Kirchenkampf im Zweiten Weltkrieg. 1. Lebensvernichtung und Klostersturm, 1939–1941." In *Katholische Kirche und Nationalsozialismus: Ausgewählte Aufsätze von Ludwig Volk.* Edited by Dieter Albrecht. Mainz: Matthias-Grünewald, 1987. 83–97.

———. "Episkopat und Kirchenkampf im Zweiten Weltkrieg. 2. Judenverfolgung und Zusammenbruch des NS-Staats." In *Katholische Kirche und Nationalsozialismus: Ausgewählte Aufsätze von Ludwig Volk.* Edited by Dieter Albrecht. Mainz: Matthias-Grünewald, 1987. 98–113.

———. "Die Fuldaer Bischofskonferenz von der Enzyklika 'Mit Brennender Sorge' bis zum Ende der NS-Herrschaft." In *Katholische Kirche und Nationalsozialismus: Ausgewählte Aufsätze von Ludwig Volk.* Edited by Dieter Albrecht. Veröffentlichungen der Kommission für Zeitgeschichte ser. B, vol. 46. Mainz: Matthias-Grünewald, 1987. 56–82.

———. "Zur Kundgebung des deutschen Episkopats vom 28. März 1933." *Stimmen der Zeit* 173 (1963/1964), 431–56.

———. *Das Reichskonkordat vom 20. Juli 1933: Von den Ansätzen in der Weimarer Republik bis zur Ratifizierung am 10. September 1933.* Mainz: Matthias-Grünewald, 1972.

———. "Der Widerstand der katholische Kirche." In *Gegner des Nationalsozialismus. Wissenschaftler und Widerstandskämpfer auf der Suche nach historischer Wirklichkeit.* Edited by Christoph Kleßmann and Falk Pingel. Frankfurt: Campus, 1980. 126–39.

———. "Zwischen Geschichtsschreibung und Hochhuthprosa. Kritisches und Grundsätzliches zu einer Neuerscheinung über Kirche und Nationalsozialismus." In *Katholische Kirche und Nationalsozialismus. Ausgewählte Aufsätze von Ludwig Volk.* Edited by Dieter Albrecht. Mainz: Matthias-Grünewald, 1987. 225–347.

———, ed. *Akten deutscher Bischöfe über die Lage der Kirche, 1933–1945.* Vol. 5: *1940–1942.* Mainz: Matthias-Grünewald, 1983.

———, ed. *Akten deutscher Bischöfe über die Lage der Kirche, 1933–1945.* Vol. 6: *1943–1945.* Mainz: Matthias-Grünewald, 1985.

———, ed. *Akten Kardinal Michael von Faulhabers 1917–1945.* 2 vols. 2nd ed. Mainz: Matthias-Grünewald, 1984.

———, ed. *Kirchliche Akten über die Reichskonkordatsverhandlungen 1933.* Mainz: Matthias-Grünewald, 1969.

Vuletić, Aleksandar-Saša. *Christen Jüdischer Herkunft im Dritten Reich: Verfolgung und Organisierte Selbsthilfe, 1933–1939.* Mainz: Philipp von Zabern, 1999.

Wagener, Ulrich. "Unterdrückungs und Verfolgungsmaßnahmen gegen Priester des Erzbistums Paderborn in der Zeit des Nationalsozialismus: Ergebnisse einer Untersuchung der Kommission für Zeitgeschichte." *Theologie und Glaube* 75 (1985), 51–62.

Walser, Gaudentius, O.F.M. Cap. *Carl Lampert: Ein Leben für Christus und die Kirche, 1894–1944.* Dornbirn: Vorarlberger, 1964.

———. *Dreimal zum Tod verurteilt. Dr. Carl Lampert ein Glaubenszeuge Für Christus und die Kirche, 1894–1944.* Aschaffenburg: Paul Pattloch, 1985.

Weber, H. *Das Wesen der Caritas: Caritaswissenschaft.* Vol. 1. Freiburg: Caritas, 1938.

Webersinn, Gerhard. "Prälat Karl Ulitzka: Politiker im Priester." *Jahrbuch der Schlesischen Friedrich-Wilhelms-Universität zu Breslau* 15 (1970), 146–205.

Weindling, Paul. *Health, Race, and German Politics between National Unification and Nazism, 1870–1945.* Cambridge: Cambridge University Press, 1993.

Weiß, Hermann. "Wilhelm Kube." In *Biographisches Lexikon zum Dritten Reich.* Frankfurt: S. Fischer, 1998. 285–87.

Wittschier, J. Bernd. "Joseph Lenzel, Pfarrer in Berlin-Niederschönhausen." *Theologisches* 10 (1988), 551–52.

Yahil, Leni. *The Holocaust: The Fate of European Jewry.* New York: Oxford, 1990.

Zahn, Gordon C. *German Catholics and Hitler's Wars.* New York: E. P. Dutton, 1969.

Ziegler, Walter. "'Haben die deutschen Bischöfe im Dritten Reich versagt?' Kritische Überlegungen zu einem vielbehandelten Thema." In *Festgabe: Heinz Hürten zum 60. Geburtstag.* Edited by Harald Dickerhof. Frankfurt: Peter Lang, 1988. 497–524.

Zuccotti, Susan. *Under His Very Windows: The Vatican and the Holocaust in Italy.* New Haven, Conn.: Yale University Press, 2000.

Index

DATE DUE

MAY 2 7			